Teaching Learning Strategies in Higher Education

Teaching Learning Strategies in Higher Education

(Ed.)
Dr. Kandi Kamala

GenNext Publication

Published, 2020

Published by

GenNext Publication
5, Ansari Road
Daryaganj, New Delhi-110002
Phone: 9811692060
E-mail: gennextpublication@hotmail.com

Printed at: G. Print Process, Delhi.

Cataloging in Publication Data—DK
Courtesy: D.K. Agencies (P) Ltd. <docinfo@dkagencies.com>

Teaching learning strategies in higher education / ed., Kandi Kamala.
pages cm
Includes bibliographical references and index.
ISBN 9789353242312

1. Education, Higher—India. 2. College teaching—India. I. Kamala, Kandi, editor.

LCC LA1153.T43 2020 | DDC 378.54 23

Contents

Foreword 11
Preface 13
Acknowledgement 15

1. Heutagogy: An Innovative Teaching Learning Strategy for Higher Education 17
Dr. Sunita Singh

2. Challenges of Student Teachers During Teaching Practice 33
Dr. P.S. Pragathi

3. Issues Related to Teaching-Learning Strategies in Teacher Education 43
Dr. Qudsia Hafeez

4. Impact of Technology in Indian Education System 53
D. Yedukondalu

5. Challenges of Teaching in College Education 61
S. Uma Devi

6. Social Sciences Higher Education Pedagogy Issues in India 69
Dr. Rama Rao Bonagani

7. Framework for Creation of Learning Resources E-Content: An Effective Tool for Teaching and Learning in a Contemporary Higher Education System 81
G. L. Rajani

8. Issues and Challenges in Higher Education System 93
Dr. K. Govindu

9. Methodological Approaches: A Study 105
Dr. Elisha Kolluri

10. Efforts towards Internationalization of Higher Education in India 117
Dr. G. Kamalakar

11. Emerging Challenges of Indian Higher Educational Institutions 145
P. Murali Krishna

12. Bench Marking Practices; Creating Practical Exposure to Commerce Graduates –A Case Study of TSWRDCW, Nalgonda 153
N. Aparna, T. Shashikala, J. Janakamma

13. Using Technology in the class: A Study on Role of Social Media in Enhancing Learning Experience 163
Anitha H S

14. Revisiting Critical Pedagogy: Issues and Challenges of Tribal Education in the State of Telangana 173
Ade Jyothi

15. Effect of Context on Teaching and Learning - Integrating CTL in to Teacher Education 181
Jakkinaboina Sridevi

16. Critical Pedagogy and English Language Teaching at the Tertiary Level in India 189
Roopna Ravindran

18. Teaching Learning Strategies: Utilizing Technology in the Classroom 195
V. Pallavi

18. Making Education Interactive with Drama Based Pedagogy 205
Ms Rupinder Brar

19. Teaching Learning Strategies - Pedagogy Issues 211
Dr. Sama Suvarnadevi

20. Encouraging Student's Language Competence through Drama Techniques in German-as-a-foreign-language (GFL) Class by using two "Learning Plays" of Brecht 219
Sharath Kumar Velmala

21. Use of Technology to Enhance Teaching and Learning 229
Dr. Shaik. Liyakhath Ali

22. Teaching English Language Skills through Mathematics 237
Smt. T Vijaya Gouri, Sri P. Janardhan Rao

23. Utilization of the Technology in the Government College of Teacher Education's Classroom 245
J. Vishwanath

24. Implementation of Right to Free & Compulsory Education Act 2009 Challenges in India 255
Dr. K. V. R. Srinivas

25. Combating the Challenges: Education and Nation Building 265
Dr. T. Sasikanth Reddy

26. Impact of Co-Curricular Activities on Leadership Qualities of UG Students 277
Rubeena Research scholar

27. Pre-Service Teachers' Attitudes towards Blended Learning 283
Navitha S. Nair and Pheiga Gangmei Dinjanglu

28. A Study on Emotional Expressivity and Social Adjustment Among Adolescents 295
Dr. Eswari Vadlamudi

29. Methodologies of Teaching and Training in Higher Education 301
Dr Jahangeer Ahmad Bhat

30. Human Resources Management in Higher Education 307
Dr. Mohd Husamuddin

31. Right to Education – A Fundamental Human Right of Children 315
Dr. Y. S. Kiran Kumar

32. Causes of Female Student Dropouts: An Analytical Study of Medak District 323
T. Neelima

33. A study on Impact of Higher Education on Women's agency in Household and in the Society 327
Dr. P. Radhika, O. Pranathi

34. Nutrition Education for Adolescent Girls in the Slums of Twin Cities under IPP-VIII, Hyderabad 333
Dr. Kalpana Toran, Dr. Kalapatapu Ravikiran Sharma, Dr. Kavita Toran

35. Relevance of Massive Open Online Courses in Higher Education 343
Dr. Vinod Kumar Singh

36. The Changing Role of Teacher in Higher Education 351
Dr. K. Geetha

37. Amplificationon Curriculum Renewal for Value Based Education System 357
Kumaraswamy Manepalli MBA

38. Utilization of Digital Technology in Class Room 363
K.V. Satya Prakash

39. Impact of Open Source Technology in Higher Education 369
P. Swathi, V. Srujanamma

40. Attitude towards Computer Education among B.Ed. Students – A Study 373
Gollapudi Manikya Rao

41. Contemporary Classroom Management 385
Prof. T.V.R. Mohan, R.K. Chithiraa

42. The Foundation of Higher Education is Mother Tongue an Astute Study 399
Dr. C.S. Sukumar Reddy, Dr. G. Gangaiah

43. Preparation of Curriculum: A Futuristic Perspective 403
Dr. B. Prathima, Dr. M. Trimurthi Rao

44. Influence of Imagination and Culture on Curriculum Development... 413
Glaze George K

45. A Critical Reflection of Indian Higher Education in the Context of Infrastructure 419
Umme Salma

46. Student Centric Guidance and Counseling in Higher Education 427
Dr. Prashanthakumara T. M

47. Integrating Technology in Classroom Studies 433
Geetha Sai Kumari

48. 21st Century Skills: Life Line for Student in the Modern Digital Era of Education:-Role of a Teacher 437
D. S. L. Aryani

49. Digitalization, Modernity and Inclusiveness; the Case of Special Needs Students in the Smart Class Rooms: A Study at the University of Hyderabad 445
Aysha Farhana

50. A Comparative Study on Achievement Motivation and GRIT among Government and Private School Children 455
Dr. Eswari Vadlamudi

51. Utilizing technology (Digital Classes) in the class room of Government schools in Telangana state 463
Shaik. Asif Ali

52. Higher Education in India: Emerging Challenges Teaching Learning Strategies With Respect To Student Centric Approaches 467
Kalpana Yerragokula

53. Developing Creative Writing Skill among Degree College Students through The Authentic Materials 477
Gidde Rajinikanth

54. Health Education on Anaemia to Rural Adolescent Girls in Erstwhile Medak District 485
Dr. Kalapatapu Ravikiran Sharma, Dr. Kalpana Toran, Dr. Kavita Toran

55. Nutrition Education for Adolescent Girls in the Slums of Twin Cities under IPP-VIII, Hyderabad 491
Dr. Kalpana Toran, Dr. Kalapatapu Ravikiran Sharma Dr. Kavita Toran

56. Right to Education – A Fundamental Human Right of Children 501
Dr. Y. S. Kiran Kumar

57. Causes of Female Student Dropouts: An Analytical Study of Medak District 509
T. Neelima

58. A study on Impact of Higher Education on women's agency in household and in the society 513
Dr. P. Radhika, O. Pranathi

59. Reforming Higher Education in India 519
P. Sujatha

60. Gender Issues in Indian Higher Education: An Analytical Study 525
Nithya Kalmekolan

61. The Changing Role of Teacher in Higher Education 533
Dr. K. Geetha

Index 539

Foreword

I am happy to write the foreword to the book titled "Teaching Learning Strategies in Higher Education''. "Teaching is not a lost art, but the regard for it is a lost tradition" commented Jacques Barzun. Requests for changes in teaching at all educational levels are normal consequences because of the rapid technological development and today's dynamic and complex reality. To improve educational achievements and students vocational training at the university and colleges, it is required to use alternative methods and procedures of teaching, blended in a combination of original strategies that promote active learning. It's a continuous challenge to comprehend a continuing willingness of students towards intellectual and emotional involvement in the learning process and taking responsibility for learning on their own.

The consequence of the ever more important role of knowledge for the economic and social prosperity and of the focus on the active role of individuals in the building of his knowledge is the tendency to implement the new guidelines in the organisation of the teaching process where the teaching – learning relationship is more flexible, students are encouraged to take an active role in instruction processes and the teaching outcomes must include the acquisition of knowledge but also the gaining of competences. The goals of education defined through the learning outcomes or development of competences cannot be realised by sheer usage of traditional didactic strategies, approaches and methods of teaching.

Turbulent social processes require a flexible and dynamic university ready to change and accept the fact that it is no longer the exclusive place where information is gathered and knowledge acquired. Any demand for a change involves innovative approaches to teaching and learning as a response to the challenges set by new media and learning theories, such as cognitivism and social constructivism. An especially important role is played by active teaching methods and procedures which recognize different needs of individual students, asking them to assume liability for personal learning and promoting critical thinking and independent learning. The leader of these changes is the teacher who must be able to implement various different teaching methods and procedures and to alternate them strategically encouraging creativity, problem solving, experience-based learning and metacognition.

India is in the throes of great developments in the field of higher education. This book identifies the needs and gaps in the strategies and tools of pedagogy which is a crucial input and is a valuable resource for teachers in higher educational institutions.

Prof. G. Gopal Reddy
Member, University Grants Commission,
New Delhi.
Former President, Indian Political Science Association.
Former Dean, Faculty of Arts and Social Sciences,
Palamur University.
Former Principal, University Post Graduate College,
Osmania University

Telangana State Council of Higher Education
(A statutory body of the Govt. of Telangana)
Opp: Mahavir Hospital, Mahavir Marg, Masabtank, Hyderabad - 500 028.
Ph : 040 - 23331118
Website: www.tsche.ac.in - Email: vicechairman1tsche@gmail.com

Preface

Higher education in India witnessed many shifts during the last six decades. The Mudaliar Commission, S. Radha Krishanan Commission, Kothari Commission and the recent knowledge Commission, have reflected on earlier paradigms, perspectives and priorities. In the era of globalization, the challenges of higher education have become more pronounced and accentuated. India, taking the lead as an emerging world economy must orient its policies, strategies and perspectives to the global challenges in terms of quality. At the same time, it must be sensitive to its local, grassroots realities of equity and inclusive character.

Education has been one of the major issues in India . Efforts have been made by the Government to solve the problem through various measures, i.e., by paying close attention to individual needs, education and equality between women and men. From these perspectives, along with other efforts, 'Education' as an innovative project is being experimented in India since early 1970's. Realising its importance, modified NPE 1992, stated that "Education must be viewed as an important part of nations' strategy to address all other issues: 'Moreover, the concept of Education itself has .been changing frequently as a result of changes in the perception of education and its relationship with other developmental variables, requiring a fresh look on the subject. Keeping the above points in mind, an effort has been made in this book, 'Teaching and Learning Strategies in Higher Education', to cover the recent trends and issues relating to the content and methodology of Education.

The present work was planned in consultation with experts who know the nerves of the field. The volume examined the two main approaches to quality teaching: the top-down approach (those quality teaching initiatives taken by the institution collectively, and determined by its leadership) and the bottom-up approach (those quality teaching initiatives taken by the teachers and which may nevertheless have an influence on the institutional policy on quality teaching). The focus of the articles is mainly on the reasons for, and the effectiveness of those initiatives. It is less concerned with the practical aspects and the concrete mechanisms used to put them into practice which are heavily dependent on the circumstances of each institution.

This volume also examines the conclusions in the context of changing socio-economic and political realities and growing optimism. It analyses three conceptual issues purpose, diversity and competition and examines the status and prospects of Indian higher education in terms of three key cross-cutting themes access and expansion, equity and inclusion and quality and excellence.

My special thanks are due to the authors of various articles. It is hoped that the book will prove useful to teachers, educational planners, school teachers, student-teachers and others interested in the eld.

Prof. Dr. R. Limbadri
Dept. of Public Administration, Osmania University
Vice-Chairman-I,
Telangana State Council of Higher Education

Acknowledgement

I express my special thanks to Prof. Jandhyala B G Tilak, Key note address and Prof. Ramabrahmam who has been a constant source of inspiration. I feel highly honoured and greatly indebted to him for sparing time to guide this work and motivating me for completion of the seminar proceedings in the form of book. I would like to express my gratitude to Prof Ram Reddy, academic colleagues and students who took part in the seminar and shared their valuable views and experiences of quality evaluation in the higher education sector. It is a good and nice experience for me to conduct two day National seminar on "Higher Education in India: Emerging Challenges. It's really a great challenge for me to accept the programme where our college does not have any infrastructure as we are accommodated by Govt. Junior College, BHEL, and Hyderabad with only two rooms. I am very thankful to ICSSR, New Delhi, RUSA and TSCHE for financial support. I am very much thankful to our Principal (FAC), Dr. K. Aruna Bai, for her encouragement and support without which I would not be able to conduct the programme and thanks to Smt. C. Jyothi, Head, Dept. of Commerce, Smt. Farhath Nazneen, Asst. Professor of English, Shri. P. Murali Krishna, Asst. Professor of Economics, Dr. N. Gopal, Asst. Professor of History, Smt. B.N.Surekha, Asst. Professor of Commerce and other staff members, Non-teaching staff, Technicians, BHEL Township.

Dr. Kandi Kamala

Chapter - 1

Heutagogy: An Innovative Teaching Learning Strategy for Higher Education

Dr. Sunita Singh

Abstract

From cradle to grave the importance of education cannot be denied. Since it not only surrounds our life, but is also the basic foundation of our society. Technological expansion generate knowledge outburst that have great impact on fast growing modern society and undoubtedly on education. Education is the way to progress. It not only surrounds our lives but is also the foundation of our society. It develops our mind and convert inquisitive mind into intellectual one. Education is not only about high score in entire subject, rather it involves in depth knowledge and insight learning as well. Now a day's most important topic of discourse for educationist is the paradigm shift of teaching towards learning. Today's students learn things faster. The students of higher education have abilities to learn new things with their own manner. But we treat them just like students of lower classes and we use all those methods of teaching at higher level that we use at primary and secondary level. Students do not need spoon feeding at this level. There is a need to change our way of teaching learning from pedagogy to heutagogy. Such teaching –learning strategy will accomplish requirement and need of modern society's learner. Heutagogy is a form of self-determined learning. It is holistic and based on the principle of learner centered approach in formal as well as informal situations. This theory is grounded in humanistic and constructivist model. Constructivism is basically philosophical believe that advocates individual construct their own understanding of reality. The theory of constructivism is grounded on the cognitive psychology that focused how the learner constructs knowledge from experience, which is unique to each individual. It is observed that the students of higher education should be given more space for self-exploration so that they can develop the competency or ability to attain the necessary skills to accomplish their educational goals, and the capability or confidence to construct and follow through on their own learning plan. The heutagogical approach gives them a suitable learning environment that is much needed in today's educational systems. This paper will discuss the heutagogy's concept, responsibilities of teacher and especially focus on significance of heutagogy at higher level in present scenario.

Introduction

We live in world that is constantly changing; advances are rapid, aided and facilitated by the fast use of and developments in technology. Promoting authentic learning opportunities is demanding. Information to support the development of knowledge is readily and easily accessible. Discipline based knowledge is no longer appropriate for living in today's complex society, communities and workplaces. Learning is increasingly concerned with what we do, and the development of those key skills and abilities appropriate for this changing, dynamic and contested workplace, as emphasised by Barnet, "the twentieth first century is calling for human beings who are themselves flexible, able to respond purposively to new situations and ideas" (Barnett 2014). Capable people are more likely to be, respond and lead effectively within the dynamic environment characterised by contemporary global society and those skills and qualities required by the modern day graduate.

Today's students learn things faster. The students of higher education have abilities to learn new things with their own manner. But we treat them just like students of lower classes and we use all those methods of teaching at higher level that we use at primary and secondary level. Students do not need spoon feeding at this level.Hence there is an urgent need to promote quality teaching in all classrooms of the country to raise the status of teaching as an advanced knowledge based profession.Therefore, the formal education must be transformed for facilitating new forms of learning and to inculcate competencies and skills (Figure - 1) that are needed to tackle complex global challenges (Scott, 2015).

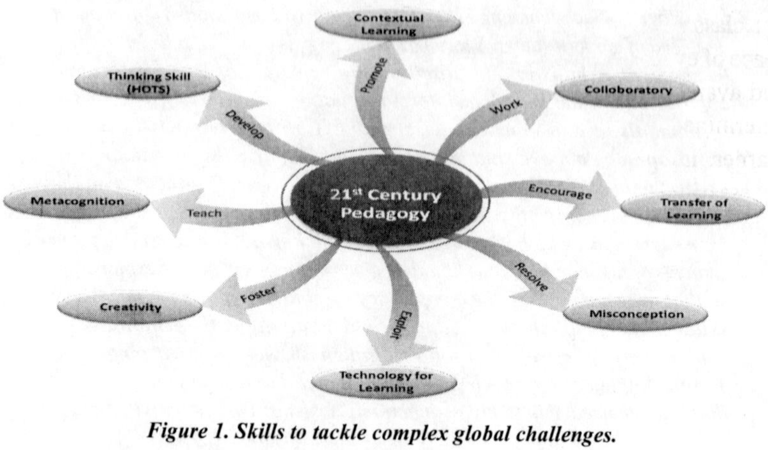

Figure 1. Skills to tackle complex global challenges.

The traditional teaching practices can be transformed by incorporating constructivism, collaborative and cooperative learning, heutagogy strategies as innovative teaching practices that can develop necessary competencies and skill in our learner to meet the challenges of 21st century. Such teaching –learning strategy will accomplish requirement and need of modern society's learner. Heutagogy is a form of self-determined learning. It is holistic and based on the principle of learner centered approach in formal as well as informal situations. This theory is grounded in humanistic and constructivist model. Constructivism is basically philosophical believe that advocates individual construct their own understanding of reality. The theory of constructivism is grounded on the cognitive psychology that focused how the learner constructs knowledge from experience, which is unique to each individual. It is observed that the students of higher education should be given more space for self-exploration so that they can develop the competency or ability to attain the necessary skills to accomplish their educational goals, and the capability or confidence to construct and follow through on their own learning plan. The heutagogical approach gives them a suitable learning environment that is much needed in today's educational systems.

Heutagogy: An Innovative Learning Strategy

The higher education environment stimulates learning through various systems and structures and these determine, when, how and what is learned; these systems can either promote or inhibit the choice of what is learned and what skills are developed (Barnett, 2012 Barnett, R. (2012). But the present teaching learning approach or traditional method of teaching do not give any scope of learner to develop their inner ability with their own way of learning. definitely we believe that individual differences exist in our class so there is need to adopt a such teaching strategy that give the space of every learner to develop their ability with their own learning speed and available time. so the newer way of learning i.e. heutagogy or self-determined strategy may fulfil the demand of today's higher education learner. in this strategy—an instructor, teacher, or other arbiter is not necessarily involved, unless the individual chooses to involve one at some point. It is important to think of it as self-determined learning, not "informal learning" as contrasted to "formal learning" (Brandon 2016).The goal of heutagogy is to teach lifelong learning. Heutagogical learning is not necessarily linear or planned, but much more informal and parallel with how people learn best outside of a school setting. The teacher serves more as a coach—a valuable resource to be tapped if necessary, but not the primary source of knowledge.

Heutagogy is a student-centered instructional strategy that emphasizes the development of autonomy, capacity, and capability. this approach encourages students to find their own problems and questions to answer. Instead of simply completing the tasks teachers assign, these students seek out areas of uncertainty and complexity in the subjects they study. Teachers help by providing context to students' learning and creating opportunities for them to explore subjects fully. The origins of heautogogy (Hase, S., & Kenyon, C. (2013) are in the pedagogy that lies complexity theory and capability development, and it expands upon the notion of life-wide and life-long learning in presenting an approach that harnesses self-determined learning.There is an ever increasing interdependence of events, and that the ability to predict future events and authentic learning is becoming increasingly challenging. Subsequently, learning is becoming much more emergent as a process, and develops a more natural, adaptive and realist phenomena where predictability and outcome becomes much less certain.it is the process of acquiring not only skills and knowledge, but the ethics and judgement required to solve unfamiliar problems in unfamiliar contexts.

As the image below illustrates, heutagogy requires the most student maturity and the least instructor control. Pedagogy, on the other hand, is on the opposite end of the spectrum.

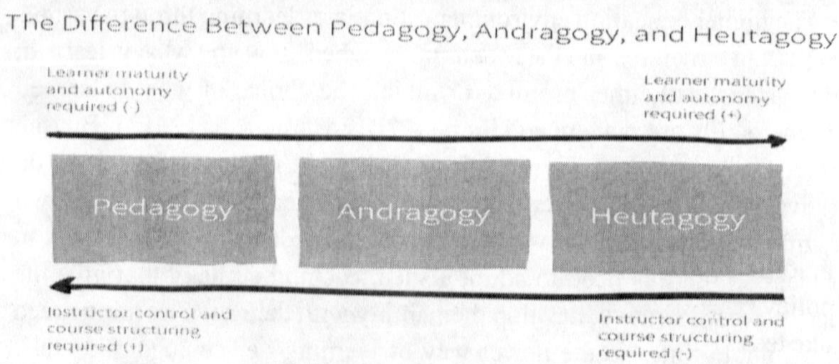

Image based onimages by Lisa Marie Blaschke and N. Canning.

Heutagogy is an attempt to develop a holistic approach to learning, and developing new skills and knowledge in developing independent capability and the capacity to question self, values and assumptions (Canning & Callan, 2010). Heutagogy looks to the future in which knowing how to learn is a fundamental skill. Snowden and Halsall (2014) suggest that there are two key collaborative strategies that support heutagogy: solution focused approach to teaching and learning, and mentor assisted learning. Solution focused teaching and learning is a transformative learning and teaching experience, activating learners to become committed, engaged citizens, and to recognise that development requires change to take place at individual, societal and cultural levels. Solution focused approaches are concerned with constructing solutions, an approach that looks forwards, towards solutions, rather than backwards, by studying problems. It is based upon the discovery of challenging beliefs, values and solutions, introducing the learner to concepts such as social injustice, oppression, inequality, and domination. The approach develops critical consciousness, collective identity, and solution oriented strategies for change. Above all, it adopts a real world approach to pedagogy; it encourages teaching and learning that focuses upon strengths, abilities, hopes, and distinctly, encourages thinking in terms of possibilities (Snowden & Halsall, 2014).In this approach, for educators to be creative in their pedagogy, encouraging learners to utilise their learning spaces to negotiate how, what and when they learn.

On the basis of above discussion we can say that heutagogy strategy letting learners set their own completion dates for assignments and allowing learners multiple completion attempts as well as having learners design their own course projects, and organizing modules so that learners can start with whatever interests them most.

Characteristics of Heutagogy

Learning in heutagogical approach is self-determined, which directs the learners acquire both competencies and capabilities (McAuliffe et al., 2008, Hase & Kenyon, 2000, 2007). Through this approach it is believed that learner can develop creativity to apply competencies to new and unfamiliar situations and became more adaptable and flexible in approach (Hase & Kenyon, 2000; Gardner et al., 2007). Day by day there is various modification and changes are implemented in educational system from policy making to teaching methods of classroom. In professional courses like teacher education can only be imparted as theoretical knowledge about various competencies such as like teaching competencies, competencies in organise and managing the school, competency of handling the group, working in team, social relationship etc. a bunch of information but these competencies in real sense can be developed only when learner would be self motivated and self directed for enhancing their capabilities, where huetagogy may prove suitable approach (Yaduvanshi & Singh, 2017). Following characteristics of heutagogy can be utilised to develop professional competencies among students:

1. Double-Loop Learning:

   An important concept in heutagogy is that of double-loop learning.

In this style of learning, students not only think deeply about a problem and the actions they have taken to solve it, but also reflect upon the problem-solving process itself.(Figure 2) The idea is that students will begin to question their assumptions and gain insight into not only what they are learning, but also how they learn. With its emphasis on providing a learner-centered environment that supports students in defining their own learning path, heutagogy also equips students with skills that will help them transition into the workforce. (Davis 2018)

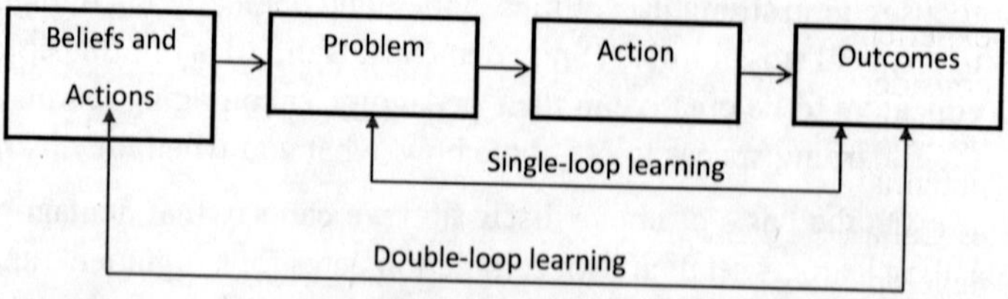

Figure (2)

The double loop learning involves challenging learner's own concept, theories, values, assumptions rather than simply encountering and reaching problem as found in single loop learning. In this situation learning is an active process in which individual either seeks education or experience or gain feedback and evaluate as they move through life's experiences. Through the process of double-looping, learners become more aware of their preferred learning style and can easily adapt new learning situations to their learning styles, thus making them more capable learners. With its dual focus on competencies and capability, heutagogy moves teachers a step closer towards better addressing the needs of adult learners in complex and changing work environments (Bhoryrub et al., 2010).

Self Directed

Teaching adults is not the same as teaching children; done well, it affords the adults a level of autonomy, even including the opportunity to determine and direct their learning. There is vast explosion of knowledge in every field most of things are governed via ICT (Information and Communication Technology). Therefore, competency of subject knowledge and digital competency can develop effectively via heutagogical approaches because no conventional instructional practices in teacher education programme can inculcate these competencies in prospective teachers unless or until they are willing to expand their subject and digital knowledge or to do innovations. When learners are capable, skills and knowledge can be solve the problems in unfamiliar situations.

Reflective Learning

One of the important characteristic of heutagogy is that of *reflective practice,* "a critical learning skill associated with knowing how to learn" (Hase, 2009). According to Schon (1983), reflective practice supports learners in becoming lifelong learners, as "when a practitioner becomes a researcher into his own practice, he/ she engages in a continuous process of self- education" Heutagogy takes into account the learner's prior learning experiences and the way in which these influence how she or he learns; by considering these past experiences and the learner's current experience and reflecting upon these, the learner moves into a growth process that has the potential to lead to transformative learning – a process described by Canning & Callan (2010) as "spirals of reflection". It may prove very fruitful in developing competency of inquiry (competency of science teaching) among students and enable them to master in problem solving skills may prove very helpful to sort out their future life problems.

Flexible Curriculum

A heutagogical approach is only possible when the curriculum is flexible and takes into consideration the learners' questions, motivations, and how thinking shifts as a result of what they've learned. Students must be able to create a curriculum for themselves that can adapt to their individual needs. Student may be required to build their plans based on a set of defined learning objectives, but they have the freedom to identify what and how to they learn. This personalization can help students feel empowered and encourage greater engagement.Thus, learner himself determines what is of interest and relevance to them. It proves helpful in modifying and adopting new and modern teaching competencies according to the demand of contemporary needs. It seems very useful in developing competency for innovation and improvement which highly significant for development professionalism in them.

Action Learning

Action learning or action research methods are consistent with heutagogical approaches that focus on the problem of learner and their immediate resolution for the benefit of learner. This can develop capacity lifelong learning. Therefore, future citizen can update and modified their competencies according to the need of new situation or problems. It provides lot of help to students to solve their local problems. In case of teachers it can helpful to solve the problem relate to school management, handling with problematic learners, dealing with community or parents thus play significant role in developing the competencies in organise and manage the school, handling group dynamics and social relations.

Flexible And Negotiated Assessment

Assessment is an important part of all instructional approaches, including heutagogy. However, in this style of learning, students design their own assessments rather than undergoing standard tests. This creates a less threatening environment for students and can encourage deeper learning.

It is important that the assessments students design include ways of measuring the understanding of content and skills they have acquired, because at the end of the process students will be assessed to determine if the agreed upon outcomes have been achieved.

Collaborative Learning

Due to its independent nature, learning in a heutagogical classroom can cause inner conflict for the learner, especially if they are not accustomed to taking responsibility for their learning. However, once students have a taste for self-determined learning, few want to revert to the confines of a rigidly structured curriculum. One way to ease the transition into heutagogy is to encourage collaboration in the classroom. By design, this approach facilitates students working together to share knowledge and reflect on their progress. Since learners are encouraged to work together—in person and digitally—to achieve a common goal, they can solve problems and reinforce their knowledge by sharing information and experiences, practice concepts, and experimenting. These collaborative sessions are an opportunity for students to learn from each other, as well as think about how they can apply their new skills in practice.

Significance of Heutagogy teaching learning strategy in higher education

India has the second highest population of the working age individuals in the world. In India, education plays a vital role to build skill based society of the 21st century. It is the quality of education that decides the quality of human resources of the country (More 2017). it shows that there is a need of quality education so that we can develop a quality citizen. Presently most of the teachers at every level use the teacher centered approach rather than student centered approach. Hence, there is a need to change our way of teaching because the needs of students at every level have changed. At primary level they are not much aware about their surroundings and also not clear and confident about their learning but the students of higher education want more freedom and space for learning because now they are able to search new things and evaluate such knowledge. In such situations heutagogical approach gives them a suitable learning environment. These are the points that focus the significance of heutagogy at higher level:

- **Give Importance of Students' freedom in learning:** Heutagogical process of learning is the place of the learner—who is at the heart of the learning—and the learner drives what it is to be learned rather than the constraints of a prescribed syllabus or curriculum that works in partnership with the academic tutor/lecturer who acts as a facilitator of learning. Heautogogy provides a framework for learning that harnesses and manages this dynamic and complex notion of learning, providing a curriculum approach that offers a twentieth first century approach to learning and teaching congruent with the demands of contemporary society.Heautogogy, as described by Hase and Kenyon (2013).is a pedagogy that facilitates self determined learning, where participants are encouraged to research their learning and practice interests and base their learning on these interests and their aspirations. In this approach to learning the learner and their place in community and society becomes the fulcrum of learning. Traditionally the learner in the learning process was often a passive recipient in the development of knowledge, where the lecturer/teacher adopted the role of knowledge expert who simply converted their knowledge, determining what was learned and how it was to be learned.
- **High degree of self-efficacy:** Heutagogy asserts that people make sense of the world around them and generalize from these perceptions, conceptualize and perceive in variances. People consequently have the potential to learn continuously and in real time by interacting with their environment they learn throughout their lifespan leading to ideas rather than the force-fed knowledge of others they enhance creativity and learn how to learn. Rogers (1951)suggests that people have a strong desire to learn and have a natural inclination to do so, and Stephenson and Yorke (1998)suggest that capable people are those that know how to learn and have a high degree of self-efficacy, and who have a

higher degree of competence- capability when working in new and unfamiliar situations. Heutagogical approaches to education place great emphasis upon holism, self, capability, community, needs of society and a focus upon learning as opposed to teaching. So we can say that in this strategy students have space to understand the concept with their own way or own learning style. Individuals also aware about his/her learning style because they learn the things in different way. The knowledge of learning abilities helps to the teacher and learner too to make their lessons or teaching pattern according to learning style of an individual.

- **Spirit of openness:** Canning (2010) provides a valuable insight into how heutagogical principles have been adopted within an early years foundation degree, demonstrating that students quite early in their programme acknowledged "gaps in their knowledge and seek out ways in which they can use the learning community that they have engaged with to support them in developing that knowledge" and by embracing a culture of openness students will become their own regulators of reflective learning However, key to successful learning is adopting a spirit of openness by all parties involved in the learning process.
- **Develop Higher Level Cognitive Abilities:** In a heutagogy, learners are highly autonomous and self-determined and emphasis is placed on development of learner capacity and capability with the goal of producing learners who are well prepared for the complexities of contemporary workplace.(Prahallada 2013) Students in heutagogical learning environment get a conducive environment for developing the skills of critical and reflective thinking, ability to communicate effectively, innovate, and solve problems through negotiation and collaboration. Action learning recognizes reflection and therefore the prospect of double loop learning in processes designed to facilitate learning. The teacher here takes the back seat and becomes a learner like everyone else enabling people to become learners as well to find solution or even put questions. Heutagogy also gives importance to creation of a learning environment in which students are encouraged to think carefully and critically and communicate their thoughts in which they wish to confront and resolve difficulties rather than gloss over them (Murugavel, 2009). It involves constantly monitoring and reflecting on the processes of teaching and student understanding and seeking to improve them.

Barnett (2007) suggests that there are risks for adopting this approach. These can be associated with "epistemological risk"; by following their interests, learning what they want to learn and creating their own curriculum, students may end up with a "warped perspective or a skewed understanding of a field" There is also a "practical risk"; the students may not have the practical skills to respond effectively to this learning approach, failing to develop and progress new skills. The pedagogical risk is concerned with developing a "space-for-being" where the risk is "ontological" shaping the learner's "being" and subsequently their personal identity. Nonetheless, Barnett (2014) does encourage educators to take risks with pedagogy, to be creative in their approaches to teaching and learning, ensuring that the needs of graduates are met and prepared effectively to fulfil the demands and needs of communities and society.

A heutagogical approach recognises the need to be flexible in the learning where the teacher provides resources but the learner designs the curriculum, not just the learning process, by negotiating the learning. Thus learners might read around critical issues or questions and determine what is of interest and relevance to them and then negotiate further reading and assessment tasks.

A recent study by Junco, Heiberger, and Loken (2010) showed that students who used Twitter (as compared to those who did not) were more actively engaged in their learning processes and had higher GPAs. Junco et al. (2010) also found that the use of Twitter boosted student-student and student-instructor interaction, as well as promoted active learning. Active use of social media in creating learner-generated content seems to contribute to development of skills of self-directedness. Initial research findings by Blaschke, Porto, and Kurtz (2010) indicate that active use of social media, for example, development of learner-generated content, supports cognitive and meta-cognitive skill development, whereas passive use (consumption) is less effective in supporting development of these skills.

Role of Teacher in Heutagogical Learning Environment

There are many duties of teachers in higher education which involves provision of a broad context of knowledge within which students can locate and understand the content of their more specific studies. Teachers of higher education play various roles like information provider, facilitator, assessor, planner, resource developer etc. Role of the teacher is same in primary and secondary level, but the need of students are differing. The primary level students do not have their understanding about creation of knowledge etc. So, at this level the role of teacher needs to be change.

Self-determined learning assumes that people have the potential to learn continuously and in real time by interacting with their environment, they learn through their lifespan, can be lead to ideas rather than be force fed the wisdom of others, and thereby they enhance their creativity, and re-learn how to learn (Kenyon 2003). Heutagogy recognizes that people learn when they are ready and that this is most likely to occur quite randomly, chaotically and in the face of ambiguity and need. To implement a self-determined learning environment, instructors need to alter their teaching approach, primarily by placing value on learner self-direction of the learning process. Such a shift would require minimal change within distance education environments as distance education teaching methods support self-directed learning and the role of instructor is already one of guide-on-the-side. They would also need to accept the heutagogical approach as one that is unconventional, where the instructor becomes a facilitator in students' learning process (Cristiano, 1993).

As teachers in heutagogy, we should concern ourselves with developing the learner's capability not just embedding discipline based skills and knowledge. We should relinquish any power we deem ourselves to have. Some of the work-based learning possibilities that are heutagogical in nature are action learning, and coaching and mentoring, and their associated techniques. These approaches emphasise processes that provide the opportunity to access learning 'moments', tacit learning, and develop the notion of a learning organisation.

Instructors should ensure that they explain this type of learning to their students from the very start of class. As in a distance learning environment, students also need to understand that a heutagogical learning environment is quite different from the traditional learning experience with which they are familiar. Expectations of instructor from learners should be clearly stated: learners are responsible for knowledge creation and deciding upon the learning path (Ashton & Newman, 2006; Schwier, Morrison, & Daniel, 2009). Empathy helps create a comfortable learning environment for learners unaccustomed to self-determined learning, and, as with self-directed learning, it is important to create a climate of mutual trust and respect with a clear delineation of instructor and learner roles and one that supports dialogue (Knowles, 1975). Ongoing guidance and feedback, as well as sharing of resources, support students along their learning journey, and learners will require ongoing instructor guidance and support throughout the learning process if they are to develop the capability of self-direction (Collis and Moonen, 2001, as cited in Ashton & Newman, 2006).

Conclusion

A modern French philosopher has said that the task of the educator is to act on the mind and the conscience of the students to render them capable of thinking and judging themselves to promote initiative, arouse spontaneity and fashion human beings into freedom. This can be done through developing will-power of the child. Success brings confidence of will and the desire changes itself into decision.In the course of time the nature of knowledge, its creation, acquisition, comprehension, assimilation and application, etc. has also been continuously changing. This has had a substantial effect on the teaching learning process and the institutional effort in providing an ambience to the learner in conformity with the changing characteristics of learner and learning process. A glance of the learning theories developed by the eminent theorists and practitioners in the past suggests that nature and characteristics of the learner and their learning style are the cardinal factors which have formed the fundamental postulation of almost all the theories._Teachers are the most important asset for any educational system. They are founders, creators and executors of educational system. Therefore, quality concern of higher education catches immense attention of educationists in present time. When we talk about capabilities of students in twenty first century, it is realized that traditional practices may not seem most effective to resolve the debate of quantity versus quality debate in higher education. To input quality we need self directed capable students who constantly effort to become more competent to meet the challenges of changing scenarios of society. In this situation heutagogical approaches may prove effective way of learning to develop capabilities in students. It is one of the ways of learning originated from constructivism. Constructivism gives importance to individuals' potentials, experiences and freedom for construction of new knowledge. Heutagogy also provides space to adult learner. Freedom is the basic requirement for natural development of an individual. The concept of heutagogy offers certain principles and practices that can be considered when designing a learning environment. Such learning environment facilitates the learner to become capable and competent individual that can handle any situations in their own ways. It is suggested that heutagogy is appropriate to the needs of learners in the twenty-first century, particularly in the development of individual capability. Therefore, a shift in thinking towards heutagogy will enable the control of learning to move more appropriately to the learner. Furthermore it will enable a far more creative approach to learning on the part of learners. If a teacher does this job then the goal of heutagogy that is self realization will be achieved.

References

1. Ankesh L more (2017). Skill development in higher education: trends opportunities and prospects. University news: 55(28). July 2017.
2. Ashton, J., & Newman, L. (2006). An Unfinished Symphony: 21st Century Teacher Education Using Knowledge Creating Heutagogies. *British Journal of Educational Technology*, 37(6) 825-840.
3. Barnett, R. (2007). *A will to learn: Being a student in an age of uncertainty*. Maidenhead: McGraw Hill/OUP.
4. Barnett, R. (2012). The coming of the ecological university. *Oxford Review of Education,37*, 439–455.
5. Barnett, R. (2014). *Conditions of flexibility: Securing a more responsive higher education system*. York: HEA.
6. Blaschke, L.M.(2018) Heutagogy and Lifelong Learning: A Review of Heutagogical Practice and Self-Determined Learning, The International Review of Research in Open and Distance Learning. Retrieved December 15, 2018, from https://files.eric.ed.gov/fulltext/EJ979639.pdf.
7. Blaschke, L.M., Porto, S., & Kurtz, G. (2010). Assessing the Added Value of Web 2.0 Tools for e-learning: The MDE experience. In Proceedings of the European Distance and e- learning Network (EDEN) Research Workshop, October 25-27.
8. Brandon B. (2016). Two transformative Learning strategies: Heutagogy and personalization. retrieved from www.learningsolutionmag.com on 30.12.2018
9. Brooks, J. & Brook, M. (1993). The care for the constructivist classrooms. Alexandria, VA 'ASCD'.
10. Canning, N. & Callan, S. (2010). Heutagogy: Spirals of Reflection to Empower Learners in Higher Education. Reflective Practice, 11(1).
11. Canning, N. (2010). Playing with heutagogy: Exploring strategies to empower mature learners in higher education. *Journal of Further and Higher Education,34*, 59–71.10.1080/03098770903477102
12. Cristiano, M.J. (1993). *I want to learn what I want to learn in the way I choose to learn it: Using learning contracts*. Paper presented at the Western States Communication Association Great Ideas for Teaching Speech (GIFTS), Community College Interest Group, February 14, 1993.
13. Davis L. (2018). heutagogy explain a self determined Learning in education.retreived from www.schoology.com on 6.1.19
14. Dwivedi, R.D. (2010). From Behaviorism to Constructivism: A Paradigm Shift in Teaching-learning Process, *University News, A Weekly Journal of Higher Education*, Vol. 48, no. 07.
15. Gardner, A., Hase, S., Gardner, G., Dunn, S.V., & Carryer, J. (2007). From Competence to Capability: A Study of Nurse Practitioners in Clinical Practice. *Journal of Clinical Nursing*, 17(2), 250-258. doi: 10.1111/j.1365-2702. 206.0188.x
16. Hase, S. (2009). Heutagogy and e-learning in the Workplace: Sum Challenges and Opportunities. Impact: *Journal of Applied Research in Workplace e-learning*, 1 (1).

17. Hase, S., & Kenyon, C. (2007). Heutagogy: A child of complexity theory. *International Journal of Complexity and Education,4*, 111–119.
18. Hase, S., & Kenyon, C. (2013). *Self determined learning: Heutagogy in a action*. London: Bloomsbury.
19. Kenyon C.(2003): Heutagogy and developing capable people and capable workplace: strategies for dealing with complexity southern cross university. epublication@SCU retrieved from https/epub.scu.edu.au on 2.1.19
20. Knowles, M. (1984). *The Adult Learner: A Neglected Species*. Houston, Gulf publishing.
21. McAuliffe, M., Hargreaves, D., Winter, A., & Chadwick, G. (2008). *Does pedagogy still rule?* In Proceedings of the 2008 AAEE Conference, December 7-10.
22. Powell, J. L. (2012). *Understanding the voluntary sector: Critical success factors - A case study*. New York, NY: Nova Science.
23. Prahallada, N.N. (2013). Heutagogy as a Learning Approach, *University News, A Weekly Journal of Higher Education*, Vol. 51, No .33.
24. Ray S. (2018). Pedagogy ,andragogy and now heutagogy. retrieved from https/ upcea.edu on 6.1.19
25. Rogers, C. (1951). *Client-centred therapy: Its current practice, implications and theory*. London: Constable.
26. Schwier, R.A., Morrison, D., & Daniel, B. (2009). A preliminary investigation of self-directed learning activities in a non-formal blended learning environment. Online Submission. Retrieved from EBSCO host.
27. Snowden, M., & Halsall, J. (2014). Community development: A shift in thinking towards heutagogy. *International Journal of Multi Disciplinary Comparative Studies,1*, 81–91.
28. Stephenson, J., & Yorke, M. (1998). *Capability and quality in higher education: Teaching and learning in higher education)*. London: Kogan Page.
29. Yaduvanshi & Singh (2017). Developing Professional Competencies among Prospective Teachers through Heutagogical Practices. *International Journal of Information Research and Review*. Vol. 4 (2).

Chapter - 2

Challenges of Student Teachers During Teaching Practice

Dr. P.S. Pragathi

Abstract

Teacher education is an important aspect of our educational system. It involves the preparation of teachers who are responsible for transforming our educational theories and policies into practice. Teaching practice is an important component of teacher training. It provides an actual teaching experience to the student teachers. The main aim this paper is to identify the challenges faced by the student teachers during teaching practice. The investigators explore the experiences of student teachers during 8 weeks' of teaching practice in different schools of Tirupati city. To investigate of the aim of this study, three research questions were formulated by the investigators. Survey design was adopted. The population consisted of 100 student teachers from 2 years of Bachelor of Education course. A structured questionnaire which consisted of 22 items in three sections was used to elicit information from the respondents. The data collected from the investigation were organized in tables and analyzed. The result of data analysis of the study revealed challenges facing by the student teachers during teaching practice which includes classroom supervision, curriculum, and instruction. Based on the findings, some suggestions were addressed on the challenges that affect student-teachers performance during teaching practice.

Introduction

Teacher education is an important aspect of our educational system. In the broader sense 'teacher education' refers to the total of educative experience which contribute to the preparation of a person for a teaching position in schools, but the term is more commonly employed to designate the programme of courses and other experiences offered by an educational institute for the announced purpose of preparing persons for teaching and other educational service and for contributing to their growth in competency for such service. The National Council for Teacher Education (NCTE) was established in 1993 by an Act of Parliament. It is the all-powerful regulatory body for the teacher education system in the country, consisting of the Teacher Education Institutions (TEIs) that run bachelor of education (B.Ed) and diploma in education (D.Ed) programmes to prepare teachers, and master's in education (M.Ed) programmes to prepare teacher educators. The teacher education has mainly two aspects at B.Ed. level. They are Pre-service and In-Service Education. Pre-service education is concerned with handling over to the would-be teacher a set of skills and knowledge assumed to be useful her/him. In-service education is concerned with providing effective feedback to teachers in schools. Pre-service education has two broad aspects- theory and practicals. The practical work is called practice teaching at school level.

Teaching practice is a form of work-integrated learning that is described as a period of time when students are working in the relevant school to receive specific in-service training in order to apply theory in practice. Teaching practice is a segment, which provides opportunity to prospective teachers; apply theoretical knowledge practically in real situation. It is an activity, which can play an important role in preparing teachers for future challenges in a classroom. Its effectiveness for the nation is beyond any doubt. It is a milestone for professional adolescence. It is a fuel for an endless journey and a combination of personality, professional skills, knowledge and training. According to Perry (2004:2), teaching practice can be conducted in a number of forms depending on the institution. Some institutions send student teachers to go for teaching practice once a day each week; others do this over a semester; while others send student teachers in a two- to six weeks' block. This period allows students to learn, to plan, to teach and evaluate lessons independently. The staff of the teacher-training college teaches practice-based components to help students gain this ability. Each student also has mentors among the teaching staff at his or her school to provide help and advice. The period of work as a trainee teacher is intended to enable trainees to practice their profession.

Stages in Teaching Practice

Primary Stage

The student teachers have to attend to that particular school, where they are going for practice teaching. The main aim of going school is to see the concerned teacher, class teachers and school staff in order to acquire information about school and its environment. Student teachers must observe the teaching methods of school, methods of concerned class teacher and notebooks of the students and their usual routine. On return from the school student teachers must have the details about scheme of studies, age of the students, strength of the class, abilities and specific problems of the students, timing of the school, textbooks and teaching aids.

Lesson Preparation

For the preparation of lesson by student teachers must know the subject, the relevant books and audio visual aids which he / she is going to teach. Well prepared lecture gives confidence to the teacher in the class. Student teachers and supervisor can reform the teaching- learning process after its evaluation.

Good Lesson-Qualities

A good lesson has the following qualities:

- Lesson planning should be in complete detail.
- Lesson should be interesting.
- Effective and timely use of teaching methods and teaching aids.
- Student should be ready for learning.
- Students should be involved practically in teaching learning process.
- Lesson should be taught in professional and friendly environment.
- All students should be given same attention by keeping in view their individual differences.

Class room Teaching

The stage of teaching in the classroom is known as practice teaching. Student teachers while teaching in the classroom passes through different steps of his / her teaching (Introduction, presentation, recapitulation) and concerned teacher / supervisor assesses / observes his / her lesson.

Teaching Practice–Evaluation

In order to evaluate the teaching practice supervisor observes the student teacher while teaching in the classroom. Supervisor evaluates / observes the punctuality, lesson planning, teaching methods, use of audio visual aids, adequacy of audio visual aids, pitch of voice, dress, start and end of lesson, interest of the students, discipline of class, use of black / white board, students' notebooks and objectives of the lesson.

Trainee teachers spend their working hours in two locations

The teacher-training college

Student teacher trainees attend theoretical classes, demonstration lessons, write assignments, projects, participate in practice-based seminars on one to two days per week, taught by college staff. The training they receive here ranges from educational and social sciences to the subject or subjects trainees are being prepared to teach.

The school

Student teacher trainees' work in their schools in centered on-

- sitting in on lessons,
- teaching lessons under supervision
- teaching lessons independently
- taking part in school meetings, working with parents, accompanying school trips etc.

Definitions of Teaching Practice

A number of terms such as the practice teaching, student teaching, teaching practice, field studies, infield experience, school based experience or internship are used to refer to this activity (Taneja, 2000). The term practice teaching embraces all the learning experiences of student teachers in schools (Ashraf, 1999). The term practice teaching has three major connotations: the practicing of teaching skills and acquisition of the role of a teacher; the whole range of experiences that students go through in schools; and the practical aspects of the course as distinct from theoretical studies (Stones and Morris, 1977).

Teaching practice is the name of the preparation of student teachers for teaching by practical training. It is the practical use of teaching methods, teaching strategies, teaching principles, teaching techniques and practical training and practice / exercise of different activities of daily school life.

Statement of the Problem

Teaching practice is one of the most important aspects of teachers training programme aimed at exposing the student teachers to the field to carry out the theoretical knowledge and experience into practice in real classroom situation under the supervision of a good teacher. In some cases, the objective of teaching practice may not be fully realized, this is because, most student teachers after their student teaching experiences or even after their graduation from college, still lack the required and necessary skills for which they were sent on teaching practice. The inability to fully realize the objectives of teaching practice or the inability of student teachers to perform to expectation can be attributed to certain challenges or inadequacies of the programme. The challenges that face student teachers during teaching practice is what necessitates the need for the study and hence the problem of the study.

Main objective of the study

The main purpose of this study is to find out the challenges facing student teachers during teaching practice.

Specific objectives of the study

- Determine the classroom supervision challenges faced by the student teachers during teaching practice.
- Find out the curriculum and instruction challenges faced by student teachers during teaching practice.
- Find out the supervisory challenges faced by the student teachers during teaching practice.

Research Questions

The following research questions are developed to follow the study,

1. What are the challenges of classroom supervision faced by student teachers during teacher practice?
2. What are the curriculum and instruction challenges faced by student teachers during teaching practice?
3. What are the supervisory challenges faced by student teachers during teaching practice?

Research Methodology

Population and Sampling

The population of the study consisted of all the future teachers who are admitted to Bachelor of Education programme in the Institute of Advanced study in Education, Tirupati. The sample of the study consist 100 student teachers. These students were selected from one teacher training institution from two semesters.

Tool development and Data collection

Since the study was descriptive in nature, therefore, survey approach was considered appropriate to collect the data. For the purpose, a twenty two item questionnaire was developed with the option of "yes" and "No".

Administration of Research Tool

The questionnaires were administered on prospective student teachers personally and responses were received.

Data Analysis

The data collected through questionnaire was coded and analyzed through in terms of percentage.

Table 1: Responses of student teachers on the challenges of classroom supervision during teaching practice

S.No	*Item Statement*	*Response type-Yes*	*Response type-No*	*Total*	*Remarks*
1.	Poor arrangement of the seating and sitting position of students	18%	82%	100%	Accepted
2.	Control over students' movement in and around the class	13%	87%	100%	Accepted
3.	Supervision over noise making	10%	90%	100%	Accepted
4.	Set inducing students	85%	15%	100%	Accepted
5.	Improvisation in teaching	19%	81%	100%	Accepted
6.	Writing on the chalkboard	89%	11%	100%	Rejected

Table 1:The table shows that items 1, 2,3,4,5 respectively were accepted upon by the student teachers because these items receive highest percentage above which is within the acceptance range and item 6 was rejected by the student teachers. All the items apart from item 1, 2, 3, 5 have highest percentage which explains that student teachers accepted that these items contribute challenges to the classroom supervision during teaching practice.

Table 2: Responses of student teachers on the challenges of curriculum and instruction challenges during teaching practice

S.No	*Item Statement*	*Response type-Yes*	*Response type-No*	*Total*	*Remarks*
7.	Lack of ability of student teachers to master the subject matter	84%	16%	100%	Accepted
8.	Lack of ability of the student teachers to utilize instructional materials properly	12%	88%	100%	Rejected

(Contd...)

9.	Lack of ability of the student teachers to apply appropriate teaching skills.	17%	83%	100%	Rejected
10.	Inadequacy of relevant textbooks	89%	11%	100%	Accepted
11.	Non availability of curriculum guiding principles	10%	90%	100%	Rejected
12.	Writing of lesson notes	84%	16%	100%	Accepted
13.	Giving of written exercise	91%	09%	100%	Accepted
14.	Marking student exercise	92%	08%	100%	Accepted
15.	Inability of student teachers to improvise instructional material	86%	14%	100%	Accepted
16.	Nervousness.	83%	17%	100%	Accepted

Table-2: The table above shows the responses of the respondents on the curriculum and instruction challenges facing student teachers during teaching practice. So far items in 7, 10, 12, 13, 14, 15, and 16 were accepted while items 8, 9,11were rejected.

Table 3: Responses of student teachers on the supervisory challenges during teaching practice

S.No	*Item Statement*	*Response type-Yes*	*Response type-No*	*Total*	*Remarks*
17.	Supervisors spent only few minutes in the class.	19%	81%	100%	Rejected
18.	Supervisors impatience to go through the lesson notes	04%	96%	100%	Rejected
19.	Lack of cordial relationship between the supervisor and the student teachers	91%	09%	100%	Accepted
20.	Uncooperative attitude of the regular teachers with student teachers	88%	12%	100%	Accepted
21.	Short of feedback from supervisors on students' performance to enable them obtain improvement	82%	18%	100%	Accepted
22.	No supervision by some supervisors	85%	15%	100%	Rejected

Table-3: The table above shows the responses of the respondents on the supervisory challenges facing by student teachers during teaching practice. So far items in 19, 20 and 21 were accepted while items in 17, 18 and 22 were rejected.

Findings of the study

After the presentation and analysis of the above data on the challenges faced by student teachers during teaching practice, the following findings were made.

- Classroom supervision creates challenges to the student teachers. The aspects like poor arrangement of the seating and sitting position of pupils/ student, supervision over noise making, pupil's movement in and around the class, improvisation in teaching constitute to challenges student teachers faces during teaching practice.

- Curriculum and instruction pose a challenge to student teachers in the sense that the curriculum- lack of ability of student teachers to master the subject matter, inadequacy of relevant textbooks, and inability of student teachers to improvise instructional materials also constitute a challenge.
- Even though the supervise faculty visit the student teachers in their practicing school regularly, some of them (faculty) lack cordial relationship with the student teachers and does not give them feedback on their performance to enable them to obtain improvement. Another aspect i.e. non co-operative attitude of the regular teachers with student teachers also creates challenge to student teachers.

Implications of the Study

Based on the findings of this research, the following implications are made:

- Proper attention should be given to the classroom supervision by the student teachers in order to achieve the specific objective at the end of the lesson in the classroom.
- Care must be given to the application of good teaching methods and techniques are very essential for quality training, developing confidence, competency and skills, which are helpful in transfer of learning and knowledge comprehensively.
- Adequate curriculum guidelines, facilities, reference materials like textbooks etc should be made available to facilitate effective and efficient teaching and learning.
- Competent and dedicated supervisors should be used in teaching practice supervision. They may stay whole day in school to check the activities of the students and observe honestly.
- There is need for the government to provide good library facilities and laboratories.
- Students' teachers should be sent to high quality schools with enabling learning environment.

Conclusion

Teachers play key roles in instructional process in schools. Teachers are the main determinants of quality in the schools. When student teachers are uncomfortable they will not put in their best during teaching practice. There is the possibility that the investment put into this course is wasted because the student teachers may not improve for the simple fact that their problems remain unsolved. The study also confirms that within the student teaching practice, student teachers come across difficulties that result to problems associated with the classroom supervision, curriculum and instruction and supervision by faculty. Classroom supervision represents one of the major challenges identified by student teachers during their teaching practice. Classroom supervision is challenging for student teachers due to the difficulty providing realistic situation in the classroom. Student teachers are expected to get the supervisors feedback to enable them to obtain improvement. The attainment of quality education will be a mirage without adequate preparation of manpower that will dispense the knowledge. This calls for serious consideration of stipulated strategies to be adopted in tackling the challenges which student teachers face in the period of teaching practice.

References

1. Akbar, R.A. (2002).A study of Teaching practice of Prospective Secondary School Teachers and Development of a Teaching practice Model, Arid Agricultural University, Rawalpindi (Unpublished PhD Thesis).
2. Agarwal (1993). Teacher and Education in Developing Society, Vikas Publications, New Delhi.
3. Ali Murtaza, (2005). Comparative Study of Practice Teaching in Formal and Non formal Systems and Development of a Model, Arid Agricultural University, Rawalpindi (Unpublished PhD Thesis).
4. Bajwa (1977).Student Teaching, Ashish Publications, New Delhi.
5. Brwn, P.D. & Brown N.R. (1990). Effective Teaching Practice. Stanley Thornes, England
6. Cohen, A. & Carver, N. (1970). A Students' Guide to Teaching Practice. University of London Press, London.
7. Cohen, L. & Manion, L. (1983). A Guide to Teaching Practice. Methuen, London.
8. Education and Training in transforming Education. New York: Sunny Press.
9. Government of Pakistan (1998). National Education Policy 1998-2010, Ministry of Education, Islamabad.
10. Gall, N.U (2003).Teaching practice in the republic of Maldives, issues and challenges. Pacific Asia
11. Garg (2000).Issues in Teacher Education,The Indian Publications, Naiwali Gali, Kacha Bazar.

12. Gupta, N.K. and Mrs.Kusum Sham Sherry (1982).Prediction of teaching efficacy through teacher's attitude toward professional training, The Educational Reviews, 88(3).
13. Loknath Mishra (2007).Reactions of pupil teachers of two years B.Ed. course towards teaching and teacher education, Edutracks, January ,Vol.6,No.5
14. Maduewesi K. (1990). Communication between theory and practice: how student teachers develop theories of teaching. Australian Journal of Education 21(1) 18-22.
15. Mohanty (1984).Student Teaching, Ashish Publishers, New Delhi.
16. Malik, S.R. (1992). The System of education in Pakistan. National Book Foundation, Lahore.
17. Ram Mohan Babu, (1992). Job satisfaction, attitude towards teaching, job involvement, teacher efficacy and the perception of organizational climate of teachers of residential and non residential schools. Doctoral thesis in Edication, S.V.U.,Tirupati, India.
18. R, A, Farooq, (1994). Education System in Pakistan: Issues and Problems, Asia Society for Promotion of Innovation and Reforms in Education, Islamabad.
19. Richert (1992).A study of student teachers in Calfornia,WWW.student teachers performance.com.
20. Saylor, J. G., Alexander, W.M., & Lewis, A.J. (1981).Curriculum planning for better Teaching and learning. (41th Ed.) New York: Holt, Rinehart and Winston.
21. Surendra Kumar Patnaik, (1979). The good school teachers as per students, The Educational Review,LXXXV(7)
22. Taneja, R.P. (2000). Encyclopedia of Comparative Education, Vol.4. Anmol Publications Pvt. Ltd., New Delhi.

Chapter - 3

Issues Related to Teaching-Learning Strategies in Teacher Education

Dr. Qudsia Hafeez

Abstract

The term higher education in India includes the entire spectrum of education beyond the twelve years of formal schooling. Higher Education in India is undergoing a big transformation, which is reflected not only in the choice of students with respect to the programme and institutions, but also in the methods of teaching and learning from instruction mode to student-centered learning. The resource now is varied from print material to e-learning. A change is also evident in the assumption of higher education from public to private good. Internalization of higher education adds a newer dimension to it. The process of change calls for a debate to understand the dimensions of the problem along quantity and quality axes. The competition rather than control, and autonomy and innovation rather than protection and inbreeding, are the hallmarks of quality in higher education. Higher Education is one of the most important indicators of quality in education in the country. The base of Higher Education lies on the foundation of Primary, Secondary and Higher Secondary Education. Teacher Education becomes one of the key determinants of reviving quality in all sectors of Education. In this paper the investigator critically examines the system of Teacher Education within the broader curricular framework of School Education; thus reflecting on the principles of NCF-2005, RTE-2009, & NCFTE-2005. And to review the Teacher Education in the light of present day demands. There are many pedagogic issues related to teaching-learning strategies in teacher education; from basic availability of resources to integrating technology in education. Higher education provides people with an opportunity to reflect on the critical social, economic, cultural, moral and spiritual issues facing humanity. It contributes to national development through dissemination of specialized knowledge, skills and innovations. It is therefore a crucial factor for survival.

Key Words: *National Curriculum Framework (2005), Right to Education Act (2009), National Curriculum Framework for Teacher Education (2009), Teacher Education, Secondary Education, National Knowledge Commission (2007).*

Introduction

Education as a social science and as a discipline is academic on one hand and professional on the other hand. For a quality process component of teacher education there is a need to redesign the teacher education system, to encompass and satisfy itself in meeting the needs of the society through implementing programmes that requires development of innovative instructional modules and strengthening of research inputs. As we are witnessing three types of Explosions, viz., explosion of knowledge, population and expectation; there is a dire need to opt for latest trends in education (i.e. both Teacher Education and School Education) to suit the needs of today's learner. Being at the apex of the educational pyramid, it has also a key role in producing teachers for the education system. In the context of the unprecedented explosion of knowledge, higher education has to become dynamic as never before, constantly entering uncharted areas.

1. Pedagogy Issues: In a science-based world, education and research are crucial to the entire developmental process of a country, its welfare, progress and security. Secondary Education Commission has defined Curriculum as totality of experiences the pupil receives through the manifold activities that go in the school, in the classroom, library, laboratory, workshops, playground and in the numerous informal contacts between the teacher and the pupil. (Babu Sai Bandla, 2012). According to National Focus Group on Teaching of Science (NCF-2005), a major area of concern is the gradual decline of practical work and experimentation at secondary and senior secondary levels, even when the concept of activity-based teaching has been initiated in the Science Curriculum on the lines of constructivism. Experiments are hallmark of science, and for science learning, they are essential. Though activity-based teaching has been accepted as a paradigm for science education and is also reflected in some measure in the textbooks developed at the national and state levels, it is hardly translated in actual classroom practice. Often practical difficulties are cited as an excuse for this lack of commitment and awareness that experiment is fundamental to doing and learning science. The degeneration of rigour in practical examinations has also lent weight to the argument to first remove them from the ambit of evaluation and then to trivialize or totally remove them from teaching practice itself. Cost cannot be an excuse for neglecting experiments since it is possible to imaginatively design low cost science experiments. Ultimately, there is no alternative but to invest heavily in improving school laboratories and workshops while reducing the importance of external examinations and promoting experimental culture in our schools. We should also have computer-interfaced experiments and projects, besides projects utilizing database from the public domain.

2. Brainstorm Ideas: Higher Order Thinking Skills is the backbone for Brainstorming Ideas in novel situations. It is a concept based on educational reform in learning taxonomies from Bloom's Taxonomy (1956) to Anderson and Krathwohl Taxonomy (2001) such as Remember, Understand, Apply, Analyze, Evaluate, and Create. Similarly, the concept of Six Thinking Hats (White for Facts; Green for Creativity; Yellow for Benefits; Black for Cautions; Red for Feelings; and Blue for Process) designed by Edward de Bono (1985) also promotes individual thinking process cohesively. The most important and urgent reform needed in education is to relate it to the life, needs and aspirations of the people and thereby make it a powerful instrument of social, economic and cultural transformation necessary for realization of the national goal. For this purpose the following five-fold programme has been suggested:

1. Relating education to productivity;
2. Strengthening social and national integration through educational programmes;
3. Consolidation of democracy through education;
4. Development of social, moral and spiritual values; and
5. Modernisation of society through awakening of curiosity, development of attitudes and values and building up certain essential skills.

Varma. Subodh (2016) reported in a Times of India article that if Science Congress is a joke, it's because Science in India is a tragedy. There is a shocking state of Science in our country, 59% of secondary schools in India don't have an integrated science laboratory although science is compulsory till class 10. So, a vast majority of students 'study' science without ever seeing any experiment, let alone doing it. At the +2 level where students opt for science, just 32% schools have separate rooms for laboratories and a quarter of them are 'partially equipped'. Perhaps they are being taught via the web; but just 37% of schools have a computer with net connection. Since the problem begins in schools and colleges, students who do go through the grind and finally get into science and technology related jobs see their dreams die in India's vast but faltering science establishment. Science education has moved from being a curiosity-driven exploration to a mark-scoring exercise to get admission in elite institutions and bag a fat corporate salary. In the process, academia has also lost high quality teachers who shape young minds. There are serious problems facing Indian Science, ranging from resource crunch to policy confusion. The goal of spending at least 2% of GDP on scientific research, outlined in the government's science policy of 2003 has not been achieved. As per latest available figures, India is spending less than 1% on research and development compared to 1.9% in China and 2.75% in US. India has just 4 scientific researchers for every 10,000 people in the workforce, much lower than not just advanced countries like the US or UK 79, but even China 18 and Brazil 14. Given the low input, the best minds have left India for greener pastures. Scientific papers published by Indians numbered about 90,000 in 2013 compared to 4,50,000 by Americans and 3,25,000 by Chinese. Citations too were below the world average. Indians filed just 17 patents per million population compared to 541 in China and 4,451 in South Korea. India still contributes less than 1% of the world's top 1% of research. Another key problem is the way science is being practiced in the country- the project mode. In today's environment of research in project mode with well-defined objectives, milestones and deliverables; curiosity-driven research is a casualty. Research objectives too are increasingly disconnected from society.

3. Student Centric: National Curriculum Framework (2005) stresses a learner centered curriculum, which is flexible and encourages learner autonomy where teacher plays the role of a facilitator supporting active participation of learners. According to an article given in Times of India dated 29/09/2015, a report by Ministry of Human Resource Development says that only 28.84% schools in Telangana have computer and internet facility, leaving more than one crore students across the state unexposed to the World Wide Web. "According to the Flash Statistics 2014-15 for Secondary Education in India highlights the poor condition of schools across the state in terms of basic facilities. In Telangana only 30.09% secondary schools and 23.17% higher secondary schools have computer and internet facility. Adding to the woes, less than 40% schools in the state have fully equipped physics, chemistry, biology and computer labs." Apart from this, only 24.96% secondary schools have integrated science laboratory. For subjects performable experiments are put up on screens, here the question arises, "Are we achieving all the aims, objectives enshrined in Constructivist Curriculum?" being taught in our schools. If this is the situation, then how can one implement Student Centered Instruction?

4. Academic Leadership: Its one of the crucial steps in the success of controlling education. It is important for effective management of programs, promotion of scholarship and excellence in teaching and student centred learning. For, communication and relationships within and outside the institutions with key stakeholders, professional associations and accreditation bodies. Leading course teams to achieve strategic outcomes; understanding contemporary teaching and learning methodologies and building and developing strategic relationships. It is important to understand the diverse roles played by an Academic Leader as Developer, Monitor, Deliverer, Innovator, and Broker and the various challenges faced by the Academic Leader in inappropriate use of roles. Similar challenges are faced

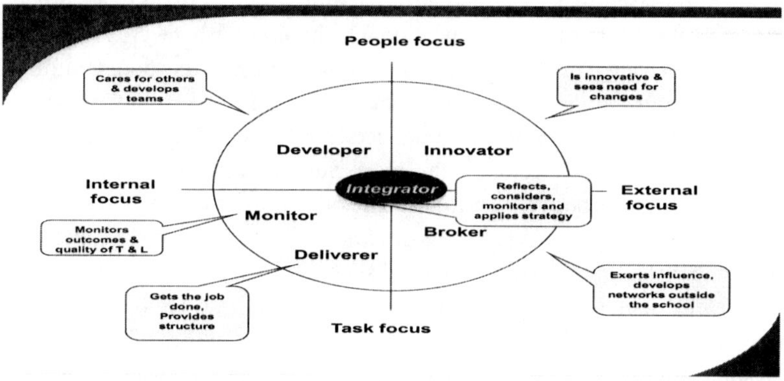

Figure 1: Roles of Academic Leader, Source:

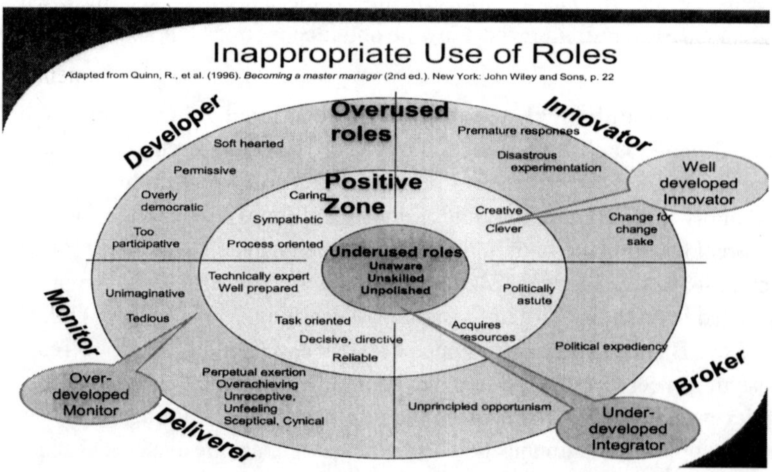

Source: https://academicleadership.curtin.edu.au/local/docs/learnlead program_resources/module _ resources/Dev_Academic_Leadership_Capability_1/Developing_Academic_ Leadership _ Capacity_1.ppt

Figure 2: Inappropriate Use of Roles and Challenges of Academic Leader

by many institutions thereby decreasing the efficiency of managing higher education and the needs of the people. It is also due to lack of awareness and understanding of this multitasking job operating in higher education environment on one hand and the lack of understanding of the expectations of the followers on the other hand.

5. Utilizing Technology in the Classroom: Though, National Policy on Education 1986, as modified in 1992, has stressed upon employing educational technology to improve the quality of education. According to an articlegiven in Times of India dated 09/12/2015, Between High Tech & No Tech; reported that, "The Indian Education sector is quickly adapting to technology. More than 400 educational technology firms were launched in the last decade. Most of the initiatives like smart class rooms, online teaching programmes, teacher evaluation, in-school learning, sharing through tablets or laptops and personalized educational content are thriving mainly in the private sector or the more autonomous higher education institutes. There is a need for a government policy framework to be expedited to make the same available for those who cannot afford these, such as government schools. However, in the absence of such a policy, private and non-government initiatives are trying to extend these technologies to government schools. Educomp, considered a pioneer in the field, has also had some progress in getting involved with government schools. But several hurdles has emerged such as poor internet penetration and low internet speeds, besides the lack of infrastructure. If these are not fixed, the great Indian classroom divide won't just be about economics but about tech as well."

6. Methodological Approaches: Educational Innovations fetch educational excellence. Since innovation is considered to increase productivity, it is considered to be critical for policymakers to integrate and apply innovation in the field. Educational Innovations in the form of different teaching methods and models of teaching such as Activity Based Learning, Active Learning Method, Individualized Instruction, Computer Assisted Instruction, Virtual Classroom, E-learning, Massive Open Online Courses, Blended Learning, Flipped Classroom, Google Classroom, Team Teaching, Peer Group Learning, etc should be developed and tried out at all levels of education to facilitate and improve student learning outcomes. Information and Communication Technologies are making dynamic changes in the society and influencing all aspects of life; much of the credit goes to Globalization and Modernization process in Education. It has shifted the role from how to use technologies to understand how to teach and learn with technologies. Lack of pedagogical knowledge amongst educators and practitioners is the foremost reason why emerging technologies remain unexplored in education or underutilized. Pathetically, to add to this problem is the chunk of lack of resources available in our country. Yashpal Committee Report (2009) argues that knowledge generation in a university system requires that different disciplines must grow in organic unity. Fragmentation of knowledge by creating boundaries of disciplines is not conducive for knowledge generation. University should be autonomous in allowing the balanced growth of various branches of knowledge. Over-regulation and interference in the functioning of university creates distortions in the knowledge generation and therefore be rationalized.

The report refers to various dichotomies in the higher education. Dichotomy between central and state university and between state university and affiliated colleges and between school and college level of education are principally the result of the fragmentation in knowledge. Similarly, undergraduate, teaching in affiliated colleges and postgraduate teaching in universities departments and university colleges cannot be treated separately. Both should co-evolve together and be treated in terms of organic unity. In fact, undergraduate and postgraduate should be the part of university and knowledge created at both the levels should feed each other. The less favorable treatment to undergraduate level of education will impact postgraduate and higher levels of education and the same is true for school and college levels of education. There has been further dichotomy between teaching and research due to the fragmented way of looking at the creation of knowledge. Teaching and research should also co-evolve together. Teaching promotes research as creative minds work together and pose questions which cannot all be answered in the classroom but taken up for research and the research understanding further develops the teaching. This integrated approach leads to qualitative improvement among students, teachers and researchers and provides the basis for further knowledge. (Bhushan, 2009).

7. Student and Faculty Mobility: As we witness three types of Explosions, viz; Explosion of Population, Explosion of Knowledge and Explosion of Expectations; then it becomes paramount for Higher Education to open doors for student and faculty mobility enriching integrated work experiences, internships, projects, collaborations, widening research network, promoting international competitions, short term teaching assignments, knowledge exchange, etc. But so far there are very few cases of such endeavors permitted in Higher Education in India. Education is a discipline, which is, on the one hand, liberal–academic, and on the other, professional. Hence, one needs to be careful to preserve its focus whether academic or professional during transaction of courses. Research programmes in Education, especially at the doctoral and post-doctoral levels while they generate and validate theory should be translated into development programmes. Teacher education institutions need to build up functional links with the school education sector and the higher education sector. In the absence of these links, teacher education institutions and schools may develop in isolation sans mutual rapport. This needs to be checked. Academic dialogue between teacher education institutions and higher education sector of which they are a part would keep alive the interdisciplinary nature of the field of education.

Conclusion: India's higher education system is the third largest in the world, next to the United States and China. The main governing body at the tertiary level is the University Grants Commission, which enforces its standards, advises the government, and helps coordinate between the centre and the state. Higher Education must be relevant to the individual and society needs at large thereby aiming at raising skills, creating high wage employment and enhancing economic growth. It is an indicator for better living standards, well-being and holistic development. It should create active mindsets that are adaptive to innovations and research, along with developing the human resource potential. Higher education in India should solve problems ranging such as income and gender disparities in enrolment, poor quality of faculty and pedagogy, lack of motivation and interest amongst students, lack of Industrial employability skills as one of the major factors contributing to the mounting number of unemployed graduates, and unnecessary political pressures dividing the nation. Henceforth, a fresh outlook towards the running of this higher sector is crucial and urgent steps should be taken to protect the system from degradation. Courses and programmes must be redesigned and inter-disciplinary approach must be followed. To increase and improve the quality and quantity of output; internal and external efficiency at all levels of education must be maintained.

References

1. Academic Leadership Retrieved from
2. https://academicleadership.curtin.edu.au/local/docs/learnlead/program resources/module resources/Dev Academic Leadership Capability 1/Developing Academic Leadership Capacity 1.ppt on 18-01-2019
3. All India Survey on Higher Education (2011-12), Government of India, Ministry of Human Resource Development, Department of Higher Education, New Delhi, (2013). Retrieved from
4. http://mhrd.gov.in/sites/upload_files/mhrd/files/statistics/AISHE2011-12P 1.pdf on 14-01-2016.

5. Altbach G. Philip & Umakoshi Toru (2004) Asian Universities Historical Perspectives and Contemporary Challenges Baltimore & London: The Johns Hopkins University Press.
6. Arulsamy. S. (2014) Educational Innovations and Management (1st.e.d.) New Delhi:
7. Babu Sai Bandla (2012). Perspectives in Education (1st.ed) Hyderabad: Bandla Publications.
8. Bhushan, Sudhanshu (2009). Restructuring Higher Education in India Jaipur: Rawat Publications.
9. Biswas, Preeti (2015, September 29). Only 28.84% schools in Telangana have Internet, Times View. The Times of India, p.5.
10. Curriculum Retrieved from
11. https://www.ugc.ac.in/oldpdf/modelcurriculum/edu.pdf, on 16-12-2018
12. Ghanta Ramesh, Dash. B.N. (2005). Foundations of Education Warangal: Neelkamal Publications Private Limited.
13. Kumar. Chethan (2015, December 09). Between High Tech & No Tech. The Times of India, p.7.
14. Natesan. A. K; Jahitha Begum. A; Sridevi. S. (2010) Quality Concerns in Teacher Education New Delhi: APH Publishing Corporation.
15. National Knowledge Commission Note on Higher Education, 29th November 2006. Retrieved from
16. http://knowledgecommissionarchive.nic.in/downloads/recommendations/Higher Education Note. pdf on 14-01-2016.
17. National Knowledge Commission, Wikipedia, The Free Encyclopedia Retrieved from https://en.wikipedia.org/wiki/National Knowledge Commission on 14-01-2016.
18. NCERT, NCF Retrieived from.
19. http://www.ncert.nic.in/rightside/links/pdf/framework/english/nf2005.pdf on 4-1-2019
20. NCFTE Retrieved from http://ncte-india.org/ncte_new/pdf/NCFTE_2010.pdf on 3-1-2019
21. Teacher Education Retrieved from

Chapter - 4

Impact of Technology in Indian Education System

D. Yedukondalu

Abstract

The impact that technology has in schools today is quite significant as technology in education has the power to transform how people learn. Technology in the classroom became more predominant by improved learning, increased engagement of students and virtual programs. Technology now can be seen as an investment for productive learning as teachers want more technology in their classrooms. So is the case in India as well with its own challenges. With both opportunities and challenges, technology in Indian Education System is rather a debatable phenomenon. When many schools are adapting the advancement in technology, yet there are some schools that strongly believe in old practices than going with the wind. The widespread adoption of technology in schools has changed the entire scenario of how students learn. Teachers are working on how to teach with emerging technologies and students are using advanced technology to enhance their learning and knowledge. The students have their own restrictions, teachers have there own and the administration is also admitting the fact that the education system is really in a poor shape today. The goal of this paper is to outline how information technology can help to create an education system that is based on the principles of helping teachers, students and administration to be effective in what they do, improving the quality and relevance of teaching learning process.

Introduction

Advancement of Technology has affected everything and everyone around us. Why not, education then! From computers to smart phones and their role in education, the journey has been very illuminating. Soon, mind hacking devices would be taking the position of our books and notebooks. No doubt, the human brain is also evolving and getting sharper day by day, the result of which is a 5-year old kid can operate smart phones. When it comes to education, India bags 92nd position among 145 countries. India must work on the rate and level of education provided to the preliminary and secondary schools. Moreover, it must ensure that every child gets education. However, now people are very much interested in getting their children educated as they have understood the importance of it. Evolution of technology has a greater impact on developing the foundation of future India. Conventional methods of mugging up words & definitions and limited learning are not prevalent anymore. The hectic schedule and getting good grades should not be the perspective. The advent of technology has released the pressure imposed on children's brain and has encouraged them to incline towards learning and become life-long leaner's.

Literature Review

The first Education Commission (1948) under the Chairmanship of Dr. Radhakrishnan was appointed to examine the state of education in India and to make recommendations for its improvement. For the proper financing of education, the Commission recommended that education should be placed in the Concurrent List so that it welcomes the responsibility of both the Central and the State government. Pillai et al., (1962) attempted to study the history and problems of educational finance in the primary and secondary education sectors in Kerala. It was found that the cost of education in relation to the total revenue of the state was far more excessive. The study made positive suggestions for reducing the expenditure on education and finding additional resources or bridging the gap between the expenditure and revenue. Education Commission (1964-66) while commenting on the university finances, recommended that the University Grants Commission should be enabled to pay both development and maintenance grants and the State governments be induced to pay their share of the university expenditure by means of block grants. It also gave a rather innocuous recommendation that the Universities should be immune from direct public accountability of their expenditure. Probably the first attempt on the part of the Government after Independence to look into the problem of financing of education in India was the constitution of a Committee on the Wages and Means of Financing Educational Development in India (1965). This committee recommended that ten percent of the central and twenty per cent of provincial revenue should be earmarked for education. Panchamukhi (1965) while presenting the estimated cost of education in India from 1950-51 to 1959-60, figured our resources costs as well as opportunity costs of education. According to his calculations, the total cost of education constituted 6.2 per cent of Gross National Product (GNP) in 1959-60.

Kothari (1966) who made a study of the total cost of education in India for three independent years, viz., 1950-51, 1955-56 and 1959-60 after estimating separately 52 the components of costs of education, namely, private costs and institutional costs calculated the foregone earnings (opportunity costs) for male and female, rural and urban students separately, which according to his estimates formed a large part of the total factor cost of education. The total cost of education was found to form 5 to 6.5% of the national income in 1960- 61 and not 2.5% as was generally believed based on calculations of institutional cost alone. Shah (1967) stated that till conflict between the motives of reality and the dictates of ideology is resolved, it would be meaningless to have a guess regarding the financial cost of and the resources likely to be available, for a satisfactory programme of development in the field of higher education. Indian Yearbook of Education (1968) also focused on the problem of educational finance specifically in the field of higher education. It lamented that, unlike other developing countries, India spent only three per cent of its Gross Domestic Product (GDP) on higher education, which was the main obstacle in meeting requirements of higher education. The Robbins Committee (1968) appointed to review the pattern of higher education and to advise the Great Britain government regarding the rules to be adopted for a long term development of higher education so as to cater to the national needs and resources, pointed to the huge rise in public expenditure, both recurring and nonrecurring, during 1954-63. This Committee also noted that expenditure on higher education in India was higher than Great Britain. Vaizey et al., (1968) indicated the dramatic changes happening in Britain and the expenditure on education from 1920-1965, pointing to the rise of share of educational expenditure in GNP from 2.5 per cent from the wars to 5 per cent in the mid sixties while its share in total expenditure had increased from 13.5 per cent to 18.9 per cent during the same period. Coombs (1968) has tried to assemble in one place the root facts about the world crisis in education to make explicit their inherent tendencies and to suggest some of the possible elements for a strategy to deal with the crisis. In his opinion, "sharp increase in polar aspirations for education which has laid siege to existing schools and universities" 53 is one of the reasons for crisis in higher education throughout the world. Severe scarcity of resources constraining the system of education from responding fully to new demands is the other reason for this crisis. Datt (1969) analyzed the cost of education in colleges. Data were collected from 28 colleges and the expenditure was specified into salary, equipment and co-curricular activity and miscellaneous. He studied the factors influencing unit cost of education using the technique of correlation and regression and came to the conclusion that a positive relationship existed between unit cost and the entire factors other than enrolment and a negative relationship existed between unit cost and enrolment. Blaug et al. (1969) computed unit cost of education to analyze the causes of graduate unemployment in India with the purpose of facilitating the estimation of rates of return to education. They relied on the data contained in the Report of the Education Commission in India (1964-66), studies conducted by the Institute of Applied Manpower Research and the official statistics available with the Ministry of Education, Government of India. They analyzed effect of wastages and stagnation on the cost of education taking into account social as well as private costs and found that the cost of education increased with the level of education and also found that while the social cost of technical education was higher in relation to general education; its private cost was lower. Raj (1972) while noting the ever growing growth in the number of students going in for higher education, laid stress on more allocation of funds on technical education. Coombs and Hallack (1972) have given explanation as to why the cost analysis has become imperative in these changing times, how costs on education behave and why they behave as they do, how various system and educational institutions have used cost analysis and with what results, how educational analysts can go about applying cost analysis in their own institutions etc. They further recommended cost analysis as a powerful and necessary tool for effective educational management and planning so as to get better results from the available resources. India might not have readily adopted education technology but it's heartening to see how a traditional sector like education is using technology as an enabler so far. Today, some cutting-edge technologies are being used to further enhance this sector, while grabbing the attention of entrepreneurs, venture capitalists, corporate and governments.

Factors enabling growth of digital education:

1. Personalized and adaptive learning

Learning platforms, software's and digital devices are together creating countless new ways to modify education. This way, the academic potential, strengths, weaknesses, aptitude and learning pace of every single student is catered to. Precise, mobile and reliable applications are being created to teach students, help them practice their learning's, take assignments and manage their schedules.

Schools are now providing their students with digital devices like desktop computers, laptops and tablets. These devices are aiding them in the teaching process while also helping them understand how students learn and how to enhance their learning process.

The 'one size fits all' teaching model is being supplemented by adaptive, personalized learning pedagogies. Going forward, this will be the new trend in formal learning that will enable students to be technologically skilled and equipped for modern workplaces.

2. Two-way conversations in E-Learning

In the traditional classroom seating scenario, students are unable to get the individual attention they need due to time constraints. In contrast, the one-to-one context of learning in digital mediums currently students to learn through videos and chat with an expert.

The upcoming 'Learning Management System' will continue the two-way communication model between students and experts. More importantly, it will let students track their coursework progress, identify improvement areas and offer ways to make the most of them.

Through the help of 'Big Data', experts will be able to capture student feedback within the framework of the content provided. With this alone, they'll be able to improvise and enhance their offerings in new ways to further benefit students.

3. Mobile-based learning

Over the past few years, mobile learning has picked up by the populace who have gradually assimilated it in their lives. It has offered students the flexibility to access educational content seamlessly across multiple digital devices like desktops, laptops, tablets and smartphones.

The smartphone user base in India continues to increase, in both urban and rural areas. The coming years will witness users accessing most of their educational content through internet powered smartphones in a massive way. Most educational content, including even online courses, will be optimized entirely for mobile devices.

4. Video-based learning

Video learning has always appealed to students since it closely mirrors the traditional classroom teaching style. Earlier, students watched video lectures as a form of homework and then discussed them during the next class. Over time, this habit brought about a remarkable improvement in their performance, with a noticeable improvement in grades.

Video lectures allowed students to learn subject syllabi at their own pace and dedicate time spent in class towards interactions. This will continue to be a trend in the future where students will have access to rich and interactive content, that will be useful for both formal training as well as performance enhancement. The increase in video-based learning on mobile devices will eventually account for 80 per cent of all internet traffic by 2019.

5. Open educational resources

Open digital education resources have commonly been used in distance learning courses. They consist of freely accessible media for learning, teaching and research purposes. They are licensed to be revised and disseminated freely by teachers among students. This allows the latter to gain access to an extensive arrive of study material that is otherwise restricted indigenously. Open educational resources also facilitate the creation of a flexible environment where teachers can customize educational content for individual sessions or classroom sittings. This is applicable for typical curricular subjects like mathematics, sciences and languages, as well as business and fine arts.

6. Usage of Virtual Reality (VR) and Augmented Reality (AR) for learning

Virtual Reality and Augmented Reality are already buzzwords in the technology space. Their advent in e-learning has massively impacted the efficiency with which it is offered to students and the way it assesses their performance.

VR allows students using e-learning platforms on mobile devices to directly interact with study material. This keeps their engagement levels high and motivates them to learn more and better. On the other hand, AR facilitates teachers and trainers in performing tasks, they previously haven't or cannot, in a safe environment.

Benefits of technology

From classroom teaching to online teaching, blackboards to interactive whiteboards and textbooks to iPads, technology brought in a continuous transformation in the educational sector.

Technology has made our learning world smaller allowing everyone to have access to the education of the global classroom. With the emerging technologies in education changing the perception of learning, schools have integrated technology in the classroom to enhance better learning and teaching. On the other hand, the technology in the classroom can also be used to simplify and fasten the daily school scores When talking about a school administration as a whole, it requires managing admissions, managing courses, student-based information, timetable management, online exam, conveyance management, attendance management, fee management, hostel management, inventory management and result management.

Various challenges for preschool education today. But my three main observations are

Mushrooming of preschools – To curb unemployment or to earn extra, preschools are being set-up within houses campus without proper infrastructure, knowledge & system. Lack of training – Preschool education is vital foundation for higher education and personality formation. It is dynamic process, which needs proper and practical training of staff at every level. These are not available and there is a lack of training. Lack of awareness among parents – Nowadays, preschool education is essential part of child education. But parents send their kids to nearest preschool considering nearness and assuming sending to preschool is only for being accustomed to going to high school and its routine life. Parents are unaware about objective and utility of preschool in child's life.

Conclusion

Technology can reduce the tremendous effort given by students to gather number of printed book and journals for acquiring knowledge and increase students' focus on more important knowledge gathering process. Equally important, technology can represent education in ways that help students understand latest concepts and ideas. The Education Technology also enables teachers to integrate project based learning. With guidance from effective teachers, students at different levels can use these tools to construct knowledge and develop skills required in modern society such as presentation skills and analytical skills. In the present time the teacher's role in teaching is facilitator. The teacher has to facilitate the learning by providing students with access to technology. The teachers can find the means to engage students more easily in learning and to cater to the various needs of different students.

References

1. Kessler Sarah, 210, http://mashable.com/2010/11/22/technology-in-education/.
2. Richey, R.C.,2008, Reflections on the 2008 AECT, Definitions of the Field. TechTrends

3. Durham University News, 2012, ur.ac.uk/news/news item/?item no=15991
4. Jagannath Mohanty ,Modern Trends in Indian Education , Second Revised & Enlarged Edition, 2004, Deep &Deep Publication Pvt. Ltd.
5. Research Report of NCERT, 2009,
6. ICT in Education in India, 2012-13, *http://www.icbse.com/ict-education*
7. Research Findings and Implications for classroom Practice (Texas Instruments), 2005,
8. *http://education.ti.com/sites/US/downloads/pdf/CL2872*.pdf
9. The National Policy on Education (NPE,)2009, *www.ncert.nic.in/othanoun/npe 86. pdf.*

Chapter - 5

Challenges of Teaching in College Education

S. Uma Devi

Abstract

Education is the most potent tool for putting the society on the path of development. Teaching is considered as the most noble and respected professions. Teachers instill values in the minds of the students and ultimately become the custodians of character build and consequently nation building. Teaching is a multifaceted task. It involves preparation, delivery of the subject matter, class management, making the students inquisitive about the subject and collaborating with the students. Teaching and interacting college students are different from teaching school students. With changing times, the teaching job has become very challenging. New challenges have emerged like plethora of information available on the internet, influx of technology and changing values of the society. The traditional concept of students' obedience has become rare.

With the mushroom growth of private educational institutions, the teacher has to face additional challenges. This paper attempts to focus on the professional challenges faced by college teachers and tries to give suggestions to overcome them.

***Key words**: Teaching, higher education, students, challenges, college*

Research Objectives

1. To find out the challenges faced by college teachers
2. To determine the efforts to be made by the teachers to overcome these challenges and contribute to effective teaching.
3. To see if the management can help the teachers overcome these issues.

Methodology: Based on formal interviews and personal interactions with the teachers and also secondary sources.

Challenges for the teachers can be classified in to two types:

1. Academic
2. Non-Academic

Academic challenges are issues related to preparation for the lecture and class management . Non-academic challenges are problems other than teaching like dealing with problematic students, lack of proper infrastructure etc.

These following are the different challenges faced by the teachers

Require Multitasking abilities

A teacher should be multi-skilled. She or he should be creative and should have the ability for critical thinking and critical analysis. She should possess life skills, pedagogic skills, technological skills, social skills and emotional intelligence. She should have proficiency in the subject as well as in the language of instruction. She should be efficient enough to integrate all the skills so that it benefits the class room teaching. On one hand, preparing for the class is an important task, on the other hand managing all kinds of students and maintaining class discipline is a more difficult task for the teacher. Sometimes, a student may not be listening in class at all due to problems like depression and not understanding the subject etc. Students from regional medium background may not understand the language of instruction thoroughly. Some students may be in disciplined and may be disturbing the class.

Disinterested Students

Situation can sometimes become tricky when inspite of having a perfect lesson plan and sufficient preparation the teacher fails to capture the attention of the students . It may sometimes happen the teacher tries her best to catch the imagination of the students with an interesting fact or trivia, but result is not as expected . It is possible that when she goes to class enthusiastically after a lot of preparation, she sometimes faces the indifference of the students. The reasons could be divergent. The student may find the points outdated or redundant as everything is available online or may find the subject dry and boring or may not connect with the teacher. Sometimes they don’t find the subject practical and useful. This is a common problem in Social Sciences subjects like History or Economics and other subjects as they are theoretical. Earlier the teachers did not face as many as challenges as the present day teachers. The students were traditionally obedient and be respectful to the teachers, but now with changing times the behaviour of the students towards teachers has degraded. Another concern is that with the advent of technology, all the information is available with the click of a button, the students might feel that the teaching is superfluous. Students feel even if they don't attend the classes, they can get all the information online. These issues made the teaching and class management challenging. Students feel they can learn things by heart just before the exams and write without understanding the importance and concepts of the subject.

Misuse of mobile phones

Though technology is very useful in gaining knowledge and making our work easy, it becomes a disruption from time to time when the students misuse it. The motivated students in the class will find a way to learn despite the distractions. Other students are engrossed in mobile games or chatting on phones. The teacher finds himself helpless and finds the whole preparation futile. If it continues over a period of time, the teacher as well as the students lose interest and the class becomes monotonous and becomes a ritual.

Misuse of newly found freedom

The children who just passed out of school want to enjoy the freedom they get in college. Unless they concentrate in class and work hard, they cannot cope with the syllabus. In such cases, the teacher has more responsibility to advise the student about the importance of time and hard work which will ultimately help them settle in life.

Dealing with diverse students

Wide variation in backgrounds and academic abilities of the students enrolled in the courses becomes a challenge for the teacher to take everybody along and see that they understand the subject. If the teacher tries to teach at the pace of the bright students, others get left behind. If she tries to give additional attention to academically weaker students, the fast learners get bored.

In most of the classes, there are students come from different social and economic backgrounds and sometimes they belong to different linguistic groups. Some students may be from rich families and some may belong to middle class or poor families. Their attitudes toward life and educational goals may vary considerably. In this diverse environment, the teacher needs to be very efficient, socializing, flexible and articulate.

Dealing with Students' problems

Students often struggle to balance studies, personal responsibilities, social relationships and peer pressure. The teacher should be responsible and tactful enough to help the students manage peer pressure. The teacher needs to understand the problems and temperament of students and deal with them cautiously. Vinay is studying in a college. He has a big family business. He does not study and considers college as a mere instrument to get a degree. Other students should not take his example and become lethargic towards studies. Under these circumstances, the teacher has the moral obligation to make Vinay understand the value of education in achieving physical, social, spiritual and mental development and it is not a mere collection of information.

Assessment of the students' abilities

Another important challenge is assessment of the students' understanding and abilities. Often the students may not ask for clarification even if they don't understand the subject. The teacher should test the students' understanding by asking questions and repeat the points that the students did not understand.

Long Periods

Long periods is another major problem. Students cannot concentrate for more than half an hour. In almost all the colleges each period is more than forty five minutes. Varun is a very sensible teacher and teaches very well keeping in view the students' level of understanding. But after forty minutes, students tend to lose concentration and start talking in class. Varun finds it difficult to stop them. Not having any free time and continuous classes make the students feel tired and bored and the teacher finds it difficult to get the attention of students.

Student-Teacher Ratio

If the student-teacher ratio is too high, it is difficult for the teacher to manage the class effectively . Especially in higher educational institutions where you have a batch of hundred students in front of you and there is little scope for personal attention.

Dealing with disobedient students

Keeping a positive approach to the class, with some steps to stop or avoid disturbance is mandatory for effective class room management. If a student is very ill-disciplined and causing disruption, best thing to do is to privately discuss with the student how the disruption is not in the best interest of the class and that you will not accept that behavior. If this does not work, then the teacher has to call the student's parents involving them in finding the solution.

Specific problems of co-education colleges

Co-education colleges have some unique issues like occasionally some students of opposite gender develop a very close friendship and display it in the class. It becomes awkward and embarrassing for the teacher as neither can he address it out rightly nor can he ignore it . In such sensitive situations, he has to tactfully communicate it to the concerned students and see that such behavior is not repeated.

Lack of faculty development programs

Training the teachers to deal with many situations may help the teacher. But many institutions are not conducting any Faculty Development Programs or orientation programs even for the new teachers. In every job, training is given. Ironically, the most important job where the teachers' duty is to train the future citizens and contribute to nation building, training is not given . For decades the teachers have been trying their own innovative methods of teaching to keep their students interested in learning. With increasing standards in education, accountability of the teacher and the demand for quality teaching and the need for Faculty Development Programs have become a necessity. The FDP is important from time to time to update the teachers with new technology, new methods of teaching and getting new knowledge. We cannot use the old methods for the new generations. Updation of knowledge is imminent to make the students inquisitive about the subject and be glued to the class room lecture.

Too many subjects and too many classes

In some private institutions, teachers are given too many classes and are expected to teach 4 to 5 subjects. Sometimes they are given subjects that they are not specialized in. Anupam is an English teacher in a private college. He was asked to teach sociology along with his own subject. Anupam is busy learning the new subject. His preparation for both the subjects is not satisfactory. He does not feel confident in the class.

Administrative work pressure

The teachers are given administrative work which consumes a large portion of their time and very little time is left for preparation which in turn may lead to lack of quality in teaching and justice to the subject is not done. Teacher may not get time for research which makes them professionally stagnant.

Rat race for ranking

These days, the private institutions are in a rat race for ranking, and for national and global presence to compete with other established institutions. This pressurizes the teachers to produce more research papers in a short period of time. Teachers are asked to do a lot of paperwork required by different ranking agencies which makes their schedule hectic and they do not get much time to focus on other academic activities.

Lack of infrastructure

Lack of adequate infrastructure like paucity of projectors, digital board, lack of proper class rooms is a big hindrance to teaching in the modern age. The teacher may not be able to see all the students when the class rooms are very large. The large class rooms should have stair case structure. Otherwise the students sitting at the back are not visible to the teacher.

Class management

Most critical issue that new instructors should focus on is classroom management. It is the responsibility of both students and teacher to maintain a positive teaching and learning environment.

Keeping these challenges in view, it becomes imperative for the Management , students and teachers that they take some constructive steps for the improving the standard of education.

Suggestions for the management

Institutions should give ample time for research and publications and should give incentives to the best performing teachers.

Faculty development programs can be conducted to identify the strengths and weaknesses of the teachers and to provide insights for improvements.

Feedback of students may lead to loss of freedom for the lecturer. Student feedback should not decide the continuity of a teacher's job.

There should be a good infrastructure in colleges and universities which may attract the students' enrollment. Infrastructure like good class room arrangement, projectors, computers make the class room teaching more effective and comfortable for both teachers and the students. Some teachers are very good in their respective subjects and excellent at teaching but are not good at writing articles. Pressurizing the teachers to do research in short span of time will not help.

Suggestions for teachers

Teaching should be made more practical. They understand better and feel more relaxed if they go for field trips to experience firsthand what is taught in the class. For example, Political Science students can be taken to legislative assembly to witness the proceedings and law students can be taken for a court visit.

To make the classes interesting and update with new technology and knowledge, a teacher has to be a constant learner. Go beyond the syllabus. Students should feel curious and excited to know what you are going to teach. Make classes interactive with student participation and group discussions. When the students express their opinions and when they can come out with new points, they feel a sense of accomplishment. Appreciate the students when they participate well. Instead of getting the sense of achievement in video games they should get it in class participation. Make the subject relevant to the present conditions.

Make students understand they have potential. Making students realize they can improve. Make use technology. PPTs and videos give visual effect and make teaching interesting. Address a single theme in a slide. Explain clearly all the technical terms used in the lecture. Give examples Be enthusiastic and professional for effective teaching. Prepare well and be a master of your subject. If you aren't clear, the students are never going to understand. Fluency in the language of instruction is very essential. Effective communication and personal discipline and appearance make the teacher exemplary and inspiring as the students are going to observe you a lot. Every teacher is a role model to the students Maintaining necessary rapport with students outside class will result in better class management. Easily the student will settle down instead of engaging in other activities. Maintain eye contact with students while delivering the lecture. Encourage questions and clear doubts. With this, you are encouraging thinking and analytical skills.

The students' coming late will result in disturbance to teacher as well as the other students. And the late coming student will not understand the lesson properly. Therefore , late coming of students should be discouraged. Motivate the students. Many students need motivation. Frequently you should encourage them. Unmotivated students are likely to disturb the class as they don't pay attention. When you notice undesirable behavior in a student, nip it in the bud, or the other students may think that it's OK for them to talk while you are teaching. Communicate clearly with the student using simple language. Be firm and direct. Be fair, positive and consistent.

Conclusion

Sometimes one has to accept that, despite all of their efforts, there will be some students who are not going to understand what is being taught in the class and also there will be some students in each class who are not interested in learning at all. One needs to let go of these factors and accept their limitations as a teacher in a higher education setup, where each student has a different purpose of joining the institution. Inspire of all the information, the role of teacher cannot be diminishes as the teacher guides the student .

References

1. Lewis, M. (1995). *Learning to be a Language Teacher*. ELI Occasional Publications No. .Ambrose, Susan A., Bridges, Michael, DiPietro, Michele, Lovett, Marsha C., and Norman, Marie, K. *How Learning Works: Seven Research-Based Principles for Smart Teaching*. San Francisco: Jossey-Bass, 2010.
2. Barbezat, Daniel, and Bush, Mirabai. *Contemplative Practices in Higher Education: Powerful Methods to Transform Teaching and Learning*. San Francisco: Jossey-Bass, 2013
3. Barkley, Elizabeth F. *Student Engagement Techniques: A Handbook for College Faculty*. San Francisco: Jossey-Bass, 2009.
4. Blumberg, Phyllis. *Assessing and Improving Your Teaching: Strategies and Rubrics for Faculty Growth and Student Learning*. San Francisco: Jossey-Bass, 2013.
5. A. Nicolaides " Innovative teaching and learning methodologies for higher education Institutions"
6. Educational Research (ISSN: 2141-5161) Vol. 3(8) pp. 620-626, August 2012 Available online@ http://www.interesjournals.org
7. Special Double Issue: Diversity and commonality in higher education." *Teaching in Higher Education*, 12(5-6), p. 555
8. Chickering, A. W. and Gamson, Z. F. 1987. Seven principles for good practice in undergraduate education. *American Association for Higher Education*, 39(7): 3–7
9. http://teaching.monster.com/careers/articles/9142-7-biggest-challenges-teachers-face

Chapter - 6

Social Sciences Higher Education Pedagogy Issues in India

Dr. Rama Rao Bonagani

Abstract

This paper has investigated the various opportunities of pedagogy issues in India's social sciences higher education. Higher Education in India starts after the senior secondary education. It consists of Central, State, Deemed, as well as State private universities, Institutions of national importance and colleges. Higher Education is the shared responsibility of both the Centre and the States, because education is mentioned in the Concurrent list of the Constitution of India. But, it is mostly controlled by the central government of India. This comes under an Union Ministry of Human Resource Development's department of higher education. Next to China and United States, India has the third largest higher education system in the world in terms of size as well as its diversity and largest in the world in terms of number of educational institutions. After India's independence from United Kingdom, higher education has been attaining a massive growth. The social sciences encompass mainly the disciplines of history, geography, political science, Public Administration, economics, and sociology. The popular perception of some of the social sciences disciplines are non-utility subjects. As a result, low self-esteem governs in the classroom teaching transaction process. Therefore, there is need to emphasise that the social sciences are essential to provide social, cultural, and analytical skills, which are required to adjust to an increasingly interdependent world, and to deal with political and economic realities. Pedagogy refers to instructional approaches implemented in the classroom by the teacher. This means that teacher has to follow different methods to teach the students in the class room. If this is applied in the higher education social sciences disciplines, a teacher has to follow diverse teaching curricular methods in order to fulfill aims and aspirations of students in the present ongoing globalization time. This is a major challenge before a teacher. The teacher has to maintain quality as well. This is very important because presently India is having a very lower rank compare to other countries in the world. The teacher's responsibility in this education is to provide an inclusive teaching in order to cover all students' interests. However, my paper is divided in five parts. The first part deals with an Introduction, the second part covers theories of teaching in social sciences higher education, the third part analyses the teaching principles of social sciences higher education, the fourth part describe's important teaching curricular issues in Social Sciences higher education and the final fifth part summarizes the major findings of the paper.

Theory of Constructivism

Constructivism understood learning as a construction of active learners' reorganisation, which is different from earlier ideas of perceiving learning as a linear process. The conceptualisation perceives learning as a non-linear and complex process.It says towards transformation where people actively construct their knowledge. The revisiting knowledge signifies a spiral curriculum and hence, a higher level of understanding about the same subject matter. This indicates that human beings learn by fitting new understanding and knowledge in and with the existing knowledge and, if required, supplementing it to form and understand new knowledge.

Teachers who use to practice approaches focus on completing syllabuses and course contents, without putting much effort to analytically perceive them so that it helps to construct the meaning. Teaching is thus, may not be a matter of transmitting but of engaging students in active learning, building their knowledge in terms of what they already understand. Constructivism, is seen as a matter of changing learners' perspectives, to help them find a different view of the world from their former conceptualisation. Teaching is thus, not a matter of transmission of information but engaging learners in active learning. Teaching-learning is dialogue-based, which helps shaping, elaborating and deepening learning, and incentivises construction of ideas. This can be followed in the SSs higher education in India.

Teaching as a Transmission

This theory says a common practice in many HE institutions is to define the task of teaching as transmission of content, and it must be instilled in students. Many of the teachers use to follow this method. This traditional lecture method represents an one-way approach, where the teacher is seen as a source of knowledge. The students, on the other hand, are passive recipients from the teacher. The present modern classrooms, the teacher practicing an information transmission by delivering the course content using technology, but essentially follows the same one-way approach of communication. This is can be an effective teaching method in SSs higher education in India.

Teaching as an Organising Student Activity

Teachers are perceive teaching as a supervision process where teacherarticulates the teaching to help students learn. The teaching here is not simply about lecturing , but also about engaging with students. It involves additional efforts of trying out different methods to facilitate learning. The methods include ways of motivating students so that they are willing to learn even dull subjects of SSs. This can be followed in the SSs higher education in India.

Teaching as Making Learning Possible

This theory says that teacher, student and subject content are linked together through an overarching tool. Teaching here is a cooperative process with learners to change their existing understandings. That is why, it is termed as making student learning possible. Teachers, who use this approach, focus on the critical issues of student learning and try to address them.Therefore, the traditional role of the teacher differs substantially. Teacher here is more of a mentor who facilitates the learner to discover the knowledge. Learning here is more inclined to applying and modifying one's own ideas. It is something the student does, rather than something is done to the students.

The process of learning, both for the teacher and student, is thus modifying one's own ideas. Teaching is a reflective activity, where the teacher listens to students and others in an effort to teach better. Continuous improvement of skills through knowledge development is an integral part of the process. That is why, this also perceives teacher as an active lifelong learner. This continuous improvement of skills to understand the needs to identify critical obstacles to topics gives them a special edge. This active teaching is seen as context related, and continuously improvable without any protocol to adhere to (Sayantan Mandal, 2018). So, this can be followed in the SSs higher education in India.

Theory of Participatory Pedagogy

According to an author Freire, Participatory Pedagogy is an approach in which a teacher and students become jointly responsible for the teaching –learning process and all grow together. He also stated that Participatory Pedagogy through dialogue enables both the teacher and students to be recognized as persons with knowledge , understanding, feeling and interest who come together in a shared educational process.(Samson Maekela Tsegay, Mulgeta Zemuy Zegergish & Muhammad Azeem Ashraf, 2018).This can be applied in the SSs higher education in India.

The teaching principles of social sciences higher education

Higher Education in the social sciences plays an important role in developing students sense of identity and influencing the ways in which they understand, participate in and contribute to local, national and global communities.The following principles are an effective pedagogy issues in the social sciences higher education of India.

Principle of Alignment

A, **Identify prior knowledge** : If the value of learning time is to be maximized, it is important to build on what students already know and understand. **B, Align teaching to desired outcomes**: Effective teachers carefully and deliberately align teaching activities and resources to support students in achieving the desired outcomes. **C, Provide opportunities to revisit learning:** Students need sufficient, related opportunities to revisit learning through a variety of activities that will embed that learning in their memories. These have to be applied in the SSs higher education in India

Principle of Connection

A, Draw on relevant content: Effective teachers encourage students to use their own experiences as a point of comparison when learning about other people's experiences in different times, places and cultures. **B, Ensure inclusive content**: Effective teachers use language that is inclusive of all learners and their experiences, select resources that make diversity visible, and avoid biased and stereotypical representations.These have to be applied in the SSs higher education in India

Principle of Community

A, Establish productive learning Relationships: Student learning is promoted by respectful and productive teacher as well as student relationships. **B, Promote dialogue**: Effective teachers develop in students an ability to dialogue with each other so that they can access the diverse expertise, experiences and perspectives of the group members. **C, Share power with students**: Approaches that deliberately give students power to make decisions about their own learning,encourage participation in and ownership of learning. These have to be applied in the SSs higher education in India.

Principle of Interest

A, Maximize student interest: Effective teachers design activities that arouse students' interest, increase their engagement and, as a result, generate learning that is memorable. **B, Satisfy diverse motivational Needs:** Because the sources of individual motivation differ, a variety of motivational strategies need to be employed. **C, Use a variety of activities:** Using a variety of activities helps students recall the content embedded in those experiences (www.ibe.unesco.org, dated 14-1-2019). These have to be applied in the SSs higher education in India.

Teaching curricular issues in Social Sciences higher education

India has a largest higher educational system in the world. Higher education plays a vital role in the development of India . So, it has a concern for the relevance of higher education.(Naac.gov.in, dated 11-1-2019). The social sciences disciplines are also part of this. The following curricular issues can be an effective for teaching the social sciences subjects.

Content

The content of the SSs not be to convey as many facts as possible. Instead, a focus on concepts and ability to analyse socio-political realities should be stressed. The hierarchical structure of India society is such that inequalities between individuals and house holds were overshadowed by disparities between castes and communities . These disparities have not disappeared(Andre Beteille,2010). More over, in a plural society like ours, it is important that all regions and social groups have to be cover.Relevant local content should be part of the teaching-learning process, ideally transacted through activities drawing on local teaching-learning resources. The teacher has to apply plurality of approaches and integrate certain contents from different disciplines to help students better understand a given social phenomenon.

Teachers of their respective SSs disciplines are expected to use principles of teaching SSs higher education that respect diversity; facilitate open discussion as well as social interaction , the plurality of thinking; appreciate multiple views; and ultimately facilitate the learning of students to diverse social contexts. Moreover, a concerned teacher has to develop the cognitive abilities of the students such as observation, identification and classification that are fundamental to understanding of social issues such as poverty, illiteracy, positive and negative aspects of population growth, communalism and against child marriage. While teaching, a teacher has to keep in mind urban, rural and various caste students. Students have to be allowed to express their views on different things. Simultaneously a teacher has to keep in mind open to listen to them and respect their views,encourage their independent thinking; allow thinking from different perspectives and provide opportunities to express thoughts. Knowledge of social sciences is indispensable for building a just and peaceful society. In India, it is important that all religions groups covers in teaching. Teaching of Social Sciences creates in the students a strong sense of human values such as freedom, trust, mutual respect, and respect for diversity.

Social sciences teaching should aim at generating in students a critical, moral issues. Use methods that promote creativity, aesthetics and critical perspectives. The responsibility of a teacher to respect the differences of diverse and strive towards quality teaching in SSs,which cater to the needs of every student. Learners, irrespective of their differences should feel cared by the teacher. Help the students to understand social issues better. To make the process of teaching and learning in SSs still better, teachers are required to select and use various learning resources such as audio as well as visual materials, including photographs, maps , and replica of archaeological, regalia, diorama globes, cartoons, newspapers, books as learning resources. Use digital audio recorders as well as players and documentaries as instructional material or teaching aids in SSs. Use newsletters, Social Sciences Journals, multi media digital materials, e- books etc.

The concerned SSs teachers can improve efficiency, relevance, creativity, improve quality, skill development, capacity expansion in the students of higher education(Mhrd.gov.in, dated on 11-1-2019). Introduce topics in the courses of SSs as part of curricula for the overall development of society . Teach the current affairs to produce better informed citizens and disseminate knowledge to improve standards of health, hygiene, sanitation, life expectancy and other social parameters. Curriculum materials etc which embodied in class room practices should benefit all group students. This has to be followed in SSs higher education(Peter McLaren,2017). According to Green " Public education systems must be understood in relation to the historical development of nation states, which embodied a new universalism that education was applicable to all groups in society and could serve a variety of social needs, albeit serving the interests of the dominant classes in society"(Tehmina N. Basit and Sally Tomlinson(eds), 2012). This can be followed in the SSs higher education in India.

Normative Concerns

The normative concerns of the SSs teachers carry a normative responsibility to create and widen the popular base for human values such as freedom, trust, mutual respect, and respect for diversity . Moreover,the SSs teaching should aim at investing in students a critical moral and mental energy to make them alert to the social forces that threaten these values.

The teaching can be focus on threats to the environment, caste as well as class inequality, state repression through an interdisciplinary approach. The teaching can also cover in order to stimulate the students thought process and creativity. A teacher has to be effectively engage the difficulties that students from oppressed communities face(Antonia Darder,2017). These can be followed in the SSs higher education in India.

Interrelationship among Disciplines of Social sciences

This means that the boundaries of the SSs disciplines need to be opened up, and a plurality of approaches applied to understand a given phenomenon. Certain themes that facilitate interdisciplinary in the SSs. Themes should be culturally relevant and not all themes can be discussed in an interdisciplinary manner. The teaching should be solution-focused and interdisciplinary methods of teaching, which developed to match influential academic ideas, such as self-directed learning and learning in communities, as students seek to engage with and improve conditions in their immediate environments. The teachers can offer real-world applications of foundational concepts in the modern practice of teaching, learning, and curriculum development. The teachers can deliver a community development curriculum to students with multiple identities. (**Halsall** Jamie, **Snowden** Michael (Eds.), 2017). These can be applied in the SSs higher education in India.

Values

The valuesof teaching of SSs should include, Which are enshrined in the Constitution of India such as justice, liberty, equality , fraternity and the unity as well as integrity of the nation and the building of a sovereign, socialist, secular and democratic republic society. Teach the students to grow up as active, responsible, and reflective members of society. Moreover, teach the students to learn to respect differences of opinion ,lifestyle, and cultural practices. A teacher can follow the value of life long learning for updating some of things purpose in this education. Values of democratic citizenship for playing a constructive role, human rights, respect for self and others, ability to listen, commitment to non violence, tolerance, acceptance of diversities, and respect for truth etc have to be teach to the higher education social sciences students (A. Jameela Begum, 2012).

Revitalize the social sciences teaching

This is necessary to help the learners acquire knowledge and skills in an interactive environment. Process of learning should promote the spirit of inquiry and creativity. A teacher is an important medium of transacting the curriculum and simplifying concepts(http://epathshala.nic.in, dated 15-1-2019). The Concerned SSs teachers can also teach the SSs disciplines to their respective students overall benefits in a sustainable manner for India's higher education purpose.

Higher education in the 21st century

This century's focus is on learning outcomes. It is different from the traditional input-based teaching-learning in HE, which focused on the process, instead emphasised that the focus would be on learning outcome and competencies jointly. With this shift, comes an issue of accountability. Teaching as a mix of pedagogical and operational specifications. The model followed by this stressed on the creative side of teaching, Teachers ability to respond innovatively highly valued in SSs higher education. However, teaching and learning have to be more practical and should avoid undesirable things (Sayantan Mandal, 2018). These can be followed in the SSs higher education in India.

Teaching as inquiry

Effective pedagogy requires the teachers of SSs to inquire into their priorities for learning, also into interventions that might enhance student outcomes, and into an impact of their actions on their respective students. Moreover, such inquiry increases the likelihood of student success . The SSs curriculum areas, which help students understand societies, their identities and what it means to be a contributing member of their community. It also supports learners in developing competencies for participating as informed and responsible citizens. These expected valued outcomes are the touchstone for all teachers of the SSs and can support learning across the curriculum (www.ibe.unesco.org, dated 14-1-2019). The teachers can adopt a learner-centered paradigm of education for equipping students with the skills needed to adapt to changing environments such as critical thinking skills, communication, creativity-related skills, conceptualization and problem-solving skills. The case study method of teaching can also be adopted to develop problem solving and critical thinking skills in this SSs higher education (FICCI, 2013). Follow cooperative learning method for the teaching of SSs. The multi dimensional model of productive pedagogies consisting of four dimensions such as intellectual demand, connectedness, supportiveness, working with & valuing difference. These can be utilize in SSs higher education in India(Fazal Rizvi and Bob Lingard, 2010). Without any one's supervision or monitoring, a teacher has to acquire upgrading skills ,fully committed and responsible for teaching in the social sciences higher education. (Kavita A. Sharma, 2013). The teachers should have and use the full freedom inorder to excel in the SSs higher education in India.

Technology

The rate at which the Information Technology (IT) is growing presently is evident from the fact that it has invaded almost every part of our life. Technological progress can be harnessed for augmenting both expansion as well as quality of India's SSs higher education. The Government of India is keen to use the technological resources in helping its mission to make HE accessible to all deserving students. In this regard, it has launched its National Mission on Education through Information and Communication Technology (NMEICT) in 2009 to provide an opportunity for all the teachers and experts in the country to pool their collective wisdom for the benefit of every Indian learner and, thereby, reducing the digital divide. Moreover, under this mission, a proper balance between content generations, research in critical areas relating to imparting of education and connectivity for integrating our knowledge with advancements in other countries are to be attempted. For this, what is needed is the teachers can work through networked manner with dedication. Utilization of available social sciences Education Satellite (EduSAT) lectures materials without compromising the quality and knowledge empowerment of the students purpose. (Mhrd.gov.in, dated on 11-1-2019**)**. Utilize e-learning from SSs, e-learning resources for SSs by internet websites and google etc for the professional growth of the SSs concerned teachers (S. K. Mangal & Uma Mangal, 2018). Teachers can use epathshala videos, and other available You Tube videos for teaching the SSs higher education in India.

However, the knowledge presently is spreading faster than at any time before in human history. The knowledge explosion mainly contributed by Information and Communication Technology (ICT) highlights the fact that without a sound system of education, no country can survive in the next millennium. So India has to reshape its perspectives on higher education. Globalization has fore fronted an issue of restructuring education to meet the demands of the present. Due to internet, knowledge revolution has been sweeping almost all continents across the world, which exerting tremendous pressure on entire educational system. So, the teachers have to use updated ICT materials to faster dissemination of knowledge in order to benefit to their respective Social Sciences disciplines higher education's students in India (K.N. Panikkar & M. Bhaskaran Nair (eds), 2012).

Conclusion

To sum up this paper, it is observed that Social Sciences higher education is very important for achieving and consistently maintaining overall development in India. The higher education teachers of social sciences disciplines can follow mixed curricular teaching approaches in order to fulfil overall aims, aspirations and interests of their respective students in India.

References

1. www.ugc.ac.in, dated on 14-1-2019.
2. www.india.gov.in, dated on 19-1-2019.
3. Mhrd.gov.in, dated on 11-1-2019.
4. http://epathshala.nic.in : dated 15-1-2019, position paper of NATIONAL FOCUS GROUP ON TEACHING OF SOCIAL SCIENCES, dated 15-1-2019, published by National Council of Educational Research and Training, 2006.
   Google (internet), dated on15-1-2019
5. Sayantan Mandal(2018),"Teaching-Learning in Higher Education : Evolution of Concepts and an Attempt towards Developing a New Tool of Analysis", cprhe research papers 9, New Delhi,Published by National Institute of Educational Planning and Administration.
6. Samson Maekela Tsegay, Mulgeta Zemuy Zegergish &Muhammad Azeem Ashraf,(2018), " Pedagogical Practices and Students Experiences in Eritrean Higher Education Institutions" Higher Education for the Future journal, Volume.5, Issue.1, January, New Delhi, Sage publications.
7. www.ibe.unesco.org, dated on 14-1-2019: booklet on "Effective pedagogy in social sciences"by Claire Sinnema and Graeme Aitken.
8. www.nios.ac.in, dated on 13-1-2019,
9. Peter McLaren,2017, " Critical Pedagogy : A Look at the Major Concepts" in *The Critical Pedagogy Reader*, edited by Antonia Darder, Rodolfo D.Torrers and Marta P. Battodano, New York, Routledge: Taylor &Francis Group Publication.
10. Tehmina N. Basit and Sally Tomlinson(eds)(2012), *Social Inclusion and Higher Education,* Bristol, The Policy Press.
11. Antonia Darder,2017, "Pedagogy of Love: Embodying our Humanity", in *The Critical Pedagogy Reader*, edited by Antonia Darder, Rodolfo D. Torrers and Marta P. Battodano, New York, Routledge: Taylor & Francis Group Publication.
12. Halsall Jamie, Snowden Michael (Eds.) (2017), *The Pedagogy of the Social Sciences Curriculum,* Internet, springer publications.
13. FICCI, 2013, Higher Education in India: Vision 2030 FICCI Higher Education -Summit 201, Internet, Published by Federation of Indian Chambers of Commerce and Industry (FICCI).
14. Fazal Rizvi and Bob Lingard (2010), *Globalizing Education Policy,* London, Routledge:Taylor & Francis Group Publication.

15. Kavita A.Sharma (2013), *Sixty Years of the University Grants Commission: Establishment, Growth and Evolution*, New Delhi, Published by UGC.
16. S. K. Mangal & Uma Mangal(2018), *Pedagogy of Social Sciences*, Internet, PHI publications.
17. K.N. Panikkar & M. Bhaskaran Nair (eds), (2012), *Pedagogy Issues in India's Higher Education,* Delhi, Pearson publication.

Chapter - 7

Framework for Creation of Learning Resources E-Content: An Effective Tool for Teaching and Learning in a Contemporary Higher Education System

G. L. Rajani

Abstract

Information technology and the Internet are major drivers of research, innovation, growth and social change. The growth in Internet has brought changes in all walks of life including the education. Educational system around the world is undergoing increasing pressure to use the new information and communication technology to acquaint students with the knowledge and information, they require in this techno savvy Era. To develop a knowledge society, it is essential to integrate ICT at all levels of education system. ICT offers tremendous opportunities for capturing, storing, disseminating and communicating a wide variety of information. Starting to provide an electric content service, platform for organizing learning experiences in managing learning and assessment has been changed greatly by ICT developments. ICT can promote international collaboration and networking in Higher Education in India and provide more flexible and effective ways for professional development. It can also help in pre-service and in-service teacher training programs.

Keywords: *e-content, proprietary tools, open source tools, concept mapping tools, Authoring tools*

Introduction

Electronic content (e-content) is the latest method of instruction that has attracted more attention to gather with the concept of models. It is a very power full tool of education. E-content which is also known as digital content refers to the content or information delivered over network based electronic devices or that is made available using computer network such as internet. E-content is valuable to the learners and also helpful to teachers of all individual instruction systems. Switching from traditional textbooks to digital course materials is a growing trend in Higher Education in India. E-content includes all kinds of content created and delivered through various electronic media from „old media such as print and radio to the increasingly sophisticated electronic tools with combination of sounds, images and text. E-content requires huge amounts of creativity both at 'information' level as well as the 'technology' level. This development has many advantages for students and faculty in greater interactivity, customizability, and opportunities for social collaboration. It is the valuable resource for development of information rich society where everyone is empowered to create, receive, share and utilize information and knowledge for their economic, social, cultural and political upliftment and development. Contents used in education can be from a number of sources: e-Journals, e-Books e-Research reports, electronic e-Lecture-modules, e-Lecture notes, and e-Lecture-slides.

Well trained teachers with required knowledge, skills and commitment can develop scientific and critical thinking, promote tolerance, and develop cultural and social values in their students. Innovative technologies will make it possible to achieve these by providing new ways to teachers. But these new technologies are placing more demands on teachers to learn how to use them in their teaching and learning processes. This great transformation is posing challenges to teachers and teacher educators in using technologies in creative and productive ways. Hence, teachers have to meet these new challenges by continuously acquiring new knowledge and skills to discharge their duties effectively. This study on E-content development is meant to understand the meaning and standards of E-content, learning objects, designing and development of digital resources for teaching and learning by using variety of tools and software such as proprietary software, freeware, open source software, public domain software, Microsoft Office, Libre Office, Software Package, Digital concept mapping tools, and Authoring tools which allow authors or e-contentdevelopers to integrate or use any array of media to create professional, engaging and interactive e-content, Thus this paper aims in providing the knowledge and skill for teachers to cater to present day learners and their learning styles.

Technology, in one form or another, has always been part of the teaching and learning environment. It is part of the teacher's professional toolbox. In other words, it is among the resources that teachers use to help facilitate student learning. Technology has changed dramatically over recent decades. The increasing variety and accessibility of technology has expanded the toolbox and the opportunities teachers have to use technology. Computer devices are more powerful and come in different forms, from those that sit on our desks to those that sit in the palm of our hands. The internet connects those devices and connects students to each other in the classroom, through the school and around the world.

This study considers the technologies that are available to teachers to support their teaching strategies. The study focuses on software, applications and resources that support teaching and learning. We consider the tools that teachers use to help their students use, create, manipulate and share information on computer devices and over computer networks. Technological devices and networks have changed our schools and classrooms. In India, technological investments in schools have been made at the state/territory level and at the national level through initiatives such as the Digital Education Revolution. There now are computers and interactive whiteboards in schools, and schools are connected to each other and the world at higher speeds than ever before. Technology in schools has become mobile, with laptop computers, tablet devices and smartphones now part of the teaching and learning context.

This study explore what teachers might do to support student learning through applications and resource tools, regardless of the device. It focuses on those tools that are relevant and used in the educational environment, with a particular emphasis on the Indian context.

Purpose of the study

Efforts to improve the 'quality' of higher education in India have seen a shift towards embedding technology into teaching. Validate attempts to devise an innovative teaching technique through e-content approach, This study on E-content development is meant to explore the meaning and standards of E-content, learning objects, designing and development of digital resources for teaching and learning by using variety of tools and software such as proprietary software, freeware, open source software, public domain software ,Microsoft Office, Libre Office, Software Package, Digital concept mapping tools, and Authoring tools which allow authors or e-contentdevelopers to integrate or use any array of media to create professional, engaging and interactive e-content. Rooted within constructivist thought it is believed that visually representing thoughts and relationships of past and newly gained knowledge encourages students to think critically and thus facilitate meaningful learning to take place, thus this paper aims in providing the knowledge and skill for teachers to cater to present day learners and their learning styles.

Objectives

- The objectives of the scheme are to
- Upskill the teachers with technological applications and resources used in classrooms today.
- Cognizant teachers in embedding technology through a range of teaching and learning strategies.
- Validate teachers in evaluating technological tools to support teaching and learning.
- Enable teachers to collect and organize the apt and sufficient learning resources for their students.
- Help teachers to create and manage e-content using a variety of software applications for creation of learning activities.
- Empower teachers to acquire and develop professional competences to meet the new challenges by continuously acquiring new knowledge and skills to discharge their duties effectively.

The role of Teacher in Education

The important role that technology plays in education gives teachers the opportunity to design meaningful learning experiences that embed technology. Advances and accessibility of technologies have made the possibilities seem almost endless. It is important not to use technology for its sake, but rather to embed technology appropriately. Here, teachers draw upon their expertise and experience in what to teach and how to teach it. A teacher has many considerations and influences in designing learning experiences for students, and the appropriate use of technology is but one of those considerations. Just as teachers keep up to date with curriculum developments, new educational policies and advances in the art and science of teaching practice, they keep up to date with the technological tools that are available to them. This means that sometimes experimentation and trial and-error are just as important as experience in what influences teachers' lesson plans.

Framework for creation of learning resources

These main processes include establishing demand for e-resources, harmonization of policies and processes, resources mobilization, developing ICT human resources capacity, establishing physical infrastructure, maintaining adequate e-resources, and creating awareness for e-resources.

Electronic Content (E-Content)

Electronic content (e-content) which is also known as digital content refers to the content or information delivered over network based electronic devices or that is made available using computer network such as internet. According to Oxford dictionary 'e-content is the digital text and images designed to display on web pages. According to Saxena Anurag (2011) 'E-content is basically a package that satisfies the conditions like minimization of distance, cost effectiveness, user friendliness and adaptability to local conditions. Well-developed e-content can be delivered many times to different learners. Individual course components i.e. units, lessons and media elements such as graphics and animations can be re-used in different contexts.

Developing a Topic for a classroom

Very well designed, developed and validated e-content will provide access to high quality meaningful digital content and serve as an effective virtual teacher.

Instructional design is the practice of creating instructional experiences which make the acquisition of knowledge and skill more efficient, effective and appealing. The process broadly consists of determining the current status of learner understanding, defining the end goal of the instructional material and creating some 'intervention' to assist the transition. This systematic approach provides a step by step process for the analysis of the learners' needs, the design and development of the material'. Most common and popular model used for creating instructional materials is the **ADDIE** model.

- **Analysis:** It is meant for examining the suitability of the e-content related to the learning needs, context, learner, task and content.
- **Design:** It is concerned with defining the learning objectives, structuring the content logically, specifying the instructional and evaluation strategies, and preparing for visual and technical design.
- **Development:** It is related to the creation of story board describes step by step script of the final outcome of the e-content.
- **Implement:** Developed materials are distributed to learners.

  Evaluation: Material is to be revised at all the stages based on the feedback received.

E-content Tools

E-content can be created in a variety of ways by using variety of tools and software. E-content development combines Content Management System (CMS) and Learning Management System (LMS). Several proprietary software, freeware, open source software, public domain software and so on are available for e-content development. Among available tools and software packages, Microsoft Office, Libre Office, Software Package can be used easily by the beginners of e-content development.

Freeware: It can be used without any monetary charges. However, restrictions are imposed for its use, modification and redistribution. In this source code is not provided. This tool can be passed on to any one free of cost.

Open Source Software (OSS): It is computer software and its source code are made available to the public. It is licensed with an open source license. Copy right holder provides the rights to study modify and distribute the software free of cost to anyone for any purpose. Open Source Software is very often developed in a public collaborative manner.

Proprietary software: It is a software that is owned by an individual or a company. It will have major restrictions on its use and its source code usually kept secret. These are exclusive property of their developers and can't be copied or distributed without complying with their licensing agreements.

Public domain software: The copy right holder donates it to the public. It is available free of cost to everyone and it can be used by any one for any purpose and only with very minimal restrictions.

Graphics, Audio and Video-Creating and Editing

There are several audio, video and graphic creators and editors available online. Some are free and some are proprietary.

Wevideo is a video creator and editor which allows us to edit and make video in an easy and intuitive way on this cloud-based app. It allows you to control the video sections easily in areas like the transition, fast and slow motion, adding effects etc.

Magisto is a video editor that can help you make your video in just a few steps. Upload the video than you can choose one of the premade editing styles, add a sound track, add a title and the video will be ready for download or for sharing on the social media.

Draw Pad is a Graphics editor and an easy-to-use image composition and manipulation program for all types of graphic design projects. You can make sketches and paintings on your computer, create logos, banner ads or billboards, draw diagrams, icons and other web graphics

Photo Shop is well known and widely used graphic editing software. It helps in image editing and drawing. One of the important features of PhotoShop is layer styles which allows you to create graphics quickly with ease.

My Paint is a graphics editor which can be easily used by teachers and students for digital painting. It enables people to create quick sketches and also complex artistic drawings on their computers. MyPaint is a simple and easy to use tool. Menus and interface are very simple. You can start drawing on the canvas without any distractions.

Inkscape is free, open source vector drawing and editing tool. It is a useful tool in doing line art. Inkscape can be used in all major computer operating systems like Linux, Mac, and Windows. It can be imported and exported to many major file formats.

GIMP is a robust image editor. It is well known open source software which is completely free. It is a good alternative to Adobe PhotoShop and has most of the characteristics of PhotoShop. It has the features like powerful painting tools, layers and channel support, multiple undo/redo, editable text layers etc.

Wave Pad is an audio editing software. This is a full-featured professional audio and music editor for Windows and Mac. It lets you record and edit music, voice and other audio recordings. When editing audio files, you can cut, copy and paste parts of recordings, and then add effects like echo, amplification and noise reduction. WavePad works as a wav or mp3 editor.

Audacity is free open source software. It is easy to use multi track audio editor and recorder for Windows, Mac, GNU/Linux and so many other operating systems. Using Audacity, you can record live audio and also computer playback on the windows, vista, etc. It can convert tapes and records into digital recordings or CDs. Using Audacity software, you can edit audio that is cut, copy and mix sounds together according to your requirements. You can change the speed and pitch of a recording. Numerous effects can also be given to the audio material.

Video Pad is a powerful and easy-to-use video editor that lets you import videos, add music and effects, then burn to DVD. You can edit video from any camcorder Capture video from a DV camcorder, webcam, or import most the video file format. More than 50 visual and transition effects are available to add a professional touch to your video. You Create videos for DVD, HD, YouTube etc. You can burn movies to DVD for playback on TV, or as a standalone video file to share online or put on portable devices.

Magisto is a video editor that can help you make your video in just a few steps. Upload the video, then you can choose one of the premade editing styles, add a sound track, add a title and the video will be ready for download or for sharing on the social media.

Video Pad is a powerful and easy-to-use video editor that lets you import videos, add music and effects, then burn to DVD. You can edit video from any camcorder Capture video from a DV camcorder, webcam, or import most the video file format. More than 50 visual and transition effects are available to add a professional touch to your video. You can create videos for DVD, HD, YouTube etc. You can burn movies to DVD for playback on TV, or as a standalone video file to share online or put on portable devices.

Openshot is a free, simple to use open source video editor for Linux. It is user friendly software which everyone can use and get great results. Openshot can take peoples' videos, photos and music files. It helps you to create the film as you feel like. You can easily add sub-titles and transitions. It can export film to DVD, YouTube, Vimeo and many other formats. Openshot integrates well with two other open source programs that are 'Inkscape' a vector editing program and the 'Blender 3D' animation program. It supports many video, audio and image formats. Audio mixing and editing is possible in Openshot.

Authoring tools

Various tools are available to produce e-content. Microsoft Power Point and word processors are also e-learning tools. These tools are not appropriate to present interactivity, testing and scoring. To develop interactive content various elements such as examples, illustrations, animations, audio, video, interactivity etc are assembled. For this purpose, we can use special tools which are authoring tools or authorware. An e-learning authoring tool is software packages which can be used create and modify web content for the use by other people. Authoring tool or author-ware is a program that helps to write hypertext or use multimedia applications. Authoring tools allow authors or e-content developers to integrate or use any array of media to create professional, engaging and interactive e-content. The main advantage of authoring tools is their easier and faster use. Using these tools e-content can be developed and transferred easily. These authoring tools has some common features. They are

- Scope for interactivity
- Navigation-ability to move throughout the content based on the content menu.
- Editing -e-content developers can make changes or update the material easily.
- Preview or play back -it is possible to preview or play back the material.
- Cross platform and cross browser inter offer-ability - it is possible to run on all platforms and different browsers.

eXe Learning is a free software tool that can be used to create educational interactive web contents. eXe learning can generate interactive content and it allows one to create easily navigable web pages including text, images, interactive activities, image galleries or multimedia clips. All the educational material generated with eXe Learning can be transferred to different digital formats. That can be used independently or to integrate them into a Learning Management System (LMS) like Moodle. Once installed eXe learning has its own tutorial in the help menu. eXe learning can be downloaded from www.exlearning.net

Xerte is a free and open source authoring tool which provides a full suite of open source tools for e-Learning developers and content authors producing interactive learning materials. This project is funded by Nottingham University.

Adobe Captivate is proprietary software. It is a rapid responsive authoring tool that is used for creating e-learning contents such as software demonstrations, software simulations, branched scenarios, and randomized quizzes in Small Web Formats (.swf) and HTML5 formats. It can also convert Adobe Captivate generated files formats (.swf) to digital MP4 (.mp4) formats which can be played with media players or uploaded to video hosting websites. For software simulations, captivate can use left or right mouse clicks, key presses and rollover images. It can also be used to create screen casts, and to convert Microsoft PowerPoint presentations to Small Web Formats and HTML5 formats. **Blogging** is a web blog is a Web site that consists of a series of entries arranged in chronological order, often update on frequently with new information about particular topic. The information can be written by the site owner, gathered from other sources, or contribution by an individual. Blogs are in different types viz., (i) personal (eg: twitter share); (ii) organizational (eg: marketing corporate); (iii) variety (eg: education genre); (iv) media (eg: photo blog) and (v) device (eg: mobile phone).

Digital Concept mapping tools

Digital concept mapping tools are another versatile tool for creating e-content in visual form. There are both online and offline concept mapping tools and these are some time referred as mind mapping tool. Teachers can easily create concept map on various topics, edit it, link it to the websites, and add graphics. These concept maps help students to identify connections and get the clear and deep understanding about the entire things connected together.

Open source Software concept mapping tools (ofline) are Visual Understanding Environment, freemind and freepalne.

Visual Understanding Environment (VUE): The Visual Understanding Environment (VUE) is an Open Source Application tool of Tufts University developed by its Academic Technology group. VUE 3.0 is the latest release of the Academic Technology Group and it has the features such as dynamic presentation of maps, map merging, enhanced key word tagging and search capabilities etc.

Freemind: http://freemind.sourceforge.net

Freeplane: https://www.freeplane.org

There are many open source alternatives with various features

Propriety Software concepts mapping tools (online) are XMind, Coggle, LucidChart, Mind Meister, Wise Mapping.

XMind (Windows/Mac/Linux): *www.xmind.net/*

Coggle: (Webapp): *https://coggle.it/*

LucidChart: https://www.lucidchart.com/

MindMeister: https://www.mindmeister.com/

WiseMapping: https://**www.wisemapping.com/**

There are many proprietary alternatives with various features

Advantages of e-content in higher education

Educational institutions are changing rapidly in response to the ability of individuals and universities to access digital content in ways that was unthinkable just five years ago. Students and colleges no longer rely on the traditional methods of information access and content delivery that formed the foundation of educational content in the past.

- The various advantages that digital content offers over traditional printed material are
- The ability to modify content or just a part of it easily and at a considerably low cost. The same exercise with traditional books is a time consuming and costly affair.
- Easy and cost-effective updating options allow access to the latest information as and when it's available rather than having to wait for the next edition of the book to be printed and made available at stores.
- Searching for the exact subject you're interested in is a breeze with digital content when compared with leafing through a book and reading every word before you're able to find what you're looking for.
- Teachers can put together customized lessons depending on what they think their students are interested in rather than being forced to rely on one or two books alone.
- Digital content takes up a fraction of the storage space that printed matter does, thus freeing up shelves and shelves of space.
- There's also the fact that the less paper we use, the more we're doing to play our part in saving the rain forests and the environment as a whole.
- There's no need to carry around books when you're travelling from place to place. If it's online, all you need is access to a computer and a fast Internet connection.

Conclusion

The use of e-Content in higher education benefits from hyperlinking, non-linearity, addition of multimedia, portability, customisation and automatic searching. All the above advantages have huge potential in increasing the satisfaction of students, as well as academics. As many HE institutions are introducing electronic content (e-Content) through the Web to their students, to choose the best e-content developing tools to create a proper course for E-learning. In addition, all produced learning contents are conforming to the Share-able Content Object Reference Model (SCORM) standard, which makes better the contents interoperability and reusability. Therefore, improving e-content developing tools is important and one of the main points is, to enhance them for the easily usage and having professional output. This paper proposed several proprietary software, freeware, open source software, public domain software, Microsoft Office, Libre Office, Software Package, Digital concept mapping tools, and Authoring tools with the goal of designing and creating the contents which should provide the learner with all the necessary tools. The usage of e-content development tools will cause the incremental of learner's interaction, therefore many organizations are attempting to reduce their training costs by developing e-Contents inhouse. Whatever the reason is, more trainers are finding themselves researching the features, benefits, and cost of developing tools. Choosing an appropriate developing tool in e-Content can help to solve many problems including the needs of growing communities to educate people, Lack of access to educational, shortage of training costs and economic opportunities.

References

1. Editing Software - Edit Audio, Video, Photos or Graphics www.nchsoftware.com/ software/editing. html.
2. e-Learning Standards – Course Avenue available at www. course avenue. com/ e-learning-standards accessed on 19th Jan, 2016
3. Free and Open Source Authoring Tools for e-Learning-e-Front Blog available at http://www.efrontlearning.net/blog/2010/10/open-source-authoring-tools-for-e.html accessed on 19th Jan, 2016
4. Frequently asked questions-Creative Commons' Available at https:// wiki. creativecommons.org/index.php/Frequently Asked Questions accessed on 12th Jan, 2016
5. National Repository of Open Educational Resources (NROER) Available at http://edtechreview.in/news/561-national-repository-of-open-educational-resources-by-mhrd accessed on 13-1-2016
6. Proprietary software - Wikipedia, the free encyclopedia available at https:// en.wikipedia.org/wiki/Proprietary software accessed on 18th January 2016
7. SOM Naidu 'E-learning A Guidebook of Principles, Procedures and Practices' Published by CEMCA 2003.

Chapter - 8

Issues and Challenges in Higher Education System

Dr. K. Govindu

Abstract

This article expects to highlight emerging issues and challenges in the sphere of Higher Education (HE) in India, especially in provincial and semi-urban ranges. When we realise that the India is the most noteworthy HE-System itself. I have attempted to concentrate on the issues identified with understudy and issues identified with biggest academic system in the third world, with more than of five million students taking H.E. in more than 12000 colleges & universities. India is additionally the third world examination/ research super power, spending an extensive sum over it (8%) the planning and change of higher education itself is exceptionally troublesome the most dominant politicians, who run the institution as the business & benefit making industry, principally dominate issue as it. An educationist have rightly pointed out that the Indian Higher Education in inconsistencies pockets of examination are substandard colleges, the best graduated are fruitful on the planet, however unemployment at home is a reality for some. Legislative issues frequently suppress the Grant and in numerous institutions emergency is the standards. Most likely India confronts today various issues pertaining to lack of education, poverty, unemployment, emergency of good and other worldly values. In any case, in the most recent couple of years each individual, a guardian, gatekeeper, educator, administrator or country is concerned with the issue of understudy turmoil is as under:

Introduction

It is generally hyped that India has a strong educational structure with premier education. The different yardsticks such as new courses, changing curriculum, dynamic methodologies and teacher training facilitate in delivery of quality content. E-learning, student-friendly learning, increased adoption of extra and co-curricular activities, etc. in India attract students from other countries such as China, Canada, South Africa, Germany, USA,

UK and Australia. However, if one sees the employability of the output, the status of unemployment and underemployment, the results are not encouraging. It is grieved that there is lack of quality education for the poor, and only a small fraction of students, around one tenth from schools, go for higher studies. It is criticized widely that many students study through memorization, and every programme is planned exam-oriented and not learning-oriented. Hence, India's education system is a stumbling block in achieving its objectives of economic development. This study intends to understand and evaluate the issues and challenges in the Indian educational system and to provide solutions.

Objectives of the Study

(a) To understand the status of Indian Education System

(b) To evaluate the issues and challenges to Indian Education System

(c) To ascertain the possible solutions to resolve the issues

(d) To provide suggestions for improvement

Research methodology

This research output is the outcome of an overview of studies conducted on the problems of Indian Education System. This is basically a qualitative research and follows the experiential approach. It uses secondary data for its analysis. Discussions with experts form part of the research work.

Scope of the study

The study exhibits the different structures existing in the Education Sector and their drawbacks. It attempts to narrate the problems in them and the challenges ahead. The study is concluded with recommendations for effective implementation considering the democratic nature of India.

Research limitations

Though the study has a vivid outlook on the issues of Indian Education System and provide feasible solutions, they should be taken in to consideration keeping in mind the following:

The study covers a wider view of the Indian Education System. It does not cover the intrinsic issues of every state of India.

The analysis is done based on secondary data available at various sources. It lacks primary data.

The researcher has not intended to compare Indian Education System with that of other countries.

The solutions are derived largely based on the public view and conclusions of other researchers.

Indian Educational System – A Review

India is known for its educational excellence. Indian Education has recently gained global recognition with its distinguished diversity character. Different curriculum bodies govern the school education system in India. They are:

1. The National Council of Educational Research and Training
2. The State government Boards
3. Central Board of Secondary Education
4. The Council of Indian School Certificate Examination
5. The National Institute of Open Schooling
6. Islamic Madrasah School Boards
7. Autonomous schools like Woodstock School, Sri Aurobindo International Centre of Education, Auroville, Patha Bhavan and Ananda Marga Gurukula.
8. International schools, under the International Baccalaureate, or the Cambridge There are 34 boards of secondary and senior secondary education in India (Studylib, 2017). More than 95% of the schools in India are affiliated to State Boards.

Private and Government schools

There are schools owned by Government as well as private parties (aided and self-financed). In 2006, 19% of Indian children were privately educated. This figure jumped to 38% in 2014 (MHRD., 2016). Private schooling has been growing continuously and found desirable by the people, irrespective of their socio-economic status.

International schools In January 2015, the International Schools Consultancy listed India as having 410 international schools. More than 95% of the international schools offer a dual curriculum (international and a national curriculum like CBSE, ICSE or State board).

Higher education India has about 152 central universities, 316 state universities and 191 private universities. Other institutions include 33,623 colleges, including 1,800 exclusive women's colleges, and 12,748 institutions offering Diploma Courses (Indrail, 2015). The University Grants Commission coordinates, determines and maintains the standards of higher education at various levels. The bodies responsible for the different professional programmes are: All India Council for Technical Education, Indian Council for Agriculture Research, Distance Education Council, National Council for Teacher Education, Bar Council of India, Medical Council of India, Indian Nursing Council, Central Council of Homeopathy, Pharmacy Council of India, Central Council of Indian Medicine and Dentist Council of India.

Open and distance learning At the school level, National Institute of Open Schooling provides opportunities for continuing education to those who missed completing school education. 14 lakh students are enrolled at the secondary and higher secondary level through open and distance learning. In 2012, various state governments also introduced State Open School to provide distance education. At higher education level, Indira Gandhi National Open University (IGNOU) co-ordinates distance learning. It has a cumulative enrolment of 15 lakh, serviced through 53 regional centres. The Distance Education Council an authority of IGNOU is co-coordinating 13 State Open Universities and 119 institutions of correspondence courses in conventional universities.

Vocational education All India Council of Technical Education reported in 2013 that there were more than 4,599 vocational institutions that offer degrees, diploma and post-diploma in architecture, engineering, hotel management, infrastructure, pharmacy, technology, town services and others. Total annual intake capacity for technical diplomas and degrees exceeded 34 lakhs. In 2016, 10 public and 10 private educational institutions were made world-class. Rs 1,000crore budget was provided for higher education. Rs 1,700 crore was provided for 1500 multi-skill development centres. 62 new navodaya vidyalaya were created to provide quality education. A digital literacy scheme was launched for covering six crore additional rural households. The National Skill Development Mission was initiated to impart training to 76 lakh youth (India Today, 2017). Entrepreneurship training was provided across schools and colleges along with massive online courses. Sarva Shiksha Abhiyan was introduced to increase focus on **quality of education.**

India has been a multi-cultural, multi-religious, and multi-linguistic society. Every State has a different and distinct identity. Dealing with various aspirations of such people in a democratic country is indeed a challenge to the Govt of India. The various issues are outlined here:

Lack of quality education

In the top 100 universities list by 'Times Higher Education World Reputation Rankings', none of the Indian universities could be found in the list. In the 2017 rankings by the HRD ministry, only 2,995 institutions (6%) participated from around 51,000-strong higher educational institutions in India. There is severe regional imbalance too. In the overall rankings, of the 100 best institutions, 67 are from just eight states. Among the best 100 universities, 40 are in three states. Among the best 100 colleges, 77 are from just five states (Nanda, Prashant K. 2017).

Corruption in Indian education system has been eroding the quality of education. It is one of the major contributors to domestic black money. Payment to Management at dark rooms and seeking admissions is increasing. 'Get full salary in the account, pay back part to Management by blank signed cheques' is also a practice in some private schools.

No proper value education

Value education is not offered in the schools and colleges. If offered, religion and hatred are spread in the name of value education. Many of the doctors, lawyers, CAs, politicians and Govt servants who are supposed to be the saviours of the society, suffer from serious charges of corruption. Old-age homes are increasing. Suicides are increasing. The meaning of love is eventually changing. The education-led technology, inventions and innovations are being misused.

Poor Women's education

Women have a much lower literacy rate than men. Conservative cultural attitudes prevent girls from attending schools. Despite Govt's attempts to provide incentives viz. midday meals, free books and uniforms, girls' attendance is poor. Though the minimum age for marriage is eighteen, many girls get married much earlier. Therefore, at the secondary level, female drop-out rate is high.

Lack of Facilities

As per 2016 Annual Survey of Education Report, 3.5% schools in India had no toilet facility while only 68.7% schools had useable toilet facility. 75.5% of the schools surveyed had library in 2016, a decrease from 78.1% in 2014. Percentage of schools with separate girls' toilet has increased from 32.9% in 2010 to 61.9% in 2016. 74.1% schools had drinking water facility and 64.5% of the schools had playground.

Curriculum issues

There are many different curriculum systems that confuse the students who wish to achieve the same objective such as Engineering, Medical and

Business Administration. At the higher education level, there is no uniformity in the syllabuses taught for the same programme. Syllabus revision is done quite often without considering the contemporary requirements of industries. There is lack of diversity in the subjects one can take in colleges. Flexibility to cross over streams is also lacking.

Public school workforce absenteeism

Teacher absenteeism in India is exorbitant. World Bank estimates show the cost in salaries paid to absent teachers is US $2 billion every year. In a study by Kremer, etc, they found 25% of private sector teachers and 40% of public sector medical workers were absent during the survey. Absence rates among them ranged from 14.6% in Maharashtra to 41.9% in Jharkhand.

Wrong societal outlook

For Governments, more scoring is success. English is becoming the measure of intellect. Hence, parents of today take least interest in vernacular medium of education. Due to the perceived notion of inferior quality, Govt schools are becoming the last choice for many. Education-seeking migration has become a matter of pride for many families. Most of the school students spend majority of their learning time in preparing for competitive exams. Coaching classes too flourish due to this unwarranted competition, leading to a class-divide.

Give more significance to primary and secondary education

Primary education is the backbone of education system of a country. If the teachers at primary and secondary level are unskilled, not qualified and less-paid, all further studies will be in stake. Hence, more attention is required on primary education rather than higher education. Presently, higher education institutions compete to get quality students. The weaker and less reputed colleges end-up with poor students. This affects consecutively the employability of youth, and creates a class-divide.

Give importance to technology in education

India has to embrace computer and high speed internet technology. Our educational delivery mechanisms should take the wealth of human capital to the masses. The models of brick and mortar schools, colleges and universities will have to be integrated and interlinked with ICT. The Governments should invest more in technological infrastructure that will ease the knowledge accessibility.

Encourage innovation and creativity

The system should reward those who deserves highest academic honor. The crammers should not be rewarded. Our testing and marking systems need to be built to recognize original contributions, creativity, problem solving and innovation. Ranks should be awarded accordingly.

Personalize the education

Indian education system is built on the assumption that if a thing is good for one child, it is good for all. But, one massive education system cannot be suitable to all. Some people are visual learners, others are auditory learners. Some kids learn faster, some do slow. The syllabus should be designed in such a way that every learner's latent ability is identified and motivated. Hasty and fast learning should be discouraged.

Train the trainers continuously

A teacher is an entrepreneur and creator. The performance of a teacher should not be restricted to classroom. It needs to be opened up for the world to see with internet. There has to be leaders in teaching positions, not salaried people holding their mantle. Hence, regular training is a necessity.

Change the aptitude to teach

Teaching jobs are widely regarded as safe, well-paid and risk-free jobs. Most of the teachers do not want to change. As they become experienced, they get septic, and not even think of the nature and need of the students. Understanding the present generation is the necessity. Guidelines should be made in this direction.

Provide quality education with character

Education without character is abortion and will create divisions in the society. A country that lowers the quality of education and allows score competition in exams will collapse. The mystified doctors, less skilled engineers, cowardly judges, money minded accountants, greedy businessmen, inhuman preachers and ignorant teachers cannot serve for the economy's growth. They will soon and surely doom the society with their unethical practices which no one can resist.

Deal with corruption strictly

Corrupt politicians supported by corrupt followers and corrupt police force are increasing. Frauds, burglaries, rape and sexual harassment cases are rising. Govt recruited bank managers work against the Govt's development policies. Printing of fake notes, introduction of plastic rice, egg, cabbage, etc are becoming uncontainable. Adulteration is everywhere and in everything. Fruits become ripe with chemicals. Even the small kids' products are adulterated. The Govt should deal with such unscrupulous people severely.

Make education affordable to all

If we have to see our country as a knowledge economy, we need to offer quality education to all and not rationing of education. Admissions in educational institutions should not be on caste or religion basis. Financial support to students based on caste and religion should be immediately stopped. It is seen that people earning good amount of income enjoy Govt incentives and they become inactive comparatively due to the caste/religion benefits. Baseless reservations create a societal division, and lead to brain drain. Reservation will vanish if the scarcity in education is avoided.

Nationalize education sector

Education in India has been regulated on a not-for profit basis. This encourages corrupt people, money launderers and politicians to use education institutions to hide their black money, and earn heavy income from education business through clever structuring. Govt cannot regulate them. Hence, it is high time to nationalize private educational institutions in tune with federal structure and compensate the investors sufficiently. Education up to tenth should be made free of cost.

Conclusion

Education is a country's lifeline, and it has to be given more importance than defence in any country. There is a dire need for revolutionary changes in the India's education system, not only in the syllabus and pedagogy, but also in the attitude towards the test and marks system. India can use its vast human resources productively if the learning system is made effective. As a child is born, it is painted with religion and caste by the cowardly society and is bombarded with all biased thoughts and unruly philosophies. Every child has unlimited potential and it should be allowed to be free from our ill thoughts. It should be taught to reduce the inequality. We can do a lot. But we are not working with required seriousness. If the Govt schools are failing, it is primarily because of non-availability or absence of teachers, no headmasters for governance, lack of initiatives by teachers, lack of guidance to students, lack of infrastructure, increased involvement of politicians and more bureaucratic control. Indifferent parents including Govt school teachers, MPs, MLAs and ministers send their wards to pvt schools. It is a shameful situation. The government will have to work on it seriously. The schools Kendriya vidyalaya and Navodaya vidyalaya are far better than public schools. The way of teaching is superb. The qualifications of teachers are unmatchable. These schools are doing wonders, providing not only quality education but also opportunity to excel. No private school can match their infrastructure; both are Govt schools with very low fee. Why can't we adopt the same philosophy in all Govt schools? Governments do a lot in education, but not fetching the results, since the attempts are neither completely organized nor consistent. The system of education should be learner-centric rather than mark-centric. Children must be allowed to choose subjects according to their interests. They should be encouraged to research on their own from library books and the Internet and share them in the class. This will help them to develop self-confidence, selfdependence and openness to criticism. Employability is a serious problem today. Somehow people get degrees and become unemployed or underemployed. The quality of education is directly linked to the resources available and it is important for the Govt to improve resource allocation to bring about qualitative changes in the field of education. Though the number of students and programmes increases every year, India has failed to produce world class universities both in the private sector or the public sector. The scarcity of quality education should be avoided. The central Govt should allocate enough money to open new schools, colleges and universities, overhaul the entire system and invest in technology and innovation related to the education system. Every child born in this country should have equal opportunity to learn, grow and excel in life with quality education blended with character. A vibrant nation is created by the energetic youth and active media. The youth and media can be positive only if the politicians are honest and responsible.

- Indian Govt needs to invest heavily in infrastructure and teachers' training. At least 8-10% of India's GDP must be invested in the education sector.
- Malnutrition affects the children's ability to learn. Poverty and nutrition deficiency should be taken care of, which is the bounden duty of the Govt.
- Teachers should encourage creativity in students. The latter should be exposed to economic, environmental and societal problems.
- The strength of a class should not be more than 25 at school and 50 at higher education. A child cannot get the required attention of a teacher if the strength is unreasonable.

- Exams should be tuned to assess the student's understanding of the subject.
- Reservation system and Management quota system be abolished. Ownership of educational units by politicians and religious groups should be discouraged.
- Media should become more responsible. Every news agency should publicise everyday at least one incident on the need of quality education and the change required in people for a healthy nation.

References

1. ASER, 2016, Annual Status of Education Report 2016, http://www.asercentre.org/p/289.html.
2. Bittersweet, 2017, The collapse of education is the collapse of the Nation, https://www.jamiiforums.com/threads/the-collapse-ofeducation-is-the-collapse-of-the-nation.1231557/, April 7.
3. Classbase, 2016, Education System in India, http://www.classbase.com/countries/India/Education-System.
4. Indiatoday, 2017, Budget 2017: Education sector analysis, then and now, https://www.indiatoday.in/educationtoday/news/story/budget-2017-education-958329-2017-02-01, February 1.
5. Indrail, 2015, Higher education in India, https://indrailsearch.wordpress.com/2015/06/13/education-higher-education-in-india/, June.
6. Kremer, etc. (2004), "Teacher Absence in India: A Snapshot", ''Journal of the European Economic Association".
7. Kumkum Joshi, 2017, How India's education system is breaking the country, http://www.dailyo.in/voices/school-education-englishgovernment-school/story/1/16610. html.
8. Maps of India, 2016, Education in India, http://www.mapsofindia.com/education, January
9. MHRD., 2016, Educational statistics at a glance, http://mhrd.gov.in/sites/upload files/mhrd/files/statistics/ESG20160. pdf.
10. Prayatna, 2014, Education in India: Past, Present and the Future. Ideas, Policies and Initiatives,
11. http://prayatna.typepad.com/education/datastatistics/, February 14.
12. Sanyal D. K., 2017, 14 facts about Indian education system and a remedy, https://sanyaldk.in/doing-it-in-open-source-way/14-factsabout-indian-education-system-and-a-remedy/.
13. Sasi Kumar V., 2016, The Education System in India, https://www.gnu.org/education/edu-system-india.en.html, 18th November.
14. Studylib, 2017, Private sector's contribution to K-12 education in India - Current impact, challenges and way forward.,

15. Tarang, 2017, Facts & Statistics about Education in India, http://www.tarang.org/facts/facts-statistics-about-education-in-india 2. html.
16. THE, 2017, World University Rankings 2017, https://www. times higher education.com/world-university-rankings/2017/worldanking#!/page/3/length/25/sort by/rank/sort order/asc/cols/stats.
17. World Bank, 2015, Educating India's Children, http://www.worldbank.org/en/country/india/brief/educating-india-children.

Chapter - 9

Methodological Approaches: A Study

Dr. Elisha Kolluri

Abstract

Teaching learning is a complex process which includes teacher, learner, teaching learning materials, suitable approaches and strategies and a learning environment which gives rise to a meaningful learning. Approach is a way of thinking and working in a set of direction so as to accomplish certain goals. Approaches deals with general philosophies of teaching. Approach is a theory about conceptual learning. It is a philosophy of how people learn in general. It can be psychologically focused such as behaviorism or cognitivism. An approach could be seen as your perspective, ideology, belief or theoretical stance on something. It encompasses a set of logical assumptions that could be made for better comprehension of issues. A method is a target plan or set of orderly procures that are based on a credible approach. It reveals what needs to be done in a systematic way and how to focus on achieving those goals.Method is nothing but a scientific way of presenting the subject, keeping in mind the psychological and physical requirements of the learner. Teaching learning strategy is a selection of suitable pedagogical processes by means of using appropriate techniques, such that all of these lie in the realm of approach, the teacher chooses to follow. The main aim of the methodological approaches is to provide subject knowledge to the learner comprehensively through teaching learning strategies. Methodological approaches are traditional approach or Teacher centered approach, behaviourist approach, constructivist approach, collaborative learning approach, problem solving approach, concept mapping approach, experiential learning approach, inquiry approach etc. These approaches are useful to provide subject knowledge to the learner.

Keywords: *Teaching learning strategies,methodology, Teacher, Learner, teaching learning material, traditional approach, behaviorist approach, constructivist approach.*

Introduction

Teaching learning is a complex process which includes teacher, learner, teaching learning materials, suitable approaches and strategies and a learning environment which gives rise to a meaningful learning. Learner is at the centre of learning process and teacher works as the facilitator of learning.

Approach

Approach is a way of thinking and working in a set of direction so as to accomplish certain goals. Approach is a theory about conceptual learning. It is a philosophy of how people learn in general. They can be psychologically focused such as behaviorism or cognitivism. An approach could be seen as your perspective, ideology, belief or theoretical stance on something. It encompasses a set of logical assumptions that could be made for better comprehension of issues.

The approaches for teaching can be broadly classified into teacher centered and student centered. In teacher centered approach to learning, teachers are the main authority figure. Students are viewed as "empty vessels" whose primary role is to passively receive information (via lectures and direct instruction) with an end goal of testing and assessment. It is the primary role of teachers to pass knowledge and information onto their students. Teaching and assessment are viewed as two separate entities.

Student learning is measured through objectively scored tests and assessments.In student centered approach to learning, while teachers are the authority figure, teachers and students play an equally active role in the learning process. The teacher's primary role is to coach and facilitate student learning and overall comprehension of material. Student learning is measured through both formal and informal forms of assessment, including group projects, student portfolios, and class participation. Teaching and assessments are connected; student learning is continuously measured during teacher instruction.Commonly used teaching methods may include class participation, demonstration, recitation, memorization, or combinations of these.

Method

A method is a target plan or set of orderly procures that are based on a credible approach. It reveals what needs to be done in a systematic way and how to focus on achieving those goals. Method is nothing but a scientific way of presenting the subject, keeping in mind the psychological and physical requirements of the children.

Difference between approach and method

An approach is a way of looking at teaching and learning. Underlying any language teaching approach is a theoretical view of what language is, and of how it can be learnt. An approach gives rise to methods, the way of teaching something, which use classroom activities or techniques to help learners learn. Approach is an axiomatic while method is procedural. Approach is a set of correlative assumptions while method is an overall plane, within approach there can be many methods.

Strategy

Strategy is borrowed term from military which actually means to utilize all of a nations force through large scale planning and development to ensure security or victory. According to Encyclopedia, Strategy refers to science or art of planning and directing large military movement and operations.

Teaching Strategy

In education, strategy is a selection of suitable pedagogical processes by means of using appropriate techniques, such that all of these lie in the realm of the approach, the teacher chooses to follow. Learning strategies is a teacher of learning activities undertaken with the aim of learning process that takes place in classroom can achieve the goals effectively. It is a long term plan of action designed to achieve a particular goal.

Methodological Approaches

The following are the some of the methodological approaches. They are

1. **Traditional Approach or Teacher centered approach**

   Learning is a passive process. Learners are not involved in the teaching learning process. Focus is on the teacher and teaching strategies. Teacher uses lectures to provide explanation to learners.Teacher knows everything and learners do not know anything. The teacher demonstrates and the learners observe.

   Qualities of a good lecture

   1. A good lecture should not be too long as to exceed.
   2. A good lecture should address a single theme.
   3. In a good lecture technical terms are carefully explained.
   4. Familiar examples and analogies are given.
   5. A good lecture establishes fluency in technical content.

6. A good lecture uses illustrations and examples.
7. A good lecture builds on existing knowledge.
8. A good lecture employs a variety of approaches.

Lecturing

The lecture method is just one of several teaching methods. The lecture method is convenient for the institution and cost-efficient, especially with larger classroom sizes. This is why lecturing is the standard for most college courses, when there can be several hundred students in the classroom at once; lecturing lets professors address the most people at once, in the most general manner, while still conveying the information that they feel is most important, according to the lesson plan. While the lecture method gives the instructor or teacher chances to expose students to unpublished or not readily available material, the students plays a passive role which may hinder learning. While this method facilitates large-class communication, the lecturer must make constant and conscious effort to become aware of student problems and engage the students to give verbal feedback. It can be used to arouse interest in a subject provided the instructor has effective writing and speaking skills.

2. **Behaviorist Approach**

   There are three types ofdomains in Blooms taxonomy.They are ***(A) Cognitive domain (Benjamin S.Blooms-1956)***: The objectives of this domain are Knowledge, Comprehension, Application, Analysis, Synthesis and Evaluation.***(B) Affective domain (D.R. Krath wohl-1964):*** The objectives of this domain areReceiving, Responding, Valuing, Organization and Characterization by a value complex.

   (C) Psycho-motor domain (Elizabeth, Simpson, Dave-1968,1972): The objectives of this domain areImitation, Manipulation, Precision, Articulation and Naturalization.

   Examples and applications: Classifying or chunking information, Linking Concepts (associate new content with something known), Real world examples, Discussions, Problem solving and Analogies etc.

3. **Learner Centered Approach**

   In which it is premised on the belief that the learner is also an important resource because he/she too knows something and is therefore capable of sharing something.

4. Collaborative Learning Approach

It will welcome group work, teamwork, partnerships and group discussion. Collaboration allows students to actively participate in the learning process by talking with each other and listening to others opinions. Collaboration establishes a personal connection between students and the topic of study and it helps students think in a less personally biased way. Group projects and discussions are examples of this teaching method. Teachers may employ collaboration to assess student's abilities to work as a team, leadership skills, or presentation abilities.

Collaborative discussions can take a variety of forms, such as fishbowl discussions. After some preparation and with clearly defined roles, a discussion may constitute most of a lesson, with the teacher only giving short feedback at the end or in the following lesson.

The most common type of collaborative method of teaching in a class is classroom discussion. It is also a democratic way of handling a class, where each student is given equal opportunity to interact and put forth their views. A discussion taking place in a classroom can be either facilitated by a teacher or by a student. A discussion could also follow a presentation or a demonstration. Class discussions can enhance student understanding, add context to academic content, broaden student perspectives, highlight opposing viewpoints, reinforce knowledge, build confidence, and support community in learning. The opportunities for meaningful and engaging in-class discussion may vary widely, depending on the subject matter and format of the course.

Motivations for holding planned classroom discussion, however, remain consistent. An effective classroom discussion can be achieved by probing more questions among the students, paraphrasing the information received, using questions to develop critical thinking with questions.

5. Cooperative Learning Approach

Cooperative learning gives students the opportunity to work with others and see different points of view. Research shows that students learn more effectively when working together rather than apart, and it is also known to improve self-confidence in students. The jigsaw technique is especially effective because each student is responsible for one another's learning, and students find out really quick that each group member has something equally important to contribute to the group in order to make the task a successful one. Students are exposed to and use many skills throughout this strategy: Communication, problem-solving skills, cognition, and critical thinking and all of which are essential for a successful academic career. Encourage students of mixed abilities to work together by promoting small group or whole class activities.

Through verbally expressing their ideas and responding to others your students will develop their self-confidence, as well as enhance their communication and critical thinking skills which are vital throughout life.

Solving mathematical puzzles, conducting scientific experiments and acting out short drama sketches are just a few examples of how cooperative learning can be incorporated into classroom lessons.

6. Constructivist Learning Approach

The students are expected to construct knowledge and meaning our for what they are taught by connecting them to prior experience. Constructivism is a theory that explains how an individual understands and explains what she/he has learnt and that is about the nature of knowledge. Constructivism is a theory of learning that is about how people start to learn and about explaining the nature of knowledge. This theory claims that people can create new understandings or they can combine things, ideas, events and activities they already know and believe in a manner of mutual interaction. Knowledge is gained in line with the will of a person instead of imitation and repetition. Philosophical explanations of this theory are based on J. Bruner, W. James, J. Dewey, J. Piaget and L.S. Vygotsky.

Learning should take place in authentic and real world. It should involve social negotiation and mediation. Content and skill should be understood within the frame work of learners' prior knowledge. Content and skills should be made relevant to the learner.

Students should be assessed formatively, serving to help them to acquire further learning experiences. Teacher should serve primarily as facilitator of learning, not instructor.

5E's Learning Model

- ***Engage:*** Students need to be engaged and focused on the learning tasks by asking questions, defining a problem and drawing their attention to an interesting event.

- ***Explore:*** Students get opportunity to explore through all senses
- ***Explain:*** Teacher interacts with students to discover their ideas
- ***Elaborate:***Students are allowed to expand the concept they have learned
- ***Evaluate:***Teacher sees if the students have attained understanding of concept and knowledge

Examples and applications;: Case studies, Research projects, Problem based learning, Brainstorming, Collaborative learning or group work, Discovery learning and Simulations.

7. Problem Solving Approach

Problem Solving Approach is based on the idea of involvement of students in real life problems. It gives an opportunity to the students to develop their learning by doing activities, questioning, thinking, searching for solution, visualizing the situation and arriving at conclusion on their own.

Teacher makes the students to identify the problem. So the teacher creates a situation, gives a question, performs activity or experiment, elicit inquiry from students to make students realize that a problem exists and helps them to initiate thinking and listens to their thoughts, makes them to recall their existing knowledge and reconstruct them when it is required and use that knowledge to solve problems.

Problem-based learning may include different steps of practice in the teaching of many disciplines. However, the basic steps for all problem-based learning are as follows:

1. Meeting the problem and defining it
2. Determining what one knows and what he needs to know and putting his thoughts into order
3. Gathering and sharing information
4. Producing potential solutions and hypotheses
5. Determining the learning issues
6. The application of the new knowledge to the problem and reevaluation
7. Identifying the best solution
8. Explaining the problem and its solution briefly
9. Evaluation and presentation of new learning

   Higher order thinking skills, such as summarizing, analyzing and making inferences and deductions are developed through problem solving. Tasks such as observation, collating and evaluating evidence and identifying essential information help children to make informed judgments. Discovery learning most notably takes place in problem solving situations where the learner draws on his/her own experience and prior knowledge to discover the truths that are to be learned.

8. Concept Mapping Approach

Concept maps are graphical tools for organizing and representing knowledge about certain concepts. A concept map represents an understanding of the relationship and hierarchy between important set of concepts. They promote meaningful learning.

Concept may be thought of as a mental framework of an event or an object. Any event or object is a concept because it has some identifiable properties or ideas associated with it. In addition, a concept also has a label called name.

Concept maps providing a visual representation of a particular material, develops new relationships among concepts, motivating students to think and engage in active learning and promoting reflective thinking.

9. Inquiry Based Learning

Inquiry based learning implies involving students in the learning process so they will have a deeper understanding of what they are learning. We are born with the instinct to inquire as babies we use our senses to make connections to our surroundings. Inquiry based learning strategies are used to engage students to learn by asking questions, investigating, exploring, and reporting what they see. This process leads students to a deeper understanding of the content that they are learning, which helps them be able to apply these concepts they are learning in new situations. In order for our students to be able to be successful in the 21stcentury, they need to be able to answer complex questions and develop solutions for these problems. The Inquiry-based learning strategy is a great tool to do just that.

Pose thought-provoking questions which inspire your students to think for themselves and become more independent learners. Encouraging students to ask questions and investigate their own ideas helps improve their problem-solving skills as well as gain a deeper understanding of academic concepts. Both of which are important life skills.

10. Interactive Approach

In this approach, an interactive classroom will have more student talk and less teacher talk. Students are given the opportunity to interact with teacher and with other students.

11. Integrated Approach

This approach makes the teacher connects what he/she teaches to other lessons of the same subject or connects his/her lessons with other subjects thus making his/her approach interdisciplinary and multidisciplinary.

12. Banking Approach

In this approach, the teacher deposits knowledge into the empty minds of students for students to commit to memory.

13. Disciplinal Approach

It limits the teacher to discussing his/her lessons within the boundary of his/her subject.

14. Direct Teaching Approach

The teacher directly tells or shows or demonstrates what is to be taught.

15. Indirect, Guided Approach

The teacher guides the learner to discover things for himself/herself. The teacher facilitates the learning process by allowing the learner to be engaged in the learning process with his/her guidance.

Newer teaching methods may incorporate television, radio, internet, multimedia, and other modern devices. Some educators believe that the use of technology, while facilitating learning to some degree, is not a substitute for educational methods that encourage critical thinking and a desire to learn.

16. Psychoanalytical Approach

Sigmund Freud put this approach, also known as psychodynamic approach, forth. Some other pioneers of this approach besides Freud are Alfred Adler, Carl Jung. Unconscious and intrinsic motivators are the most basic concepts that are used to explain human behaviours. The most well known elements of this approach are hypnosis, structures of conscious (unconscious, preconscious, conscious); psychic elements of personality (id, ego, superego) and psychosexual developmental periods.

17. Technological Approach

Integrating technology into the classroom is a great way to empower students to stay connected in this technological era. Technology rich lessons have been found to keep students motivated and engaged longer. Any of these technology integration strategies will have a positive impact on student learning.

An experienced teacher knows that not every teaching strategy that you use will be an effective one. There will be some hits and misses, and depending upon your teaching style, and the way your students learn, you will figure out which strategies work and which do not. It may take some trial and error, but it doesn't hurt to try them all.

Technology in the classroom

Integrating technology into the classroom is a great way to empower students to stay connected in this technological era. Incorporating technology into your teaching is a great way to actively engage your students, especially as digital media surrounds young people in the 21st century. Interactive whiteboards or mobile devices can be used to display images and videos, which help students, visualize new academic concepts. Learning can become more interactive when technology is used as students can physically engage during lessons as well as instantly research their ideas, which develops autonomy.

Some examples of utilizing technology in the classroom is to create web based lessons or a Web quest, multimedia presentations such as a video, animation, or some type of graphic, utilizing a tablet or an iPod, taking your class on a virtual field trip, participating in an online research project, or even creating a class website.

Conclusion

A teacher should have knowledge and understanding of various approaches and strategies of teaching learning so that the teacher has a choice to select the most suitable one according to the needs of the learners. This way, the teacher can take maximum advantage of whatever learning situation arises during transaction of concepts. However, approaches and strategies discussed above are not exhaustive. A teacher has much flexibility to devise a strategy, select and with over form one strategy to other as per the requirements of the teaching learning situation.

References

1. Westwood, P. (2008). What teachers need to know about teaching methods. Camberwell, Vic, ACER Press.
2. Vanaja, M. (2004). Methods of Teaching Physics. New Delhi: Discovery Publishing House.
3. Wenjiang (2012). Informatics and Management Science V. London: Springer.
4. Neeraja, K.P. (2011). Textbook of Communication and Education Technology for Nurses. London: Jaypee Brothers Medical Publishers Ltd.
5. Heidgerken, Loretta (1965). Teaching in Schools of Nursing: Principles and Methods. Philadelphia, PA: Lippincott.
6. Petrina, S. (2007) Advance Teaching Methods for the Technology Classroom Hershey, PA: Information Science Publishing.
7. Donche, V (2013). "Differential use of Learning Strategies in First-Year Higher Education: The impact of Personality, Academic Motivation, and Teaching Strategies". The British journal of Educational Psychology.
8. S.I. and Rose, A.A. (2005) "Designing a Strategic Information Systems Planning Methodology for Malaysian Institutes of Higher Learning (isp- ipta), Issues in Information System, Volume VI, No. 1, 2005.
9. Baskerville, R. (1991). "Risk Analysis as a Source of Professional Know-ledge". Computers & Security.
10. Howell, K. E. (2013) Introduction to the Philosophy of Methodology. London: Sage Publications.
11. Katsicas, Sokratis K. (2009). "Chapter 35". In Vacca, John. Computer and Information Security Handbook. Morgan Kaufmann Publications. Elsevier Inc.
12. Berg, Bruce L., 2009, *Qualitative Research Methods for the Social Sciences*. Seventh Edition. Boston MA: Pearson Education Inc.
13. Creswell, J. (1998). Qualitative inquiry and research design: Choosing among five traditions. Thousand Oaks, California: Sage Publications.
14. Creswell, J. (2003). Research Design: Qualitative, Quantitative, and Mixed Methods Approaches. Thousand Oaks, California: Sage Publications.
15. Franklin, M.I. (2012). Understanding Research: Coping with the Quantitative-Qualitative Divide. London and New York: Routledge.
16. Guba, E. and Lincoln, Y. (1989). Fourth Generation Evaluation. Newbury Park, California: Sage Publications.
17. Herrman, C. S. (2009). "Fundamentals of Methodology", a series of papers On the Social Science Research Network (SSRN), online.
18. Howell, K. E. (2013) Introduction to the Philosophy of Methodology. London: Sage Publications.
19. Ndira, E. Alana, Slater, T. and Bucknam, A. (2011). Action Research for Business, Nonprofit, and Public Administration - A Tool for Complex Times. Thousand Oaks, CA: Sage.
20. Joubish, Farooq Dr. (2009). Educational Research Department of Education, Federal Urdu University, Karachi, Pakistan.

Chapter - 10

Efforts towards Internationalization of Higher Education in India

Dr. G Kamalakar

Abstract

Higher education has now become a part of the globalization process in the form of cross-border matching of supply and demand. Consequently, higher education can no longer be viewed in a strictly national context. This calls for a broader meaning of internationalization, which embraces the entire functioning of higher education.[1] *Internationalization of higher education is seen as one of the ways a country responds to the impact of globalization, yet, at the same time, it respects the individuality of the nation. While the various meanings attached to the term internationalization illustrate its complexity and richness as a concept. A country's unique history, indigenous culture(s), resources, priorities, etc. shape its response to and relationships with other countries. Thus national identity and culture are key to internationalization of higher education. The advent of education hubs is heralded as the latest development in internationalization of higher education. The prevalence of education hubs is a token of the transformative forces at play in higher education the world over. The concept of internationalization of higher education was modeled in the wake of the United Nations' avowed interest in higher education.*

Key Words: *Globalization, Migration, GATS, Internationalization.*

Introduction

The Organization's patronage of higher education as an item of global priority was decisive in conflating manifold ideas of internationalization of higher education into the theoretical entity. "Collection and analysis of comparative educational data increased, which allowed international comparisons to be made and conclusions to be drawn thereof. Higher education started to be viewed from an international perspective when formulating and implementing national policies".[2]

Knight describes internationalization of higher education as 'the process of integrating an international/intercultural dimension into the teaching, research and service functions of the institution'. There are several key concepts in this definition, e.g. the idea of internationalization being a dynamic process and not a set of isolated activities, integration or infusion that contributes to the sustainability of the international dimension. Finally, this definition refers to the primary and universal functions of an institution of higher education, namely, teaching, research and service to society. This could suggest that internationalization is an aim in itself, while in many countries and settings it is rather seen as a means to achieve a wider goal, e.g. quality improvement, restructuring and upgrading of higher education systems and services.[3]

The Purpose of Internationalization

In many countries, cuts in public funding also forced higher education institutions to look abroad for financing. Under the policy of internationalization, many universities have been following aggressive strategies to attract foreign students, who are charged fees above the per student costs. Foreign students, thus, subsidize the higher education of local students.

It is unfortunate that even some of the best universities in the world, such as Oxford and Cambridge, also seem to be adopting the same approaches, contrary to what they did earlier, namely offering scholarships to foreign students to attract and promote the best talent. In the framework of the World Trade Organization, many countries find it convenient to sell cheap higher education degrees to gullible students from developing countries by adopting different modes under the General Agreement on Trade in Services. Universities are fast becoming entrepreneurial institutions both domestically and internationally.[4]

Rationale for Internationalization

There are a variety of ways to describe and define internationalization; there are also a number of different rational esormotivations for wanting to integratein to international dimension of higher education. Aigneretal, suggest that there are three major reasons for the internationalization of higher education: 1. interest in international security; 2. maintenance of economic competitiveness; 3. fostering of human understanding across nations.[5]

Internationalization is not an altogether unknown phenomenon in higher education in India and other developing countries. Students have for many decades gone abroad for higher studies and professionals have gone out to teach or do research. Foreign faculty have come to our shores for teaching in our institutions. The reasons behind the explosion of the phenomenon of internationalization are not difficult to fathom.

The opening up of our economy through the new policies of liberalization, easier capital flows and access to new technologies facilitated by globalization have helped expand the scale and modes of internationalization.[6]

International, intercultural, and global dimension are three terms that are intentionally used as a triad. International is used in the sense of relationships between and among nations, cultures or countries. But we know that internationalization is also about relating to the diversity of cultures that exists within countries, communities, and institutions, and so intercultural is used to address this dimension. Finally, global, a controversial and value-laden term these days, is included to provide the sense of worldwide scope. These three terms complement each other and together depict the richness in the breadth and depth of internationalization.[7]

Trends in Internationalization of Higher Education: Migration

The internationalization of higher education is already in progress in India. The following evidence, though not comprehensive, will give a sense of the directions and trends on the ground.[8] A total of 1, 50,000 Indian students are presently studying in the USA, at an annual cost of over $4 billion. This number is next to that of China which has also sent its students abroad in a big way. A good proportion of the Indian students, of course, do not return to the home country. There were 131 foreign educational programmes being offered in India in partnership with Indian institutions.

A few thousand students are enrolled in these programmes which also offer them opportunities to study in foreign countries for a part of their courses.[9] These programmes are largely in technical and vocational subjects.[10]

Study abroad by students is still the most visible mode of internationalization. The Organisation for Economic Co-operation and Development (OECD) countries dominate this arena. The United States (US) leads in this regard with 6, 00,000 visiting students. China alone has 3, 50,000 students studying abroad. India and China account for the largest proportion of foreign students in the US.[11]

Compared to the developments in China and other countries, India's forays into internationalization have been modest. As noted above, these include the liberalisation of foreign exchange for those who wish to study abroad, easing of restrictions on foreign investment, and a limited number of collaborative programmes with foreign providers. The key Indian players that have taken advantage of the new policies are from the private sector. Public universities have not been active on this front so far, nor do they have the resources to take such initiatives.

There is, however, no effective and coherent strategic or regulatory framework to monitor and assess these activities.[12] The net result is that internationalization has been dominated by foreign and Indian institutions which are not in all cases known for their high standards and educational quality.

Movement of Students for Studies Abroad

The focus here is on scaling up thismodewhichhasalreadybeenpopular for a long time. It is a way to meet the rising demand, especially in technical and professional fields. Increased mobility through liberalization has alsofacilitated the movement of teachers and other professionals to work abroad. But the down- side is that this mode can be accessed only by the elite sections of society. While it is bound to remain popular, it cannot be counted on to solve the problem of access that faces the majority of our students. For them, the answer lies in creating opportunities for higher studies within the country.

Internationalization of Higher Education in India

In sum, three types of internationalization of higher education can be distinguished: import-oriented, export-oriented, and import-and-export oriented (Huang, 2007). While many developing countries have had to adopt import-oriented models, and developed countries primarily adopt export-oriented ones, countries like India and China belong to the third category. Education is a trillion Dollar industry worldwide. Education industry groups are, therefore, attracted by the prospects of liberalization and globalization of this industry. They seek more international deregulation and generally support WTO and GATS efforts.

As demands for higher education grow the world over, the governments are also finding it difficult to provide adequate budgetary allocation. GATS cover educational services of all types for all countries whose educational systems are not exclusively provided by public sector or those systems that have a commercial purpose. Hardly any country has education exclusively in the public sector domain and therefore, almost all the world's educational systems come within the purview of GATS.[13] So far only 40 countries have agreed to all the provisions of the GATS.

Many have chosen to limit its scope. Higher education services, however, now figure in India's offer on liberalization in trade in services that the Commerce Ministry has submitted to WTO in August 2005.[14]

India has responded to internationalization of higher education later than its neighbors in the South East Asia. The present drive is fallout of the Government's expressly proclaimed policy of economic liberalism. Powar(2012) states: "The advent of globalization in the early 1990s, and the signing of the General Agreement on Trade in Services (GATS) in 1995 provided, at least theoretically, a pathway for the entry of both foreign providers and foreign investment, in to India" (p. 237). Internationalization of higher education has not been a high priority item up until quite recently.

In recent times, India has emerged as an education hub attracting students from various countries and countries from the developing world. Since education is in the state sector to a great extent, it is cheap compared to the developed countries. Technologically also India is making great strides. This is resulting in private sector boom in technical and other professional areas. Economically too, India's growth rate is high.

All these factors play a role in attracting a number of foreign students to study in India. Similarly good numbers of Indians are also going abroad for higher studies. Thus internationalization is a two way process offering opportunities for institutions, individuals and governments here.

In order to promote cultural understanding through education, the Indian government has been offering many fellowships to international scholars specializing in Indian studies in the fields of culture and social sciences through the Indian Council of Cultural Relations (ICCR). The ICCR has also established 108 Chairs of Indian Studies in various foreign universities. However, the dramatic growth of transnational education providers in the Indian higher education scene has been a more recent phenomenon.[15]

Indian Students Studying Abroad

Indian students abroad are dispersed over 50 countries of the world. Out of the 189, 472 Indian students in 2012, more than 85% students were concentrated in six countries: the United States (51%), United Kingdom (16%), Australia (6%), Canada (4%), United Arab Emirates (4%) and New Zealand (4%). It is noted that between 2008 and 2012, the popularity of Australia as a destination for Indian students has declined.[16]

Table: 1 Top Ten destinations of Indian students

Country	*Year 2005*	*Country*	*Year 2008*	*Country*	*Year 2012*
UnitedStates	84044	UnitedStates	94664	UnitedStates	97120
Australia	20515	Australia	26520	UnitedKingdom	29713
UnitedKingdom	16685	UnitedKingdom	25901	Australia	11684
United ArabEmirates	6684	RussianFederation	4314	Canada	8142
Germany	4339	NewZealand	4094	United ArabEmirates	7310
Canada	2829	Germany	3257	NewZealand	7248
NewZealand	1563	Canada	3219	Germany	4312
Kazakhstan	1003	Ukraine	1785	RussianFederation	3351
Ukraine	957	Cyprus	1076	Ukraine	2516
Malaysia	828.5	Malaysia	1065	France	1955
WORLDWIDE	146267	WORLDWIDE	176881	WORLDWIDE	189472

Source: UNESCO Institute for Statistics (UIS)

Additionally, a strategic advantage for India is related to the fact that there are easily identifiable geographic and political regions that have proven to be strongholds in terms of "sourcing" students, as it were. The foremost among them are: Afghanistan, Iran, Arabic speaking countries in Central Asia, the Gulf and Africa. The fact that these are "old faithful", so to speak suggests a steadfast brand stature, which will undoubtedly help recruit students. The following tables demonstrate the inflow of international students:

Students from SAARC Region in India

India is gradually emerging as a hub for tertiary education in the South Asian region.Table below presents mobile students from the SAARC region. It also include the students enrolled in United States, United Kingdom and Australia from SAARC region. The table shows that only in case of Bhutan that 71% of their internationally mobile students came to India. However only 2% of the students from Bangladesh came to India. Even though India gets 19% of internationally mobile students from Nepal, almost 60% of the Nepalese students go to the aforementioned countries other than India.

Table: 2 Students'Mobility from the SAARC Region to India, USA, UK, Australia and Canadain 2011-12

Country of origin	*Destinationcountries*							
	% in India	*% in USA*	*% in UK*	*% in Australia*	*% in Canada*	*Total % in USA,UK, Australia & Canada*	*% in other countries*	*Total*
Afghanistan	16.3	03.6	02.1	01.1	0.7	07.5	76.2	9754
Bangladesh	02.4	14.6	17.4	15.2	6.0	53.2	44.4	21927
Bhutan	71.3	03.0	0.6	11.5	0.9	16.0	12.7	3186
Maldives	14.1	01.5	07.1	11.1	0.4	20.1	65.8	1862
Nepal	18.7	31.9	05.5	21.8	0.4	59.6	21.7	29184
Pakistan	*	11.7	23.1	09.9	5.0	49.7	50.3	37962
SriLanka	07.0	17.3	21.6	21.1	0.9	60.9	32.1	16204

Source: UNESCO Institute for Statistics (UIS)

Table: 3 Inflow of International Students to India

Region	*1990-91*	*1995-96*	*2000-01*	*2005-06*	*2008-09*
Asia	5741	4831	3866	10493	16004
Africa	6318	4081	2964	2403	4193
N and SAmerica	263	309	327	654	614
Europe	173	127	179	206	304
Australasia	35	40	44	71	66
Miscellaneous	369	699	405	629	597
Total	12899	10087	7785	14456	21778

Source: Association of Indian Universities (as cited in Powar, 2012, p. 245)

India is becoming the educational hub in the SAARC region as India has a relatively large higher education system and capacity to absorb students from neighboring countries.

Table: 4 Country-wise Inflows of International Students to India

Countries	*2004-05*	*2005-06*	*2006-07*	*2007-08*
Iran	1120	1264	2180	2669
Nepal	1352	1411	1728	1821
United ArabEmirate	1500	2034	1878	1560
Ethiopia	226	302	1033	1289
SriLanka	582	530	466	997
Afghanistan	35	65	422	976
SaudiArabia	419	551	771	835
Bahrain	382	481	446	600
Kenya	418	523	621	592
Oman	646	505	608	548
Total	6680	7666	10153	11887

Source: Dongaonkar and Negi 2009

The factors that potentially strengthen the case for education hubs in are: the vast majority of international students hail from developing countries; additionally, the students are reportedly quite sure of their preference for English speaking higher education system and subsist on a meager budget.[17] This configuration is suggestive of India's boundless potential for internationalization of higher education. It would not be implausible to hold that India's ability to offer higher education in English at a fraction of the cost of the industrialized countries, combined with its physical proximity to regions that are teeming with higher education hopefuls points at bountiful gains that can be accrued with strategic planning.[18]

India might be the world's singlelargest market for foreign universities. The country has a significant unmet demand for higher education access. Currently, only 10 per cent of the age group attends university half the proportion in China and well below the rate in most rapidly developing and middle-income countries. Further, India has a huge unmet demand for high-quality higher education…Thus, foreign institutions see a tremendous opportunity for lucrative growth in the Indian market.[19]

Collaborations A University is interested in developing collaboration among researchers bringing them together in existing, new or larger 'Centres of Excellence'. Collaboration can take various forms ranging from offering general advice and insights, sharing data or ideas through correspondence or discussions at conferences, by visiting each other, or by active participation in a specific piece of research conducted jointly or separately and then integrating the results. Research and Enterprise can provide further advice.[20]

India's Experience with American Institutions

It may be interesting to see how India has benefited from international partnerships in the past and whether some of those models are still relevant. India's experience with the United States in selected areas of education, such as agriculture and science and technology is a good example. In the agriculture sector in the 1950s, the introduction of the 'Green revolution' in India can be traced back to Indo-US collaborations in agricultural sciences. This helped to sustain research and education in agriculture[21]. Agriculture education in India greatly benefited from government-level collaboration in education through these colleges.

In the 1960s, a consortium of American universities facilitated the establishment of educational institutions like the Indian Institute of Technology, Kanpur, and the National Council of Educational Research and Training in New Delhi both founded with academic partnerships under the umbrella of the two governments. Both institutions are now totally Indian in terms of faculty and governance.

Offering Joint Degrees

Now the government is attempting to encourage Indian institutions to enter into partnerships with foreign universities and offer joint degrees to Indian students. The foreign universities do not have to open campuses in India, but their faculty would teach approved courses in India. The student would spend part of the four year bachelor degree programme in India and the remaining period at the foreign university.

This is an attractive approach to internationalisation, giving an opportunity for 'global immersion' to Indian students, who also get a foreign degree at a reduced cost. The academic quality, financial implications and administrative arrangements for recognising joint degrees have yet to be worked out between partnering institutions. Yet even before institutions were able to explore this opportunity, the government has come up with a caveat over the choice of institutions with which private institutions in India can collaborate.

The government insists that Indian institutions can only select a 'partner' institution abroad that is in the top 500 of international rankings. As is well known, hardly any Indian institutions are ranked within the world's top 500 institutions.[22] So are top-ranked foreign institutions expected to partner with non-ranked Indian institutions? This is not an attractive offer for a partnership. Unfortunately, this approach to internationalisation does not seem to be workable, either.

Lack of Focus on International Students

The final area of an internationalization strategy pertains to sending Indian students abroad and attracting foreign students to India. The government has left it free for Indian students to study anywhere abroad. It has no plans unlike Brazil and China to provide scholarships for study in countries such as the United States.

There are also no plans to promote cultural understanding of other countries by supporting Indian students to study, for example, in China or Brazil. One has seen President Barack Obama's '1, 00,000 strong' initiative supporting American students going to China. India also has no major schemes to attract foreign students.[23] The infrastructure required to host international students, in terms of good hostels, trained staff and adequate student advice services, does not exist in the majority of higher education institutions.

Strong Regulatory Mechanism

The University Grants Commission has come out with new regulations for foreign universities degree, which make it mandatory for all foreign and Indian educational institutions to seek its approval before entering into any partnership with Indian varsities. The UGC has said, "No foreign education institution or Indian education institution shall establish or operate its educational activity in India through collaboration leading to award of degrees or post graduate diplomas without the approval of the UGC." Existing collaborative arrangements between foreign and Indian institutions have been given six months' time to ensure that they meet all the norms under the new regulations. As per the new regulation, only such foreign institutions will be allowed to collaborate and have twining agreement with Indian education institutions which are accredited with the highest grade in their homeland. "The collaboration of foreign education institutions shall be allowed with only those Indian institutions which are accredited by the nationally recognised accrediting agencies with a grade not less than B," says the UGC regulation.[24]

An analysis of developments in higher education in India during the last two to three decades shows that there has been a systematic and continuous effort towards internationalization of higher education in general without committing to the provisions the GATS framework.[25]

The government is occupied with the formulation of guidelines for allowing foreign universities into India and for Indian institutions to go abroad, even though no clear policy decision on committing education under the GATS seems to have been made. While some public institutions like the Indian Institutes of Management and Indian Institutes of Technology, universities like the Indira Gandhi National Open University (IGNOU), public education bodies like the Central Board of Secondary Education (CBSE), and several private institutions are eager to export education and, in fact, are already doing so. Ministries and other organizations of commerce and trade such as the National Association of Software and Service Companies (NASSCOM), Confederation of Indian Industry (CII), and \ (FICCI) are keen on opening higher education for trade.[26]

The NKC also favours it. While many of them favour expanding and even regulating trade in higher education, they do not necessarily argue for making commitment to the GATS. However, there have been very few serious attempts at examining the implications of trade in higher education in India. Some authors (e.g. Deodhar, 2002; Sahni and Kale, 2004; Bhushan, 2006) have highlighted the problems the GATS would pose to higher education in India; others (e.g. Bhushan, 2004) have suggested restructuring of domestic regulations; still others (e.g. Raychaudhuri and De, 2007, 2008) have described the several barriers to trade in the era of globalization. Only a few (Chanda, 2003; Ahmad, 2005; Amin, 2008) have highlighted the opportunities it offers, and very few indeed (Raju, 2006) have suggested commitment of higher education to the GATS, with gradual liberalization.

The NKC also recommends internationalization mainly for economic reasons. It pleads for allowing foreign institutions to come to India, and providing incentives to good institutions and disincentives to substandard institutions, as this will reduce the outflow of Indian students to study abroad, resulting in substantial savings in foreign exchange.[27] The NKC also recommends that Indian institutions be encouraged to create campuses abroad and has advocated special efforts to attract foreign students to India. It argues that India should increase number of foreign students in Indian universities to at least 50,000, because if every one of them were charged US$10,000 per annum, this would bring in the substantial amount of US$0.5 billion.[28] Would improve competition, provide more choices to students, and contribute towards reaching higher levels of academic excellence.

Some initiatives are already being taken to attract more and more foreign students, such as easing of entry/visa regulations for foreign students, Indian missions abroad providing personalized counseling services to students seeking to come to India for studies, empanelling of a cadre of registered trained agents for foreign students, and building of international student centres in universities. That will work as a nodal point to assist foreign students in each university. The government's intention is to make India a global knowledge hub ('Easier visas', 2009. See also Planning Commission, 2011).[29]

It is widely felt, however, that India may not be able to emerge as an important exporter, but can certainly become a large importer, as it cannot compete with the giants in international trade. Only a very few institutions in the country have the potential to export quality education and succeed in trade, and those institutions also need huge initial investments, which are still lacking. Further, it is also felt that export would come at the cost of educational development at the domestic level; after all, there is huge unmet demand for education within the country.[30]

Currently only a minority of Indian universities and colleges have significant alliances with foreign institutions for activities including development and delivery of courses, joint research, or the exchange of staff and students. Although the newly emerged private universities and colleges are very active in promoting internationalization through the adoption of foreign curriculum, twinning programmes, etc., their objectives have only a limited dimension improve their market position through the promise of preparing students for the globally integrated economic environment.The dramatic expansion in numbers of students going abroad and a significant rise in the number of partnerships with foreign institutions is not the result of a government policy.[31]

Foreign Educational Institutions (Regulation of Entry and Operation) 2010 Bill[32]

It aims to regulate the entry and operation of foreign educational institutions seeking to impart higher education. Every foreign educational institution intending to operate in India has to be notified as a foreign educational provider by the central government on the recommendation of the registrar (secretary of the University Grants Commission). The bill was introduced in the Lok Sabha in May 2010, and then referred to a parliamentary standing committee. The committee gave its report in May 2011. The foreign universities bill was approved by the union Cabinet in March this year (2010) and was introduced in the Lok Sabha on May 3, 2010.

The bill, once passed, has the potential to create the same impact on India's higher education sector as the economic liberalization and deregulation in the 90s had on India's industrial sector. The bill is unclear whether reservation of seats for OBC and SC/ST students would be an eligibility criterion for the foreign educational institutions to be notified as Foreign Education Providers (FEP). The FEPs would be treated as Indian private universities and allowed to set their own fee and would be exempt from reservations. Also, one of the concerns expressed in the monograph is the imposition of the condition that no repatriation of profits will be allowed might act as a deterrent for the foreign universities to enter India. Without a possibility of taking back its invested capital, a foreign institution might simply choose to not enter the Indian education sector.[33]

Highlights of the Foreign Educational Institutions (Regulation of Entry and Operations) Bill 2010[34]

Every foreign educational institution intending to operate in India has to be notified as a foreign educational provider (FEP) by the central government on the recommendations of the Registrar (Secretary of the University Grants Commission). Foreign educational providers have to maintain a corpus fund of a minimum of Rs 50 crore. Upto 75% of any income generated from the corpus fund shall be utilized to develop its institution in India and rest should be put back in the fund. Any surplus in revenue generated in India by the foreign university has to be invested in the development of the educational institution established by it in India. The Bill allows foreign universities to set up branch campuses without an Indian partner. But it includes requirements such as maintaining a corpus fund of at least Rs 50 crore, not allowing repatriation of funds and a track record of 20 years in the parent country. The central government may exempt any institution, on the advice of the Advisory Board, from conforming to the requirements of the Bill except the penalty provision and the ban on revenue repatriation.

The main concerns with the Bill are as follows

Thrust of the Bill - The statement of Objects and Reasons of the Bill indicate that the Bill is to regulate the entry and management of foreign educational institutions in the context of chances of adoption of various unfair practices besides commercialization. It begins with the words: "A number of Foreign Educational Institutions have been operating in the country and some of them may be resorting to various malpractices to allure and attract students. It is stated that this is necessary to maintain the standards of higher education within the country as well as to protect the interest of the students and in public interest. Thus the entire thrust of the Bill is on regulation seen in the context of unfair practices and not to encourage foreign educational institutions to set up operations in India.

1. Detailed procedure- A detailed process for recognition of a foreign educational institution in India has been laid down.
2. Corpus - A corpus fund of Rs.50 crore is to be maintained by the foreign educational Institution.
3. Lack of Flexibility in designing curriculum and deciding on qualifications of faculty is another disincentive.
4. Use of revenues - A foreign education provider shall, out of the income received from the corpus fund, utilise not more than seventy-five percent of such income for the purposes of development of its institution in India and the remaining of such unutilised income shall be deposited into the corpus fund.
5. Non-repatriation of profits - No part of the surplus in revenue generated in India by such Foreign Education Provider, after meeting all expenditure in regard to its operations in India, shall be invested for any purpose other than for the growth

and development of the educational institutions established by it in India.

6. Omnibus withdrawal clause- Withdrawal of recognition can be done if there is a violation of any provisions of this Act or UGC Act or any other law in force.

Opposition to the Bill

1. There are three views on the issue of foreign educational institutions operating in India. Opponents argue that it would limit access and lead to commercialisation. Proponents of the Bill argue that it would increase choices for students and enhance competition in the sector. There are some experts who support limited entry based on the reputation of the institution.
2. Present rules permit foreign universities to collaborate with Indian partners through various mechanisms. However, few globally renowned universities collaborate with India. It is not clear if the Bill would attract quality foreign universities given the stricter guidelines.
3. The Bill lacks clarity on what provisions the foreign institutions may be given an exemption from since they have to follow all other laws in force. This effectively means that they have to conform to standards set by statutory authorities on curriculum, methodology and faculty and mandatory publication of prospectus.[35]
4. The thrust of the Bill seems to be regulation of malpractises rather than encouraging foreign universities. It is not clear if the Bill would attract quality foreign universities given the strict guidelines. It appears to be a piece of "over-regulation" rather than appropriate regulation.
5. Lack of flexibility in designing curriculum and deciding on qualifications of faculty is another disincentive.
6. No provision to re-appropriate profits except for the growth and development of the institution established in India may act as a deterrent.
7. The Bill in the present form lacks clarity on what provisions the foreign institutions may be given an exemption from since they have to follow all other laws in force. This effectively means that they have to conform to standards set by statutory authorities on curriculum, methodology and faculty and mandatory publication of prospectus.

In 2013, the University Grants Commission notified the University Grants Commission (Promotion and Maintenance of Standards of Academic Collaboration between Indian and Foreign Educational Institutions) Regulations 2012 laying down the regulations for collaboration between a foreign and Indian educational institution.[36] Details of the Regulations are in Annexure IV. However, few globally renowned universities have collaborated with India. Under these regulations, no foreign university can set up institutions independently in India.

The collaboration route may not be the most ideal way in which foreign universities may want to participate in India. Further, in September 2013, the Ministry of HRD proposed to permit foreign universities to open their campuses in the country as companies as provided under the Companies Act. As per the powers vested with the Central Government to make rules under the UGC ACT, the ministry was in the process of finalizing the UGC (Established and Operation of Campuses of Foreign Educational Institutions) Rules by which foreign universities can set up campus in India and issue foreign degrees.

The least important mode chosen so far is setting up of campuses in India by foreign universities, which involves an inflow of foreign direct investment intothe field of education in India and the establishment of institutions. However, this mode is preferred by the government as it reduces the outflow of students for study abroad and the corresponding outflow of money to other countries in the form of fees and related expenditure, apart from the inherent attractiveness of foreign direct investment in the form of foreign capital. One hundred per cent foreign direct investment in higher education in India is now allowed by law under the 'automatic route', but this is the least preferred mode, as opening a branch campus requires huge investments in infrastructure. None of the 131 foreign education providers have set up any campuses of their own in the country, although some have entered through joint ventures. While come foreign universities have evinced interest in setting up[37] Campuses in India, so far there is no case of this kind.

Education 'imports' to India are increasing because of deficits in domestic provision of education or high interest in foreign education or both. Despite rapid expansion, there still exists huge unmet demand for higher education in the country. Foreign degrees are viewed in India, as in many developing countries, as yielding very high returns. The foreign label itself has a premium in the labour market. Hence there can be private demand for education programmes offered by foreign education providers, even if the education provided by the inferior foreign institutions is not better than the run-of-the-mill education provided by most of the accredited institutions in India. Furthermore, most of the foreign providers offer only graduate programmes in areas generating high profits.[38] But there is private demand for undergraduate programmes, as the students hope that such programmes will not only be of higher quality but also facilitate easy admission to postgraduate programmes in foreign universities or employment abroad. Students perceive foreign education programmes as practical and market-oriented with flexible curricula and examinations, attractive evaluation systems, and good job prospects abroad. For the same reason, Indian partners prefer to collaborate when they get a brand name of a foreign university to award the degree. Moreover, the twinning arrangements may help domestic institutions to obtain domestic and international validation for their low-quality programmes, some of which could be described as 'sandwich' programmes, and to attract domestic students looking for foreign degrees and also international students. It is also possible that there may be better monitoring of these programmes by the parent foreign universities, particularly if an accredited foreign university is involved in the programme. However, data about the placement record of the foreign education programmes operating in India or in other developing countries are not readily available, nor do studies estimating the cost benefit ratios of expensive foreign educational programmes seem to have been conducted.

The NKC has already recommended that the government 'formulate appropriate policies for the entry of foreign institutions into India and the promotion of Indian institutions abroad, while ensuring a level playing field for foreign and domestic institutions within the country'.[39] Accordingly, as mentioned above, the government has been busy formulating some guidelines that provide a framework for trade in education – both export and import, but essentially for importing education.

The Association of Indian Universities (AIU, 1999) prepared some guidelines essentially to grant equivalence to foreign degrees, and later AICTE (2005) prepared another set of regulations for foreign education providers (in 2003, revised in 2005) in relation to technical education. Somehow, the UGC was not involved in this. Recently, a committee chaired by CNR Rao (hereafter referred to as CNRRC; Government of India, 2006a) submitted a report on general higher education.[40]

The Yashpal Committee Government of India[41] also argues, 'if the best of foreign universities, say amongst the top 200 in the world, want to come here and work, they should be welcomed'. They should award an Indian degree and be subject to all rules and regulations that would apply to any Indian university. In fact, the Committee argues that as India wants the best learning experiences to be shared by its students, this can be done by inviting foreign scholars to come to Indian universities to teach and by making our rules and regulations more flexible in this regard. However, the Yashpal Committee does not argue for internationalization for monetary benefits or for trade in education. It categorically observes that these committees are, however, concerned mainly with the issue of allowing and regulating the entry of foreign universities into India, not with commitment to the GATS perse.

The Department of Commerce,the Government of India, has prepared a consultation paper on trade in education services, which highlighted the inadequacy of public higher education, noted the rapid growth of private education, and, like typical trade and commerce negotiators at WTO, emphasized the opportunities that commitment of education under the GATS and opening up of higher education to foreign investors offer to India in improving access, quality, and equity in higher education.

The Department of Commerce is to join the league of education-exporting countries and for this, importing of education in terms of allowing foreign institutions and foreign direct investment in higher education is suggested. There is no sound logic to the argument that India should import higher education to become a major exporter of the same. The capacity of India to become a major exporter of higher education like the USA, UK, Australia, and New Zealand is, in fact, limited, even if it is desirable.[42] Thus, some of the arguments of the Department of Commerce are unsound and others are familiar arguments. The government of India (2007) has also prepared a draft bill for regulating the entry and operation of foreign educational institutions.[43]

The University of Chicago opened a centre in Delhi on 29 March. Virginia Polytechnic Institute and State University, popularly known Virginia Tech, is opening its centre in May. Harvard Business School has an Indian research centre in Mumbai, and Deakin University, a well-known name from Australia, has a centre in New Delhi, foreign Universities branches in India.[44]

631 Foreign Education Providers were operating in the country 440 were functioning from their respective home campuses 5 had opened their own campus in India 60 had programmatic collaboration with local institutions 49 were operating under twinning arrangements and 77 had arrangements other than twinning or programmatic collaboration.[45]

References

1. Annual Report, 2009-10, Department of Higher Education, Ministry of Human Resource Development.
2. Ballal, H.S. (2009), FICCI-Higher Education Summit,Nov 6, 2009, New Delhi.
3. Barnett, R. (1992), Improving Higher Education. Total Quality Care. Buckingham. SRHE/Open University Press.
4. Bhattacharya, I. & Sharma, K. (2007), 'India in the knowledge economy – an electronic paradigm', International Journal of Educational Management Vol. 21 No. 6, pp. 543-568.
5. Blackwell, Fritz (2004), India: A Global Studies Handbook, United States of America:
6. Chauhan, S. P. C. (2008), Higher Education: Current Status and Future Possibilities in Afghanistan, Bangladesh, Bhutan, India, Maldives, Nepal, Pakistan, and Sri Lanka.
7. Colling, C. and Harvey, L. (1995), Quality control assurance and assessment in the link to continuous improvement, Quality Assurance in Education, 3(4), 30-34.
8. Draft Report of Working Group on Higher Education for the XI Plan, Planning Commission, Government of India (2007-12).
9. Elder, Joseph W. (2006), "*Caste System*", Encyclopedia of India (vol. 1) edited by Stanley Wolpert, 223–229.
10. "*Infrastructure: S&T Education*", Science and Technology in India edited by R.K. Suri and Kalapana Rajaram (2008), New Delhi: Spectrum.
11. India 2009: A Reference Annual (53rd edition), New Delhi: Additional Director General (ADG), Publications Division, Ministry of Information and Broadcasting, Government of India.
12. Knight, J. and Dewit, H. (1997), Internationalisation of Higher Education in Asia Pacific Countries,European Association of International Education, Amsterdam, Natherlands.
13. Prabhu, Joseph (2006), "*Educational Institutions and Philosophies, Traditional and Modern*", Encyclopedia of India (vol. 2) edited by Stanley Wolpert, 23–28.
14. Raman, S.A. (2006). "*Women's Education*", Encyclopedia of India (vol. 4), edited by Stanley Wolpert, 235–239.
15. Sanyal, B. C. (2001), *'New functions of higher education and ICT to achieve education for all'*, Paper prepared for the Expert Roundtable on University and Technology for Literacy and Education Partnership in Developing Countries, International Institute for EducationalPlanning, UNESCO, September 10 to 12, Paris.
16. Setty, E.D. and Ross, E.L. (1987), "*A Case Study in Applied Education in Rural India*", Community Development Journal, 22 (2): 120–129, Oxford University Press.
17. Sharma, R. (2003), 'Barriers in Using Technology for Education in Developing Countries'.

18. Sripati, V.and Thiruvengadam, A.K. (2004), *"India: Constitutional Amendment Making The Right to Education a Fundamental Right*", International Journal of Constitutional Law, 2 (1): 148–158, Oxford University Press.

19. Staropoli A. (1991), Institutional Evaluation: The Role of the Main Actors in Higher Education. Dahllöf, U., Harris, J., Shattock, M., Staropoli, A. & in't Veld, R. 1991:Dimensions of Evaluation in Higher Education. HEPS 13. London. Jessica Kingsley.

20. Thorat, S. (2006), *Higher Education in India: Emerging Issues Related to Access, Inclusiveness and Quality*, Nehru Memorial Lecture,University of Mumbai.

21. Vrat, Prem (2006), *"Indian Institutes of Technology"*, Encyclopedia of India (vol. 2) edited by Stanley Wolpert, 229–231.

Index to Frequently Cite Reports

1. Ambani Birla Report on Education 2001.
2. Foreign Educational Institutions bill 2010.
3. Gajendragadkar Report: committee on governance of universities and colleges, UGC New Delhi 1971.
4. Gnanam report: UGC committee towards new education management 1990.
5. Hartog Report: auxiliary committee report on review of growth of education in British India 1929.
6. Higher education and research bill 2011.
7. Human Development Report 2011.
8. Janardhan Reddy Report: CABE committee on policy HRD Government of India 1992.
9. Jha Report: report on the review welfare government of India 1977.
10. Kothari Report: Education commission 1964-66.
11. Mdhruri Shah Report: Committee to Enquire In to the Working of the Central Universities 1983.
12. Model act Report: UGC Committee on Model Act for Universities'Prof.D.S. Kothari 1964.
13. Mudaliar Report: report of secondary education commission 1953.
14. National Knowledge Commission Report 2009.
15. Narayana murthy committee Report 2012.
16. NPE 1968: National Policy of Education 1968.
17. NPE 1986/92: National Policy of Education 1992.
18. NPE 1986: National Policy of Education 1986.
19. POA 1986: Programme of Action 1986.
20. POA 1992: Programme of Action 1992.
21. Radhakrishnan Report: University Education Commission 1949.
22. Ramamurti Report: Committee for Review of NPE 1986.
23. Robbins Report: Committee on Higher Education London 1963.
24. Sachar Report: Social Economic and Educational Status of the Muslim Community in India 2006.

25. Sadler Report: Calcutta University Commission 1919.
26. Sapru Report: Committee of Members of Parliament On Higher Education 1964.
27. Sargent Report/Plan: Educational Development in India 1944.

Notes

1. http://www.investopedia.com/terms/i/internationalization.asp.
2. cited Guruz, 2008, p. 137.
3. ZHA Qiang, "Internationalization of Higher Education towards a Conceptual Framework Policy futures in Education," Volume, 1, Number 2, 2003. p. 249.
4. Jandhyala B.G.Tilak, "Global Trends in Funding Higher Education" *Marketization and Economic Themes,* Number 42, 2006, p P.2.
5. ZHA Qiang "Internationalization of Higher Education towards a Conceptual Framework Policy futures in Education, Volume, 1, Number 2, 2003. p. 251.
6. KRS Murthy, "Internationalization of Higher Education: Strategic Implications," *Economic and Political Weekly*, Vol. XLIV, No. 9, February 28,2009, p. 36.
7. Jane Knight,. "Updating the Definition of Internationalization," *International Higher Education International Issues,* p. 2.
8. Panchamukhi,. "Globalization and Higher Education In India," 2008, p. 27.
9. Huang, F "Internationalization of Higher Education in an Era of Globalization: What Are Its Implications for China and Japan," *Higher Education Management and Policy (OECD).* 2007.
10. Agarwal, Pawan, "Higher Education in India: The Need for Change," *ICRIER Working Paper,* New Delhi, June, 2006.
11. http://www.cgdev.org/files/15310 file Higher Ed. pdf.
12. Ibid.,
13. Sanat Kaul, "Higher Education In India: Seizing The Opportunity Indian Council For Research On International Economic Relations," May 2006, p. 9.
14. Ibid., p.10.
15. http://unesdoc.unesco.org/images/0021/002149/214997e. pdf.
16. "Status Of International Students In India For Higher Education." 2014.
17. Vidya Rajiv Yeravdekar and Gauri Tiwari,. "Internationalization of Higher Education in India: How Primed is the Country to Take on Education Hubs?," ,Volume 157, 27 November 2014, Pp.165–182.
18. Ibid., p.173.
19. PG Altbach, J Knigh, "The Internationalization of Higher Education: Motivations and Realities," 2012.
20. http://www.cisco.com/web/offer/usc/Cisco Sales Summit 2015/index.html.
21. Prabhakar J Lavakare, "Does India have an international higher education strategy?" *University World News,* 15 June 2013, Issue No. 276.
22. http://poetsandquants.com/2014/02/24/at-indias-leading-business-school-the-jobs-are-plentiful-the-students-are-satisfied/.
23. file:///C:/Users/pc/Downloads/US-Students-in-China.pdf.

24. Jandhyala B.G. Tilak, "Trade in Higher Education: The Role of the General Agreement on Trade in Services (GATS) UNESCO: International Institute for Educational Planning, p17.
25. Ibid., p. 93.
26. http://shodhganga.inflibnet.ac.in/bitstream/10603/45468/9/09 chapter%20i.pdf.
27. The approach of the NKC (2007, 2008) has been singularly pro-private and pro-trade in higher education. See Tilak (2007) for a short comment on the NKC.
28. Some might argue that if US$10,000 were charged per student per year, very few students would come to India, as it might be much cheaper to study in advancedcountries.
29. http://planningcommission.nic.in/news/pre pov2307.pdf.
30. https://www.insidehighered.com/blogs/world-view/internationalization-where-india-headed.
31. UGC provides assistance to universities for constructing residential facilities for foreign students.
32. http://www.prsindia.org/billtrack/the-foreign-educational-institutions-regulation-of-entry-and-operations-bill-2010-1139/.
33. http://www.icbse.com/universities/foreign/.
34. Some other important provisions of the Billare: A foreign education provider shall ensure that the course or programme of study offered and imparted by it in India is in conformity with the standards laid down by the statutory authority, and is of quality comparable, as to the curriculum, methods of imparting education and the faculty employed or engaged to impart education, to those offered by it to students enrolled in its main campus in the country in which such institution is established orincorporated.

    Mandatory publication of details about fees, number of seats approved by the relevant statutory authority, process of admission, details of teaching faculty and their minimum pay and other emoluments payable for each category of teachers and other employees, broad outline of the syllabus specified by the statutory authority or by the institution.
35. http://www.prsindia.org/billtrack/the-foreign-educational-institutions-regulation-of-entry-and-operations-bill-2010-1139/.
36. Philip G. Altbachand Jane Knight., "The Internationalization of Higher Education: Motivations and Realities" article SAGE Journals 210.
37. In 2007, as many as 104 institutions of technical education were offering programmesincollaborationwithforeignuniversities,allwithoutanyapproval of the All-India Council for Technical Education (Agarwal, 2009: 334).
38. http://www.aicte-india.org/downloads/nkc.pdf
39. http://prayatna.typepad.com/education/2005/09/cnr rao committ.html.
40. http://prayatna.typepad.com/education/2009/07/summary-of-full-text-of-the-yashpal-committee-report.html.
41. http://unesdoc.unesco.org/images/0021/002149/214997e.pdf.
42. It was reported that the bill, deferred earlier due to lack of political support, was likely to be introduced in Parliament in 2009. The government intended to pass

this bill in 2009, along with another bill to set up a constitutional body of the kind suggested by NKC and the Yashpal Committee, which would also have provided barrier-free entry to foreign institutions from 2010–2011 (*Hindustan Times*, Mumbai, 28 August 2009, p. 7). The bill was withdrawn and anew bill was introduced in May 2010. See Tilak (2010) for acommentary on the bill.

43. http://www.livemint.com/Politics/JtHPA61PdLaQIzSxtwgZUI/Foreign-universities-open-India-centres.html.

44. http://www.dnaindia.com/india/report-educated-in-india-narendra-modi-government-s-new-pet-project-2089923.

Chapter - 11

Emerging Challenges of Indian Higher Educational Institutions

P. Murali Krishna

Abstract

The Indian higher education institution is in an urgent need of capable leaders who can lead and manage the university affairs in the era of globalization, thus the present paper is an attempt to identify the emerging challenges of Indian higher education institutions and the important role of academic leader in bringing about the required changes. The higher education in India, particularly in last two decades or so, has remarkably transmuted and developed in a notable manner to emerge as one of the largest system of its kind. Arguably, these developments in higher education may directly be linked with the several changes that have occurred in the global economy, which calls for more knowledge and skilled worker force, and workers with profounder understandings of new business methods all over the world. In this constantly changing economic environment, higher education system around the globe and especially in the developing nation like India is in constant pressure to respond to rising student expectations and to be at per with the demands of global competition. There is no denying the fact that higher education not only provides individuals with a better chance of employment and growth, but also in turn leads to a better lifestyle, recognition and status. In the words of Sri Narendra Modi, Honble Prime Minister of India, "Good quality education is the foundation of new discoveries, new knowledge, innovation and entrepreneurship that trigger growth and prosperity of the individual as well as that of a nation. For this, we need to make our curriculum and pedagogy relevant to the needs of our society and economy and nurture qualities of problem solving and creative thinking, learning-by-doing, greater engagement with the live context, and confident self-expression from a young age.

***Keyword**: Academic Leadership, Higher Education, Autonomy, Governance.*

Introduction

The world has realized that the economic success of the states is directly determined by their education systems. Education is a Nation's Strength. A developed nation is inevitably an educated nation. Indian higher education system is the third largest in the world, next to the United States and China. Since independence, India as a developing nation is contentiously progressing in the education field. Although there have been lot of challenges to higher education system of India but equally have lot of opportunities to overcome these challenges and to make higher education system much better.

It needs greater transparency and accountability, the role of colleges and universities in the new millennium, and emerging scientific research on how people learn is of utmost important. India need well skilled and highly educated people who can drive our economy forward. India provides highly skilled people to other countries therefore; it is very easy for India to transfer our country from a developing nation to a developed nation. The current study aims to highlight the challenges and to point out the opportunities in higher education system in India. India's higher education system is the world's third largest in terms of students, next to China and the United States. In future, India will be one of the largest education hubs. India's Higher Education sector has witnessed a tremendous increase in the number of Universities/University level Institutions & Colleges since independence.

The 'Right to Education Act' which stipulates compulsory and free education to all children within the age groups of 6-14 years, has brought about a revolution in the education system of the country with statistics revealing a staggering enrolment in schools over the last four years. The involvement of private sector in higher education has seen drastic changes in the field. Today over 60% of higher education institutions in India are promoted by the private sector. This has accelerated establishment of institutes which have originated over the last decade making India home to the largest number of Higher Education institutions in the world, with student enrolments at the second highest (Shaguri, 2013).The number of Universities has increased 34 times from 20 in 1950 to 677 in 2014. Despite these numbers, international education rating agencies have not placed many of these institutions within the best of the world ranking. Also, India has failed to produce world class universities.

Today, Knowledge is power. The more knowledge one has, the more empowered one is. However, India continues to face stern challenges. Despite growing investment in education, 25 per cent of its population is still illiterate; only 15 per cent of Indian students reach high school, and just 7 per cent graduate (Masani, 2008). The quality of education in India whether at primary or higher education is significantly poor as compared to major developing nations of the world. As of 2008, India's post-secondary institutions offer only enough seats for 7 per cent of India's college-age population, 25 per cent of teaching positions nationwide are vacant, and 57 per cent of college professors lack either a master's or PhD degree (Newsweek, 2011). As of 2011, there are 1522 degree-granting engineering colleges in India with an annual student intake of 582,000 (Science and Technology Education, 2009) plus 1,244 polytechnics with an annual intake of 265,000. However, these institutions face shortage of faculty and concerns have been raised over the quality of education (Mitra, 2008).

Despite these challenges higher education system of India equally have lot of opportunities to overcome these challenges and have the capability to make its identity at international level. However, it needs greater transparency and accountability, the role of universities and colleges in the new millennium, and emerging scientific research on how people learn is of utmost important. India provides highly skilled people to other countries therefore; it is very easy for India to transfer our country from a developing nation to a developed nation. Growth of Higher Education Sector in India As higher education systems grow and diversify, society is increasingly concerned about the quality of programmes, public assessments and international rankings of higher education institutions.

However these comparisons tend to overemphasis research, using research performance as a yardstick of institutional value. If these processes fail to address the quality of teaching, it is in part because measuring teaching quality is challenging (Hernard, 2008) India has been always been a land of scholars and learners. In ancient times also, India was regarded all over the world for its universities like Taxila, Nalanda, Vikramshila and its scholars. By independence India had 20 universities, 500 colleges enrolling about 2,30,000 students. Since independence India has progressed significantly in terms of higher education statistics. This number has increased to 659 Universities and 33023 colleges up to December 2011-12. Central Government and state Governments are trying to nurture talent through focusing on the number of Universities and Colleges for expansion of higher educations. There is no doubt to the fact that much of the progress achieved by India in education has come from private sector. In fact the public sector and private sector is not in opposition to each other but they are working simultaneously in Indian education sphere. UGC is the main governing body that enforces the standards, advises the government and helps coordinate between center and states.

Challenges in Higher Education in India It is our 69th year of independence still our education system has not been developed fully. We are not able to list a single university in top 100 universities of the world. Various governments changed during these six decades. They tried to boost the education system and implemented various education policies but they were not sufficient to put an example for the universe. UGC is continuously working and focusing on quality education in higher education sector. Still we are facing lot of problems and challenges in our education system. Some of the basic challenges in higher education system in India are discussed below:

Enrolment: The Gross Enrolment Ratio (GER) of India in higher education is only 15% which is quite low as compared to the developed as well as, other developing countries. With the increase of enrolments at school level, the supply of higher education institutes is insufficient to meet the growing demand in the country.

Equity: There is no equity in GER among different sects of the society. According to previous studies the GER in higher education in India among male and female varies to a greater extent. There are regional variations too some states have high GER while as some is quite behind the national GER which reflect a significant imbalances within the higher education system.

Quality: Quality in higher education is a multi-dimensional, multilevel, and a dynamic concept. Ensuring quality in higher education is amongst the foremost challenges being faced in India today. However, Government is continuously focusing on the quality education. Still Large number of colleges and universities in India are unable to meet the minimum requirements laid down by the UGC and our universities are not in a position to mark its place among the top universities of the world. Infrastructure: Poor infrastructure is another challenge to the higher education system of India particularly the institutes run by the public sector suffer from poor physical facilities and infrastructure. There are large number of colleges which are functioning on second or third floor of the building on ground or first floor there exists readymade hosieries or photocopy shops.

Political interference: Most of the educational Institutions are owned by the political leaders, who are playing key role in governing bodies of the Universities. They are using the innocent students for their selfish means.

Students organise campaigns, forget their own objectives and begin to develop their careers in politics.

Faculty: Faculty shortages and the inability of the state educational system to attract and retain well qualified teachers have been posing challenges to quality education for many years. Large numbers of NET / PhD candidates are unemployed even there are lot of vacancies in higher education, these deserving candidates are then applying in other departments which is a biggest blow to the higher education system.

Accreditation: As per the data provided by the NAAC, as of June 2010, "not even 25% of the total higher education institutions in the country were accredited. And among those accredited, only 30% of the universities and 45% of the colleges were found to be of quality to be ranked at 'A' level".

Research and Innovation: there are very nominal scholars in our country whose writing is cited by famous western authors. There is inadequate focus on research in higher education institutes. There are insufficient resources and facilities, as well as, limited numbers of quality faculty to advice students. Most of the research scholars are without fellowships or not getting their fellowships on time which directly or indirectly affects their research. Moreover, Indian Higher education institutions are poorly connected to research centers. So, this is another area of challenge to the higher education in India.

Structure of higher education: Management of the Indian education faces challenges of overcentralisation, bureaucratic structures and lack of accountability, transparency, and professionalism. As a result of increase in number of affiliated colleges and students, the burden of administrative functions of universities has significantly increased and the core focus on academics and research is diluted (Kumar, 2015).

Opportunities in Higher Education India is a large country, with an estimated population of young people aged between 18 to 23 years to be around 150 millions. The sheer size of the market offers huge opportunities for development of the higher education sector in India. India now boasts of having more than 33,000 colleges and 659 universities, which has been quite a remarkable growth during the last six decades. The year 2012 witnessed 21.4 million enrollments, which makes India the 3rd largest educational system in the world. Unfortunately, the educational infrastructure of India is inadequate to handle such huge volumes. In spite all the government spending in the educational sector, it is just too insufficient to meet the growing requirements.

Therefore, higher Education sector has now been identified as one of the promising areas for private and foreign investments. It offers immense investment opportunities in both non-regulated and regulated segments (Nexus Novus, 26 July, 2013). Indian higher education system is growing very fast irrespective of various challenges but there is no reason that these Challenges cannot be overcome. With the help of new-age learning tools, it is easy for country like India to overcome these problems and bring a paradigm shift in the country's higher education sector. With such a vibrant country with huge population properly educated, the possibilities are endless. If knowledge is imparted using advanced digital teaching and learning tools, and society is made aware of where we are currently lagging behind, our country can easily emerge as one of the most developed nations in the world. There are opportunities for strategic engagement and capacity building in higher education leadership and management at the state level. There are opportunities for India to collaboration at national and international level on areas of systemic reform, including quality assurance, international credit recognition, and unified national qualifications framework.

Equality of educational opportunity in higher education is considered essential because higher education is a powerful tool for reducing or eliminating income and wealth disparities. The idea of equalizing educational opportunities also lies in the fact that "the ability to profit by higher education is spread among all classes of people. There are great reserves of untapped ability in the society; if offered the chance they can rise to the top. A great deal of talent of the highest level is, in fact, lost by an in egalitarian system of education" (Balachander, 1986). The need to enhance the employability of graduates is presenting entry points for collaboration in enterprise education and entrepreneurship, links with industry, research skills and the wide range of transferable skills, including English. The emerging interest in Indian higher education institutions in the vocational skills market provides areas for potential engagement with international partners. There is a need to build stronger relationships and increase mutual understanding in higher education by increasing support and participation in platforms (conferences, workshops, seminars) which enable debate and dialogue with other countries of the world.(British Council, 2014).

Suggestions Improving the System of Higher Education: There is a need to implement innovative and transformational approach form primary to higher education level to make Indian educational system globally more

4. To analyze the challenges associated in adopting such bench marking practices at degree level

Student Centric methodology in higher education

The student centric methodology is frequently termed as a Flipped classroom which is becoming a buzz word in the recent years which is turning traditional education on its head. In 2007, when two chemistry teachers from Colorado followed this method and shared their experience using online sources, this method gained some importance and attention. The flipped classroom is a pedagogical model in which the typical lecture and homework elements of a course are reversed. There is no single model for the flipped classroom—the term is widely used to describe almost any class structure that provides prerecorded lectures followed by in-class exercises. A growing number of higher education individual faculties have begun using the flipped model in their courses. The flipped model puts more of the responsibility for learning on the shoulders of students while giving them greater impetus to experiment.

Skill set required for the students

In the changing global scenario, quality in education determines the career opportunities of the student. The students basically require two types of skills. They are:

A. Domain Specific Skills

The knowledge and skills required for a specific job. This is the theoretical base required to do specialised jobs. For example, an accountant needs to know how financial transactions are recorded, summarised , analysed and interpreted. Thus for any career we choose we require domain specific skills. They include

- Subject expertise
- Knowledge in related software
- Applicability of concepts
- Basic Knowledge in related disciplines

B. Soft skills or life skills

The skills that are not specific to a particular career path but are generic across all sectors. They include

- Decision making
- Problem solving

- Critical thinking
- Coping with stress
- Coping with emotions
- Effective communication
- Creative thinking
- Interpersonal relationship
- Self awareness

In olden days, the source of knowledge was only through printed material and information given by the lectures. But now a days, there are many other sources to gather or attain knowledge. These include: You tube videos, Teacher tube videos, Audio podcast, self-recorded material, screen capturing software's, informational handouts, Skype lessons from subject experts, Case studies, Role-plays, Power Point Presentations, Blogging, Online discussions, Projects etc.

Activities that give practical exposure to students

Higher education increases the scope for acquiring more skills and knowledge to lead a decent living in the society. It also helps to increase labour workforce participation which is very important for increasing financial and social security of individuals in general and women in particular.

The Telangana Social Welfare Department initiated to start 23 women's degree colleges by name "Telangana Social Welfare Residential Degree College For Women (TSWRDCW's)" during 2016 and increased their number to 30 during the academic year 2017. These colleges provide free education to them by imparting qualitative education along with all facilities that are necessary for their overall development. These colleges were instructed by the higher authorities that the method of teaching must be student centric. So, the faculty gets more encouragement to put into practicality their innovative ideas. This paper tries to identify various innovative practices taken up by the Commerce department of TSWRDCW, Nalgonda.

The innovative practices include

1. Establishment of Student Bank
2. Establishment of Student Store
3. Proposal to establish a Commerce Lab
4. Organizing Commerce Fests

Establishment of Student Bank

The Department of Commerce started Student bank on 17th February 2017, to create practical exposure towards banking transactions. The main objectives of establishing student bank is to create awareness among students about the formalities to be followed while opening a bank account, to know about various forms used in a bank like withdrawal form, pay in slips etc. along with safeguarding their money. The student bank is managed by the students only. From each class there will be one "Bank Clerk" nominated by their co students, who will record and maintain the accounts of their class. There will be one Bank manager from the faculty to supervise the work done by these clerks and reconcile the books of accounts on regular basis and get it countersigned by the principal to maintain transparency. The students who want to become an account holder with the Student bank have to fill an account opening form and submit identity proof along with two passport size photographs.

The Student Bank concept helps in developing saving habits among students apart from keeping their money in safe hands. Short term loans will be provided to principal, staff and students of the college which must be repaid with in duration of 3 days, if the duration exceeds 3 days then interest will be collected from them and the interest thus collected will be utilized for maintenance of student bank. The maximum repayment period is 15 days on any loan extended. As of now, no interest is paid on deposits but there is a plan to set norms for paying nominal interest to the students on their deposits in the days to come. Application amount of Rs.20/- is collected from students who are willing to open an account in Student Bank from this year towards printing expenses of account opening form, passbook, pay in slips, withdrawal forms and other bank related documents. The bank is visited by the Deputy secretary and other higher officials and appreciated the concept of student bank and suggested to keep a good name for the same. On their suggestion, the student bank is renamed as "BOS – Bank of SWAEROS" during the month of January, 2018. The students also created logo for the same.

BOS

Bank of Swaeros

As a bank clerk, I know how to maintain passbook and cashbook. I will report my work to bank manager. The books are reconciled (Checked) by the bank manager regularly. Bank manager supports and helps in every aspect. I am feeling that it's a good opportunity for us to develop our skills. We are so grateful to our Commerce Department.

Various forms used by BOS are:

(a) Account Opening form
(b) With drawl form
(c) Pass Book
(d) Pay in Slip

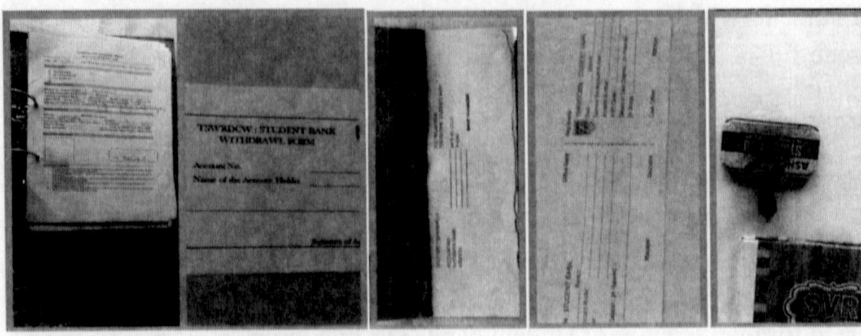

Establishment of Student Store

The degree college at Nalgonda, as a part of co-curricular practical activity took initiative to educate Commerce students how to plan a business and take up the relative activities by starting student store on a very small scale on 12th August, 2017 with the cooperation of the principal. As the college is of residential pattern, the students cannot go out of the college campus for their day to day requirements. The students will bring all the required things when they come from home itself. But sometimes, the things may not be sufficient for their use and to get additional require material, they need to depend on their house parents. Sometimes it becomes difficult for the house parent to bring the listed items for the students as the college campus is located in the outskirts and no shops are located nearby. In order to reduce this inconvenience caused to the students and to facilitate the students to purchase the basic required products a student store is established.

Apart from this, it helps to give a practical experience to Commerce students about starting a business unit and to manage business related activities and makes them competent to take business decisions. As a primary step, survey is conducted by the students to know the brand preferences of the students. A list of products that can be purchased for stores is prepared. An amount of Rs.4,750/- is taken as loan from the student bank that was established in the college during 2016-17. The amount of loan was also repaid by the student leaders with in a period of 5 months.

Four students from B.Com will be selected as store leaders to maintain the stores and they will be replaced with new leaders for every semester. The store leaders have to maintain daily sales register, cash book and bin cards and get it checked by the Faculty Store In charge and again countersigned by the principal to maintain transparency. The student store is kept open from 5.00pm to 6.00pm on working days and from 1.30 pm to 4.00pm on holidays. A survey is also conducted on Utility of Student Store, where the students gave their opinion that they are getting benefited from the store. The store will run only on cash basis and no credit is extended on purchases. The students have framed vision and mission statements to stay focused on their duties and responsibilities. These following statements are the vision and mission statements of student bank.

Vision

- To explore the practical knowledge of business
- To acquire the knowledge about business

Mission

- To develop leadership qualities by acting as a treasurer and store leaders by selling the products.
- Time management can be developed by following store timing.
- Recording and maintaining the Bin cards to know the transactions.
- Knowing about the cost and demand of particular product.
- Providing the products to college in their personal need.
- Development of roles and responsibilities.
- To continuously evaluate our performance against suitable benchmarks.

Proposal to establish a Commerce Lab

The Department is planning to establish a Commerce Lab where the students get the exposure to various aspects of business. It helps to develop the institute as a centre of academic excellence with total commitment to quality education and related fields with holistic concern for better life, environment and society.

Objectives of Commerce Lab

- To provide practical exposure of the process, procedure and practices followed by the organizations in conducting commercial practices / Businesses and expose the students with all forms / formats / formalities
- To provide practical orientation to students while teaching the subjects according to the syllabus by linking it with the lab practical
- To improve reasoning and analytical abilities of students
- To create more interest among the students in the subject.
- To make the students aware of availability and applicability of commerce lab documents/ items for their day today routine purposes
- To equip the students with practical knowledge and develop entrepreneurial abilities to start own business or to get better employment in the competitive job market
- To prepare the students to fulfill the requirements of industry and business

Organizing Commerce Fests

Commerce fests will help the students to understand the subject related concepts in practical method and they enjoy the games and activities that are involved in that. Not many colleges organize these fests as it required lots of planning and resources. The activities that can be conducted in the commerce fest are:

- Poster Making
- Collage Making
- Business Plan
- Team Building Activity
- Acting as a Business Personality
- Commerce Quiz
- AD Making
- Essay Writing & Elocution

Challenges associated in adopting such Bench marking practices

The practices that were discussed above help to develop the subject knowledge and create interest among the students. But while implementing this methodology, there some challenges need to be addressed. Those challenges include:

1. In order to conduct the above discussed activities, funds are required to procure the material and arrange the things. The financial support cannot be expected from the management in all the cases.
2. Faculty or mentor initiation must be there for the success of these programmes rather than the initiation of the management only. If faculty feels its importance then they do not feel the burden of the excess work they are taking up.
3. Student contribution is also very important as they are the central part of all the activities. They need to be motivated first and tell them the need of these activities and their importance and its impact on their future career.
4. Proper planning and allocation of limited resources in a planned and phased manner will lead to success otherwise it ends up messy.
5. Support from the college management is of utmost importance. Even if the faculty is interested to do the work, the management should not pull them back. It leads to demotivate such faculty who takes initiative.

Conclusion

Bench marking practices help to build confidence and increase motivation among the students. The faculty initiating these activities also gets recognition for their work and has a good work environment. TSWRDCW, Nalgonda could do all these activities with the support and encouragement of the higher authorities.

References

1. Angre, K. (2013, June 26). 50 per cent of Indian graduates not fit to be hired. Retrieved from NDTV: https://www.ndtv.com/india-news/50-per-cent-of-indian-graduates-not-fit-to-be-hired-report-526502.
2. Chakrabarty, R. (2016, July 16). India today in education. Retrieved from India Today: http://indiatoday.intoday.in/education/story/engineering-employment-problems/1/713827. html.
3. Vas, J. (2012, October 5). Role of Commerce Education in the Changing Business World. Retrieved From Http://Alwaysbestarticles.Blogspot.In/2012/10/Role-Of-Commerce-Education-In-Changing. Html.

Chapter - 13

Using Technology in the class: A Study on Role of Social Media in Enhancing Learning Experience

Anitha H S

Abstract

This study focuses on learning the impact of using technology in the classroom taking social media as a tool for learning. Gone are the days when blackboard and chalk were used in the classes. Today learning is going hand in hand with emerging technologies. From traditional methods of teaching and learning, education has moved to smart learning using different media.

Social media is one such tool which is not completely explored in the world of academics. It allows students to participate, involve and share ideas, which is a very important factor in classroom learning. Evolving from teacher cantered learning to student centred learning social media gives students a sense of authority in the class thus making them more enthusiastic and enjoy the process of learning. The objective of social media is connecting to people and sharing information without geographical, social or cultural boundaries. Even though social media started as a medium of entertainment, soon it became a place of sharing information, ideas and knowledge. Educational institutions also slowly realizing the importance of social media and are starting to use it for effective teaching and information dissemination.

Different types of Social Medium such as Facebook, LinkedIn, Instagram, and Blogs can be used as tool for effective teaching. The researcher has chosen Facebook and LinkedIn to analyse the impact of using social media in the classroom. This study will analyse and interpret the data collected by students using questionnaire method and also content analysis of research done in the field of education and social media. The aim of the study is to examine the effectiveness of Facebook and LinkedIn in classroom learning in relation to its effect on Undergraduate students.

Introduction

Kaplan and Haenlein (2010) define social media as the applications that are supported on the Internet and are based on the ideological and technological foundations of Web 2.0 and allow creating and interacting with contents generated by users by open and free means. Social media is now has crossed borders, becoming a platform for social connectivity. Facebook and LinkedIn are two celebrated social media platforms which people across the country are using.

Education has evolved from the Gurukula system to the concept of smart classes. With world evolving there is a need for the education system to update and provide effective methods of teaching to the students to prepare them for the competitive world.

Social media is largely considered as the medium of entertainment. Its uses in academic learning are still not completely explored. Kop and Hill (2008) suggest that in this age of information technology, learners need to connect through social media for an effective learning experience.

What keeps students interested and motivated in the class? How a teacher can deliver a lecture keeping the interest of the students and fulfilling their requirements? To answer these questions the concept of student/learner-centred learning and teacher-centred learning needs to be understood.

Teacher centred learning is where a teacher will decide on the structure of the class and students will learn according to that structure. Whereas in a student centred learning, students engage in active learning by using methods such as cooperative learning, open ended assignments, critical-thinking exercises, simulation, and problem-solving activities (Felder & Brent, 1996). This kind of learning will engage students in the class and also increase their level of understanding as more interaction will be involved. Social media allows for such interaction and also keeps interest of the students making them more attentive in the class.

McLoughlin and Lee (2011) explains the importance of Pedagogy. He says it promotes learner centred and self-directed learning and focuses on higher levels of engagement, user-generated content, and personalized learning.

Facebook: Facebook is a social media platform created to connect people together. Even though Facebook started as a medium of entertainment, its uses in academics cannot be ignored. Since Facebook is a medium of audio and visual it catches eyes of the viewers and holds the interests of the users. Apart from photo/video sharing, Facebook is home

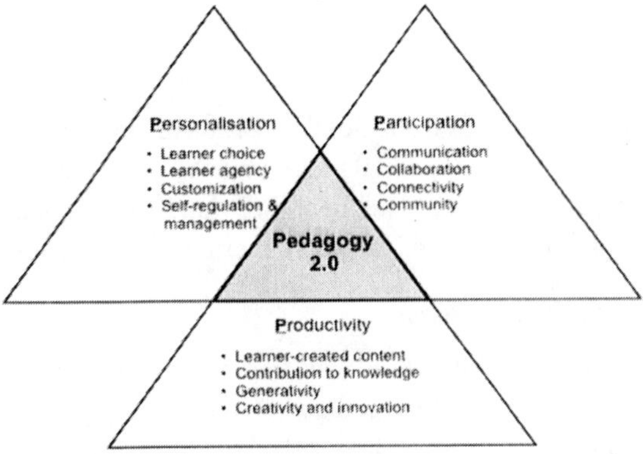

Key elements of pedagogy 2.0, McLoughlin and Lee (2011).

for many informative pages which can be used in the classroom environment for better understanding of the concepts. Since most of the students are well equipped with Facebook usage it will not be difficult to merge it in the academics.

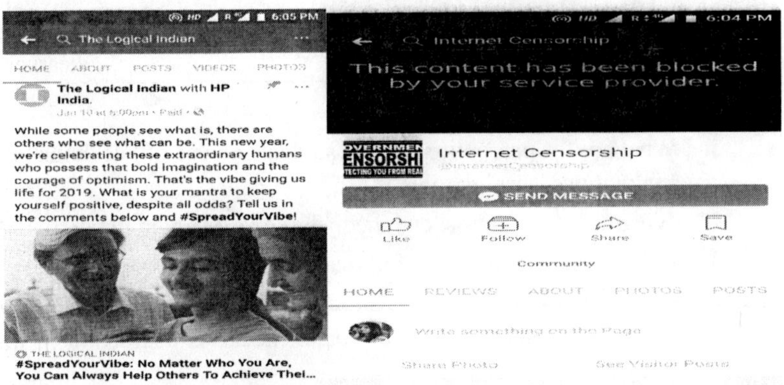

Screenshots of 'Logical Indian' and 'Internet Censorship' which publishes educational content

LinkedIn: LinkedIn was started as a business platform by Konstantin Guericke, Reid Hoffman, Allen Blue, Jean-Luc Vaillant and Eric Lysoon. This was used majorly for job search and also connecting professionally with likeminded people. Unlike Facebook LinkedIn is mostly used for professional purpose. Apart from connecting to people of similar interest, LinkedIn contains many informative articles which can be useful in understanding concepts better. Another major advantage of LinkedIn is that most of the information shared on the feed are informative and educative which avoids distraction when using it.

LinkedIn Learning is a subsidiary of LinkedIn which contains online courses taught by the professionals. LinkedIn is a platform for organisations and individuals to help them achieve their goals and aspirations through personalised and data driven learning experience (Roslansky, 2016).

1.1 Statement of the Problem

The problem of this study was that many educators and students consider social media as only a medium of entertainment. Many Educational institutions are yet to explore the uses of social media in academics. It is important to know how students perceive social media (Facebook and LinkedIn) as learning tool and how well they are aware of its uses in academics.

Another notion that prevails among teachers is that social media is merely a distraction which could possibly be the reason for not experimenting using it in the class. A secondary problem was to determine how well students can connect to the topics taught in the class by making use of Facebook and LinkedIn by the teachers.

1.2 Research Questions

1. What are the perceptions of the students on use of Facebook and LinkedIn as learning tools
2. What influence does social media has on classroom interactivity?
3. Does using social media for academic purpose promote student centred learning?
4. Do students perceive use of social media as distraction in the class?

1.3 Purpose of the study

It is important to understand students' requirements in learning and Educational institutions role in promoting and nourishing students' interests is immense. Even though traditional method of teaching is widely accepted and followed, it is important to update teaching techniques to keep students more active and interested in learning.

This study tries to analyse students requirements in classroom, what keeps them interested and motivated and what is the learning outcome by inculcating social media as a tool in the classroom. The study will also explain the uses of Facebook and LinkedIn as an educational tool which is largely considered by students and teachers as an entertainment and business medium.

1.4 Limitations of the study

2. The study only focuses on Facebook and LinkedIn as teaching and learning tools
3. The participants were selected from one college in Bangalore
4. Since technology is not accessible in every part of the country, this research holds good mostly for urban set up
5. The results were specific to this setting and might not hold true for all the colleges in India
6. The results of the study are limited to reliability of the participants

1.5 Operational Definitions

Social Media- "A group of Internet-based applications that build on the ideological And technological foundations of Web 2.0, and that allow the creation and exchange of user generated content" (Kaplan & Haenlein, 2010, p. 61).

Facebook- One of the leading social networking sites used by students in higher education. Established in 2004, Facebook allows users to connect via the Internet to create a profile, post videos, photos, and connect with friends (Dabner, 2012).

LinkedIn -LinkedIn (LI) is a professional networking website. While other social networking sites such as Facebook and Myspace focus more on personal and social networking. LinkedIn allows professionals to create and maintain career-oriented business connections and promote their services or professional skills. (https://www.techopedia.com/definition/26940/linkedin li)

Perception- A thought, belief, or opinion, often held by many people and based on appearances (http://dictionary.cambridge.org/, n.d.)

Distraction- Forgetting information needed for processing the most important task. (Speier, Valaciah, & Bessey, 1999)

Student centred learning-Student centred instruction attempts to engender active learning by using methods such as cooperative learning, open ended assignments, critical-thinking exercises, simulation, and problem-solving activities (Felder & Brent, 1996)

Technology-Technology refers to methods, systems, and devices which are the result of scientific knowledge being used for practical purposes. (https://www.collinsdictionary.com/dictionary/english/technology)

1.6 Theoretical Framework

Connectivism- Connectivism is a social theory by George Siemens which talks about learning in the digital era. Connectivism stresses on importance of technology in learning process and how it is important for people to be up to date in this fast pacing world. Drawing parallel to Behaviourism and Cognitivism, Connectivism talks about learning outside body (Simon Bailey, 2017) that is making use of technology to interact, learn and share ideas. Siemens stats that information is not only available in the individual but it occurs outside individual or within organisations (Siemens, 2005). He also tells that by using technology to learn will help in both knowledge consumption and knowledge creations (Siemens, n.d.).

3.1 Sources of Data

Data can be obtained either from primary or secondary sources. Primary data is the information obtained first-hand for the specific purpose of the study. Secondary data refers to information gathered from various sources that already exist.

In this study, primary data has been collected in the form of personal interviews

3.2 Research Instrument

The Interview questions was the only research instrument used for collecting primary data. Face to face interview with the students was also conducted.

3.3 Sample

Random sampling method was employed for this study. 10 undergraduate students were interviewed for the study

3.4 Population

Population for this study is undergraduate students between the age of 18 to 22.

3.5 Sample procedure

10 students were selected randomly and were asked set of questions to understand the use of social media in academics and its impact on learning. The respondents' views were taken into consideration and answers were analysed through interpretations and observations.

3.6 Analysis of face-to-face interviews

Face to Face interview was conducted among 10 respondents

Q1: Do you have Facebook and LinkedIn account? How long have you been using these social media?

Responses received to this question are, out of 10 respondents,6 respondents have both Facebook and LinkedIn accounts and 4 respondents have only Facebook account.

Majority of the respondents were using Facebook regularly and for long time than LinkedIn because Facebook contains information which are entertaining and visually appealing than Linked In

Q2: How do you perceive Facebook and LinkedIn as academic learning tools?

Two most common responses received to this questions were, 'Audio-visual medium' and 'Entertainment-Informative' medium

Most of the respondents use Facebook for its Audio-Visual quality. They believe that this quality of both Facebook and LinkedIn makes the class more interesting and motivating.

Even though Facebook is largely considered as an entertainment medium respondents agree that there are many informative pages and posts which can be used for academic learning

Three respondents spoke about LinkedIn learning and told they take up online LinkedIn learning course to understand the concepts.

Other three respondents had a LinkedIn account but were not using it actively because they consider LinkedIn as only a tool for job search.

Q 3: Do you think social media has larger influence on classroom interaction?

All the respondents agreed that social media has larger influence on classroom interactivity. Two common responses were 'Familiarity' and 'Sense of confidence'.

Since the younger generation is more familiar with the use of social media, when it is used as a tool in classroom teaching, students participate more because they would be familiar with the format of social media. Respondents also think that it boosts their confidence level when talking about something they are familiar about.

Other responses include the way content is shared on social media, for example conveying information through memes or other humorous way can help in indulging in classroom participation.

Q4: Does using Facebook and LinkedIn for academic purpose make you feel that teachers are acknowledging students' needs?

All the respondents agreed that this approach makes them feel important and allows them to choose the mode of learning rather than just following what the teacher is teaching.

Q5: Do you think by using Facebook and LinkedIn in the class there are chances of getting distracted?

Nine out of Ten respondents think that it causes distraction in the class. The reasons they listed out are, pool of information which can confuse them on what to read/watch or what not to. Other reason is the advertisement pop ups in these social media which could cause distraction. Unnecessary or irrelevant information, Personal photos/Videos are also reasons listed by the respondents on distraction.

Respondents feel that by they might not be distracted much by using LinkedIn because the content shared on LinkedIn are more of informative than entertainment.

Conclusion

Based on the study conducted, there were observations and recommendations as well as scope for future studies.

Students agree that use of Facebook and LinkedIn is effective in the classroom learning and it increases the interest level and participation in the class. In the interview most respondents also feel that many teachers do not use Facebook and LinkedIn as a tool for academic learning and they wish to experience these tools more in class.

Students also feel that there is a need of balance use of these tools in the class as it is also important to follow traditional method of teaching as it gives more personal touch to the class learning. In the study, it is observed that students are not using LinkedIn much for academic purposes and the reason being lack of awareness among students about the use of these tools for academics. LinkedIn being recognised as the professional application, is not explored by the students. Even though they have heard about LinkedIn learning, they are not actively using it because of lack of knowledge about it. Students feel that if proper training is given on the uses of these tools, they are open to use it as learning tools in academics.

The study answers all the Research questions by data collection and by interpretation of that data

References

1. Antoniou, A., Theodoropoulos, A., Christopoulou, K., & Lepouras, G. (2014). Facebook as teaching tool in higher education: A case study. *International Journal ofAdvances in Social Science and Humanities,* 2(3), 43-56.
2. Gruzd, Anatoliy & Staves, Kathleen & Wilk, Amanda. (2012). Connected scholars: Examining the role of social media in research practices of faculty using the UTAUT model. Computers in Human Behavior. 28. 2340–2350. 10.1016/j.chb.2012.07.004.
3. Blankenship, M. (2011). How social media can and should impact higher education. Education Digest: Essential Readings Condensed for Quick Review, , 39-42.Buzzetto-More NA. Social networking in undergraduate education. Interdiscipl J Inform Knowl Manag. 76. 39-42.
4. Suprapto, Falahah & Rosmala, Dewi. (2012). Study of Social Networking Usage in Higher Education Environment. Procedia - Social and Behavioral Sciences. 67. 156–166. 10.1016/j.sbspro.2012.11.316.
5. Bahati, Bernard. (2015). Extending Students' Discussions Beyond Lecture Room Walls via Facebook. Journal of Education and Practice. 6. 160-171.

Chapter - 14

Revisiting Critical Pedagogy: Issues and Challenges of Tribal Education in the State of Telangana

Ade Jyothi

Abstract

The issue of medium of instruction, and teacher education is highly debated in the present day tribal education. When we consider the districts of Telangana, it is found that it is one of the most populated state by tribes. Hence, in this condition it is necessary to look into the educational policies and their role in promoting mother tongue based education among the language minority groups. Role of medium of instruction is found to be crucial in promoting education among tribes. It is also seen that the drop-out ratio is increasing among the tribal population due to the lack of instruction and training. As their mother tongue, culture and socio-economic conditions differ from that of the main stream, hence there is need for imparting mother tongue based education among tribes and look into the challenges faced by them. Apart from that, the theory of critical pedagogy, also helps in imparting the socio-cultural, and economic upliftment of the tribes. Hence the paper examines the theory of critical pedagogy and provides its importance in promoting the quality education among the tribes of the Telangana state. Thus taking critical pedagogy into consideration, we can analyze the cause and effect of tribal deprivation in the field of education. The paper also uses secondary data as a source for collecting the data.

Key Words: Critical Pedagogy, Tribes, Education.

Introduction

Tribes and their educational status in Telangana

Tribes are considered to be the most vulnerable section of people in the population. These sections of people are still found to be backward in their socio-economic, cultural and educational status. In the newly formed state like Telangana, the condition of few tribes (Gond, Koya, Kolam, Sugali, Pardhan and Chenchu) is fund to be more pathetic. When we consider few other tribes (Lambada and Yerukala) from Khammam and parts of Adilabad district the enrollment ratio of these tribes in education and also in the government and public sectors has increased to greater number in the recent past.

According to the 2011 Census, Lambadas are found to be the major dominant tribal group inhabiting through the Telangana State. Their population according to 2011 census is 20, 46,117. And the tribe which is found to be less in number are Pradhan's. Their population according to 2011 census is 24,776. Though there were many schemes and policies introduced by the government, the educational status of the tribes is still lagging behind.

Quality in Education

The major challenges relating to the increase in the enrollment ratio in schools is providing access and implementing mother tongue based education in the early stage. School education should be universalized by increasing the number of ashram and tribal schools. Quality in the tribal education can also be employed through the use of culturally familiar materials.

An increasing number of researchers strongly advocate the use of the mother tongue or home language as medium of instruction in early stages of education. This assumes greater significance in the context of education of tribal children because their mother tongue is often quite distinct from the prominent languages in the state or regional languages. ST children face problems wherever teachers do not speak their dialect at all. From the perspective of language, it is desirable to have a local teacher from the same tribal community (Jha & Jhingran, 2002).

It is also found that most of the states have took an initiation in improving the quality of tribal education. The major problem that they found was the use of regional medium of instruction and appointing untrained teachers for teaching. It is also found that use of local teachers has increased the enrollment ratio in schools.

The presence of tribal teachers, especially from the same community, has shown and improved school participation of ST children. Coming from the same community, it is believed that the teachers would understand and respect the culture and the ethos with much greater sensitivity. Studies suggest that teacher motivation contributes more to teaching – learning process than teacher competence (Vaidyanathan and Nair, 2001).

It is also found that the use of mother tongue has increased the cognitive ability of the learners. Though there might problems in accepting the tribal language as medium of instruction among the tribal community, but it is also important to make them realize the importance of mother tongue based education.

Problems related to the Tribal Education

There are many problems in the field of tribal education. Few problems are listed as follows:

I. Medium of language – Language is one of the important constraints of tribal children which prevents them from the access to education. Because most of the tribes speak a language which does not have script. And the language that is used in the schools is different compared to their mother tongue.

II. Setting – The physical environment plays an important role in preventing the child to attend the school. And when we compare that in case of tribes it is found to be more vulnerable.

III. Economic Condition - The economic condition of tribal people is so poor that they do not allow the children for schools rather they prefer them to send to some petty jobs.

IV. Attitude of the parents - As education does not yield any immediate economic return, the tribal parents prefer to engage their children in remunerative employment which supplements the family income.

V. Teacher Related Problems- Most of the teachers appointed in the tribal schools are from non- tribal community. As these teachers do not understand the culture and the background of the students, the classroom transactions are not properly managed.

VI. Lack of proper monitoring- Proper monitoring is hindered by poor coordination between the Tribal Welfare Department and the School Education Department. Also the community participation is lacking which leads to lack of coordination.

VII. Improper Teaching Materials- The textbooks used in the tribal schools doesn't cater to the need of the tribal student. Students feel alienated in the classroom because the texts do not represent their tribal culture.

Objectives

1. To analyze the problems of tribes related to education.
2. Review the concept of Critical Pedagogy
3. Interrelate Critical Pedagogy and educational upliftment of tribes.
4. Theoretical constructs and practical feedback in education.
5. To analyze the socio-linguistic causes on tribal education

Critical Pedagogy and Education

In the prospect of education critical Pedagogy (henceforth CP) is considered as the oldest concept. Critical pedagogy is the term used by Paulo Freire in his book titled "The Pedagogy of the oppressed" (1960s and 1970s). Freire talks about the oppressor (feudal landowners) and the oppressed (peasants working for land owners). Freire's problem posing model focusses on the empowerment in the field of education. It criticizes the traditional method of teaching which looks at teaching as a mere vehicle of transferring the subject knowledge. The primary aim of critical pedagogy is to bring awareness about the power structure that exists in the society. According to Giroux (2001), critical pedagogues theorize that though educational institutions are part of societies with unequal distribution of power, they are considered to be the political sites and are not neutral, therefore they tend to manifest and reproduce societal power imbalance.

As critical pedagogy is known by different names, few names that refers to CP are pedagogy of oppressed, emancipatory literacy, critical education etc. When we actually see the difference between critical pedagogy and critical thinking, it can be clearly demarcated based on the ideology both the schools of thought share. Critical thinking looks at the things in a neutral way unlike connecting it to the social change as in critical pedagogy (CP). Teaching under CP focusses on the social change. The supporters of critical approaches to second language teaching and learning are more interested in connecting language learning and social change. Hence, with this perspective in mind it is clear that language is not just a means of communication to express feelings or thoughts. Rather learners use the language to connect it to the things in their social surroundings, their experiences, and the possibilities about the future.

In actual sense as Ira Short defines critical pedagogy as:

"Habits of thought, reading, writing, and speaking which go beneath surface meaning, first impressions, dominant myths, official pronouncements, traditional clichés, received wisdom, and mere opinions, to understand the deep meaning, root causes, social context, ideology, and personal consequences of any action, event, object, process, organization, experience, text, subject matter, policy, mass media, or discourse". (Empowering Education, 129).

This clearly shows that teacher works towards making the students question the ideologies and helps the students create their own understanding about the concept or ideology.

Beliefs inherent in critical pedagogy

Though there are no guidelines or limitations about any theory. Rather there are certain viewpoints shared by critical pedagogues regarding critical pedagogy. And certainly these viewpoints are not ultimate. These beliefs are viewpoints that are shared by different critical theorists including Giroux, McLaren, Delpit, Ladson-Billings, Dillard, Hooks, and others.

The three common beliefs are as follows:

1. Reflection upon the individual's culture or lived experience;
2. Development of voice through a critical look at one's world and society, which takes place in dialogue with others;
3. Transforming the society toward equality for all citizens through active participation in democratic imperatives;

   (Riasati, M. J., & Mollaei, F. 2012)

Critical Pedagogy in ESL Context

As the structure of society is found to be very unfair and unequal in terms of power and status, the educators of the critical pedagogy felt a need for critical pedagogy. Hence, they have adopted the concept of critical pedagogy into the curriculum and syllabus of English language teaching. As most of us are aware that ESL teaching deals with mostly the students of language minority groups and immigrants. Through the studies by Norton, 2000; Miller, 2003, it is clear that some second language learners without social, linguistic or cultural identity often alienated in and outside the classroom. Hence, it is said that language teaching and learning must be connected to the objectives of educating students, to understand why things are the way they are and how they got to be that way (Simon, cited in Morgan, 1998). Critical ESL pedagogy is the "pedagogy of hope" (Freire, 1992).

Few recommendations for the improvement of Tribal Education

1. Quality improvement of primary schools.

2. Developing the materials at primary level using the local heritage.
3. Ashram schools / residential schools should be established on a large scale in tribal areas.
4. Involving community in promoting quality education.
5. Monitoring attendance and retention of children.
6. Appointing maximum teachers belonging to the same community.
7. Developing dictionaries using local/regional language.

Conclusion

Critical Pedagogy emerged with the need to transform the educational needs of people from different sects of the society. If at all, critical pedagogy is integrated in our education system (teaching and learning) it will help the learners to become independent thinkers and doers. It also help in making the learners look at things in a way much different way. Incorporation of critical pedagogy into the curriculum will help (marginalized/tribal learners, language minority groups) in changing their world view.

Critical Pedagogy is considered important in the teaching-learning process because it promotes empowerment to the marginalized community in changing their outlook and helping them incorporate critical behavior. The important belief of critical pedagogy was that no education system is politically neutral and all that education system can do is to empower the students with critical behavior, which they can carry forward to the outside world.

References

1. Akbari, R. (2008). Transforming lives: Introducing critical pedagogy into ELT classrooms. *ELT journal*, 62(3), 276-283.
2. Canagarajah, S. (2005). Critical pedagogy in L2 learning and teaching. *In Handbook of research in second language teaching and learning* (pp. 955-974). Routledge.
3. Giroux, H. A. (2003). Public pedagogy and the politics of resistance: Notes on a critical theory of educational struggle. *Educational philosophy and theory*, 35(1), 5-16.
4. Giroux, H. A. (2001). *Theory and resistance in education: Towards a pedagogy for the opposition*. Greenwood Publishing Group.
5. Freire, P. (1972). *Pedagogy of the Oppressed*. 1968. Trans. Myra Bergman Ramos. New York: Herder.
6. Jha, J., & Jhingran, D. (2002). *Elementary Education for the Poorest and Other Deprived Groups: The Real Challenge of Universalization*. Manohar Publishers.
7. Riasati, M. J., & Mollaei, F. (2012). Critical pedagogy and language learning. *International Journal of Humanities and Social Science*, 2(21), 223-229.

8. Shor, I. (2014). *When students have power: Negotiating authority in a critical pedagogy*. University of Chicago Press.
9. Shor, I. (2012). *Empowering education: Critical teaching for social change*. University of Chicago Press.
10. Sujatha, K. (2002). Education among scheduled tribes. *India Education Report: A Profile of Basic Education, New Delhi: OUP.*

Chapter - 15

Effect of Context on Teaching and Learning - Integrating CTL in to Teacher Education

Jakkinaboina Sridevi

Abstract

When we acquire new information or learn, we do so in a particular context. Not only while learning, but also when the learnt material is retrieved, context plays an important role. Experiments conducted by Estes(1972) show that it is easier to retrieve a particular episode when you are in the same context in which you have encoded it. Contextual teaching and learning (CTL) is a concept that helps teachers relate subject matter to real- world situations. CTL motivates learners to take charge of their own learning and to make connections between knowledge and its applications to the various contexts of their lives: as family members, as citizens, and as workers. It provides a conceptual framework for unifying a constellation of education theories and practices and represents one approach to improving teacher education. Contextual teaching and learning includes six related teaching and learning strategies. Eick etal. (1975) who conducted experiment related to this, suggested that memory improves considerably when the internal states during retrieval matches that of encoding. Memory and retrieval would be partly dependent on the internal state during learning, this is called "state dependent retrieval". Thus the factors of contextual effect on learning is a significant one. Today, linguists, educators and psychologists make an considerable effort in creating a congenial context while teaching context language skills and other useful information so as to make the learning more effective.

Key Words: *Self-Regulated Learning, Teaching and Learning in Multiple Contexts, Problem-Based Learning, Interdependent Learning Groups and Authentic Assessment.*

Need to integrate contextual teaching and learning into teacher education.

Introduction

Contextual teaching and learning (CTL) is a concept that helps teachers relate subject matter to real- world situations. CTL motivates learners to take charge of their own learning and to make connections between knowledge and its applications to the various contexts of their lives: as family members, as citizens, and as workers. It provides a conceptual framework for unifying a constellation of education theories and practices and represents one approach to improving teacher education.

A primary purpose of CTL is to help students become self-regulated learners capable of high achievement. Beyond this primary goal, there is the recognition that students possess unique skills, interests, and cultural backgrounds.

Learning should take place in many sites, or multiple contexts, not just in classrooms. Museums, parks, government offices, and health facilities are just a few of the places where learning can occur in the community. Connected to learning in multiple contexts is the first of three teaching strategies: problem-based learning, which recognizes that students learn from real-world problems. Two other teaching strategies, interdependent learning groups and authentic assessment, contribute to the development of self-regulated learners.

Self-regulated learners need knowledge about themselves, the subject, the task at hand, learning strategies, and the contexts in which they will apply their learning. Self-regulated learners are similar to "expert" learners who know how they learn best - that is, their preferred leaming styles, what is hard or easy for them to learn, and how to use their strengths to learn. Self-regulated learners think about the contexts in which they will apply their knowledge now and in the future, connecting their present leaming to future activities. Self-regulated learners also are motivated to learn. School assignments are interesting to them because they value learning.

Teaching and learning in multiple context: Theories of situated cognition assume that knowledge is inseparable from the contexts and activities within which it develops (Borko and Putnam 1998).it is important that how and where the person learns a particular set of knowledge and skills are fundamental to what the student learns. students make sense of new information, given their internal mindsets, by relating it to their past social, cultural, and physical experiences. learning occurs naturally in a variety of contexts. both inside and outside the school.

Problem-Based Learning: Learners prepare to be self-directed, collaborative problem-solvers and encounter a situation that invites them to define one or more problems and to propose hunches, actions, and so forth. Learners prepare to be self-directed, collaborative problem-solvers and encounter a situation that invites them to define one or more problems and to propose hunches, actions, and so forth. Learners present their findings. Learners examine costs and benefits of the solutions generated and reflect on the effectiveness of their problem-solving approach.

Interdependent Learning groups: learning is a social process that can be enhanced when learners have opportunities to interact about instructional activities. The topic of collaboration in learning can be traced to the early 1900s, when John Dewey criticized the use of competition in education and proposed that educators structure schools as democratic learning communities. students interact face-to-face, rather than across the classroom. Group members seem to need each other for support, explanations, and guidance. But even though group members work together. Students learn individually accountable for leaming. Students practice collabo- ration before starting a new learning task. students monitor group processes and relationships to make sure their group is working effectively. In interactive and collaborative learning contexts, students have opportunities to adopt various perspectives and think reflectively in ways that foster social and moral development and self-esteem. Learning groups can help students feel.

Authentic assessment: authentic assessment can best be distinguished from traditional modes of educational assessment by qualities that foster formative development of teaching and learning processes.

Integrating CTL into teacher education: a quality teacher is the key to student learning. A caring, competent, and qualified teacher for every child is the most important ingredient in education reform.

Need and significance of the study

The purpose of this work is to give teachers and teacher educators an opportunity to see how contextual teaching and learning (CTL) can change classrooms and teacher education programs. Contextual teaching and learning (CTL) is a concept that helps teachers relate subject matter to real world situations. CTL motivates learners to take charge of their own learning and to make connections between knowledge and its applications to the various contexts of their lives: as family members, as citizens, and as workers. It provides a conceptual framework for unifying a constellation of education theories and practices and represents one approach to improving teacher education.

Expectations of students. As noted, the law prescribed what learner should know and be able to do to be successful in today's world. Each learner should:

Use basic communication and mathematics skills in finding, organizing, expressing, and responding to information and ideas. Apply core concepts and principles from science, arts and humanities, mathematics, practical living studies, social studies, and vocational studies.

Become a self-sufficient individual who demonstrates independent learning, self-control, a healthy lifestyle, flexibility, and an appreciation for diversity. Become a responsible group member who demonstrates consistent, responsive, and caring behaviour; interpersonal skills; respect for the rights and responsibilities of others' worldviews; and an open mind to other perspectives. Think and solve problems, including the ability to think critically and creatively, develop ideas and concepts, and make rational decisions. Connect and integrate experiences and new knowledge throughout the curriculum, question and interpret ideas from diverse perspectives, and apply concepts to real-life situations in the community and at work.

Thus the factor of contextual teaching and learning is a significant one. Today, linguists, educators and psychologists make an considerable effort in creating a congenial context while teaching context language skills and other useful information so as to make the learning more effective.

Objectives of The Study

- Main objective of the study is to find out effect of context on learning.
- Learning happens in multiple context apart from classroom learning.
- Importance of integrating contextual teaching and learning into teacher education.

Hypothesis

- Context facilitate learning.
- Learners learn the content in multiple contexts.
- Contextual teaching and learning is important to integrate into teacher training programs.

Material required for context facilitate learning

- A set of 18 cards having incomplete sentences with relevant and irrelevant words printed on them.

- Stop watch
- Intervening task
- Wooden screen

Description of the tool

Each card has an incomplete sentence. There will be two words printed on top left and top right corners out of which one will be relevant word and the other will be an irrelevant word. The subject is seated comfortably and each card was presented for 5 seconds each and after presenting all the cards, the subject was given intervening task for 2 minutes. Later the subject is asked to recall the words and the experimenter notes them for 5 minutes. The number of relevant and irrelevant words were counted and percentage will be calculated.

Discussion

CTL motivates learners to take charge of their own learning and to make connections between knowledge and its applications to the various contexts of their lives: as family members, as citizens, and as workers.

Self-regulated learning makes a sequence of learning and they question themselves about How have you spent your time? What do you know? (what did you learn recently) What don't you know? How can you find out what you don't know? What are your frustrations?

Problem-based learning /(PBL) is a student-centered approach in which students learn about a subject by working in groups to solve an open-ended problem. This problem is what drives the motivation and the learning. Examine and define the problem. Students learn to solve a problem or learn a matter or a content in a systematic procedure and the following are the steps followed - Explore what they already know about underlying issues related to it. Determine what they need to learn and where they can acquire the information and tools necessary to solve the problem. Evaluate possible ways to solve the problem. Solve the problem. Report on their findings.

When new learning activates information already in memory, this gives students multiple paths to access that learning is now stored with a variety of related memories in multiple areas of the brain. Students can retrieve the information from a number of areas in response to different cues.Mentally manipulating new and already known information increases memory and understanding, so providing learners multiple ways to apply their learning in new applications or situations helps their brains build increasing awareness of the concepts behind that new information. These mental manipulations guide students to progress from an initial concrete fact to more abstract conceptual knowledge. The contexts may be home community, or workplace, or less tangible context such as cyberspace and the imagination.

Learning is a social process that can be enhanced when learners have opportunities to interact about instructional activities. In interactive and collaborative learning contexts, stu- dents have opportunities to adopt various perspectives and think reflectively in ways that foster social and moral development and self-esteem. Learning groups can help students feel safe about sharing their ideas and actively participating in the learning process.

Authentic assessment makes Involving students in in-depth situations in which they develop and habitually solve problems and employ higher-order thinking. by using CTL strategies, we can creates self-regulated, life-long learners.

A caring, competent, and qualified teacher for every child is the most important ingredient in education reform. Teacher education is under pressure to improve the preparation of the nation's teachers. Teachers must be capable of giving directions to students learn in different context. For this teachers must be well trained about how students can understand different content and the context related to it. Teachers must be able to relate and teach content with different life situations. A best teacher take the classroom teaching into the society where they live by giving live examples from the society.

Conclusion

When we acquire new information or learn, we do so in a particular context. Not only while learning, but also when the learnt material is retrieved, context plays an important role. It is easier to retrieve a particular episode when you are in the same context in which you have encoded it. Context is not always external to th memorizer, such as a physical location or specific face, what is happening inside of us when we encode information i.e. our internal state also becomes pat of the context. Memory improves considerably when the internal states during retrieval matches that of encoding. Thus the factors of contextual effect on learning are a significant one. Today, linguists, educators and psychologists make an considerable effort in creating a congenial context while teaching context language skills and other useful information so as to make the learning more effective. Teachers must develop portfolios that present evidence that they can meet the Beginning Teacher Standards before receiving their teaching licenses. All teacher education standards are aimed at developing students' abilities to communicate effectively, apply core instructional concepts, be self-sufficient as individuals, be responsible team members, solve problems, and integrate knowledge.

Educational Implications

- CTL requires that teachers plan lessons that are developmentally appropriate for students. Include interdependent learning groups, provide for an environment that supports self-regulated learning, consider the diversity of students, addresses the multiple intelligences of students.
- Further research must be conducted on the higher education and the ways to relate the curriculum with the community.
- Further studies must be conducted on the multiple contextual learning.
- Inservice and preservice programs must be conducted regularly.
- Teaching and learning of all subjects should be contextual.

References

1. https://psycnet.apa.org/record/1986-10995-001.
2. https://link.springer.com/article/10.3758/BF03197465.
3. https://link.springer.com/article/10.3758/BF03196157.
4. https://www.uv.uio.no/iped/english/research/projects/.../artikkelen-dissemination. pdf.
5. Introduction to Contextual Teaching and Learning Susan Sears file:///A:/phd/introduction%20to%20contextual%20teaching%20and%20learning. pdf.
6. RG Berns, PM Erickson - 2001 – ERIC.
7. Contextual teaching and learning: What it is and Why it's Stay. here to Elaine B Johnson, Ph D.

Chapter - 16

Critical Pedagogy and English Language Teaching at the Tertiary Level in India

Roopna Ravindran

Abstract

Critical Pedagogy advocates that teaching/learning process is a political act. Critical Pedagogy considers the educational system as one of the means to contest the hegemonic systems existent in the society. The origin of Critical pedagogy can be associated to the Brazilian Educator and Philosopher, Paulo Freire. In his Pedagogy of the Oppressed, Freire criticised the banking system of Education which is still widely used in majority of the Degree Colleges in India. The teacher deposits legitimate knowledge into the student who comes with an empty head to the Indian College classrooms. English Language can no more be taught in isolation from the society. Students need to be aware of the power relationships through their interactions inside and outside the classrooms. Critical Pedagogy would place ELT in the grounds of critiquing undemocratic and oppressive social relations. Students should be actively engaged in the teaching learning process through classroom transactions, curriculum making and assessment processes. This paper aims to make a survey of the theoretical framework and praxis in the area of Critical Pedagogy at tertiary level in India. It will also try to draw insights from different works on critical pedagogy to theorize a way to practice Critical Pedagogy in the Degree Colleges in India.

Introduction

Critical Pedagogy is born out of the Neo-Marxist school of thought. Critical pedagogy has applied the concepts of the Critical Theory in Education and Culture. There was an attempt for critical enquiry in the fields of Sociology, Political science, Education and Psychology even from the beginning of 20th century. Dewey (1902, 2016), Gramsci (1971) and Vygotsky (1978) are some of the thinkers who have incorporated a critical quest in their respective disciplines.

Dewey (1933) theorized that students who are actively concerned about their learning may become responsive participants in a democracy. He believed that rote memorisation contributed to the passive acceptance of one's oppression in society, whereas learning through problem-solving would lead students to acquire an additional active role and position in the society.

In the traditional mode of education, the teacher is the sole agent to impart information. The data transferred to students are deposited in the minds of students. The students never rise to question that data transferred by their authoritarian teachers. In this old method the teacher thinks but the learners do not have to think on their own. The teacher chooses the content, students obediently receives it. They receive, memorise and repeat mechanically. They are not asked to individually relate this information imparted in the classroom to the issues and injustices in society. Consequently, the students are stuck to the passive role during this transaction of knowledge in the classroom environment.

According to Vygotsky's (1978) theory of social construction, a person's intellectual development results from social interactions in the culturally specific contexts.

The notion of Critical Pedagogy was initiated by Paulo Friere, the Brazilian educator and philosopher in his *The Pedagogy of the Oppressed* (1970). His main aim was to create a philosophy of adult education for the poor in Brazil by involving them in a critical dialogue with real life circumstances. His propositions are very much valid and adaptable to the Indian tertiary level education. There should be a change from learning for the examination perspective to learning for practicing in life.

According to Friere, Teaching Learning process cannot be neutral. It has apparent and hidden ideologies working behind it. Hence, it is an inherently political act. The main aim of Critical Pedagogy is to involve the teachers and the learners democratically and thereby emancipate the learners from the oppression that they face in a teacher centred classroom and in a larger scale hegemonic society. Paulo Freire clearly demarcates the traditional banking education and problem posing education. In banking education the teacher deposits knowledge in students. Within the latter, the teacher is the agent of change. In this new situation all of them, students and teachers mutually learn and all of them teach one another.

The critical pursuit of knowledge has to be paralleled by a quest for mutual humanization among those engaged in such a pursuit. Unlike 'banking education' that inhibits creativity and domesticates students, a radical pedagogy requires non-authoritarian social relationships that support dialogue and communication as indispensable for questioning the meaning and nature of knowledge and peeling away the hidden structures of reality"

The education process need to be a constant course of action involving "unlearning", "learning", "relearning", "reflection" and "evaluation." The learners need to be made aware of the power relation exorbitantly existent in the society. Critical pedagogy demands for a curriculum whose main aim is to have a critical out view of the social and political scenario existent in everyday life. Freire's praxis necessitates the effective implementation of educational practices for a conducive learning situation and in a larger scale an all inclusive society. Critical Pedagogy cannot be viewed merely as an educative technique it is a practice with extensions in the student's life. Learners get a makeover to active participants of a democratic classroom. Students, from being objects of education get transformed to subjects of their own autonomy and emancipation. Due course of education, students get emancipated to transform their societies. Through problem posing education the students incorporate in them a habit to think critically. This can in turn help them to fight the oppression and inequalities latently existent in the larger society. Hence, Critical pedagogy prepares the students to challenge any form of dominance, subjugation and inequality with the aim of emancipating the marginalized sections of the society.

This philosophy of education was later developed by Henry Giroux (1983, 1988). Henry Giroux is mainly concerned with the pervasiveness of power relations in the socio-cultural sphere, especially schooling. In schools hegemony functions not only "through the significations embedded in school texts, films, and `official' teacher discourse" but also "in those practical experiences that need no discourse, the message of which lingers beneath a structured silence." Ira Shor (2013) defines critical pedagogy as:

"Habits of thought, reading, writing, and speaking which go beneath surface meaning, first impressions, dominant myths, official pronouncements, traditional clichés, received wisdom, and mere opinions, to understand the deep meaning, root causes, social context, ideology, and personal consequences of any action, event, object, process, organization, experience, text, subject matter, policy, mass media, or discourse."

Bell Hooks (1994) with her Engaged Pedagogy, Joe Kincheloe (1991, 2008) with his critical cognitive theory and Michael Apple (1983, 1990, 2013) with his experimentations on education and power, critical thinking , critical teaching and development of democratic schools have developed Critical Pedagogy far ahead.

In the following section, the paper attempts to find out how Critical Pedagogy can be incorporated into the English Language Education in India.

Critical Language Pedagogy at Tertiary Level

Language is ideological in one way or another. It is important to realise whose interests are satisfied by the way in which language is used and also who are the resultant beneficiaries.

English language teaching in Post Colonial India presents a particularly complicated context in this regard. The history of Colonial education shows that India was forced to establish a unified, textbook-centred system in the past. However, there have been changes in this regard. Attempts have been made to reduce the presence of Literary Canon from the English text books and thereby integrate simpler and relatable content.

English language is taught as Common Course for any CBCS Bachelors programme in India.There are universities which still follow hard core literature syllabus for their common course of English. Most of the Universities include Communication Skills as compulsory under this Common Course. English Language teaching learning process need not be reduced to merely a tool for communication. Language offers varied opportunities for learners to engage in a fluid relationship between societies and also confront its power relations during the course of its discourses. For instance, the Bachelor programme of Calicut University, Kerala offers common courses on Critical Reasoning, Writing and Presentation, Literature and Contemporary Issues and Culture and Civilisation in addition to the common course on Communication Skills. Such initiatives offer possibilities for implementing critical language pedagogy during its classroom discourses.

English language skills are a significant demand for obtaining access to opportunities and privileges, even supposing the sort of skills needed dissent wide from context to context. However, apart from the urbanised lot, the English language skills are also considered necessary by a huge majority in the rural areas, particularly within the marginalized population. The latter lose out many opportunities due to their detachment with English language. Majority in the urban areas have been introduced to English since their pre primary education. But, the marginalised lot has to bear the brunt of the differences in the education system. Majority of the rural students have learned English bilingually and lack confidence even when they come to the tertiary level of education. Therefore, it is indeed problematic to adopt an all surpassing Common Course curriculum for Degree Colleges in a University in India. Even the pedagogy needed for one section of the population (the English medium school educated social class urban students) are completely different from another section of the society (for example, the marginalized rural population, for whom English is important to have an admittance to opportunities and privileges).

Both the "What" and "How" of teaching are problematical. Curriculum, Textbooks need to be revived to make the students belonging to different social strata more socially conscious and inclusive. Textbooks need to be divided into sections giving ample space for socially conscious pieces of information which has relevance in the contemporary Indian scenario.

Language Learners cannot be alienated from the Society. Text books should include readings from the previously excluded groups of the society. Hence, Learning English language in India needs to be a political act.

Praxis in the tertiary level of language teaching and learning

Kumaravadivelu emphasizes on the classroom being essentially "politically motivated and historically determined". Classroom discourse, according to him, contains the social, political and historical conditions of the learners and teachers, making it a "racialised", "stratified", "gendered" experience.([8])

In a language classroom, textbooks, supplementary materials and classroom activities are a few essentials for the execution active critical language pedagogy. Freire worked with "generative themes" that offered possibilities of generating productive discussions in the classroom. Teachers should give ample opportunities for the students to explore the content of every lesson from multiple perspectives. This permits students to grasp differing types of social relationships that are existent in Indian society. Students need to learn to give equal importance to the multitude of critical perspectives that are produced in the classroom discussion. A teacher dominated classroom usually has huge potential in class rooms to reveal the hidden agendas during the delivery of a lesson. A teacher can certainly work on the alternative realties, different perspectives of incidents described in the lesson to create a sense of inclusiveseness for the students from marginalized communities. In certain cases, the teacher can also produce materials in addition to the text. The text is most often considered to be a pretext. The main aim should be to enable all the students understand alternative perspectives. The other important tool for practicing critical pedagogy is classroom activities. The teacher should engage the students in sufficient speaking and writing activities to generate more discussions and debates in the classroom. These classroom activities play a major role in serving the students to develop critical perception.

Conclusion

India is a land of diversities. Language pedagogy has to critically mirror on these diversities of culture, gender variations, inequality in castes and class, differences of vernacular languages of the learner, urban or rural regions they belong to, spiritual variations, food, and customs etc. it's to form the scholars acknowledge and revere the democratic culture in India. And also, the final aim has to be a mirrored image on the consciousness of the learner to attain self-emancipation. Language is often a best tool to empower the learners. This paper aims to conclude with the findings to suggest that the students, at the end of their education at the tertiary level, need to have a critical awareness and should be ready to fight for their rights in this country.

References

1. Apple, Michael. (1990). Ideology and curriculum. London: Routledge.
2. Canagarajah, Suresh. (1999). *Resisting linguistic imperialism in English teaching*. Oxford: OUP.
3. Freire, Paulo, 1921-1997. (2000). *Pedagogy of the Oppressed*. New York: Continuum
4. Giroux, H. A. (1981). *Ideology, Culture & the Process of Schooling*. Philadelphia: Temple University Press, 20-25
5. Hooks, Bell. (1994). *Teaching to Transgress. Education as the Practice of Freedom*. London: Routledge.
6. Kincheloe, Joe L. (2008). *Critical Pedagogy Primer*. New York: Peter Lang.
7. Kumaravadivelu, B. (1999). *Critical Classroom Discourse Analysis*. TESOL Quarterly, 33(3), 453-484.
8. Shor, I. (1992). *Empowering Education: Critical Teaching for Social Change*. Chicago: University of Chicago Press, 129.

Chapter - 18

Teaching Learning Strategies: Utilizing Technology in the Classroom

V. Pallavi

Abstract

Elementary and secondary school teachers participated in focusgroup discussions and completed a survey to examine barriers and supports to computer integration. Although teachers used computers at home and school, they were not wholly comfortable with the technology. Familiarity with computers predicted greater comfort with technology and greater comfort was related to greater integration in the classroom. Thematic analysis of the focus groups yielded six major themes, including issues related to: support, teachers, context and access, students, computer hardware and software problems, and external or other priorities. The discussion of computer integration also inspired substantial emotional responses on the part of teachers. Despite increases in computer access and technology training, technology is not being used to support the kinds of instruction believed to be most powerful. In this paper, we examine technology integration through the lens of the teacher as an agent of change: What are the necessary characteristics, or qualities, that enable teachers to leverage technology resources as meaningful pedagogical tools? the literature related to four variables of teacher change: knowledge, self-efficacy, pedagogical beliefs, and subject and school culture. Specifically, we propose that teachers' mindsets must change to include the idea that "teaching is not effective without the appropriate use of information and communication technologies (ICT) resources to facilitate student learning." Implications are discussed in terms of both teacher education and professional development programs The availability of new technology tools that can help the teacher in making teaching interesting and engaging. The technology skills and knowledge that students gain in the classroom will create the foundation for the skills and knowledge they will need in the future. Technology integration is the use of technology tools in general content areas in education in order to allow students to apply computer and technology skills to learning and problem-solving. Generally speaking, the curriculum drives the use of technology and not vice versa. Technology integration is defined as the use of technology to enhance and support the educational environment. Technology integration in the classroom can also support classroom instruction by creating opportunities for students to complete assignments on the computer rather than with normal pencil and paper.

Introduction

However, to truly understand the future of technology in education, and in order to give any recommendations for the future usage of technology, we must come to an understanding of the major issues pertaining to the use of technology. Primarily, the major issues in technology can be divided into three main areas: the integration of modern technology into existing learning theory, the evaluation of the effectiveness of technology within instructional settings, and the trials of successful technology integration into similar fields. Unless technology can be supported by previous learning theories, then technology is merely a distraction to the educational process . Historically accepted learning theories have a great deal of research and design principles exploring their assumptions and tenets. It is of great importance to the validity of its use that technology is compatible with previous learning theories and methodologies. Learning theories provide insight into how individuals learn and thus provide methods for designing effective lessons. Thus, technology can be used most effectively for educational purposes if it is compatible with previously developed learning theory frameworks.

Technology in education is defined as an array of tools that helpful in advancing student learning and measured in how and why individuals behave. Educational technology is the study and ethical practice of facilitating e-learning, which is the learning and improving performance by creating, using and managing appropriate technological processes and resources. Educational Technology relies on a broad definition of the word "technology" which significant the tools and the sources to enhanced, to develop the skill of the Education.

Technology has the ability to enhance relationships between teachers and students. When teachers effectively integrate **technology** into subject areas, teachers grow into roles of adviser, content expert, and coach. **Technology** helps make teaching and learning more meaningful and fun.

What is Technology Integration?

Technology integration is the use of ***technology*** tools in general content areas in education in order to allow students to apply computer and ***technology*** skills to learning and problem-solving. The ***technology*** should become an integral part of how the classroom functions—as accessible as all other classroom tools.Technology integration is the use of technology like.,

Technology integration is using computers effectively and efficiently in the general content areas to allow students to learn how to apply computer skills in meaningful ways. Discrete computer skills take on new meaning when they are integrated within the curriculum.

Technology integration: the effective implementation of educational technologies to accomplish intended learning outcomes. Educational technology: any tool, equipment, or device—electronic or mechanical—that can help students accomplish specified learning goals. Educational technology includes both instructional and learning technologies. Instructional technology: educational technologies teachers employ to provide instruction. Learning technology: educational technologies learners use to accomplish specific learning objectives and tasks.

Technology integration: the effective implementation of educational technologies to accomplish intended learning outcomes. Educational technology: any tool, equipment, or device—electronic or mechanical—that can help students accomplish specified learning goals. Educational technology includes both instructional and learning technologies. Instructional technology: educational technologies teachers employ to provide instruction. Learning technology: educational technologies learners use to accomplish specific learning objectives and tasks.

Technology integration: the effective implementation of educational technologies to accomplish intended learning outcomes. Educational technology: any tool, equipment, or device—electronic or mechanical—that can help students accomplish specified learning goals. Educational technology includes both instructional and learning technologies. Instructional technology: educational technologies teachers employ to provide instruction. Learning technology: educational technologies learners use to accomplish specific learning objectives and tasks.

1. Computers
2. Internet
3. Software application.
4. CD-Rams.
5. Digital cameras
6. Video cameras
7. Mobile phones
8. Tablets

Why Technology Integartion

The availability of new technology tools that can help the teacher in making teaching interesting and engaging. The technology skills and knowledge that students gain in the classroom will create the foundation for the skills and knowledge they will need in the future.

Technology integration is the use of technology tools in general content areas in education in order to allow students to apply computer and technology skills to learning and problem-solving. Generally speaking, the curriculum drives the use of technology and not vice versa. Technology integration is defined as the use of technology to enhance and support the educational environment. Technology integration in the classroom can also support classroom instruction by creating opportunities for students to complete assignments on the computer rather than with normal pencil and paper.

Technology has become integrated in the classroom in so many ways, that we often don't even think about how we are using it. The Education World Tech Team offers lessons and activities to help educators make better use of technology tools for instruction, and to help students improve their technology skills within the context of the regular curriculum. Included:

Integration activities that utilize the Web, PowerPoint, Excel, digital photography, SMART Boards and more.

What are The Benefits of Technology?

1. Keeps students focused for longer periods of time.
2. Makes student more excited to learn.
3. Enables students to learn at their own pace.
4. Caters to different learning styles.
5. Improves Knowledge retention
6. Encourages individual learning
7. Encourage collaboration.
8. Student can learn useful life skills through technology.
9. Benefits for teachers.
10. Improves engagement.

How Does Technology Help The Teacher.

It **helps teachers** in managing their classroom very efficiently and **Teachers should treat the adoption of technology as part of lesson planning.** The teacher plays an essential role in every student's education, behavior and development. In the present competitive environment, it's a tough task for a teacher to manage a classroom by concentrating on every student. Classroom management is the process of ensuring that classroom lessons run smoothly despite the disruptive behavior of students. Technology nowadays makes everything easy and effective. The most important thing a teacher needs to have is self-confidence.

1. Helps in producing interesting, diverse and student friendly material.

2. Makes teaching interesting and fun.
3. Gives access to more information and ideas.

What are The Benefits of Technology To The Students?

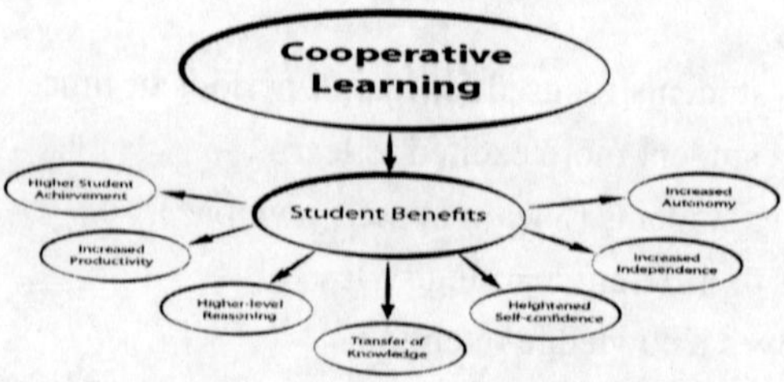

Students can gain the skills they will need to be successful in the future. Modern learning is about collaborating with others, solving complex problems, critical thinking, developing different forms of communication and leadership skills, and improving motivation and productivity.What is more, technology can help develop many practical skills, including creating presentations, learning to differentiate reliable from unreliable sources on the Internet, maintaining proper online etiquette, and writing emails. Students can practice collaboration skills by getting involved in different online activities.Students who are engaged and interested in things they are studying, are expected to have better knowledge retention. These are very important skills that can be developed in the classroom.

Co-Ordinate Live Video

You don't have to limit yourself to pre-recorded videos, as conferencing technology can allow subject matter experts to deliver lessons.

Whether it's a contact from another school or a seasoned lecturer you reach out to, bringing an expert into your classroom will expose your students to new ideas and can lighten your workload.

Get Creative

Technology is just another tool. Used judiciously and creatively. It can bring about a change in the teaching learning process.

The role of the teachers and classroom settings is an important influence upon student beliefs and development of their own creativity.

Gather Student Feedback

To encourage student input about content-processing activities, create and distribute surveys.

Feedback is an essential part of education and training programmes. It helps learners to maximise their potential at different stages of training, raise their awareness of strengths and areas for improvement, and identify actions to be taken to improve performance.

Negative Side of Using Technology

There is a need for school counselors to assist parents and school personnel in protecting their students from harm and victimization.

Each aspect of our life has become modernized and has become more technological advanced due to portable internet availability, Television, iPods, PDA, cell phones, laptop computers, mp3, players of every brand, Communication in shape of text messages & emails, business system i.e. online banking and e-buying and selling, online gaming, online liberalities and much more.

The role of Technology in Education is a well-written article to help you understand how education and technology are related. Students have potential gain from using Wi-Fi at their educational institutions to do research, create and complete assignments and projects. Also, they are able to utilize specific software which helps them complete projects.

Conclusions

In terms of its present status and use for educational purposes, technology is fulfilling an ever increasing role in both the traditional education field, and in other fields which are utilizing technology for educational purposes. Within the educational field we can see technology as a means of removing barriers for students and teachers alike. First, technology can remove financial and geographical barriers through distributed learning.

This allows students and teachers to experience educational opportunities that they might have otherwise never been able Technology and its use in Education: Present Roles and Future Prospects 16 to encounter. Second, technology is bringing about a new focus on problem and skill based learning. Information databases, such as EPSS, are being used to assist teachers in the acquisition of new knowledge and provide professional support outside of the traditional professional development seminar. In addition, information databases are assisting students in making the transition from knowledge retention to real world problem solving. Furthermore, technology has been shown to have sound theoretical foundations within the educational field. Various learning theories have been shown to be compatible with the usage of technology in education, especially those that attribute social interaction and simulation to forms of learning. Evaluative frameworks, normally reserved for traditional training programs, have also been successfully applied to technology based training. In other words, while providing benefits for students, the use of technology does not detract from the effectiveness of education or violate long standing educational principles. Technology can work within the educational system and does not need to be viewed as in conflict with the historical precedence of the field. As further evidence of the educational effectiveness of technology implementation, other fields have adopted technology for their own educational and training programs. Corporations are integrating their training sessions with technology.

The healthcare field is using technology to prepare doctors for a future in an age of excessive information, where skills related to research and knowledge application are valued at a higher level. Each successful implementation of educational technology into other fields only serves the argument for integrating technology at every level of the traditional educational process. If technology is successful in assisting the continued development of our Technology and its use in Education.

References

1. Masani, Zareer, India still Asia's reluctant tiger, BBC Radio 4, 27 February 2008.
2. Mitra, Sramana, How To Save The World's Back Office of Forbes, 03.14. 2008.
3. Newsweek, Special Report: The Education Race, August 18–25, 2011.
4. Nexus Novus, Higher Education Opportunities in India,
5. http://nexusnovus.com/higher-educationopportunities-india, Jul 26, 2013 accessed on 30/07/2016.
6. Science and Technology Education". Press Information Bureau, Retrieved 2009 08-08.

7. Shaguri, Obadya Ray, Higher Education in India Access, Equity, Quality, EAN World Congress.
8. Sharma, Sahil, Sharma, Purnendu, Indian Higher Education System: Challenges And Suggestions.
9. Electronic Journal for Inclusive Education, Vol. 3, No. 4, 2015, pp.3-4. International Cooperation, 2014.
10. Journal of Arts, Humanities and Management Studies, Volume 01, No. 2, Feb 2015.

Chapter - 18

Making Education Interactive with Drama Based Pedagogy

Ms Rupinder Brar

Abstract

One of the most demanding skills for teachers to acquire is how to move away from structured routines of teaching and to lead disciplined improvisation in education. Mastering the ability to lead interactive and creative teaching is a difficult challenge for teacher students even though it is part of their teaching. The persistent tension between scripted teaching and creative teaching is a demonstration of deeper, competing conceptions of teaching. Students find it cumbersome to move away from scripted teaching. There are various methods to stimulate a change in the teaching learning process and based on the fact that good teaching is based on confidence, rich interaction and creative passion, drama comes into existence. Drama and improvisational exercises such as verbal spontaneity games, role playing, and physical movement can train the interaction skills of the students. Coaching can be done through activities that develop teaching skills, new ideas and thoughts. By coaching, interaction skills we have new experiences using our sense organs. These can reshape our mental pictures, help us rethink and analyze our representations of reality – often in a creative way.

Introduction

In the history of education different art subjects have been understood as helping to develop human creativity (Gardner, 2006). Still a continuous struggle is seen in curriculums between creative art education and structured teaching. One way to solve this problem has been illustrated by Keith Sawyer (2009), who has discussed structured and creative teaching. Sawyer criticizes traditional structured teaching. According to him, this kind of teaching is too heavily based on instructions, where knowledge is only a collection of static facts, figures and procedures which teachers should put into students' heads. An alternative to structured schooling is creative teaching, which aims for deeper conceptual understanding by preparing students to create new knowledge. The teacher's role is to facilitate than to teach in a traditional way. The curricula of creative teaching consist of non-static facts, which are integrated into contextualized knowledge from culture. Creative learning is also built on the learner's (both the teacher's and the student's) prior knowledge, and this constructively leads to a classroom where the core is founded on synergistic conversations. The creative part of constructivist learning is based on the fact that classroom conversations are improvisational. This means that the teacher and the students build knowledge together, and unexpected insights emerge. These dimensions show that creative teaching is suitable for postmodern knowledge society (Sawyer, 2009.)

Creative teaching is possible through Drama-based pedagogy. This pedagogy depicts a assemblage of drama-based teaching and learning strategies to engage students in learning. Drama based pedagogy describes a collection of drama-based methods of teaching and learning strategies to engage students in learning. Drama-based pedagogy depicts a collection of drama-based teaching and learning strategies to engage students in learning. 21st century learning requires interactive classrooms to produce smart students, who are not only successful in their own endeavors but contribute equally in the development of the nation. Skills that are the need of the hour are, character education, citizenship, collaboration, communication, creativity, and critical thinking. There are different teaching strategies that can be used for making class rooms effective and one such teaching strategy to make class room effective is DBP. Drama based pedagogy is a collection of drama based teaching and learning strategies to engage students in teaching and learning process. It is the collection of teaching tools like dialogue, theatre games, image work, and role work, active and dramatic approaches to engage students in academic, affective and aesthetic learning through dialogic meaning-making in all areas of the curriculum (Dawson & Lee, 2016). It is an, non-exhibitional, process-centered improvisational form of drama in which participants are guided by a leader to imagine, enact, and reflect upon human experiences." The best part of these techniques is that they engage students with ease and help create an environment for cross examination and cross-curricular learning opportunities. In addition, these techniques support a variety of learning styles and thinking styles and keep students actively involved in the learning process. The use of drama as a teaching tool across the curriculum gained popularity in the United States in the 1920s as "creative dramatics." Over the years, teachers in countries around the world have continued to experiment with and further develop these creative teaching tools. There are many other terms also used for drama-based pedagogy that includes: creative drama, informal drama, creative play acting, improvisational drama, educational drama, role drama, and process drama.

Applications of creative drama pedagogy for classroom

Learning problems are normally not related to the difficulty of the subject matter but rather to the type and level of the cognitive processes required to learn the material (Keefe & Ferrell, 1990). It is believed that when teachers are able to analyze the individual differences and needs of their students, the educational process is likely to become optimized for both teachers and students. One way to achieve this is integration of Drama-based pedagogy into numerous curricular areas. It can be used to introduce a new concept or to revise a previously done concept or to check for knowledge, or extend the learning of the students. It can be used to explore a character's motivations, infer a story's outcome, or to illuminate facts and concepts. The teaching techniques emphasize the broader goals of problem-solving and creative thinking through the creation of a kinesthetic, interactive experience in the teaching learning process. In short we can say that the curriculum that is full of dramatic moments and tensions, Drama helps to extract those tensions from the pages of textbooks and worksheets and "enact" them with students. Ideally this will lead to a classroom of engaged learners who have new critical and different perspectives on the topic at hand .Understanding the philosophy behind the this work is important as a facilitator of drama based pedagogy. Through constructivist practices in the teaching learning process , aim is to invite students to actively enter this process. The resulting "creative chaos" can, at times, be disconcerting for some educators, but the learning that results will be worth it. Drama requires the ability to teach creatively, to be a teacher who is ready to become as part of a group as one of the learners in the drama education situation. To implement this kind of teaching, which is both creative and dialogic (Frijters, Dam & Rijlaarsdam, 2008), the school teacher must have capacity to manage unrest, uncertainty and unpredictable situations. There is always a strong element of incompleteness in drama activity (Heikkinen, 2005). Living in incompleteness is typical of the process of drama education and improvisation. The in-completeness gives both the teacher and the learner permission to examine, and indeed to fail, but above all, it provides the opportunity to find functional and evolving solutions. Drama mirrors the ways in which students learn through their early experiences of dramatic play. As a more structured and organized kind of improvisational role-playing, Drama-based pedagogy generates and cultivates many cognitive and affective skills. Of these skills, the following are important for ensuring a student's success in school:

- communication abilities & skills
- problem-solving abilities
- critical thinking skills
- decision making capabilities
- creativity
- imagination
- Collaboration skills

Drama-based pedagogy, when used with organized periods of oral or written reflection, provides an excellent link between various classroom curricula and the specific knowledge and skills required for success. The goals of drama and improvisation as teaching methods are

- To increase awareness of the student's self i.e mind, body and voice and others like collaboration and empathy;
- To increase the interaction skills of students; to improve clarity and creativity in the communication of verbal and nonverbal ideas;
- To increase the understanding of human behavior, motivation and diversity in educational situations.

Drama and improvisation can improve the quality of learning and the quality of life in education because drama can be used to extend the worldview of the human being and deal with difficult situations .Students gain experience in various roles (teachers, parents, pupils etc.) that explore human tensions and conflicts with drama conventions and techniques. Drama and improvisation has both an emotional and intellectual impact on the participants. It holds up a mirror for us to examine ourselves and deepens our understanding of human motivation and behavior. It broadens our perspective through stories that portray life from different points of view (Howard-Jones, Winfield and Crimmins, 2008).

Conclusion

Compared to planned teaching, creative improvisational teaching is "a very different vision: teachers are knowledgeable and expert professionals, and are granted creative autonomy in their classrooms." Planned teaching is performance at the lowest level: teachers stand on the "classroom stage" in front of a student "audience" and relay simple facts.

An alternative is creative teaching based on improvisational performance. This means that "effective classroom discussion is improvisational, because the flow of the class is unpredictable and emerges from the actions of all participants, both teachers and students." (Sawyer, 2004). Drama requires of the teacher an ability to function simultaneously in many kinds of roles. The teacher is always in the role required of a teacher, as Buchmann (1986) has stated. However, the teacher is always in the educational situation also as a person. Commanding this wholeness is tiring and challenging, so the ability to be in this situation as a teacher requires daring and risk and drama based pedagogy is worth the risk . (Saweyr, 2004).

References

1. Edmiston, B. (2013). *Transforming teaching and learning with active and dramatic approaches: Engaging students across the curriculum*. Routledge.
2. Frijters, S., ten Dam, G., & Rijlaarsdam, G. (2008). Effects of dialogic learning on value-loaded critical thinking. *Learning and Instruction*, *18*(1), 66-82.
3. Heikkinen, R. K., Luoto, M., Kuussaari, M., & Pöyry, J. (2005). New insights into butterfly–environment relationships using partitioning methods. *Proceedings of the Royal Society of London B: Biological Sciences*, *272*(1577), 2203-2210.
4. Howard-Jones, P. A., Winfield, M., & Crimmins, G. (2008). Co-constructing an understanding of creativity in drama education that draws on neuropsychological concepts. *Educational Research*, *50*(2), 187-201.
5. Gardner, H. (1999). Intelligences reframed: multiple intelligences for the 21st century. New York: Basic.
6. Papavassiliou-Alexiou, I., & Zourna, C. (2016). Teachers' professional competences: what has Drama in Education to offer? An empirical study in Greece. *Professional Development in Education*, *42*(5), 767-786.
7. Sawyer, K. (2004). Creative Teaching: Collaborative Discussionas Disciplined Improvisation. Educational Researcher, Vol. 33, No. 2, 12–20.

Chapter - 19

Teaching Learning Strategies - Pedagogy Issues

Dr. Sama Suvarnadevi

Abstract

Education is the process of reforming diameter. On the other hand, it is the recondition to development. Indian epics Peru se education as a Process which helps in reframing characters and brings qualitative changes in human behaviour by inculcating the Sterling qualities of heart like prudence, humbleness circumspection, self-composure, self-confidence, modesty, love and thus helps to lead a harmonious and orderly life. Indian philosophy is his repository of all knowledge, wisdom and virtues. It contains an outline of the entire universe covering all the matters relating to animates and inanimate. This philosophy of education is not only to meet the personal welfare or individual exhalation of a chosen taw, But for the welfare of the entire whole universe and thus it provides the basis of total aspects of education. Indian schools of thoughts believe that human development starts at the very outset of formation not embryo in the Mother's Womb and requires proper care since then, to be a complete man throughout the ages, Indian experienced and experimented the philosophy of education and on the basis of lice it advise us the sense of true Indian education. Our Sages like S.Radhakrishnan, Swami Vivekananda, Sri Aurobindo, Rabindranath Tagore and others advocate in favour of these eternal values in their work and deeds.

Importance of Higher Education

"Education is Lamp of Life." Education is a crucial input in human resource development which is fundamental to the realisation of the goals of national planning for development. It prepares the individual for assuming his role as a responsible citizen, develops in him scientific temper and rational outlook, sensitizes him to ethical, social and cultural values and equips him with fundamental knowledge, skills, attitudes and values which would enable him to contribute to the productive programmes of national development. Education is an important means of meeting once basic needs since it provides the necessary knowledge for change in current practice and skills to better use the service provided. It plays a critical role in development by infusing in an individual the ability to play a constructive role in the society.It has been observed that development programmes are well implemented only when investment of capital and transfer of Technology are supported by adequate human knowledge and skills. Education is found to be a powerful force in raising the consciousness of a population to deal with proper managemental and natural resources. Education and development are two factors which have presently engaged the attention of planners and administrators in most of the developing nations of the world. Education, in its widest meaning "encompasses the whole field of human growth and development." The fundamental concern of education is infact to facilitate the fullest growth and development of individual potentialities in harmony with the larger interest of the society. Education therefore, has a dual role to play in the society. According to Sarvepalli Radhakrishnan, "state can organise and organisation which is in its premises. University can inaugurate the future society." In 1995 WTO affected our education field. In these 10 to 13 years period there are many changes in our higher education.Meaning of pedagogy: The method and practice of teaching especially as an academic subject or the theoretical concept.

Issues and discussions of pedagogy and its forms

Pedagogy refers to the "interactions between teachers, students and the learning tasks. This broad term includes how teachers and students relate together as well as the in instructional approaches implemented in the classroomImportance of subject:Destiny of the nation is shaped classroom. Advancement and development of quality education plays a crucial role in Nations progress full stop especially the quality of Higher Education has a very pivotal role for technology advancement, creation of wealth and modernization of society full stop Para change the advancement of Higher Education promotes the national coalition, scientific temper and independence of the mind and spirit the furthering the goals of socialism, secularism and democracy ensured in our constitution. The education is an unique investment in the present and future parrot change with the effect of globalisation economical, rural regional and rural and urban inequalities increased in manifold. The study of National Sample Survey and Arjun Sengupta committee revealed the startling facts of economic and other inequalities. In this context 11th plan gave more importance to the education and health.

Steps of project method

1. Creating situation: In the first step teacher creates the proper situation to the students in the class. He puts up the knowledge about the project method procedure, steps and uses to the students, A project should arise out of a need felt by students and it should be never before on them. It should be purposeful and significant.
2. Selection of the problem: the teacher helps the students to select the problem and guide them. Students are having freedom to choose the topic or problem based upon their interest and ability.Before choosing the topic the principal should be taken into an account to stop such as school tasks are to be as real and as purposeful and they are of such a nature that the student is genuinely eager to carry them out in order to achieve a desirable and clearly realised aim.Teacher should only tempt the students for a particular project by providing a situation but the proposal for the project should finally come from students.
3. Planning: The teacher discuss with the students about the problem in a various angles and point, After the free expression of the student's opinion about the problem, the teacher write down the whole program of the action stepwise on the blackboard.

   In the process of planning teacher has to act only as a guide and should give suggestions at the time but actual planning should be left to the students.
4. Execution: The students are stating their work in this step full stop they are collecting the relevant information and materials. At first the teachers should give the time and write to the students according to their own speed interest and ability. During this check the teacher should carefully supervise the pupils in manipulate your skills to prevent waste of materials and to Gaurd accidents. Teacher should constantly check up the relation between the Chalked out plans and the developing projects.
5. Evaluation: Evaluation of the project should be done both by the students and the teachers. Here the students evaluating their task. They determine whether the objects are achieved or not. After that they criticise and Express their feelings about the task freely.

   The evaluation of the project has to be done in the light of plans difficulties in the execution and attitude results.
6. Reporting and Recording: it is it is the last step of the project method in which each and every step of the worker reported. The

reported things are recorded in a certain order in a book form.It should include the proposal, plan and its discussion duties allotted to different students and how far they were carried out by them. It should also include the details of places visited and serve as guidance for future and all other possible details.The book format of report is submitted to the teacher at the end.

Advantages of project method It helps to develop social skills and values among the students.

A. It gives an opportunity to correlate the subject matter to real life situations.
B. Students are more receptive and learn faster when they work together.
C. Students get proper freedom to execute the project in accordance with their interest and abilities because of which they get their psychological level satisfied to be considered extent.
D. This method is not only subject centred but due to importance it is been provided to the students also.
E. Through these method students are provided with various opportunities by which day can satisfy their interest and desires.
F. Habit of critical thinking is developed among the students through this method.
G. With this method students get the sample chances in which they can develop coordination among the body and mind.
H. Through this method teacher can read well balanced development of the students.
I. Through this method science teaching can be done with considerable success, as science is practical subject and this method is also scientific and practical in nature.
J. This method helps in promoting social interaction and cooperation among the students has they have to work in groups and have no interact with various persons for gathering information.
K. Students gain knowledge directly through their own efforts does the acquired permanent kind of information which is returned by them since a long period of time.
L. Mostly the projects undertaken in classroom my classroom assignments, because of which load of homework from the students get reduced it to considerable extent.

M. It helps to widen the mental horizon of students. It setups a challenge to solve a problem and this situation stimulates the constructive and creative thinking.

Disadvantages of project method

A. This method takes a lot of time to plan and execute a single project.

B. It is not possible to design different projects for different topics and it is also not possible to cover all the topics are contained in a single project.

C. For proper execution of a project, large number of financial resources is required.

D. Search methods can only be proved successful if the teacher is highly knowledgeable, alert and exceptional gifted.

E. Systematic and adequate learning is not provided by this method as it is a method of incidental learning point through this method; students learn only what is required by them in relation to the completion of the project.

F. Generally it is found that the teachers do not possess much information regarding the manner in which this method should be used as a result of which the hesitate from using this method, as a result of which, its utility remains more or less limited to negligible extent. Sometimes the projects may be too ambitious and beyond students capacity to accomplish.

Role of teacher

A. In project method of teaching the role of teacher is that of a guide, friend and a philosopher.

B. The teacher is not a dictator or a commander that a friend, guide and a working partner.

C. He encourages his students to work collectively, and cooperatively.

D. He also helps students to avoid mistakes.

E. He makes it a point that each member of the group contributed something to the completion of the project.

F. If the students face failure during execution of some steps of the project that teacher should not execute any portion of the project but should suggest them some better methods of techniques that may be used buy them next time for the success of the project.

G. We should help the students in developing the character and personality by allowing them to accept the responsibilities and discharge them efficiently.

H. Who should provide democratic atmosphere in the class so that the students can express themselves fully without any fear of the teacher.

I. He should be alert and active at that time to see that of the student's projects is running in guidelines.

J. He should have Tharo knowledge of individual children so as to all of them work accordingly.

K. He should have initiative, and just for learning.

L. Teacher should always remain alert and active during execution step and see that the project was the completion successfully.

M. During execution of the project teachers should maintain a democratic atmosphere.

Types of projects

1. Individualproject
2. Socialproject
3. Groupproject
4. Simpleprojectand
5. Complexproject

According to Kilpatrick there are 4 types of projects

A. Constructive project practical or physical tasks such as construction of article, making a model, digging a well and playing a drama are done in this type of projects.

B. Esthetical project appreciation powers of the students are developed in this type of project through the musical programs, beautification of something appreciation of poems and so on.

C. Problematic project in this type of project develop the problem solving capacity of the students through their experiences. It is based on the cognitive domain.

D. drill project it is for the mastery of the skill and knowledge of the student and increase in the work efficiency and capacity of the students.

Conclusion

This project presents a method for increasing security of the information requested by the users with the use of steganography method in this method, instead of direct selling of information; it is a hidden new picture by the password. After entering the password, the user can witness the information extracted from the picture with the password is entered correctly the project is an economically in terms of time it is not possible to fit into the regular and table.

References

1. Methodology B.Ed, Telugu academy
2. Pedagogy of social sciences, Telugu academy
3. Internet
4. www.learning portal.iiel.unesco.org.

Chapter - 20

Encouraging Student's Language Competence through Drama Techniques in German-as-a-foreign-language (GFL) Class by using two "Learning Plays" of Brecht

Sharath Kumar Velmala

Abstract

Drama texts are different from poem, novel, and other literary texts. In a language class drama texts can be taught using drama techniques rather than using conventional methods of teaching and learning. In this paper I would like to explore encouraging the students' language competence, especially speaking and writing skills, through drama in German-as-a-foreign-language (GFL) class. By that students can attain not only the academic goals but also the social objectives. As an example two "learning plays" (Lehrstücke) of Brecht named "The Yes Sayer" (Der Jasager) and "The No Sayer" (Der Neinsager) are chosen. The themes of these plays interest the students. The language of those plays is not difficult and the characters can be identified by the students themselves.

Introduction

This work is based on the curriculum of BA German (Hon.) fourth semester students of Delhi University. In the curriculum short stories, novels, poems and also dramas are dealt in the literature class. The level of their language is B1-B2. According to the Common European Framework of Reference (CEFR) it is an intermediate level. Students are able to use the already learned foreign language in and outside the class.

The main objective of using drama in GFL class is overall development of the student. Verbal skills (i.e. speaking along with different intonations) and nonverbal skills (body posture, group cohesion and social competences) of the student can be encouraged. Another objective of didactics of drama can be that the student can interact in foreign language with real persons in a particular context in the class. And the main focus is on spoken language. According to Haßler (1985), an educationalist, when the characters and situations are nearer to the real life, it is, then, more useful for students to learn.[1]

In this work different approaches of drama teaching which are useful for GFL class, are analyzed and an alternate approach is discussed. Waldmann's 'productive approach' (*productiver Ansatz*) and the 'concepts of drama didactics' (*die Konzepte der Dramendidaktik*) by Lösener, are discussed. For Waldmann 1) a drama pre-school (*dramatische Vorschule*) should happen to give an insight into the forms and structures of drama. 2) And then the different techniques can be applied on drama text and learned. Also Steinweg's outline of drama class (Skizze) is discussed in this work based on "The Yes Sayer" and "The No Sayer".

1. Concepts of drama didactics (*die Konzepte der Dramendidaktik*):

The concepts of drama didactics are helpful in encouraging the performance ability and thereby encouraging the speaking and writing ability of students in the class. There are 3 kinds of drama didactics approaches. They are genre theory approach, theatrical approach, and production-oriented approach.

1.1. Genre theory approach

In the postwar years the focus of drama was still as an ideological function. And in 1950's and 60's the aesthetic value was brought to the foreground. A prominent representative of this genre theory approach was Harro Müller-Michaels. He developed in the beginning of 1970's a course (Lehrgang) in which genre specific structures of characters, plot, conflict, space, time, and dialogue were developed by examining puppet show, improvisation theater, theater for children and young people, folk theater, radio play, film and television plays, one-act and multi-act plays.[2] Here the individual structural elements were revisited and strengthened in every learning level, whereas the emphases can vary. Müller-Michaels combines methodically six different didactic approaches together with form of action and corresponding learning objective. The methods can be expanded through the learning objectives and variation in forms of action.[3]

1.2. Theatrical approach

By the end of 1970's play-oriented pedagogic methods were developed. Besides Walter Beimdick, Herta-Elisabeth Renk was a prominent personality. Beimdick focused mainly on mediation of knowledge about the professional theater work. Renk's approach, which is established semiotically, combines verbal and nonverbal communication skills in order to aware students for the effect of dramatic expressions and make them curious about it.[4]

Franz-Josef Payrhuber, a German educationalist, says that while reading any drama text student can become aware of implementation of it into an actual play. For that, Payrhuber adds further, student should visit theater performances to have a greater significance on them. The perception of a play can be completed by performing it. After the experience of completeness another function of play comes which is interpretation. It is shown to student that there is a practical dramaturgic interpretation with performed play, in which director presents his individual interpretation, where as in classroom discussion it can vary.[5]

1.3. Production-oriented approach

In 1960's appears production-oriented approach. This approach indicates a class in which students listen, read, analyze and interpret literature receptively. They design themselves. They work with text. They elaborate and rewrite the text in order to perform it. In the book *Produktiver Umgang mit dem Drama* (Productive engagement with drama, 2004) Günter Waldmann deals with the whole concept of drama didactics. Herald Frommer is considered as a representative for the production-oriented approach. Reading is, according to him, an activity of enactment and concretizing a drama text is a creative and personal analysis which can be achieved by writing pre-texts and post-texts, further writing of a scene, and formulating subtexts. As a result of this, dramatic dimension of a text can be experienced which leads to the different approaches and also to the implicit enactment of drama texts.[6]

2. Concepts of drama didactics according to Lösener

Another kind of concepts of drama didactics are used by Hans Lösener. It is to understand that reading and enacting of a drama text are two fundamentally different activities. Lösener introduces three kinds of enactments of drama texts which are performed enactment (*aufgeführte Inszenierung*), mental enactment (*mentale Inszenierung*) and implicit enactment (*implizite Inszenierung*). With this differentiation it is possible to break the classic polarization between theatricality and text.[7] In the next step Lösener assigns an approach to those concepts of enactments and apply them to conceptualize a drama class.

2.1. Performed enactment

The enactment which is performed on stage is the result of a collective work process and it assumes an inner theater work. Lösener combines the performed enactment with the approach of play-oriented class and refers to the concept of scenic interpretation (*szenische Interpretation*) by Ingo Scheller who puts the scenic presentation in helping the interpretation process.

2.2. Mental enactment

Mental enactment takes place in the head of reader and it requires training for specific reading abilities. It is to understand that a drama text aims at performance. And performed enactment is like a prerequisite for mental enactment which creates textual prerequisite. Production-oriented teaching concepts are assigned to the mental enactment. Lösener discusses, as an example, Waldmann's concept which originates from a drama text as concept and produces a close relation between text and performance.[8]

2.3. Implicit enactment

Implicit enactment is created by drama text itself and also by various enacting factors like body and speaking. Characters, plot, etc of a play can be developed through the interrelation of those enacting factors. Lösener refers to text-oriented teaching concepts and he cites Frommer's concept of reading and enacting (Lesen und Inszenieren). For Frommer text is more than a linguistic reception, and with self-esteem of reader he finds textual enactment.[9] By that dramatic moment would be ceased with pure writing of summery of a drama scene since the dialogue process would have been removed.

2.4. Relation between performed, mental, and implicit enactments:

Lösener puts all three concepts of enactments together in a relation with each other and clarifies their dependency on each other. He operates here with the concept of drama-specific rhythm which comes from the specific expression of big and small units of meaning of a text, because performed enactment, which ignores rhythm of mental enactment, neglects the concept underlying the direction, and also the play itself.[10]

2.5. Summary

Drama texts these days at BA level are read mostly as epic texts which doesn't encourage student to enact it. Lösener connects it to the fullness of interpretation aids and reader's guides which make clear that which interpretation skills would be demanded by learner. The interpretation aids and reader's guides are structured mostly according to the outline of summery, background knowledge and information regarding form and genre, and final conclusions of interpretation. But reducing knowledge about plot neglects dramatic dimension of a text, opines Lösener.[11]

Drama pre-school by Waldmann

Günter Waldmann, drama pedagogue, discussed about drama pre-school (*dramatische Vorschule*) in his productive approach with drama texts. To be productive with drama texts students should become aware of basic concepts of drama. Waldmann introduces drama pre-school in his productive approach (*produktiver Ansatz*). It has several phases. In the first phase dramatic pre-school focuses on free writing of a drama text to understand the characteristics of drama. In the first hour of writing students work on characters, dialogues and plot. Based on a shot scene characters can be developed and observed the possibilities of how a situation changes when various characters enter on to the stage and gains dramatic effect according to the behavior of characters.

In the second phase of drama pre-school a dramatic dialogue can be developed. Waldmann suggests a situation, as an example, in which a store detective calls an alleged suspect. Now students should make dialogues between store detective and suspect and improvise the situation. At the end of the first hour a group of students are able to create beginning and end of the given situation and connect it to the main plot.

The second hour of writing session deals with dramatic conflicts. One should aware that dramatic plot is formed, developed, escalated and solved with conflicts.[12] Thoughts can be added to a given situation in order to be solved by conflicts. Possible salvations of conflicts are supposed to be established by students through writing dialogues between characters.

The third and last hour of writing session has an objective which is to develop a situational drama (*Sitationsdrama*). The results of first and second hour of writing sessions should be connected with each other and made a short play. The third hour aims to experience that drama cannot be developed a whole rather by adding various drafts together.

At the end of drama pre-school drama text becomes play. The functionsof main texts (Haupttexte) and instructions (Nebentexte) were found in which the instructions of a scene can be omitted. Some drama scenes are written with main text along with instructions and are analyzed regarding the question of their effect. Drama text should lead to the performance and cannot be treated as a plain text. Waldmann says that students immerse in their respective roles and empathize with timing and handling of character and are aware of the behavior of each character.

3. Learning plays (*Lehrstücke*)

Learning play concept was developed by Bertolt Brecht along with Kurt Weill in 1929. It is developed from classic theater. Learning play was not basically developed for the theatrical considerations rather for the development of music. And as the next step it is developed as school opera (Schuloper) to incorporate with reform-pedagogical objectives. In the beginning this play was used also to address the problems of layman. Learning play model appears to offer academic use due to its pedagogical intention.[13] With leaning plays Brecht wanted to give an experience to his readers and public, with which they can learn. He says, "Learning play teaches through performing it, not by watching it. No audience is needed for learning play."[14] All involve in the plot and become actors. According to Brecht an actor should acts freely without any mechanical training.

Together with the authors Kurt Weill und Paul Hindemith, Brecht wrote six learning plays. They are *der Lindberghflug*, *die Maßnahme*, *der Jasagerund der Neinsager*, *die Ausnahme und die Regel* and *die Horatier und die Kuriatier*. For this work *der Jasager* and *der Neinsager* are chosen. Each play has six actors and a mass-chorus. These roles can be performed in class by the students of BA (Hon.) fourth semester of Delhi University. They can be performed in an easy and curious way to attain teaching objective.

3.1. The Yes Sayer

This is a two-act play. It deals with consent of a boy with his sacrifice in the interest of society. An unknown disease outbreak happens in a city. A teacher from that place makes an expedition with three of his students to fetch medicine to cure the disease. In the middle of the journey one of the boys, whose mother is ill, falls sick and cannot walk further on to the mountains. His fellow students would not like to help him to go further. They ask him, should they all go back to save the boy's life or should they throw him into valley. According to the "norm" there the boy should agree with the society – large section of people – and when he "agrees" he must be killed. At the end the fellow students throw him into valley. Because of a "great norm" the boy is supposed to sacrifice his life.

3.2. The No Sayer:

With some changes and additions in the text of The Yes Sayer Brecht wrote The No Sayer. It is also written in two acts. The plot of these two plays is almost identical with each other except the second half of the second act. In The No Sayer the boy doesn't sacrifice his life. He refuses his agreement with society and doesn't follow the "norm" and continues the expedition. The boy says.

4. Outline of drama class by Steinweg

The German peace researcher Reiner Steinweg made an ideal outline for drama based teaching and learning especially for Brecht's learning plays. He was an experienced pedagogue for theater. He opines, the outline can work based on the interests and focuses of participants. Steinweg outlines learning plays drama course in six steps which depend on each other. They are introducing of rules (*Einführung der Regeln*), activation and adaptation of text (*Aktivierung und Textaneignung*), perception (*Wahrnehmen*), transfer (*Übertragung*), transmission (*Veränderung*), andconclusion (*Ergebnis und Abschluss*).

4.1. Introducing of rules

For performing leaning plays in class one should consider the following rules.

(a) Artistic perfection is not necessary.
(b) Person in the role is different with the character.
(c) After every performance student should discuss what they saw and feel. (association)
(d) Literary interpretation of drama text is avoided.
(e) All students must do activities before performance.

4.2. Activation and text adaptation

Various activities and exercises activate mind and body of students. Text adaptation doesn't require the sense of text. In the class all students read out the text and analyze it. Then a conversation begins between the students without considering the grammatical and semantic structures. After that students are allowed to connect their personal experience with the text or to a sentence in the text.

4.3. Perception

In this phase teacher suggests students to decide a role and reflect how they perceive it and how they want to play it. And then they play. After every performance all students discuss about their reflections and observations about every act. It is called association (to real social situations). Then the unclear ideas are discussed. Observations regarding body posture, movements, gestures, tone, etc can be shared by saying "Das war wie …" (that was like …).

4.4. Transfer

After perceiving and observing play teacher discusses his own experience along with the roles of the boy, the mother and the teacher in learning plays. Every group in the class should develop a small scene from the two plays (Yes-Sayer and No-Sayer) by including their perceptions and observations. The vocabulary should be used from the plays itself. Like that the newly written text is alienated.

4.5. Transmission

Every student can select three scenes and should say why he/she selected those scenes. With this discussion some ideas about characters can be cleared. And now only one scene should be selected by the students and work further with it. According to Steinweg transmission can occur in two ways. The first is by changing the role of student and the second is by changing the plot. For example, a small change in the plot of Yes-Sayer, when the boy disagrees with the teacher, it leads to No-Sayer. So No-Sayer is alternate plot for Yes-Sayer and vice versa.

4.6. Conclusion

In this phase students are asked to write a page full of their personal problems. They can write in any form like a picture, a story or a letter to a friend, etc. The objectives of learning plays are to realize the social objectives, to understand the contradictions between intension and conduct of a person. The text of learning plays provides a context for experiencing personal and social conflicts.

References

1. Brecht, Bertolt: Über das Lehrstück. In: Mittenzwei, Werner (Hg.): *Bertolt Brecht Schriften*. Band 5. Frankfurt am Main: Suhrkamp 1973.
2. Even, Susanne: Kognitives und affektives Lernen im dramagrammatischen Unterricht. Lernstile, Lernstrategien und Lernanschauungen. In: *Materialen Deutsch als Fremdsprache* 2003.

3. Knopf, Jan: Brecht Handbuch Band 1. Stücke. In: Jan Knopf (Hg): *Brecht Handbuch in fünf Bänden*. Stuttgart, Weimar: Metzler 2001.
4. Haßler, Ingrid: Theater im Konversationsunterricht. In: Wilhelm Krull/Fritz Wefelmeye (Hg): *Textarbeit – Literarische Texte*. München: Iudicium 1985.
5. Lösener, Hans: Konzepte der Dramendidaktik. In: Günter Lange/Swantje Weinhold (Hg.): *Grundlagen der Deutschdidaktik. Sprachdidaktik – Mediendiaktik – Literaturdidaktik*. 3. Aufl. Baltmannsweiler 2007.
6. Steinweg, Reiner: *Lehrstück und episches Theater, Brechts Theorie und die theaterpädagogische Praxis*. 2. Aufl. Brandes & Apsel : Frankfurt am Main 2005.
7. Waldmann, Günter: Produktiver Umgang mit dem Drama. Eine systematische Einführung in das produktive Verstehen traditioneller und moderner Dramenformen und das Schreiben in ihnen; für Schule (Sekundarstufe I und II) und Hochschule. 3. Aufl. Baltmannsweiler 2001.
8. Müller-Michaels, Harro: *Dramatische Werke im Deutschunterrricht*. 2., überarb. Aufl. Stuttgart 1975.
9. Denk, Rudolf / Mobius, Thomas: *Dramen- und Theaterdidaktik*. Eine Einführung. 2., neu bearb. Aufl. Berlin 2010.
10. Payrhuber, Franz-Josef: *Das Drama im Unterricht. Aspekte einer Didaktik des Dramas, Analysen und empirische Befunde – Begründungen – Unterrichts modelle*. Rheinbreitbach 1991.

Notes

1. Ingrid Haßler: Theater im Konversationsunterricht. In: Wilhelm Krull/Fritz Wefelmeye (Hg): Textarbeit – Literarische Texte. München: Iudicium 1985.
2. Harro Müller-Michaels: *Dramatische Werke im Deutschunterrricht*. 2., überarb. Aufl. Stuttgart 1975, P. 205.
3. Vgl. Harro Müller-Michaels: *Dramatische Werke im Deutschunterrricht*, P. 205.
4. Rudolf Denk/Thomas Mobius: *Dramen- und Theaterdidaktik*. Eine Einführung. 2., neu bearb. Aufl. Berlin 2010, P. 88.
5. Franz-Josef Payrhuber: *Das Drama im Unterricht. Aspekte einer Didaktik des Dramas, Analysen und empirische Befunde – Begründungen – Unterrichtsmodelle*. Rheinbreitbach 1991, P. 78.
6. Vgl. Rudolf Denk/Thomas Mobius: *Dramen- und Theaterdidaktik,* P. 96.
7. Hans Lösener: Konzepte der Dramendidaktik. In: Günter Lange/Swantje Weinhold (Hg.): *Grundlagen der Deutschdidaktik. Sprachdidaktik – Mediendiaktik – Literaturdidaktik*. 3. Aufl. Baltmannsweiler 2007, P. 298.
8. Vgl. Hans Lösener: Konzepte der Dramendidaktik, P. 302.
9. Ebenda P. 311.
10. Vgl. Hans Lösener: Konzepte der Dramendidaktik, P. 303.
11. Vgl. Hans Lösener: Konzepte der Dramendidaktik, P. 299.
12. Vgl. Günter Waldmann: *Produktiver Umgang mit dem Drama,* P. 9.
13. John Knopf: Brecht Handbuch Band 1. Stücke. In: Knopf, Jan (Hg): *Brecht Handbuch in fünf Bänden*. Stuttgart, Weimar: Metzler 2001. P. 28.
14. Bertolt Brecht: Über das Lehrstück. In: Werner Mittenzwei (Hg.): *Bertolt Brecht Schriften*. Band 5. Suhrkamp : Frankfurt am Main 1973, P. 91.

Chapter - 21

Use of Technology to Enhance Teaching and Learning

Dr. Shaik. Liyakhath Ali

Abstract

Technology provides numerous tools that teachers can use in and out of the classroom to enhance student learning. This article provides an introduction to some of the most common tools used in and out the classroom for teaching and learning of the students.There are specific types of Teaching , learning tools like presentation software, classroom response systems(clickers), Online projects and collaboration tools, information visualization tools, Flipping the classroom, podcasts, Games, teaching with table computers and converting a face to face course to an online course. The author has tried to explain the implementation of above said technologies in classroom as well as outside classroom to give a boost and enhance quality of teaching and learning.

Keywords: *Podcasts, flipping, information visualization, Presentation software.*

Introduction

In order to enhance student learning in and out of the classroom, Technology provides numerous tools for the use of teachers .There are numerous on - line resources about using technology to enhance teaching in a number of ways. For example, Teaching with Technology2, from the learning Technology consortium offers 17 peer reviewed essays on using different kinds of educational technology. Merlot is a huge, peer – reviewed, multi-disciplinary resource for learning and online teaching.

Below are resources on using specific types of teaching and learning tools.

1. Presentation Software

Sometimes it's helpful to provide visual aids to complement teaching, stimulate discussion, or allow out-of class teaching, Tools designed for this purpose, such as PowerPoint, can be used well or used badly. There are many resources that provide advice for thoughtful use of PowerPoint, as well as a few additional presentation tools. For example:

What is Good Power point Design? – Garr Reynolds, Presentation Zen.

Twelve Active Learning Strategies for Power Point – University of Minnesota.

Top 10 Evidence-Based, Best Practices for PowerPoint in the classroom (John Hopkins professor emeritus).

Think Outside the Slide - Dave Paradi.

Active Learning with PowerPoint – Sharon Huston.

Other tools

Prezi (make your presentations Zoom).

Thoughts on Using Prezi as a Presentation tool.

Comparison Chart: PowerPoint and Prezi.

Xtranormal (animation tool for you and your students).

2. Classroom Response Systems ("Clickers")

One way to encourage student engagement is by utilizing electronic devices that facilitate students to record their answers to multiple choice questions and allow us instantly display the results. The anonymity encourages participation and their answers help the teacher know when further discussion is needed. Use of clickers can also serve as a catalyst for discussion.

Clickers allow teachers to poll attitudes, check comprehension, stimulate discussion and more.

The following are few classroom response systems:

Teaching with a Classroom Response System (Overview from Vanderbilt).

Classroom Response Systems: A Teaching with Technology White Paper (Carnegie Mellon)

How to Use Clickers Effectively (University of Colorado Science Education video)

Poll Everywhere (classroom polls with images, equations and more using student smart phones or laptops).

Socrative (student response system that works with any internet-connected device, allowing multiple question types, quizzes, exit tickets and more. No clicker necessary because students use their own devices).

3. Online Projects and Collaboration Tools

Technology can support student collaboration on creating new knowledge, reflecting on what they are learning, or working together to achieve a deeper understanding of course material.

Online tools provide many new options. Students can collaborate on projects, collects and synthesize information and write for different types of audiences. Here are some examples:

Online Collaboration Generally

Teaching in the Cloud: Using online Collaboration tools to Enhance Student Engagement. Those jointly edited Google Docs, Google sites, wikis; cloud storage of video projects, crowd sourced research, Google spreadsheets, for data aggregation, Piazza and class blogs and it also considers issues of IT support, ease of use and student privacy.

Wikis

Vanderbilt's Center for Teaching provides this helpful overview.

Wikis in Higher Education (University of Delaware report)

Wikify Your Course: Designing & Implementing a Wiki for your Learning Environment (advice from Educase)

Teaching with Wikipedia (Indiana University Bloomington's Center for Innovative Teaching & Learning has these suggestions for using the mother ship of wikis)

Blogs

Student Expectations for Technology and Uses of Blogs –Venderbilt's teaching center. *Class Blogs*: Discusses learning goals, ways to use blogs, need for student training and ways to assess student blog – writing.

Pedagogy and the Class Blog: This blog is created by English Professor at George Mason which throws reflections on grading and assessing blog posts from "Sample Reality."

Twitter

Professors use Twitter to increase student engagement and grades. *The Twitter Experiment:* Twitter in the classroom can be used in reporting on and demonstrating Twitter Experiment in a class at UT Dallas.

Revisiting Twitter as an Educational tool:

To engage students with each other and with the outside world and for the professional development of teachers Twitter is helpful. It is designed by University of Oregon's teaching centre.

Other Online Collaboration Tools

Piazza

Piazza is a free online gathering place where students can come together to ask, answer and explore under the guidance of their instructors. With Piazza you can easily answer questions, manage course materials and track student participation.

Using Xtranormal against Straw Men

A professor describes assigning students to make Xtranormal videos to demonstrate the ability to realistically grapple with counter arguments.

4. Information Visualization Tools

Technology can also clarify and stimulate thought through transforming words into pictures. Here are some tools to help lead your to think more critically by encouraging them to visually structure information.

Visualization tools can help you make information clearer to students either by providing you with clearer visuals or better yet assigning them to use visuals to make connections.

46 tools to make Info graphics in the classroom

These tools help your students deepen their understanding by showing connections, mapping, creating timelines, etc.

A quick look at Instagrok

It is a web – based tool that creates a web-like visualization based on semantic relationships between terms, and also serves as a search engine. It remembers stranger in a strange land?

Classroom Assessment Tools

This is a video designed from the center for Instructional Innovation, Western Washington University.

5. Flipping the Classroom

To make the best use of the classroom time we have with our students, sometimes a great way to move them toward higher levels of understanding is to move the lecture out of the classroom and use in-person time for interactions that require applying, synthesizing and creating."Flipping" doesn't have to use technology but tools such as videos, podcasts, online quizzes and the like can help in and out of class activity work together. These resources explain the theory underlying this teaching method and provide practical suggestions for making it work.

6. Podcasts

Whether for a flipped class or just as resource for your students, you may want to create a podcast that conveys information students need for initial learning or review.

7. Teaching with Games

What could be more engaging than a good game, used well? The games may lead to deeper learning and give some examples of their use in higher education.

8. Video games are good for learning

Video games are good for learnig.we should use the learning principles built into good video games in and out of schools even if we are not using games. These learning principles can be built into many different curricula. Different types of games can have different effects. Puzzle games like *Tetris* and *Bejeweled* may very well exercise pattern recognition capacities. *Trivial Pursuit* games may well make learning facts fun.

9. Teaching with Tablet Computers

We're only beginning to explore their many possibilities for higher education. Here are some ideas. Thinking about buying a tablet computer that will provide lots of computing power and also provide lots of teaching options.

iBooks Author

Create and publish amazing books for iPad, iPhone, and Mac.Available free on the Mac App store, iBooks Author is an amazing app that allows anyone to create beautiful textbooks-and just about other kind of book – for iPad, iPhone and Mac. With galleries, video, interactive diagrams, 3D objects, mathematical expressions and more these books bring content to life in ways the printed page never could.

10. Converting a Face-to-Face Course to an Online Course

Teaching online, whether in a hybrid course or a wholly-online course, requires different techniques and different tools. Without the F2F contact, professors will need to be even clearer about setting and articulating expectations for digital work and participation. Encouraging interaction between professor and student and among students is an additional challenge, as is monitoring student learning as the course progresses. The online environment requires the use of basic technologies to digitalize course materials as well as mastery of the university's learning management system. And various tools like *Skype* allow synchronous interaction. Here are some ideas to get you started.

Using course components that are online rather than face-to-face creates both new challenges and new opportunities. Here are a few resources to help start that journey.

Duke center for Instructional Technology

The Online Teaching Guide was developed by faculty members from the Duke University school of Nursing (DUSON) under the guidance of the Duke center for instructional Technology(CIT).The work of this group culminated in this resource for faculty members who want to enhance their ability to plan effective online learning experiences for students. This guide serves as a user – friendly and practical tool to assist faculty in planning and implementing online courses.

Conclusion

At present we are in brain century, explosion of knowledge in every field. Science and Technology has become part and parcel of our lives. Without Science and Technology we can't expect our life. Education field is not exception to this. It has become indispensable to move forward without the implementation of Technology in education field. No doubt Teacher plays pivotal role in teaching, nobody can substitute his place, and whatever may be the technology. But it is in the hands of teacher who can how best utilize Technology for effective implementation of his teaching and thus enhance the teaching learning process and elicit the set objectives and percolate the teaching at the grass root level.

References

1. https://www.smu.edu/Provost/CTE/Resouces/Technology.
2. https://www.smu.edu/cox/Learning-culture/Academic-Departments.
3. www.merolot.org/merlot/index.htm.
4. Presentationzen.blogs.com.
5. www.cmu.edu/teaching/resources/publications.
6. www.cmu.edu/teaching/technology/tools/information.
7. www.edutopia.org/blog/flipped-classroom-best-practices.
8. www.academiccolab.org.
9. Itlatnd.wordpress.com.

Chapter - 22

Teaching English Language Skills through Mathematics

Smt. T Vijaya Gouri, Sri P. Janardhan Rao

Abstract

English language is the most valuable treasure that one can possess. The globalised era has brought English communication skills and soft skills to the forefront of professional world. Writing skill is a component of language skill with important role in human life. Language is unique human trail the enable on express own ideas, views, logical thinking, creative thinking etc., The use of Mathematics in the ELT classroom enjoy a great revival now. Many mathematics problems provide rich resources of Reading, Writing and Communication for students to express themselves in second language learning. They can also be used to intensive or exclusive reading, thinking, and writing mathematics problem can help learner practice the language learning skills through reading and writing skills. Reading besides systematic presenting as new. When students write explanations of their work and give examples, teachers can better assess student understanding and progress throughout time. Writing is an ideal vehicle for formative assessment, providing teachers with the information they need to adjust their instruction.

***Key words**: Importance of ELT, LSRW skills, Problem solving.*

Introduction

Mathematics always thinks, logical and describes our world. Understanding the facts, concepts, principles and laws of mathematics helps learners to solve not only theoretical problems but also real life problems. Towards the end of the 20th century English became a truly global language and since then it has kept its privileged position among other world languages. It is estimated that English spoken by about 1.5 billion people all over the world (Crystal 1997:5). Undergraduates require an ever-increasing range of skills to maintain relevance with the global environment of the new millennium.

Communication skills are a vital component of this, recognised by academia and industry alike. Reading and Writing skills are essential for undergraduate who aspires to carry out his/her proficient practice in the global arena. Multilingual skills are considered a salient element in the make-up of the new global undergraduate. Yet there is ample evidence that undergraduate lack the required standard of communication skills, particularly when compared to the needs of industry internationally. Communication skills are a regular feature of graduate job in industry; some graduates employed in industry have identified that education in communication skills needs to be improved given the demands encountered in industry. Indeed, communication skills are considered to be a valuable career enhance. Inadequate and ineffective communication skills reflect badly on the individual and the profession. An insufficient level of communication skills instruction in engineering education generally only serves to undermine the whole profile of the graduation. Writing Skills are essential component in the education of graduates to facilitate not just students' education but also to prepare them for their future careers. In this article, the author discusses various important writing skills required of current graduates, such as foreign language skills. Also discussed are various elements of communication skills education, such as oral, listening, written, visual, interdisciplinary and intercultural. These studies have gone a long way to modernize education, and aimed to improve teaching and learning in education by stressing the role of reading and writing in the classroom. According to Martinez and Martinez (2001), "Reading and writing are essential to both develop problem-solving and concept discovery processes". These theorists stressed the need for using a variety of exploratory methods and technology to improve learning, also stressing the positive effect of using writing assignments in mathematics. The topic of "Language and Communication in Mathematics Education" covers a wide range of areas of interest, ranging from the question of what constitutes "language" in mathematics, through investigations of communicative interactions in mathematics classrooms and study of issues involved in teaching and learning mathematics in multilingual settings.

The purpose of this study was to explore the relationship between problem solving ability and content knowledge of first year Bachelor degree students in mathematics.

Reading

Reading can be considered a two part process. First, it is the transfer of encoded information from written text to the reader. Several cognitive psychologists (Gough, 1972; Rumelhart, 1977; Chall, 1983) suggest theories on how this might occur. Second, and of more importance to the paper, reading is the comprehension of the information by the reader. Rosenblatt (1978), in her transactional theory of reading, maintains that reading comprehension occurs as the reader actively shapes what is being read by bringing background knowledge, cultural orientation, personal reading history, beliefs and feelings to bear on the text. Thus, as the reader or the context in which the text is read changes, the comprehension of the text changes.

Writing

Writing is a powerful tool because it provides a unique form of feedback. As the student writes, information from the process is immediately and visibly available, which allows the learner to review the reasoning for correctness. Moreover, writing clarifies and organizes a student's thoughts. Since writing prepares a product for another Volume 8 Number 1 19 person, the author must make sure that the writing flows and that all points are made clearly. Finally, Emig asserts that the slow pace of writing is conducive to student learning. Since writing is comparatively slow to reading, talking, or listening, it forces thinking to slow down to the pace of the writing. This allows students to reason through thoughts carefully to make sure they are correct and complete before they are stated. Writing can be beneficial to students in other ways as well. Moore (1993) claims that effective writing can be used to influence opinions of the public and colleagues, which is a crucial skill in a wide variety of occupations. Also, writing is often necessary for occupational success. He notes that many employers both want and expect their employees to be good writers. Writing may also have beneficial aspects for student learning that are specific to mathematics courses. In a research study of writing in mathematics, Grossman, Smith, and Miller (1993) suggest that a student's ability to explain concepts in writing is related to the ability to comprehend and apply mathematical concepts. This is applicable in both short and longer time frames.

Objectives of the study

1. To find out the extent of language learning ability through problem solving aptitude and content knowledge of undergraduate students in mathematics.
2. To find out the influence of content knowledge on problem solving ability in mathematics among first year degree students.

Tools

Test for assessing content knowledge in Language learning.

Test for assessing problem solving ability in Mathematics.

Both tests were developed based on 5 major concepts at undergraduation level namely, 1.

Elimination theory

Elimination theory is the classical name for algorithmic approaches to eliminating some variables between polynomials of several variables.

Obstruction theory

Obstruction theory is a name given to two different mathematical theories, both of which yield chorologicalin variants. In the original work of Stiefel and Whitney, characteristic classes were defined as obstructions to the existence of certain fields of linear independent vectors. Obstruction theory turns out to be an application of cohomology theory to the problem of constructing a cross-section of a bundle.

Approximation theory

Approximation theory is concerned with how functions can best be approximated with simpler functions, and with quantitatively characterizing the errors introduced thereby. Note that what is meant by *best* and *simpler* will depend on the application.

Automata theory

Automata theory is the study of abstract machines and automata, as well as the computational problems that can be solved using them. It is a theory in theoretical computer Science and discrete mathematics (a subject of study in both mathematics and computer science).

Character theory

Characters of irreducible representations encode many important properties of a group and can thus be used to study its structure

The Reading and writing skills test consisted of 15 mathematics problems on the chosen 5 concepts. These problems were selected from Graduation based level.

Sample for the Study

The sample in the study comprised of 30 students persuading undergraduate degree in mathematics. Sample were selected from Rural Area Government Degree College.

Procedure of the study

Afford opportunities for students to clarify key terms and words.

Dissimilar the language used in everyday communication, the language of mathematics is precise and concise. Each word and phrase used in mathematics has a definite meaning that must be grasped to assure that the student fully understands the mathematical concept. Therefore, it is essential for students to learn the key terms and words used in mathematics. This requirement, however, does not imply that students be "taught" the terms in isolation (e.g., "Here are the terms for the lesson; what do they mean?"). On the contrary, the terms should be used in the same context in which the students will encounter them. Students need to be given opportunities to read the terms and definitions, ask questions about them, use them in sentences, and if possible, describe them using visual or concrete materials. Language can be made comprehensible through a variety of means, such as demonstrations, hands-on materials, visual aids, and manipulation of content (Krashen and Terrel 1983). Furthermore, mathematical terms are best understood when students use the language of mathematics in a meaningful setting (Krashen 1981; Cummins and Swain 1986).

Keep a classroom environment to English writing skills are encouraged to participate.

The teacher can design whole-class instruction in a manner that encourages the participation of all students. Reducing the amount of time the teacher talks gives students more time to use English in class. One basic "truth" applies in language learning: One can become proficient only if one uses the language. An essential part of the process of learning the language is to give students the freedom to make errors when writing English. The teacher should deal with grammatical errors tactfully. Students can be corrected through modeling; for example, if a student states that "the root squares are five," the teacher can respond, "Yes, the square root is five. Would you repeat your answer, please?"

Give students opportunities to examine and discuss problem-solving processes.

A number of procedures can often be helpful when working through mathematical tasks. By verbalizing the processes used to solve problems, students who may not be confident about their English-language skills can be assisted in their problem-solving endeavors. For example, they can routinely be encouraged to discuss such questions as these:

1. What are the important facts or conditions in the problem?
2. Do you need any information not given in the problem?
3. What question is asked in the problem?
4. Describe how you solved the problem.
5. How did you feel while you were solving this problem?
6. How do you feel after having worked on the problem?

Results and Findings

Giving students explicit guidelines for their written work can reduce the amount of time needed to evaluate their writing. Annalisa Crannell (Franklin and Marshall College) has students staple a problem solving to their papers. J.J. Price (Purdue University) includes dos and don'ts in his article 'Learning Mathematics Through Writing: Some Guidelines (Price, *Coll. Math. J.*, 20 (5), 393-401, 1989). Bruce Crauder (Oklahoma State University) and others provide students with a few exemplary problem solutions, whose style they are encouraged to emulate. Melvin Henriksen (Harvey Mudd College) and Jennifer Szydlik (University of Wisconsin at Oshkosh) report that grading students' first efforts severely results in dramatic improvement. Extent of Reading ability with understanding through mathematic problem among undergraduates. Range of content knowledge in mathematics through reading. To find out the extend content knowledge, how to solve in mathematics among under graduates. Sentence construction knowledge, structure of knowledge in mathematics. Relationship between English language and mathematics problem solving ability in mathematics for tool. That is, for increase knowledge about reading and writing skills.

These papers were concerned with the construction of mathematics and mathematical thinking and, in particular, the ways that teachers and teaching methods shape the possibilities for students' mathematical thinking and the ways in which mathematical knowledge is developed in interactions between teacher and students and among groups of students.

Drageset characterised different ways in which teachers respond to student contributions, offering a framework for analysing how different practices may have potential to help student thinking to progress. Milani also discussed how different forms of interaction may relate to learning, identifying dialogic questioning as a form that involves students as active participants in the learning process. Focusing on the development of spatial perception in undergraduates, Schuette's study investigated the different ways in which this domain is talked about in the three contexts of Rural area Government degree college. Theories used a semiotic approach to analyse and describe students' proportional reasoning, finding that multiplicative strategies were more successful than either additive or formal strategies.

Conclusion

The study of mathematics becomes meaningful when the student attains the true content knowledge and effective language learning ability through problem solving. For effectively writing skills in mathematics learners must have knowledge about the ideas, concepts, logical thinking sentence construction and structural arrangements embedded in the problem. This paper not only measure learners ability to use mathematical procedures, but also measures breadth of their knowledge and depth if their conceptual understanding. There has been a longstanding interest in the issues involved in teaching and learning mathematics in different languages. This originated to a large extent in the context of post-colonialism at a time when many countries with a legacy of education in the language of the ex-colonial power were struggling to value their own national and local languages and to develop the use of these languages in education.

References

1. Charles, Randall, Frank Lester, and Phares O'Daffer. *How to Evaluate Progress in Problem Solving*. Reston Va.: National Council of Teachers of Mathematics, 1987.
2. Cuevas, Gilbert J. "Increasing the Achievement and Participation of Language Minority Students in Mathematics Education." In *Teaching and Learning Mathematics in the 1990s*, 1990 Yearbook of the National Council of Teachers of Mathematics, edited by Thomas J. Cooney and Christian R. Hirsch, 159-65. Reston, Va.: The Council, 1990.
3. Cummins, James. "The Role of Primary Language Development in Promoting Educational Success for Language Minority Students." In *Schooling and Language Minority Students: A Theoretical Framework*edited by D. P. Dolson, 3-50. Los Angeles: Evaluation, Dissemination and Assessment Center, California State University/Los Angeles, 1984.
4. Cummins, James, and Merrill Swain. *Bilingualism in Education.* London: Longman, 1986.
5. Dishon, David, and Paul O'Leary. *A Guidebook for Cooperative Learning.* Holmes Beach, Fla.: Learning Publications, 1984.

Chapter - 23

Utilization of the Technology in the Government College of Teacher Education's Classroom

J. Vishwanath

Abstract

In this context it is very important that the utilization of technology in the college of education's classrooms to provide hand on experience, involvement, concentration towards the subject matter students learn, newness from the conventionality has been the basic criteria for the introduction of the technology in the teacher education. Palamuru University, Mahabubnagar caters the educational needs of four districts that is Mahabubnagar, Nagarkunrool, Alampur Jogulamba and Wanaparthy areas. University placed Information Communication Technology (ICT) in the curriculum of teacher education. The major interest is to make the teachers and learners abreast with the present world's technology that is the chief expectation of the world. University has opened the door for the better understanding of technology through teaching learning practices of the teachers, teacher trainees and ultimately the students, who inspired by the new technology and gadgets and learn efficiently. Main objective of this empirical research paper is to find out whether teacher trainees in the government teacher educational institutions have utilized the new technology in their teaching practice session in an efficient manner or it is a state of burden for them to use in the classroom teaching practice. For this empirical research, I have taken up the Government District Institute of Education and Training and Government College of Teacher Education, Mettugadda, Mahabubnagar district teacher Trainees of various Mathematics, Science and English methodologies. The tools used to collect the data is a checklist with yes or no responses in which the teacher trainees should have to respond by choosing an appropriate option by ticking in the box given at the right side of them.

Key words: *Technology: ICT technology,*

Introduction

This study finds the utilization of the technology in the government college of teacher education as the demand of the 21st century. In this direction Government has taken great initiative to introduce ICT in the Teacher Education Institution as the part of the B.Ed. course to meet the demands of the society. Presently the world is changing rapidly that present day tool and technic has been stale for the next instance. So it is very important for the people to be upgraded to sustain in the market. Most of the developed countries have exploited the potentials of ICT to transform their educational landscape at the tertiary, secondary and even primary levels particularly through the instructional process (Kosakowski, 1998). Generally ICT holds out the opportunity to revolutionize pedagogical methods, expand access to quality education improve the management of education systems (World Bank, 2002). Hence curriculum in the 21st century of Teacher Education urgently demand for teachers capable of effectively handling ICT resources for the purpose of helping students to radically obtain and manipulate information for their educational resource development.

As per the demands of the education system every teacher have to be thorough knowledge regarding the digital equipment's to dispense thoroughly the subject matter by attracting the students' attention and engage the students perfectly in the learning process.

It is challenging to the teacher that he should always be in touch with the present change to abreast in the competition of education and in the world of education.

The present technology has changed a lot and is easily available to the students and they are more acquainted the present day technology rather than the teachers who are busy with their daily routine.

ICT Means

ICT is an interdisciplinary science primarily concerned with the collection, classification, manipulation storage retrieval and dissemination of information (Wikipedia, 2008). Abimbade (1996) saw ICT as a concept, method, function, process or system of collecting, analyzing, processing and sharing of information using electronic equipment. According to Ezekoka (2007), it is a means of accessing or receiving, storing, transforming, processing and sending ideas, perception or information through computer and their telecommunication facilities. ICT encompasses all that is involved in modern communication satellites, radio, television, video, tape recorders, compact discs, floppy diskettes and personal computers and other related equipment so that the output generated can reach the user at reasonable cost and in good time to the overall benefit of mankind

Integrating ICT in Teaching and Learning at Secondary School Level

Integrating ICT into teaching and learning refers to the process of determining which products and processes of ICT should be appropriate for give classroom situation and problems (Ifegbo, 2005). Referring to the instructional uses of ICT, the teacher is expected to acquire competencies and expertise in the utilization of ICT so as to be able to use it properly for lesson delivery. In the teaching and learning process the learner the curricular contents, the specified objectives, the materials/methods and the teacher interact in the instructional system to achieve the expected result.

Statement of the Problem

Present paper consists of Utilization of the technology in the government college of teacher education's classroom teaching practices in Mahabubnagar district.

Research Questions

The study was guided by the following research questions.

1. What are the available ICT resources used in teaching and learning in secondary schools in Mahabubnagar?
2. To what extent do teachers use ICT resources in the teaching and learning process?
3. To what extent do teachers involve students in the use of ICT resources in the teaching and learning process?
4. What are the challenges encountered by teachers in colleges in the integration of ICT in the teaching and learning process?
5. What alternative resources do teachers use in the absence of required ICT resources?

Methodology

Descriptive research design was adopted in this study to ascertain the actual utilization of ICT resources in the teaching and learning process by the secondary school teachers. The sample population consists 100 teacher sampled from teachers students in Mahabubnagar district Teacher Educational Institutes with random sample method.

Toot: A questionnaire titled "Utilization of the technology in the government college of teacher education's classroom teaching practices in Mahabubnagar district." The tool was used as the instrument to collect data. 100 respondents out of the 100 returned their questionnaire appropriately completed.

Statistical Tool: Mean, Median, Mode, SD and T-test is served as the statistical tool for data analysis for research questions.

Finding

1. 2 % of people saying that they are using CD for explaining new concepts.
2. 3% of people said that they can arrangement computer system without taking the help.
3. 12% of the student teachers said that they prepare digital lesson plans and present them.
4. 60% of student teachers feel that it is there is no need for the digital lesson as it is very difficult to prepare the lessons.
5. 20% of student teachers responded that they find digital classroom facilities will find in the schools to present my topic.
6. 6% of student teachers said that they can prepare my lesson plan without having the help of others.
7. Only 18% of student teachers interested in presenting the concepts with the help of computer with projector.
8. 18% of teacher students said that they can prepare digital lessons innovatively by using various softwares.
9. 2% of student teachers said that they readily prepare a digital lesson.
10. 2% of students teachers said that they prepare a soft copy of my work regularly.
11. 42% of student teachers said that they regularly go to the computer lab.
12. 32% of student teachers said that their college has provided me ample of practice through lab timings.
13. 22% of Student teachers said that computer sir/madam regularly rectifies my doubts.
14. 25% of student teachers said that Computer lab slats has been provided to them by the institution.
15. 56% student teachers have shown interest in going to the lab.

16. 23% student teachers said that their lecturers have explained them the concepts through the computer projector.
17. 24% of Student Teachers have the opinion that there is no need of the computer lab in the College as plenty are available in outside.
18. 3% of student teachers said that they can copy the file into the pen drive or into the C.D.
19. 4% said that they get a computer system readily available to them at the college.
20. 100% of student teachers said that they have no internet facility in the computer lab.

Discussions on Findings

1. Maximum number of Student teachers have not got the knowledge of the computer CD of various subjects to explain new and difficult concepts.
2. Very few student teachers got the knowledge regarding arrangement of the new computer system without taking the help.
3. Very few student teachers have the knowledge of preparation of the digital lesson plan and present them.
4. Maximum Number of student teachers felt that there is no need for the digital lesson as it is very difficult to prepare the lessons.
5. A Few student teachers responded that they find digital classroom facilities in their schools to present their topic.
6. Few number of student teachers said that they can prepare their lesson plan without having the help of others.
7. Few strength of student teachers interested in presenting the concepts with the help of computer with projector.
8. Few teacher students said that they can prepare digital lessons innovatively by using various softwares.
9. Very few of student teachers said that they readily prepare a digital lesson.
10. Very few student teachers said that they prepare a soft copy of my work regularly.
11. Less than 50% of student teachers said that they regularly go to the computer lab.
12. Few student teachers said that their college has provided me ample of practice through lab timings.

13. A few Student teachers said that computer sir/madam regularly rectifies my doubts.
14. Only quarter of the student teachers said that Computer lab slats has been provided to them by the institution.
15. More than fifty percentage of student teachers have shown interest in going to the lab.
16. A few student teachers said that their lecturers have explained them the concepts through the computer projector.
17. A few percentage of Student Teachers have the opinion that there is no need of the computer lab in the College as plenty are available in outside.
18. Very few percentage of student teachers said that they can copy the file into the pen drive or into the C.D.
19. Very few student teachers said that they get a computer system readily available to them at the college.
20. All student teachers said that they have no internet facility in the computer lab.

Conclusion

Even if Government has placed various revolutionary amendments in the field of education to provide a qualitative education it is very difficult for the dream to be fulfilled unless every Teacher Education Institute work together in providing qualitative education to every student teacher So as to make the world citizen rather local.

Monitory mechanism will definitely make certain changes by making proper change in the ICT introduction in the teaching learning process very clearly. To become the world citizen and specially a model teacher means to have a better understanding of the present tempo of the world and its demands. So having the great interest in ICT knowing is one of the important factor for the students and meet with the demand of the world. So, it very essential to the Educational Institutions to strictly follow the educational implementation by the NCTE and SCERT.

Recommendations

1. It is very essential to make the awareness of the electronic goods to the student teachers so as they can meet the challenges easily done.
2. Practical knowledge should have to provide to every student to become good citizen.

3. Every student teacher will have to get the knowledge of preparation of digital lesson plan and present to them so that regular orientation with various tasks will be given.
4. It is very essential to equip the class with the digital lesson presentation purpose.
5. It is mandatory for the student teachers to get the good knowledge to the student by making proper groups and make them to learn how to prepare digital lesson. And the government has to help the institutions by making initiation of compulsory outcome of the student teacher.
6. As very small amount of student teachers have the ability to prepare the digital lesson and present them in the classroom so by providing orient all the student teachers must obtain the knowledge of the digital knowledge.
7. Preparation of lesson plan innovatively is very essential for the student teachers as per the competition of the present market.
8. Very few of student teachers said that they readily prepare a digital lesson.
9. Giving orientation towards digital presentation is very important so as the student teacher can prepare a soft copy of my work regularly.
10. Regular provision of timing for every student teacher on the compulsory basis bring regular changes in the learning of Digital lesson preparation.
11. Providing sufficient time for the student teachers is very essential so as to rectify their doubts.
12. Profession development in the field of digital has been very important and it provides essential need for the student teacher in their professional period.
13. Computer slats were prepared and maintained more strictly interest in going to the lab.
14. It should be very essential to give them special classes should be provided to the students where student teacher can learn the subject manner easily.
15. It is even very important to the students teacher to update in the field of digital lesson as it is the present world.
16. Every skill of the computer knowledge will have to provide to the student teacher so he can use the knowledge for his/her development.

17. Maintaining infrastructure facility and providing the system is very essential to the institute management and it is very important for getting the knowledge to the student teacher for the best provision of the next left.
18. Internet is very essential for all in the present day usage. College management necessarily taken the action for the provision of the internet connection so as the student can have very good help.

Reference

1. Abimbade, A. (1996). Principles and practice of educational technology. Ibadan: International Publishers mLimited.
2. Adekunle A. (1997). Educational opportunity through technology:A comparative analysis of Ghana and Nigeria. In the annual convention of the Nigeria Association for Educational Media and Technology.
3. Adeya, L. N. & Oyelaran-Oyeyinka, B. (2002). The internet in African Universities: case studies from Kenya and Nigeria Accessed from URL: http// www.intech.unu.edu
4. Afolabi, A. O., Adedapo, Y. A. & Adeyanju, O. L. (2005). Why college Teachers do not use ICT facilities in teaching. Journal of Learning
5. Anao, (2003). Using the computer in enhancing the accuracy of the trapezoidal rule. Nigeria Journal of Coomputer Literacy 3(1) 67-71.
6. Anekwe, J. U. (2006). Effects of constructionist based instructional model on students' interest and academic
7. achievement in French Language in Anambra State. Unpublished PhD Thesis University of Port- Harcourt Rivers State,
8. Babalola, I. & Efunbajo, (2002). The impact of teachers' access to ICT on students' achievement. Journal of Computer Assisted Learning 9(3) 63-71.
9. Ekukinami, T. U. (2002). The status of application of information technology in primary schools
10. AKSJEMT.Ile-Ife: Obafemi Awolowo University
11. Elkin, R. (1985). Attitude of Special Education personnel towards computer. Educational Technology 22(7).
12. Ezekoka, G. K. (2007). Evaluation of secondary school teachers' use of ICT for curriculum implementation.
13. Journal of Women in Academics 4(1) 210-219.
14. Ezekoka, G. K. (2008). A survey of learning resources for the teaching of Education Technology in Nigerian
15. Educational Communication and Technology Journal 33(3)
16. Kosakowski, J. (1998). The benefit of information technology in education. Retrieved June 24, 2007 from
17. http://www.Askeric.org/Uhoime/Digest
18. Liverpool, L. S. O. (2002). Information and communication technology in teacher education. In A. M.

19. Mohammed & A. Umar (Eds.) Teacher education in Nigeria: past, present and future. Kaduna: National Teachers Institute.
20. Mutula, s. M. (2003).Assessment of African telematics policy and regulatory infrastructure: potential for learning.
21. Okebukola, P. (1997). Old, new and current technology in education. UNESCO Africa 14, 1517-1518.
22. Oxfam Educational Report, (2008). A review of good practice in ICT and Special Education needs in Africa.
23. UNESCO (1998). Teachers, Teaching and New Technologies In World Education Report. Paris: UNESCO pp. 78-94.
24. World Bank, (2002). Information and Communication Technologies: A World group strategy. Washington D.C: The World Bank Group

Chapter - 24

Implementation of Right to Free & Compulsory Education Act 2009 Challenges in India

Dr. K. V. R. Srinivas

Introduction

The emerging knowledge-based economy, characterized by rapid technological changes and open and competitive economies, has placed education systems all over the world under tremendous pressure. Economic and social progress in the coming years will clearly depend on the quality of human resources-well-educated and healthy people capable of adapting to the knowledge and skill demands of the fast-changing economic scene. The education system in India is also in the midst of this fluid situation, faced with rising expectations of the people on the one hand, and the pressures of an economy undergoing structural reforms on the other. The critical requirement at this point of time is to take a long-term view and initiate strategic measures, in both policy-making and operational spheres, in order to create an education system. Having acknowledged the importance of eight years EE, the foundation of the pyramid in the education system, India first amended its Constitution by inserting Article 21-A in 2002 and then passed the RTE Act, 2009 in the Parliament.

Table 1: The Right of Children to Free and Compulsory Education Act, 2009-an Abstract

Chapter	*Title*	*Contents*
1	Preliminary	Name of the Act and Definitions
2	Right to Free and Compulsory Education	Right of child, Special provisions for children not admitted / completed EE, transfer rights

(Contd...)

3	Duties of Appropriate Government, Local Authority and Parents	Duties like provision of infrastructure, teacher"s training, quality education: Sharing of financial and other responsibilities
4	Responsibilities of Schools and Teacher	Extent of school"s responsibility, no capitation fee, no corporal punishment, no denial of admission, school recognition, no denial of admission, norms and standards for school
5	Curriculum and Compilation of Elementary Education	Examination and Completion certificate
6	Protection of Right of Children	Monitoring, grievance redressal
7	Miscellaneous	Power to make rules, issue directions
The Schedule	Norms and Standards for a School	Norms and standards for teaching and infrastructure

Source: Right to Free and Compulsory Education Act 2009

The Table gives a snapshot of the RTE Act, 2009. The Act consists of seven Chapters accompanied by Schedule. The Act effectively sums-up all actions which are required to achieve UEE. The Act has been framed keeping holistic view of education, equity, access to all especially traditionally excluded categories, gender concern, centrality of teacher, moral compulsion on all stake holders, convergent and integrated system of educational management. It also provides flexibility for States to modify some norms as per requirement.

The Act lays down minimum norms and standards for all schools, government and private, through a mandatory Schedule. This includes number of teaching days per year, number of teaching hours per day, number of rooms, availability of teaching learning materials, library, toilets, safe drinking water, playground, kitchen for mid-day meals, TPR, subject teachers in classes VI to VIII, part time art, work and physical instructors and so on.

Studies conducted on quality of education and the role of communities

Moral compulsion is imposed through the RTE Act on parents, teachers, educational administrators and other stakeholders. Pre-RTE Act some studies have been conducted to know the quality of education received by children especially impact of public participation. The study "Findings from Baseline Surveys in Three Indian States", assessed public participation, teacher accountability and school outcomes in states of MP, UP and Karnataka. It was found that at the end of grade IV only 22% in UP, 33% in MP and 73% in Karnataka could read a simple sentence. Knowledge in Mathematics was more miserable. Teacher attendance and engagement in teaching were low in MP and UP and much higher in Karnataka. One basic reason for low ratings in UP and MP was that the communities were largely uninformed or unprepared or did not have the capacity to hold teachers accountable.

The scope of the study was further extended and the researchers launched structured campaign providing information to communities about their oversight roles in schools in Karnataka, MP and UP. They found a positive impact on process and behaviour outcomes, delivery of inputs to students, teacher effort and learning outcomes in all three States. Outcomes at baseline were much higher in Karnataka suggesting greater efficiency in delivery than in MP and UP. The differences in impact may be due to the differences in the initial conditions and also in the different decentralization set-ups in different States.

Sarva Shiksha Abhiyan and RTE

The Sarva Shiksha Abhiyan ("Education for All" movement) was initiated in 2001 for achievement of Universalisation of Elementary Education (UEE). It is the flagship programme of GoI. Sarva Shiksha Abhiyan (SSA) is the culmination of all previous endeavors and experiences in implementing various education programmes. While each of these programmes and projects had a specific focus – Operation Blackboard on improving physical infrastructure; DPEP on primary education – SSA has been the single largest holistic programme addressing all aspects of elementary education. SSA is being implemented in partnership with State Governments to cover the entire country and address the needs of 192 million children in 1.1 million habitations. SSA seeks to provide quality elementary education including life skills with special focus on girls education and children with special needs. SSA will act as a vehicle for implementing the RTE Act. SSA will assist State governments in implementation. The funding for RTE will be shared by central government and State Governments in the ratio 65:35. The provisions under SSA need to be aligned with the legally mandated norms and standards and free entitlements mandated by the RTE Act.

Status of Implementation of RTE Act, 2009 in India

SSA has reviewed the implementation of RTE in all the 35 States / UT (Union Territories). The table below shows the status of implementation of RTE Act, 2009, till mid March 2011. Except two states where data is not available, almost all states / UTs have initiated the process to make EE free and compulsory though none have yet implemented RTE Act in totality.

State Rules: The appropriate Government, may, by notification, make rules, for carrying out theprovisions of RTE act. Two states have adopted the central rules on RTE, 9 States have made and notified their own rules. Only one-third of the States / UTs have notified rules and the rest are still in the process of making rules. Foremost for implementation of the Act is to prepare and notify rules. If States are lagging behind in this stage, then it indicates that they are not aware, which is not true or they do not have the required skills, which again is debatable or they are not serious in implementing the Act.

Constitution of NCPCR / SCPCR: The National Commission for Protection of Child Rights(NCPCR) or State Commission for Protection of Child Rights (SCPCR) is authorized to examine and review the safeguards for rights provided under the Act, inquire into complaints and recommend measures for effective implementation of the Act.

NCPCR is the apex monitoring body for implementation of the Act. As part of monitoring, they have initiated social audits of Government schools under 250 Gram Panchayats across 10 States. They are also studying how SDMCs can effectively monitor the administration and management of primary schools under Section 21 of the Act.

Where the SCPCR has not been constituted in the State, a temporary authority i.e., Right to Education Protection Authority (REPA) should be constituted which has the same powers and responsibilities as SCPCR. As depicted in the Table, 3 states / UTs have constituted REPA and 8 have constituted SCPCR. Two-thirds of the states are yet to constitute the Commission which monitor s childs RTE.

Academic Authority: The Academic Authority will look into the academic matters. Thecurriculum and evaluation procedure shall be laid down by the said authority. The Authority has been notified in twenty States, in three States dual authorities have been notified. Generally States have notified SCERT (State Council of Research and Training) as the academic authority.

Eight years Elementary Education Cycle: Elementary education of eight years forms thefoundation for future education and to gain better life skills. The States can be grouped into two: those having seven year EE and those having eight year EE cycle. But now all States need to follow eight year EE cycle. Two-thirds of the states have adopted eight year cycle.

No Detention policy: No child admitted shall be held back in any class or expelled from schooltill the completion of EE in a school. The instructions have been issued by 26 States and 5 States are in the process of issuing. But child-centered teaching and continuous evaluation are alien to a system accustomed to eliminating a majority of children by declaring them „fail' sooner or later. Also, the quality of education a child receives has to be continuously monitored.

No corporal punishment: As per this Act no child shall be subjected to physical punishment ormental harassment. Whoever contravenes the provision shall be liable according to the disciplinary action under the service rules applicable to such person. Such instructions have been notified by 27 States / UTs and 4 are in the process of adopting.

No Board Examinations: No child shall be required to pass any Board examination tillcompletion of EE. Twenty-five States/UTs have notified the rules. To counteract the ill-effects of this rule that may lead to decline in educational quality received by the child, the act envisages for comprehensive and continuous evaluation of childs understanding of knowledge and his / her ability to apply the same.

Private tuitions, Screening procedure and Capitation fees: As per RTE rules, no school orperson shall collect capitation fee and subject the child or his parents to any screening procedure during admission. Also, teachers are banned from engaging in private tuitions. Instructions on these rules have been issued by 19 States.

Working days / Instructional hours: The Act has fixed minimum number of working days andinstructional hours in an academic year separately for primary and upper primary classes. For primary classes (first class to fifth class), a minimum of 200 working days and 800 instructional hours have been fixed. For upper primary (sixth class to eight class) a minimum of 220 working days and 1000 instructional hours have been fixed. Notices on these instructions have been issued by 13 States and 20 are in the process of adopting.

As per DISE Flash Statistics 2009-10, the average working days in all states for all schools is Manipur, Meghalaya, Nagaland and Kerala have less than 200 working days on an average. The percent of Lower Primary Schools with Less than 200 Working Days (Government & Aided Managements) is 5.92 %. The percent of Upper Primary Schools/Sections with Less than 220 Working Days (Government & Aided Managements) is 30.28 %. This indicates that more Upper primary schools have to increase their working hours as compared to primary schools to meet the minimum requirement.

As can be seen from the above Tables, only three States of Haryana, Madhya Pradesh and Sikkim have fully adopted the various rules mentioned in the Act. Various States are in different stages of enforcing RTE Act. Various circulars have been issued to notify the rules. The timing of issue of circular is also important. Goa government issued circular for not detaining any students and infact promote them to the next class, after the schools already had declared their results, in which several students were failed. But no State / UT has implemented the Act even after completion of one year of RTE act enforcement. To know how many States will actually implement the Act, one has to wait till the next academic year 2012-13.

Other Provisions in the RTE Act

Reservation of 25% seats in schools: As per the Act, Private unaided and special categoryschools shall admit atleast 25% of students from weaker sections and disadvantaged groups. This provision has been widely challenged. There is pressure on Ministry of HRD as several petitions are lined up in the Supreme Court by private schools for excluding them from this reservation.

Teacher Pupil Ratio: The schedule of the RTE Act prescribes minimum TPR for classes I to Vas 1:30 and for classes VI to VIII as 1:35. TPR for all States is at 1:33. At primary level it is 1:33 and at upper primary level it is 1:31. But the problem is the disparities across various States. In Bihar, U.P. and Jharkhand the number of pupils per teacher is 57, 47 and 45 at primary level and 61, 44 and 47 at upper primary level respectively. While allocating resources the *status quo* in various States has to be analyzed and accordingly allocation has to be done.

Duties of appropriate authorities: There is a certain overlap and complementarities infunctioning of authorities. However, the appropriate government shall lay down policy, prescribe curriculum, make arrangements for teacher recruitment and their proper deployment, and make financial arrangements, and provide technical support. The local authority on the other hand will ensure the enumeration, admission and attendance of children, school mapping and availability of neighbourhood schools, and monitoring.

Challenges with RTE

The main challenge is with respect to the allocated budgets to fructify this act. The Center and the States have to share the financial responsibility of RTE in the ratio of 65:35. The Finance Commission has already provisioned '24,000 crore annually and the Center has also made a provision of '15,000 crore and '21,000 crore in Budget 2010-11 and 2011-12 respectively towards the same. Going by the RTE and its objective, this budget is considered much lower than the requirement.

Academic experts are of the opinion that though the budget may have presented an optimistic picture with an overall increase for allocation to education it does not reflect on the preparedness of the States with respect to RTE on counts related to finance and infrastructural facilities.

According to experts, RTE Act is a non-starter because of grossly inadequate budgetary provisions for rolling it country-wide. Although the Expenditure Finance Commission has suggested a 65:35 Centre-State share, most state governments with huge deficits are demanding for larger Central assistance. For instance, Uttar Pradesh Government has refused to implement the Act unless the contribution by the Centre is 90% while a few other State Governments like West Bengal, Gujarat, Goa and Haryana are demanding for a 75:25 funding pattern.

Now, the next challenge is to implement the 25 percent reservation for disadvantaged and economically weaker section children, keeping all children in school until class VIII while reaching acceptable standard learning levels, monitoring private schools recognition, establishing School Management Committees that function well, and all done with similar mechanism in all States and Union Territories.

RTE has made it compulsory for all aided and unaided private schools to reserve 25 percent of total seats in elementary education for disadvantaged and economically weaker section children. These so called reserved seats, that promise free education, would only give relief from tuition fees and not from other expenditures – which are quite considerable. The RTE does not consider the cost of school books, education tools, co-curricular fees, extra tuition needed and fees demanded in other development activities, which are quite high in good private schools.

To ensure proper school mapping and availability of neighbourhood schools, a GIS (Geographic Information System) mapping of schooling facilities could assist the appropriate Governments to understand the geographic dispersal of schools, the distance to schools from the habitations and the physical barriers, if any, as some State Governments are already doing. This would require the appropriate Government and the local authority to work in unison.

RTE Act has already made it compulsory for all schools to maintain a student to teacher ratio of 30:1. Various pan-India surveys indicate that currently schools are struggling with a ratio of 50:1 (and some schools with 80:1), not to rule out those schools which are running with just a single teacher. With many teacher positions vacant, the attainment of such globally-practiced ratios seems quite challenging. In addition to this an equal amount of untrained teachers are at the primary level, who have to be trained to match the qualification prescribed by the RTE within the next five years.

Besides having parameters to measure the inputs to ensure the UEE, there is an unequivocal requirement for ensuring the quality of the outcomes achieved. Quality of outcomes refers specifically to the learning levels of the children, the difference which has come about in retention and survival rates of children, and whether or not the coming about of this act has had any positive impact on the transition rate of children from primary to upper primary levels.

A direct co-relation needs to be established and strictly monitored periodically as to how input in terms of infrastructural guarantees, accessibility to neighbourhood schools, availability of qualified teachers assures the certificate issued on the finishing of eight years of free and compulsory education actually reflects the enhanced reading and writing skills of the children between the age of 6 to 14 years.

There is an urgent need to expedite the execution of the provisions of this Act, which is primarily the responsibility of the central and state governments working alongside local authorities. There needs to be an in-built mechanism to ensure that the adoption of the provisions of the Act is done with reference to concrete goals, which can realistically be achieved through inputs being fed into the system by the means of the RTE Act.

Conclusion

Education is a key to economic development and the enjoyment of many other human rights. Education provides a means through which all people can become aware of their rights and responsibilities, which is an essential tool for achieving the goals of equality and peace. Half a century after the Constitution of India directed the States (Concurrent list) to ensure free and compulsory education for every child aged 0-14 in the republic, followed by the Millennium Declaration of United Nations and amendment of the Constitution in 2002, the Right to Free and Compulsory Education Act, 2009 was unanimously passed by Parliament in August 2009 and became effective from April 1, 2010.

We are yet to get the Act off the ground; State Rules which govern the implementation of the Act have been notified by very few States. There is shortage/excess of teachers in places; basic facilities like toilets, drinking water are also not available in required number. One of the major issue is inadequate budgetary provisions and the debate of who (Centre or the State) should bear a larger share. The Right to Education does not limit education to the primary or the first stage of basic education, or among children of a particular age group. The Right to Education is also not an end to itself, but an important tool to acquire basic human skills thus improving the quality of life. The RTE Act mandates several substantive reforms that are systemic in nature. States/UTs would need to issue appropriate rules and government orders for implementing the entire gamut of provisions. The biggest challenge is to have an integrated approach to synthesize and integrate the wide variety of provisions, strategies and interventions.

References

1. Madhav Godbole, *"Elementary Education as a Fundamental Right"*, Economic and Political Weekly December 15, 2001.
2. Arun Mehta *"Elementary Education In India"*, Analytical Report 2006-07 and 2007-08,NUEPA.
3. Tooley, James,"*The Global Education Industry"*, 2nd edition, Institute for Economic Affairs, London 2001.
4. Mohammad NiazA sadullah and Nazmul Chaudhury, *"Madrasas and NGOs:*
5. *Complements or Substitutes? Non-State Providers and Growth in Female Education in Bangladesh"*, World Bank Research Paper, 2008, WPS 4511.
6. Felipe Barrera-Osorio1,*"The Impact of Private Provision of Public Education: Empirical.*
7. *Evidence from Bogotá Concession Schools, Impact Evaluation"*, Series no. 10,WPS4121.
8. B.C. Mehta &KrantiKapoor, "*Implementing Right To Education Act*", 07 March, 2010.
9. GoK,*"Human Development in Karnataka"* 1999, Planning Department, Government of Karnataka, Bangalore.
10. The Indian Express, June 16, 1998.
11. Kaul, Rekha, *"Caste, Class and Education: The Politics of the Capitation Fee*
12. *Phenomenon"*, Sage Publications, New Delhi, 1993.
13. Bhatty, Kiron, *"Educational Deprivation in India: A Survey of Field Studies"*, Economic and Political Weekly, Vol XXXIII, Nos 27 and 28, July 4 and 11, 1998, pp 1731-40, 1858-63.
14. 1996 estimates of the Department of Public Instruction, Government of Karnataka.
15. Ramachandran, Vimla, *"Bridging the Gap Intention and Action: Girls' and Women'sEducation in South Asia"*, ASPBAE, UNESCO- PROAP, New Delhi, 1998.

16. Swaminanthan, Mina : *"Where have All the Children Gone?"*, The Hindu, November 14, 1999.
17. J.N. Panday, *"Constitutional Law of India"*, 24th edition, Allahabad publication.

Chapter - 25

Combating the Challenges: Education and Nation Building

Dr. T. Sasikanth Reddy

Abstract

Education contributes significantly in the development of any nation. It makes the nation economically, culturally, socially and morally rich. To enable a child morally strong, education has its significant contribution. It is well known fact that a nation is a group of people who share history, tradition, culture, religion, and language. The subject of any nation generally has a common national identity. Thus, nation building is the building or development of that common identity. Nation building is a social process and it takes a long time. All these aspects will be possible only when the citizens of a nation are educated.

This paper first attempts to give an overview on education, briefly depicts primary, secondary and higher education. Then the paper highlights the contribution of education in nation building, aims at the present challenges in women's education, disabled students' education and SC/ST students' education and throws light on the equal opportunity of education to all.

***Key Words**: nation building, modernization, globalization, women education, disabled students' education, SC/ST students' education*

Objectives of the Paper

1. Globalization and nation building.
2. Contribution of education in nation building.
3. Women's education and nation building.
4. Education of disabled students and nation building.
5. SC/ST students' education and nation building.

But before analyzing the proposed issues, it would be apt to discuss briefly the concept and forms of education.

Education: A General Overview

David E. Bloom asserts that 'general education emphasizes on the development of the whole individual, and not just occupational training. It highlights the ability to think, communicate and learn and to adopt a broad historical, comparative and disciplinary perspective on different Issues' *(Universities and Globalization,* 146). Education literally means 'to learn or to train'. In the largest sense, education is any act or experience that has a formative influence on the mind, character, and ability of an individual and in the technical sense, education is that entity which is transformed by society to the coming generations such as its accumulated knowledge, skills, merits, values, familiarity, and insights. Dr. Upasna Sharma has noted 'the term 'education' is derived from the Latin word educate' which means bringing up a child, both physically and mentally' *(Education in Third World and India,* 95). Schools, colleges and universities are the temples of learning. But the basic fact can never be overlooked that we all start learning since the time of our and that it lasts till our last breath. The first educational institution is one's own home and mother is regarded as the first teacher.

Primary Education and Secondary Education

The first five-seven years of formal and basic education that is five or seven years of schooling beginning from the age of five or six is called primary education. The education for children aging 6-14 has been made compulsory as well as free in many countries. Primary education is regarded as the fundamental right of the children and various articles of Indian constitution insists for primary education for all children irrespective of sex, colour, religion, and region. Although Indian government has banned child labour but still a large number of children are working in hazardous factories. Dr. J.C. Pant has noted 'a quality basic education will better equip girls and boys with knowledge and skills needed to adopt healthy lifestyles, to protect themselves from HIV/AIDS and other sexually transmitted diseases, and to take an active role in social, economic and political decision-making as they transit to adherence and adulthood'. *(Education in Third World and India,* 247). Secondary education is the education which one gains after completing their primary education and just before college life. Thus, it is a bridge between primary education and college or higher degree.

Higher Education

The meaning of the term higher education differs from country to country. It is sometimes called as third stage or post-secondary education.

It is not compulsory for everyone to achieve higher education like primary education. Colleges and universities are the institutions where one gets higher education that comprises teaching as well as research. In many developed countries, nowadays, people are interested in getting higher education. For the national economies, higher education is very important. To quote Goolam Mohamedbhai: 'Universities are not places where one simply goes to be educated. They are institutions where the young meet to learn, reflect and debate on their society, and to develop intellectually, culturally and physically. Campus-based higher education provides the students with a unique personal experience that helps them to become better citizens later'. *(Universities and Globalization, 156).*

Globalization and Nation Building

Globalization is that process by which people, nations, governments, and companies around the globe interact and integrate with each other. The process plays a crucial impact on culture, political systems, environment, entrepreneurship and economy of the country which influences the welfare of the society as a whole. Integrating the cultural, economic and political systemof the economy is its main target and it is supposed to be a driving force for the democracy, economic growth and prosperity of a nation. All over the world it has greatly influenced the use of language. It has mixed various cultures together making it something completely new. In this globalized age nation building is a great challenge before us. R.P. Pathak writes: The modern societies of today are globally connected and interdependent. No society can remain isolated today because easy means of transport and communication are available nowadays. Besides, all the nations are committed to global co-operation for common problems (Education in the Emerging India, 101).

As far as expansion of globalization is concerned it is a time consuming process and at times it even takes centuries to track up the desired goal. The globalization in the present era has picked up the pace particularly in the past five decades. It is in practice since the Second World War resulting mainly because of planning by economists, politicians and business interests. The globalization has brought change in economic development. The economy has been affected by globalization to a large extent as it makes a lot of profit. This has become possible only because of the common ground of exchange of goods and services provided to them. Financial markets have also been affected by globalization. The financial institutions are getting every facility in the provision of lending and borrowing. Globalization has its informational aspects too that is another factor in nation building. The inflow and outflow of information having no barriers as well as easy and quick access to information is possible only when globalization pervades. Because of globalization satellites, communications, telephony, and Internet have a more and easy access. Politically, globalization tends to generate a world government, which has a much wider scope as compared to local, state or national governments. The social and economic rights to the citizens have also been influenced by globalization. When globalization infuses in a country, a strong impact on standard of living, level of consciousness, and behaviour pattern is experienced.

The above discussed points give a clue to the positive aspects of globalization. Although, the term globalization seems very small but it covers a wide range and has changed the entire global scenario. There is no meaning of distances in this global era. Despite having positive aspects of globalization, it has negative aspects also. Because of globalization the financial differences between the privileged and underprivileged countries widens. The affluent nation progresses day by day for they have sufficient resources while the poor nations are left deprived because they do not have sufficient material. The physical boundaries are not given any consideration when a country enters into a global market and the entire world is regarded as one and only one nation. In such a situation the labourers are being exploited. The rich countries get workers at cheap rate and in this way maximum exploitation of such countries are done. The next negative aspect of globalization is in the field of competitions. It is something else that competitions are considered as a congenial token of growth but on the other hand over indulgence in the same proves a disaster. In the words of Teboho Moja 'one of the key features of globalization is increased competition, which has become a driving force for innovation and entrepreneurship. Competition in higher education has increased and has become unfair'. (Universities and Globalization, 168). If a nation becomes a part of globalization, its companies ultimately enter the cut-throat competition and the entry of new companies even intensifies the competition.

From globalization's destructive and transformative effects, the nation is suffering to a large extent. The autonomous places and the kind of democracy that will be left to local politics and civil initiatives will have to be able to protect themselves within the global framework in which the mutual material and cultural dependence of a global democracy is valid. Those who take the nation-state as a line of defense assert that every local and traditional difference is preserved because of this condition. However, they ignore the reality that it is because of this same condition that entire local and regional units have altered into structures that can be thrown into the melting pot of globalization. The seeds of the globalization have been sowed by the nations and now it is reaping what it had already sown. A fundamental approach is needed by us so that we should maintain our traditions as well as criticize those traditions which are more harmful rather than helpful. We should take into account those strategies that are ready to join and contribute new proportions which are universal and helpful in nation building.

Contribution of Education in Nation Building

The aim of every nation is to have learned and educated citizens. No country will lead the path of progress until and unless its citizens are educated. For overall development of any nation, the pre-requisite factor is that its citizens should be educated. It is a critical factor in nation building. Education leads to:

Better Life

Enjoying the quality of life is every one's dream but this dream can be fulfilled only when we will have education. Educated people are less likely to suffer depression. They are more motivated to achieve the goal of life and are healthier than those who leave school at a young age because through education they become aware of the hygienic and sanitary condition.

Contributes in Democratization

In earlier days education was reserved only for a few selected persons. The rest of the population was deprived of education. They were unable to participate in the intellectual discussion. Those people were not able to understand their proper right. It is necessary that a democratic country should promote education for every citizen; only then a nation's development is possible. R. Pathak asserts 'almost all the civilized nations have organized themselves on democratic principles of freedom, equality and justice. Hence, modern man is able to exercise his rights and do his duties as well as responsibilities as citizen. He participates in making laws and elects his choicest government. He can change the government, if it is dysfunctional. Democracy is the key to modernization and civilization of today. (Education in Emerging India, 100).

Promotes Peace and Stability

Educated people generally do not want to indulge in antisocial activities. One of the major concerns of international security and harmony is the operation of peace and stability. Peace and stability operations are now regarded as a first-order, integral component for the success of any nation building. It can be generated only by educating the subjects of the nation.

Productivity and Earning is Increased

Educated people are liable to earn more in comparison to uneducated or less educated people. The more we are educated, the more we have access to technical means of promotion production. If we will have higher degree, we can have better oriented job where we can earn sufficient money for the welfare of our family as well as nation. In this way, productivity and earning is ensured.

Reduces Inequality

Uneducated people are not given proper consideration by educated people. They look at them with contemptible eyes. The problem of untouchability and outcaste are seen more among uneducated people. If the entire citizen will be educated, they will look forward for the welfare of their country and not in such trifle things of casteism.

Reduces Poverty

Poverty is another greatest hurdle in the development of any nation. More than 70 per cent of Indian population resides in villages whose main occupation is agriculture. They are not aware with .the development of new scientific inventions that are helpful in agriculture. Different sorts of fertilizers are produced day by day, but these people are unaware of these things. In this way they are not in a position to grow crops in such a way as it can be grown. If they will be educated they can utilize these facilities and, thus, they can increase the economy of the nation. In the words of V.C. Pandey: 'education is at the heart of development. The countries which have made the greatest progress in reducing poverty in recent decades are those which have combined effective and equiitable investment in education with sound economic policies. Education enables people to use and extend their capabilities, develop skills, improve their livelihoods and increase their earning potential'. (Girls Primary Education, 170).

Concern for the Environment

To promote sustainable development, the government has introduced a number of policies and different laws whose aim is to alleviate the pressures of social imbalances on natural resources. These policies are the reconstruction and development programme, a white paper on population policy, and the national crime prevention strategy. The problems of pollution, health hazards, and inadequate housing and service provision, contributing to informal sector activities and crime may result in uncontrolled settlement development. In the areas of less dense human habitation, the natural resources are under less pressure comparatively than that of those having dense population. The impacts of poverty on the environment are due to deforestation from excessive collection of wood for fuel and soil degradation through cultivation of unsuitable soils. If people will be educated, they will be conscious of the deterioration of polluted environment and its impact on their health. They will try their best to keep their environment neat and clean by different means.

Women's Education and Nation Building

V. C. Pandey acclaims: 'Educating girls has benefits at the personal, community and social levels that make it one of the most important investments that any developing country can make.... Educated women are more likely to enter the formal labour market, earn higher wages and thus contribute more directly to a nation's economic productivity.' (Girl Primary Education, 11). No one can ignore women's role in nation building. Around fifty per cent of the population of the whole world is of women. If they will be educated, they will contribute in every form for the development of their nation. But it is sad to say that women all over the world have been looked down as the weaker section. Various initiatives have been taken by Indian government to improve the educational status of women but still a lot has to be done in this field. There are several reasons that hinder women's entry into the educational field. They have to assist their mother in domestic works—cooking, bringing water, managing fuels (especially in villages), taking care of the younger children and so on. But nowadays, women cannot be regarded as the weaker section of the society. The biological distinction between male and female is an accepted truth, but now it is no longer acceptable to women in general and feminist in particular. Simone de Beauvoir in her oft-quoted book The Second Sex (1949) writes 'One is not bom, but rather becomes, a woman... it is civilization as a whole that produces this creature... Only the intervention of someone else can establish an individual as an Other'(A Reader's Guide to Contemporary Literary Theory, 130).

Women are the architect of the society. To establish the institution of family life, building the home, bringing up the children and making them good citizens, etc., depends to a large extent on women. In making an ideal family, ideal society and ideal state, they contribute positively. Men should not brush the importance of women's education aside. Women should also move forward and show their hidden talent that what they can do for the development of their nation. V.C. Pandey states, 'education is central to the achievement of greater equality in society, including between men and women. Investment in education for girls has been shown consistently to be one of the most important determinants of development, with positive implications for all other measures of progress.' (Girl Primary Education, 170).

If women will be educated, they can help in nation building by reducing maternal mortality rate as well as infant and child mortality rate. They will earn themself and will not depend on their husbands or other male members for their livelihood. They will share in their family planning and will have their own voice and suggestions in spending their earnings. V.C. Pandey underlines: 'Education for girls means that as women they will be able to exercise their rights to participate in political and economic decision-making in the community as well as in the households; that they will be able to participate in development efforts in both the household and the community.' (Girl Primary Education, 11).

Education of Disabled Students and Nation Building

The term 'disability' has been variously defined and is applied synonymously for 'handicapped', 'crippled', 'physically challenged', and so on. The disability may be of different forms— vision, speech, hearing, movement, and mental. A person who is not able to see clearly or who can partially see may be called visually disabled while speech disability means a person who is dumb. Moreover, those whose words are difficult to understand by a listener of normal comprehension and hearing will also be considered having speech disability. Hearing disability means those who cannot hear at all or who can hear only loud sounds. Similarly, those who lack limb or are unable to use limbs normally will be considered as having movement disability. And those who lack comprehension ability according to their age are mentally disabled. V.C. Pandey acclaims: 'There are many definitions of disability, not only across but also within countries. These varied definitions demonstrate that disability is a social construct as much rooted in cultural, social, political, legal and economic factors as in biology.' *(Girl Primary Education,* 247).

It is necessary to teach disabled students. Education is that organism which cannot be affected by the outer structure or beauty of a person. But generally it is seen that these disabled students are not able to continue their studies. A sense of discomfiture or inferiority is experienced by such students while studying in regular schools and colleges. To quote Jane K.

Scale, 'more seriously, some students felt that breakdowns in communication reinforced their disabilities by forcing them to identify themselves as disabled to many different people all of whom were seen as strangers" (E-Learning *and Disability in Higher Education,* 11).

Illiteracy among disabled persons living in rural areas are higher than that of living in urban areas mainly because most of the educational institutions for disabled students are located in towns. Private organizations working for the welfare of disabled students are also located in urban areas. Illiteracy among female disabled is higher than male disable because of the social mind setup of the guardians who think that girl's education is not necessary especially if she is disabled. To quote V.C. Pandey: 'Girls with disabilities are a large and diverse group whose educational needs have gone largely unnoticed by those committed to promoting either gender equity or disability equity. Evidence is scarce, but it seems clear that these girls are not faring well'. *(Girl Primary Education,* 246). Furthermore, he adds: 'Disabled children are at severe risk of exclusion from school and other social activities. Especially in the case of girls, the victims may be a burden on the family because marriage prospects may be hampered'. *(Girls Primary Education,* 246). These disabled persons are also parts of the nation. If they will be educated, they will not be burden on their family or society. They will earn their livelihood themselves. For educating such students neither special teacher nor any special books are required. The government should take stern steps for the education of disabled students.

SC/ST Students' Education and Nation Building

The condition of Schedule Castes (SC) and Schedule Tribes (ST) are still miserable. They are considered as outcaste or untouchable. Most of these people are not only uneducated but also illiterate. Dr. C.P.S. Chauhan says 'due to low level of literacy, the SC/ST parents do not appreciate the value of education for their children. They are sometimes opposed to the idea of sending their children, especially daughters, to school. The evils of child marriage and child labour are more prevalent in SC/ST communities than in non-scheduled population'. (*ModernIndian Education,* 279). For the development of any nation in the proper sense of the term, it is necessary that its whole citizen should be educated. But children belonging to these groups are not getting proper education. The children with disability from these groups and other marginal groups are entirely deprived of education. Because of their status, these people experience social discrimination, segregation, and lack of access to resources and opportunities. Schedule Tribes are living an isolated and neglected life. They do not have their own places where they can live properly. On this ground their culture is also different than others. All these aspects are responsible for the backwardness of their education. Therefore, the emphasis is given on expanding physical access to schooling for SC and ST children. Schools are being established in the areas where these people are residing. Although access to schools at primary stage is now almost universal, there still exists a gap at upper primary stages. Even if the schools which are available in the neighbourhood of SC population, have minimum facilities of infrastructure. Facilities of free textbooks, mid-day meal, stationery, uniform, transport and so on should be available to these students easily. Discrimination against SC children on the basis of their caste status as reflected in school practices and teacher's attitudes adversely affect the quality of schooling that children receive. Such type of discrimination should be uprooted to ensure quality education. In remote tribal areas, especially at upper primary stage, the physical access to schooling is still a crucial issue in some nations. The facilities of hostels for children coming from educationally deprived communities should also be maintained and expanded. Separate hostels should be monitored for girl students so that they may have a secure life.

Conclusion

To conclude it may be added that education is an important factor for the development, progress, advancement of any nation. The public life of a nation is very closely associated with education. In a situation of development and progress, education embellishes public life. By the total development process, education by its very nature gets influenced. To keep in tune with the changing requirements, expectations and call of the society, it is necessary to renew the content and process of education. Education and society are interlinked and each strengthens the other. In adverse and difficult circumstances, the citizens of a nation face many challenges and in this way nation becomes weak. For the smooth and sound progress of any nation, the entire citizen including , women, disabled persons, weaker section of the society should be highly educated. The challenges such as-political interference, shortage of teachers, outdated examination system, lack of infrastructure, caste-based reservation, problem of quality education, lack of teachers should be solved. We should never forget the fact that education is a tool for developing an economically flourishing and successful society and for establishing equity and social justice.

References

1. Abraham, M. Francis, *Contemporary Sociology, An Introduction to Concept and Theories,* Oxford University Press: New Delhi, 2006.

2. Agrawal, Meenu (Dr.), *Education in Thirt World and India,* Kanishka Publishers: New Delhi, 2008.
3. Breton, Gilles; Lambert, Michel; (eds.), *Universities and Globalization,* UNESCO Publishing: Canada, 2003.
4. Chauhan, C.P.S. Pr.), *Modern Indian Education, Policies, Progress and Problems,* Kanishka Publishers: New Delhi, 2005.
5. Pandey, V.C., *Girls Primary Education,* Isha Books, Delhi, 2004.
6. Pathak, R.P., *Education in Emerging India,* Atlantic Publishers and Distributors (P) Ltd.: New Delhi, 2007.
7. Scale, Jane K., *E-Learning and Disability in Higher Education,* Routledge: London and New York, 2006.
8. Selden, Raman, Widdowson, Peter, Brooker, Peter, *A Reader's Guide to Contemporary Literary Theory* (Quoted in this book) New Delhi, 2005.

Chapter - 26

Impact of Co-Curricular Activities on Leadership Qualities of UG Students

Rubeena Research scholar

Abstract

This study investigates the impact of co-curricular activities on leadership qualities. College graduates recognized as a community leaders we're selected from Government degree college of Nizamabad district. The study was delimited to sports, Elocution, debates, essays and athletic. The sample of 450 students was selected. Data were collected by questionnaire of leadership qualities which was developed by researcher. The data was analyze by using statistical techniques mean, standard deviation, Pearson coefficient of correlation, and t-test. On the basis of data analysis was found that co-curricular activities how significant impact on leadership qualities of undergraduate students.

Introduction

The function of education is to guide and control the formation of habit and character on the part of the individual as well as to develop his capacities and powers, so that he will become an efficient member of society (Maribeth1990). Education is, then, the great mean of controlling habit and character in complex social group. It is the basic need of every society. The society uses educational institutions as its agent of socialization. The curriculum is devised to provide desirable attitudes and experiences among youth.

Most of the classical and almost all modern educationists admit that education is not just the memorization of certain facts, figures and skills but it is all-round development of the students. So it is logical to think that co-curricular activities are the integral part of educational system. Kumar et. al (2004) commented that co-curricular activities hold a place of great importance in the field of education for the all-round development of children. Mentions have been made in various educational books, commission reports and educational plan regarding the policy, programme, activities and significance of these activities. They further added that for social, physical and spiritual development co-curricular activities are prerequisite.

Society needs mentally and physically healthy persons having qualities like creativity, leadership, hard work and honesty. Such qualities need training and practice. Textbook alone cannot develop such qualities. These qualities also acquire co-curricular activities as well. Co-curricular activities are, therefore, a series of activities related with the institutional program, which help to bring out all round development of the students, outside the subjects for examination schedule. Co-curricular activities stimulate playing, acting, singing, recitation, speaking and narrating in students. These activities guide students how to organize and present an activity, how to develop skills, how to cooperate and co-ordinate in different situations these helps in leadership qualities.

Statement of the Problem

The problem under investigation was to find out the impact of co-curricular activities on leadership qualities of UG students.

Objectives of the Study

The following were the objectives of the study:

- To find out the relationship of co-curricular activities with leadership qualities in UG students.
- To find out the impact of co-curricular activities on leadership qualities of UG students.

Hypotheses

1. There is no significant relationship of co-curricular activities with leadership qualities in UG students.
2. There is no significant impact of co-curricular activities on leadership qualities of UG students.

Tools for data collection

1. **Leadership qualities questionnaire:** researcher, by consulting the experts, developed a questionnaire containing 40 items.

2. **Proforma for Participation in Co-curricular activities:** In the Proforma co-curricular activities are listed and students are required to put a tick mark in the activity he has participated, mention the total no. of participations.

Data collection and Analysis

Data were collected by administering the questionnaire to the sample of 450 students of government degree collage of Nizamabad district. Co-curricular activities were measured by five items. Each item was assigned the value of 4. Student who responded as "Yes" to 3 items was given value of 12, student who responded as "No" to 4 items was given value of 4. In this way co-curricular activities were measured. sample was divided into two groups. Students, who scored 5 or above in cocurricular activities, were placed in participant group and students, who scored 4 or below were placed in nonparticipant group. For the analysis of data Mean, standard deviation, variance, correlation and t-test were applied.

Table 1: Data of Male Sample Non-participant and participant Group

Groups	*mean*	*SD*	*Variance*
Non-participant	4.75	.603	.364
Participant	8.76	1.90	3.63

Table 2: Data of Female Sample Non-participant and participant Group

Groups	*mean*	*SD*	*Variance*
Non-participant	7.12	2.38	5.70
Participant	8.53	2.08	4.33

Table 3: Correlation coefficient between co-curricular activities and leadership qualities of male and female sample

Groups	*variable*	*Correlation coefficient*
Male	Correlation coefficient between co-curricular activities and leadership qualities	0.630
Female	Correlation coefficient between co-curricular activities and leadership qualities	0.260

* correlation Significant at á=0.01

Table 4: Mean difference between Participant and Non-participant groups on leadership qualities for male sample

Groups	*mean*	*t value*
Non-participant	4.75	12.52
Participant	8.76	

*p< .0001

Table 5: Mean difference between Participant and Non-participant groups on leadership qualities for female sample

Groups	*mean*	*t value*
Non-participant	7.12	4.15
Participant	8.54	

*p< .0001

Findings

Following results have been obtained from the analysis of data.

The data from male sample reveals that Correlation between co-curricular activities and leadership qualities is 0.630, which is significant at α=0.01. And The data from female sample reveals that Correlation between co-curricular activities and leadership qualities is 0.260, which is significant at α=0.01.

T-test was applied on male sample for finding out mean difference between Participant and Non-participant groups on leadership qualities The data revealed that mean difference between co-curricular activities and leadership qualities is significant (t = 12.52)

T-test was applied on female sample for finding out mean difference between Participant and Non-participant groups on leadership qualities The data revealed that mean difference between co-curricular activities and leadership qualities is significant (t = 4.15)

Conclusion

The results obtained by the study reveal that co-curricular activities play a significant role in developing leadership qualities of UG students. These activities are unavoidable for achieving curricular objectives. conclusions drawn from the findings of the study are Co-curricular activities have stronger relationship with leadership qualities of male and female UG students. Co-curricular activities have stronger impact leadership qualities of male and female UG students. Co-curricular activities have significant impact on leadership qualities of UG students.

Co-curricular activities provide a chance to students for utilizing his potentials. Study also reveals that educational institutions are well aware of about importance of these activities and are managing these activities. The result show that student is availing the opportunities of enjoying these activities in society also.

References

1. Ganyon (1995). Importance of Co-Curricular Activities. Retrieved May 11,2003 fromhttp://www.moe.bsn.bn/ Co curriculum/departments.html.
2. Marsh, H. W., & Kleitman, S. (2002). Extracurricular activities: The good, the bad, and the nonlinear [Electronic version]. Harvard Educational Review, 72, 464-512.
3. Sewan. (1999). Purpose of Co-Curricular Activities. Retrieved May 7,2003 from http://www.redlands.nsw.edu.au./ Pdf/cpdfs/preparatory school.pdf.html
4. Soderberg, Melissa Boocock TITLE Student Leadership and Participation in Independent School Activities: Culture Created in Schools. Columbia Univ., New York, NY. Esther A. and Joseph Klingenstein Center for Independent School Education.
5. Thomas and Morrison (1995). Characteristics of Leadership. Retrieved May 7,2003 fromhttp://www.redlands.nsw.edu.au./df/leadership preparatory school.pdf.html.
6. Wellon, S.J. (2000). Definition of Co-Curricular Activities. Retrieved April 13,2003 from http://www.galaxy.edu.np/abtgal.html.

Chapter - 27

Pre-Service Teachers' Attitudes towards Blended Learning

Navitha S. Nair and Pheiga Gangmei Dinjanglu

Abstract

The influence of information and communication technologies can be visible in all segments of modern society, namely, economy, medical service, international relations, education, etc. Contemporary education has to follow this global change in order to meet the goal of education and today, educational stakeholders appreciate the endeavor of both online learning and face-to-face learning environment in enhancing the quality of education. Blended learning is one of the relatively versatile concepts emerged as a result of the intervention of information and communication technology to education. Blended learning has been introduced as an opportunity to improve the teaching and learning process by harmonizing the pros and cons of on-ground and online learning settings (Caner, 2012).The purpose of this research work is to investigate the attitudes of pre-service teachers' towards blended learning. The current study also examines the relationship between various aspects of blended learning, such as online learning, learning flexibility, study management, technology, classroom learning, and online interaction. This study is quantitative in nature, an adopted survey questionnaire is utilized for gathering data from 75 pre-service teachers', and purposive sampling technique is used for sample selection. Mean, standard deviation, t-test and Pearson moment correlation are used to analyze the data statistically. Based on the statistical analysis, results are discussed and conclusions are arrived at.

***Keywords**:* Blended learning, face-to-face learning, and online learning.

Introduction

Information technology has an indispensable role in the current century with each passing day a unique software or gadget is being introduced into the world. Rapidly changing internet technologies have forced our education institutions to transform and challenge the way it delivers discourse to the diverse needs of the students. This change has an effect upon the higher education institutions and continuously demanding to improve the quality of learning and teaching at these institutions. Learning is a social process, where teachers, as well as the learners, utilize effective learning strategies to achieve the demands of the school and higher education curricula. This statement is supported by Garrison and Vaughan (2008, pp: 32) "Education *is a structured learning experience designed to achieve intended outcomes effectively and expeditiously"*. In recent years, the most striking invention in the field of education is the incorporation of information and communication technology in education. The information and communication technology (ICT) has become a tool for enhancing student's learning, teacher's instruction and institutional administration (Kirschner and Woperies, 2003). Also, this technology has accelerated the process of teaching and learning by providing more flexible ways of learning. In the opinion of Livingstone (2015) higher education institutions must make every attempt to replace teacher- centered strategies with more student- centered approaches. In teacher- centered learning, learners' put all their focus on the teacher, students work alone and as a result collaborative learning is discouraged. It also prohibits the learners to express their thoughts and moreover, they become passive learners' in the entire learning process. On the contrary, in student centered approach, students act as the fulcrum where the entire learning process happens. Gibbs (1995) stated that student-centered learning as emphasizes on learner activity rather than passivity, students' experience on the learning outside the institution and prior to the course, process and competence, rather than content of learning (as cited in Wijayanthi & Listiani () pp.1). Weimer (2012) stated the characteristics of student- centered learning: explicit skill instruction encourages students to reflect on what they are learning and how they are learning, encourages collaboration and motivates students by giving them some control learning process. Over the past several decades, a wide range of technologies has emerged with an intention to assist teaching and learning. Blended learning is one of the relatively versatile concepts emerged from the influence of information and communication technologies on education. It is one of the strategies many higher education institutions have opted for student centered learning. The term blended learning first appeared around 2000 and was at that time often associated with simply supplementing traditional classroom learning with self-study e-learning activities (Khan, 2015, pp. 160). Today this mode of learning has been obtaining significant attention and its purpose is to establish a balance between face-to-face learning and online learning.

Blended learning- A shift from traditional classroom learning

According to Singh and Reed (2001) blended learning is the transfer of "right" skills to the "right" person at the "right" time by matching the "right" learning technologies with the "right" learning style for the purpose of achieving the learning objectives (as cited in Shivam & Singh, 2015, pp. 369). Tayebinik and Puteh (2012) discussed blended learning as a combination of instructional modalities, especially face-to-face and online learning. Graham, Woodfield, & Harrison (2013) viewed that, this pedagogical approach combines on- line (asynchronous and / or synchronous) and face- to –face contact time between lecturers and students and / or between students in a course. Likewise, Watson (2008) defined blended learning as combining online delivery of educational content with the best features of classroom interaction and live instruction to personalize learning, allow thoughtful reflection, and differentiate instruction from student-to-student across a diverse group of learners (as cited in Caner, 2012, pp. 24). Garrison and Vaughan (2008) observed this form of learning as one that effectively included the right mix of learning environments to enhance the learning experience and offer a student- centered, self-paced, flexible and multifaceted approach to the learning and teaching process (as cited in Birbal et al., 2018, pp. 9). Furthermore, (Zurita, et al., 2015) stated that blended learning assists in developing skills, namely, communication, creativity, information literacy and collaboration. These are the relevant skills which are required for a learner in this twenty- first century, thus their potentiality to earn these skills is dependent on their preparedness as well as readiness to learn in a technology driven learning environment. In order to acquire these skills, blended learning can be used as an excellent pedagogical approach which provides opportunities to lecturers and students to indulge in meaningful interaction and discussion in an asynchronous and synchronous environment. It is now a standard part of the education and training lexicon (Dzakiria et al., 2006. pp: 12).

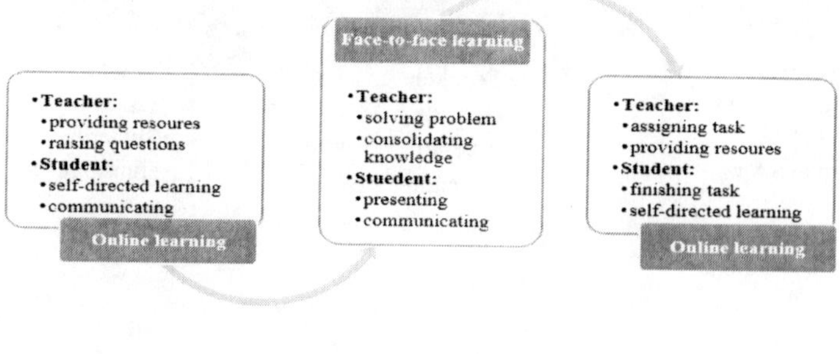

The Framework of Blended Approach.

Adapted from "Blended Learning versus Traditional Learning: A Study on Students' Learning Achievements and Academic Press", by Wei et al., 2017.

Comparing blended learning to traditional classroom learning, there are many potential benefits the former mode of learning has. At first, assisting learners' in their learning achievements.Secondly, nurturing creative and critical thinking and also assist them to instill control over learning followed by increasing learners' level of satisfaction in learning and reducing the stress level. Finally, to develop a sense of sharing attitude amongst students. While the latter mode of learning gives emphasis on teacher and furnish pedagogy which is content- oriented. In addition to this, traditional classroom learning does not promote the interaction between the instructor and students, which further blocks collaborative learning amongst learners. The aim of blended learning is not to replace the teacher but alters the role of the teacher from a mere disseminator of knowledge, which a traditional classroom demands, to a facilitator and a mentor. In a conventional learning process, prior to discourse students examine the content which the teacher is going to address and during the class, the instructor delivers new knowledge and information, which is devoid of students' interaction. As a result of blended learning, now classroom instruction has become student-oriented, interactive, and learning becomes independent of time and place, rather than teacher- centered.

However, technology integrated instruction maintains a suitable balance between online instruction and teacher-led instruction but does not lessen the role of the teacher. As we all know that the persistent concern of every teacher is- provide a better learning experience, who offers a personal learning experience, guidance, compassion and encouragement to the learners, which no technology integrated learning can offer.

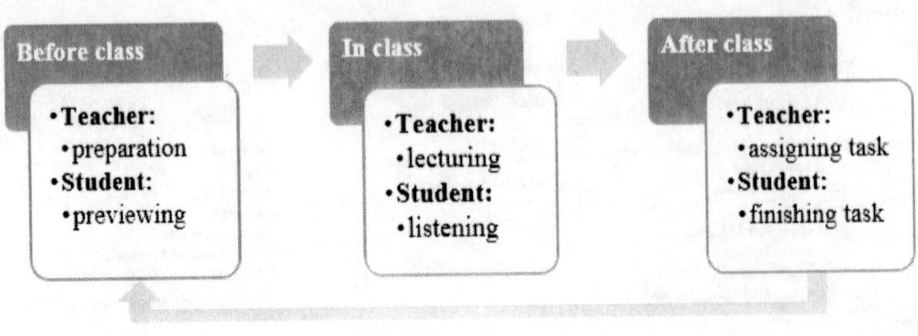

The framework of Traditional approach

Adapted from "Blended Learning versus Traditional Learning: A Study on Students' Learning Achievements and Academic Press", by Wei et al., 2017.

To sum up, blended learning is a robust model of teaching, an intermix of e-learning and classroom instruction to accomplish the goal of education. In this context, we can infer that blended learning has become an incitement to rethink traditional and rediscover the learning community (Garrison &Vaughan 2008) and an integrating platform that seamlessly connects the real and virtual educational world (pp. 32). In recent years, the relevance of blended learning has increased, the American Society for Education and Development ((Rooney, 2003) defined blended learning as one of the top ten trends in the knowledge delivery industry (as cited by Graham, 2006).

Literature Review

An increasing amount of research works have been carried out on blended learning which indicated that technology integrated learning is more efficacious and systematic in ameliorating students' learning achievements. A recent study by Akbarov et al. (2018) investigated university students' attitudes toward blended learning and traditional classroom in EFL context among 162 participants. The study reported that students prefer blended learning over traditional classroom learning and also revealed moderately positive attitude infographics and paperless classroom within EFL environment. Along the same lines, Senn (2008) surveyed 51 graduate students' and conducted case studies on students' attitude towards blended and face- to- face instruction and reported that students preferred blended learning over face-to-face, because they enjoyed the flexibility of the online format but were eager to meet in the face-to-face setting for extra instructional support. Findings from similar research conducted by Thiyagu (2011) among 150 B.Ed trainees' demonstrated that students had positive perceptions of blended learning.

In 2009, Larson and Sung had done a survey study among 168 college students on blended learning and face- to- face learning and found that students were more motivated and satisfied with blended and online learning in comparison to face-to-face interaction. In an investigation to blended learning: Uncovering its transformative potential in higher education, Garrison and Kanuaka (2004) showed that blended learning is consistent with the values of traditional higher education institutions and also proved that it has the potential to enhance the efficiency and effectiveness of meaningful learning experience. In a study which is set out to determine the effect of blended learning model on high school students' biology achievement and on their attitudes towards the internet, Yapici and Akbayin (2012) revealed that the blended learning model contributed more to the students' biology achievement than traditional teaching methods and that the students attitudes towards the internet developed statistically significantly. A similar study by Hoic-Bozic et al. (2009) inquired the effects of blended learning at a university in teaching methods in information science course by using a learning management system and reported that students' were satisfied with this new pedagogical approach and their academic achievement was above par. In addition, Tang et al. (2013) investigated the university students attitude towards readiness for blended learning and found that students had a positive relationship towards blended learning, had a negative relationship towards classroom learning and technology integration in education was not an impediment to the students. Overall, these studies outline the need for combining face-to-face instruction with an online delivery mode and also promote collaborative learning experiences among learners.

Research Questions

In light of the above literature studies, the purpose of this study is to investigate pre-service teachers' attitudes towards various dimensions of blended learning. Few research questions are formulated in order to accomplish this purpose:

1. Which aspect of blended learning is perceived more by the participants?
2. What is the relationship between the different dimensions of blended learning?
3. Are there any significant differences in pre-service teachers' attitudes towards blended learning related to their gender?

Methodology

This study is quantitative nature which utilized a survey research methodology. A total of 75 pre-service teachers' participated in the present study, out of which 30 (40 %) were males and 45 (60 %) were females. Age group of the samples ranged from 22 to 30 years and all these participants were at their first year, pursuing B.Ed course from a private college located in Ranga Reddy Dist, Telangana. Purposive sampling technique was used to select the participants. An adapted survey questionnaire from Bribal et al (2018) was used to inspect students' attitude towards various dimensions of blended learning. This tool comprised of 37 items which intended to measure pre-service teachers' attitude towards six dimensions of blended learning: Technology (4 items), Learning Flexibility (4 items), Online Learning (10 items),Study Management (5 items), Classroom Learning (5 items), and Online Interaction (9 items). Respondents were asked to express their attitude to each of these dimensions on a five-point Likert scale ranging from Strongly Disagree to Strongly Agree. Items on learning flexibility raised issues such as students' access to learning materials and how far they have the freedom to learn at their own pace. Classroom learning focused on learners' preferences for face-to-face interaction and items on technology aimed at measuring how far students' are acquainted with virtual learning techniques. Online learning comprised of items on students' opinion on delivering instructions online and self- directed learning. Study management referred to how capable and motivated students' are in organizing their time and studies through online mode. Online interaction referred to learners' ability to cope with digit technology to collaborate with other students and to interact with lecturers.

Analysis of Data and Findings

Descriptive and inferential statistics, such as Mean, Standard deviation, t-tests, and Product Moment Correlation were used to analyze the data. These tests were performed with the help of the Statistical Package for Social Sciences (SPSS-v- 22).

Research question 1: Which aspect of blended learning is perceived more by the participants?

Descriptive statistics like mean and standard deviation was used to determine which aspects of blended learning are perceived more by the respondents. Out of the six blending factors participants rated technology (M = 4.73) followed by learning flexibility (M = 4.28), then online interaction (M = 4. 25) as the important factors of blended learning. Classroom learning was observed (M= 2.23) as the least perceived aspect of blended learning.

Table 1: Mean and Standard Deviation of pre-service teachers' attitudes towards blended learning aspects.

Aspects of blended Learning	*N*	*Mean*	*Standard Deviation*
Technology	75	4.73	.444
Learning Flexibility	75	4.28	.464

(*Contd...*)

Online interaction	75	4.25	1.184
Study Management	75	3.81	1.162
Online Learning	75	3.37	1.429
Classroom Learning	75	2.23	.855

Research question 2: What is the relationship between the different dimensions of blended learning?

Inferential statistics Pearson Moment Correlation was used to investigate the relationship between various dimensions of blended learning. Results showed that technology and study management had the strongest correlation ($r = .462$, $p < .01$). However, significant positive relationship was found between technology and online interaction ($r = .321$, $p < .01$). On the other hand, positive relationship was observed between learning flexibility and study management ($r = .281$, $p < .05$), and online interaction and study management ($r = .277$, $p < .05$).

Table 2: Pearson Product Moment Correlations: Relationship between the Blended Learning dimensions

Dimensions	*Technology*	*Learning Flexibility*	*Online Interaction*	*Study Management*	*Online Learning*	*Classroom Learning*
Technology	1	.210 .071	.321** .005	.462** .000	.036 .760	-.037 .754
Learning Flexibility		1	.199 .086	.281* .015	.177 .130	-.085 .468
Online Interaction			1	.277* .016	-.019 .869	-.117 .317
Study Management				1	-.053 .653	-.032 .782
Online Learning					1	-.135 .247
Classroom Learning						1

**Correlation is significant at the .01 level.

*Correlation is significant at the .05 level.

Research question 3: Are there any significant differences in pre-service teachers' attitudes towards blended learning related to their gender?

Results from Table 3, revealed that there were no significant differences in male and female participants attitudes towards various dimensions of blended learning.

Table 3: Comparing pre-service teachers' attitudes towards blended learning based on their gender, using t-tests.

Dimensions of blended learning	*Gender*	*N*	*Mean*	*S.D*	*t*	*Sig*
Technology	M	30	4.733	.443	.915	.731
	F	45	4.727	.446		
Learning Flexibility	M	30	4.308	.463	1.00	.536
	F	45	4.261	.465		
Online interaction	M	30	4.250	1.185	.740	.604
	F	45	4.251	1.185		
Study Management	M	30	3.806	1.185	.864	.710
	F	45	3.827	1.141		
Online Learning	M	30	3.386	1.146	.851	.906
	F	45	3.366	1.403		
Classroom Learning	M	30	2.141	.768	.129	.157
	F	**45**	**2.301**	**.908**		

Discussion

The answer to the first research question was technology. Technology integrated learning offers a plethora of learning opportunities like communicate with lecturers, and other students across the world and also, limitless access to course materials. Hence, this aspect of blended learning was perceived and appreciated more by the respondents. In addition to this, learners' valued the contributions of learning flexibility and online interaction furnished by blended learning which enabled the students to work at their own pace and permitted them to collaborate well with others through a virtual medium. However, classroom learning was the least perceived dimension of blended learning which indicated that participants are not comfortable with the teacher-oriented and content-centered pedagogical model. This lines up with the findings reported by Akbarov et al. (2018, pp.66) revealed that students prefer blended learning to the traditional classroom in the EFL context.

Regarding gender impact, there were no significant differences in male and female participants' attitudes towards various dimensions of blended learning. This aligns with the findings reported by Bunz et al. (2007) and Hung et al. (2010) found that there were no differences in attitudes toward online learning between male and female students.

Furthermore, the correlation analysis in this study showed a strong positive relationship between technology and study management and technology and online interaction. This shows that pre-service teachers' are comfortable with web-platform, learn effectively through online interaction and also be capable to organize time while virtual learning.

The positive relation between technology and online interaction has been proven with previous studies on blended learning done by Bribal et al (2018, pp.28). Similar findings were reported by Hauser et al (2012) and Vance (2012) on students' attitudes toward technology and success in blended learning.

Conclusion

As the findings of this study revealed that student teachers' have positive attitudes toward blended learning, hence it is imperative to educate all educational stakeholders about the concept of blended learning, its benefits, and shortcomings. Additionally, during online learning due importance should be given to the varied learning styles of the learners' in order to cater to the learning needs of our students. Most importantly, while imparting blended learning lessons balance between online and classroom strategies should be maintained in order to attain the lesson objectives.

Effective teaching and learning happens when the instructors use a variety of methods, strategies, and approaches in their discourse and good learners will employ different learning strategies. This type of teaching and learning will maximize knowledge acquisition and offer diverse learning opportunities for both students and teachers.

The rapid development, as well as the convergence of technology and integration of this technology into education, has opened up novel opportunities to learners. By virtue of this blending, learners' are no longer being hitched to a standardized curriculum; instead, learning has become more collaborative, flexible and lifelong. Thus, blended learning or paperless classroom or virtual classroom or digital learning should be inevitably being a part of every education institutions as a way to enrich teaching and learning. I would finally conclude with the Wagner (2016) definition "blended learning as a blend of different learning modes and materials coordinated to help learners to meet their own educational goals and objectives more effectively than learning in the traditional environment".

References

1. Akbarov, A., Gonen, K. & Aydogan, H. (2018). Students' attitudes toward blended learning in EFL context. *Acta Didactica Napocensia, 11 (1),* 61- 68.

2. Birbal, R., Ramdass, M. & Harripaul, C. (2018). Student teachers' attitudes towards Blended Learning. *Journal of Education and Human Development,7 (2),* 9-26.
3. Bunz, U., Curry, C., & Voon, W. (2007). Perceived versus actual computer-email-web fluency. *Computers in Human Behavior, 23(5)*, 2321–2344.
4. Caner, M., (2012). The definition of blended learning in higher education. In P. Anastasiades (Ed.), Blended Learning Environments for adults: Evaluations and Frameworks (pp. 19- 34). Retrieved from http://www.academia.edu/2115266/
5. Dzakiria, H., Mustafa, C. S., & Bakar, H. A. (2006). Moving forward with blended learning (BL) as a pedagogical alternative to traditional classroom learning. *Malaysian Online Journal of Instructional Technology (MOJIT), 3*(1), 11-18.
6. Garrison, R., & Vaughan, H. (2008). *Blended learning in higher education: Framework, principles and guidelines*. New York: John Wiley & Sons.
7. Garrison, D. R. & Kanuka, H. (2004).Blended learning: Uncovering its transformative potential in higher education. *Internet and Higher Education,7, 95–105.*
8. Graham, C. R. (2006). Blended learning systems: Defnition, current trends and future directions. In *Handbook of blended learning: Global Perspectives, local designs*. San Francisco, CA: Pfeiffer.
9. Graham, C. R., Woodfield, W. & Harrison, J.B. (2013). A framework for institutional adoption and implementation of blended learning in higher education. *The Internet and Higher Education. 18*, 4-14.
10. Hauser, H., Paul, P., Bradley, B., & Jeffrey, L. (2012). Computer self-efficacy, anxiety, and learning in online versus face-to-face medium. *Journal of Information Technology Education, 11*(1), 141-154.
11. Hoic-Bozic, N., Mornar, V. & Boticki, I. (2009).A Blended Learning Approach to Course Design and Implementation. *IEEE Transactions on Education*, 52 (1), 19-30.
12. Hung, M. L., Chou, C., Chen, C. H., & Own, Z. Y. (2010). Learner readiness for online learning: Scale development and student perceptions. *Computers & Education, 55*, 1080–1090.
13. Khan, Ms. S. (2015). Blended Learning vs. Traditional classroom settings. *International Journal of Nursing,* 2 (1), 158- 161.
14. Kirschner, P. and Woperies, I. G. J. H. (2003). Mind tools for teacher communities: A European perspective. *Technology, Pedagogy and Education, 12 (1)*, 127-149. Retrieved from https://www. triangle.co.uk/jit/
15. Larson, D. K. & Sung, C. H. (2009). Comparing student performance: Online versus blended versus face-to-face. *Journal of Asynchronous Learning Networks, 13*(1), 31-42.
16. Livingstone, K. (2015). Teaching faculty's perception about implementing e-learning practices at The University of Guyana. *International Journal of Education and Development using Information and Communication Technology (IJEDICT), 11*(2), 85-103.
17. Senn, G. J. (2008). Comparison of face-to-face and hybrid delivery of a course that requires technology skills development. *Journal of Information Technology Education, 7*, 267-283.

18. Singh, H. & Reed, C. (2001). A white paper: Achieving success with Blended Learning. Central Software. Retrieved from http://www.centra.com/download/whitepapers/blendedlearning.pdf.
19. Tang, C. M. & Chaw, L. Y. (2013). Readiness for blended learning: Understanding attitude of university students. *International Journal of Cyber Society and Education, 6, (2),* 79-100.
20. Watson, J. (2008). *Blending Learning: The Convergence of Online and Face-to-Face Education.* Retrieved from ERIC database.
21. Wei, Y., Shi, Y., Yang, H., & Liu, J. (2017). Blended Learning versus Traditional Learning: A Study on Students' Learning Achievements and Academic Press. Retrieved from https: //www. researchgate.net/publication/319052091.
22. Wijayanti, P. R., & Listiani (). Students' satisfaction in the implementation of student centered learning. Retrieved from https://www.academia.edu/attachments/57238983/.
23. Yapici, I. U. & Akbayin, H. (2012).The effect of blended learning model on high school students' biology achievement and on their attitudes towards the internet. *The Turkish Online Journal of Educational Technology, 11 (2)*, 228-237.

Chapter - 28

A Study on Emotional Expressivity and Social Adjustment Among Adolescents

Dr. Eswari Vadlamudi

Abstract

Adolescence is a crucial period in an individual's life due to physiological changes due to which major personality and behavioural changes can be observed. Emotional expression refers to how a child conveys his or her emotional experience through both verbal and non verbal mode of communication. Social adjustment is the ability of child to adjust to the norms and standards set by the society. The major purpose of the research was to examine the relationship between emotional expression and social adjustment in adolescents. The design of the research is quantitative and descriptive. The method used was simple random sampling. The scales used are Berkeley expressivity questionnaire by Gross et al 2013 which is a 7 point scale with 16 items measuring the facets of expressivity mainly negative , positive expressivity and impulse strength. The second scale is social adjustment inventory developed by Roma Paul (1985) with 60 items and validated by Sibnath Deb and Aparna Mukherjee (2009) the research was conducted on children between the ages of 10 – 19 years of age in both sexes. Factors such as age, family type, religion and other important environmental factors were taken into consideration. Data interpretation is yet to be done. For the same, SPPSS version 21 will be used, to calculate measures of central tendency, correlation and t-test.

Key Words: *adolescence, emotional expression, social adjustment, communication.*

Introduction

Adolescence is described as the period between the ages of 13-19 years, it is described as a transitional stage between childhood to adulthood. It is also a time when several physical and psychological changes start to take place, It is a time when children start to develop specific developmental knowledge and skills, as well as learn to regulate their emotions and manage relationships. These are the attributes, abilities and skills which will later be necessary to assume adult roles.

The onset of adolescents can start early i.e preteens, and the changes during this time play an essential role in teen maturity as they start to think of themselves as individuals behavioural changes occur as they experience certain internal conflicts, challenges. The three stages of adolescents - early adolescence 12-14 where they experience certain confusion about their identity and middle adolescence is 15-17 the time when physiological changes start and finally from 17-19 when they start to make their own decisions about life and cognitive development starts.

Social Adjustment: Adjustment can be defined as 'The process of adapting or becoming used to a new situation'.(Oxford dictionary)

Thus social adjustment is 'Getting along with the members of society as best as one can' Adolescence is a period that bridges the gap between childhood and adulthood and as explained above many of the crucial behavioural changes occur with regards to adjustment and communication.

This can be defined as a conscious, intentional and continuous effort made by humans and many other creatures that live in a society/sect or together. This is in order to fit in and belong in a group. In accordance with the society's standards, values, rules and expectations one usually alters their behaviour to meet those standards. It is a psychological process that starts to happen through the process of socialization. Both animals and humans follow a pattern specific to their species during one's lifetime. All these attempts are made in order to be accepted by society. Many every day phenomenon are a result of social adjustment. To explain in simpler terms we behave in accordance to the situation and environment that we are in, for example a child in school may act in a disciplined manner since he is expected to by his teachers and he might behave in a friendly way when he is with his friends and in a relaxed manner at home. The difference is the environment not the child and as one grows and experiences cultures, values he adjusts accordingly and may change his or her values in accordance or may choose not to as well in some cases. Many concepts such as gender roles, moral values, culture, and traditions are shaped like this. All these change with time as society too changes.

Social adjustment manifests in two forms that is both in interpersonal relations, how we treat our parents, friends, siblings, colleagues, spouses our expectations etc, gender roles are of significance here. And social relations as a part of a community. The cause of adjustment is primarily the social setting and effect is the impact it has on one's behaviour. This has both positive and negative effects both for the individual and the society as one learns social skills, coping mechanisms and also many verbal and non verbal skills and important life skills, It further enhances social performance and social competence.

Emotional Expressivity

Emotional expression – The term refers to how an individual conveys his or her emotional experience through both verbal and non verbal mode of communication. Emotional experience and emotional expression are different as one could experience emotions without expressing them. Emotional expression is an important aspect of emotional regulation and affects health outcomes as well.

Feeling certain emotion such as sadness, pain, frustration and anger is a universal aspect as a living being but the expression of such emotion differs from one creature to other and one individual to another. emotional expression is often a form of communication among people thus a person may understand, interpret and judge another person when he watches the others facial expressions, body language and gestures. For example an individual cries if he is sad and slouches if he feels dejected or sorrowful and a range of expressions showcase on one's face as disgust, shame, surprise and anger etc...

These often come naturally to us and the expression at most times is unconscious but there are times an individual makes a conscious effort to alter or manipulate and make slight changes to their non verbal communication means mentioned above to form an impression on another person so that they will be judged as desired this is usually done during interviews and presentations. The manipulation is also done in art like dance, theatre and acting to tell a story. Non verbal expression though not as direct and happens naturally sometimes is a quite strong and powerful mode of transmission of emotions. Emotional expression in adolescents is an interesting feature to observe since it is the period when many experience a range of new situations and experiences occur both biologically and otherwise. It is also a time when peer pressure, societal expectations specific to gender and gender roles, major decision regarding education and career are made due to all these a regulation and control over one's emotion is put into practice and a contrast before adolescence and after can be observed. Biological changes contribute a lot to this but social situations influence just as much or if not more since one alters his or her emotional regulation according to the societal rules and standards Social rules strongly regulate expressivity for example in Japan people tend to mask displays of fear or disgust when the authority figure is present.Emotional intelligence, expressivity, personality are closely interlinked to each other as the first two have an impact in formation of one's personality.

Adolescence is the bridge between those two phases. The interesting detail to observe is that some of the trends observed are reversed during the period of adolescence in some individuals because it coincides with the onset and appearance of what are known as pubertal changes or puberty which actually refers to whole set of shifts and changes in the body system caused by the activation of sex glands. Due to the onset of many biological changes during this transitory state and also because of the inconsistencies in social environment in which they are sometimes treated as children and at other times expected to behave as an adult resulting in overly sensitive, insecure, sometimes violent and disproportionate emotional behaviour which psychologist Stanley Hall described as emotional instability but subsequent research proved that though it may not lead to things mentioned above, to a great extent the instability depends on social and cultural factors for example in simpler tribal societies where the social and cultural conditions are not very demanding the stress on the adolescent is minimal therefore instability is also minimal. Apart from this psychologists have found that emotional behaviour or expressivity is very intense as well as teenagers finding it difficult to control emotions as they are easily aroused. Mood fluctuations also play a huge part especially for young girls who start their menstruation cycle.

Objectives

1. To study the profile of the respondents.
2. To study the levels of emotional expression and social adjustment
3. To know the relationship between impulse strength and social adjustment
4. To know the relationship between negative emotional expression and social adjustment
5. To know the relationship between positive emotional expression and social adjustment
6. To know if there is a difference in emotional expression with regard to impulse strength, negative and positive expression with gender.
7. To know if there is a difference in social adjustment and gender.
8. To know if there is any relationship between certain independent variables like age, religion, economic status. Family type and number of siblings.

Hypothesis

H1: There is a correlation between impulse strength and social adjustment.

H2: There is a correlation between negative emotional expression and social adjustment.

H3: There is a correlation between positive emotional expression and social adjustment.

H4: There exists a difference between social adjustments based on gender

H5: There exists a difference between impulse strength, negative emotional expression, positive emotional expression.

Population and Sample

The researcher has taken adolescents and young adults to do the research i.e., the age group of 13 to 19 year old were taken who where students of either school or college. The research was conducted in the twin cities of Hyderabad and Secunderabad. The research used random simple sampling method to get the sample.

Research Design

The researcher has used descriptive research design which is a scientific method which involves observation and description of the behaviour of the respondent without influencing them.

Research Instruments

For this study, the researcher used interview schedule wherein a questionnaire were given to the respondents and they were supposed to choose the correct response which is best suitable for them . The two scales which were used in the question were berkely emotional expressivity scale and social adjustment inventory developed by Roma Paul (1985) with 60 items and validated by Sibnath Deb and Aparna Mukherjee (2009) .

Data Analysis

After the data collection data analysis was done by using SPSS version 20 by using various test like co-relation, t-test and measures of central tendency which are mean median and mode.

Results This study helps us to understand the relationship between Social adjustment Mean 25.11 SD is 6.226 and Emotional expressivity is mean 61.4700 and SD 12.27.

It is interesting to observe that there is difference with regard to subscales in emotional expression where mean for impulse strength is 24.14 SD 7.091 and negative expressivity mean 20.70, SD IS 4.631 positive emotional expression mean 16.63 and SD 4.469.. There is negative correlation between social adjustment and negative emotional expression r = -.269 sig = .003. there is also a negative correlation between negative emotional expression and social adjustment r = -.269 sig = .003. t- test has also been conducted to compare and know the difference between social adjustment and emotional expression with regard to gender with t = -2.271, df = 98 sig = 0.25 i.e. the mean of emotional expression in females is 65.7069 is much higher than males 55.6190And the social adjustment among women is comparatively lower than men the mean for women is 23.93 and men is 26.74.

References

1. Saarikallio, S., Vuoskoski, J., & Luck, G. (2014). Adolescents' expression and perception of emotion in music reflects their broader abilities of emotional communication. Psychology of Well-Being,4 (December), 1-16. doi:10.1186/ s13612- 014-0021-8.
2. Journal published by Kyongboon Kwon, Jessica B. Willenbrink, Amanda R. HanrahanUniversity of Wisconsin-Milwby Kaukee, USA Volume: 38 issue: 7, page(s): 908-922 Article first published online: April 20, 2017; Issue published: August 1, 2018.
3. Polliasre, Alisha & Raftery-Helmer, Jacquelyn & V. Cardemil, Esteban & E. Addis, Michael. (2016). Social Context, Emotional Expressivity, and Social Adjustment in Adolescent Males..Psychology of Men & Masculinity. 19. 10.1037/ men0000081.
4. Adam (2004). Beyond Quality: Parental and Residential Stability and Children's Adjustment, School of Education and Social Policy, North western University, pp. 56-60.
5. Cutronaet (1994). Middle childhood antecedents to progressions in male substance use: An ecological analysis of risk and protection. Journal of Adolescent Research, Vol. No. 14, pp175–205.Cutronaet (1994). Middle childhood antecedents to progressions in male substance use: An ecological analysis of risk and protection. Journal of Adolescent Research, Vol. No.14, pp175–205.
6. Raju & Rahamtulle (2006). Adjustment problem among school students journal of Indian academy to applied psychology, Vol. No.33 (1), pp. 45-50 V. Ramaprabou (2002). The effect of Family environment on the adjustment pattern of adolescents, Department of Psychology, Tagore Arts College, Pundhcherry, India, pp. 89-90.

Chapter - 29

Methodologies of Teaching and Training in Higher Education

Dr Jahangeer Ahmad Bhat

Abstract

"Educate" for higher school is largely, in our opinion, means to build a system of relationships between people. A efficacious educational bustle of students of higher educational institutions (HEI) depends not only on the degree of knowledge of methods of intellectual activity; it is also due to the individual settings of educational activity – constant method of affairs of the student to the world and to itself. The requisite quality, which must wisdom a student in a higher educational institution, is, essentially, the capability to learn, which put a fundamental bearing on his professional development, because it governs its prospects in University continuing education. Learning to learn is sine quo non than to learn a specific set of knowledge, which in our time is nippily becoming antediluvian. Thus, research and exploration to figure out useful and effective teaching and learning methods are one of the most important necessities of educational systems; Professors have a determining role in training such people in the mentioned field. The research paper will mostly focus on different dimensional methods of teaching and learning in higher education.

Introduction

More important is the ability to self-knowledge, based on creative thinking. Especially rapidly in the period of University education is the development of special abilities. The student is first confronted with many activities, which are components of his future profession, so at the senior courses should be paid special attention to dialog forms of communication with students, in particular, in the process of implementation of their course and degree projects, training, etc. The transfer of "personal knowledge" can usually only in the dyad "teacher – student".

Higher education research is a multidisciplinary field, engaging researchers from across the academy that makes use of a wide range of methodological approaches.

There is a wide range of methodological approaches (e.g., experimental design, action research, self-study, case study research, grounded theory research, classroom ethnography, implementation analysis, phenomenological study, program development/evaluation research, survey research, longitudinal study research) (Bogdan & Biklen, 2006)

Each methodological approach is rooted in particular ontological and epistemological assumptions, as well as embodying important ethical considerations for the processes and outcomes of conducting research (Hubball, H. T., & Albon, S, 2007).

Rapid changes of modern world have caused the Higher Education System to face a great variety of challenges. Therefore, training more eager, thoughtful individuals in interdisciplinary fields is required (Anderson A, 2012; 8:15–28.). Thus, research and exploration to figure out useful and effective teaching and learning methods are one of the most important necessities of educational systems ; Professors have a determining role in training such people in the mentioned field (Khodaparast Haghi A., 2005;7(28). A university is a place where new ideas germinate; roots strike and grow tall and sturdy. It is a unique space, which covers the entire universe of knowledge. It is a place where creative minds converge, interact with each other and construct visions of new realities. Established notions of truth are challenged in the pursuit of knowledge. To be able to do all this, getting help from experienced teachers can be very useful and effective.

Key Words: *Teaching, Higher Education, methods of teaching, methods of education, personality,*

Research Methodology: Most of the existing published material pertaining to the topic has been studied in order to extract pieces of information that were found relevant for the Research work. Along with that, historical method has been used to have in-depth insight for the background and nature of the work.

Teaching and learning methods

In the process of learning it is impossible to learn any concrete issue by using only one method. The teacher has to use different methods during the teaching process; also a combination of methods is frequently used. In the process of teaching methods often supplement one other. The most widely spread teaching and learning methods as well as their definitions are given below. A teacher should choose the proper method according to the concrete aim and problem.

1. **Discussion/debates.** This is the most widely spread method of interactive teaching. A discussion process greatly increases the quality of students' involvement and their activity. A discussion may turn into an argument and this process is not merely confined to the questions posed by the teacher. It develops students' skills of reasoning and substantiating their own ideas.
2. **Collaborative work;** using this method implies dividing students into separate groups and giving each group its own task. The group members work at their issues individually and at the same time share their opinions with the rest of the group. According to the problem raised, it is possible to shift the functions among the group members in this process. This strategy ensures the students' maximum involvement in the learning process.
3. **Problem-based learning** (PBL) is a method which uses a concrete problem as the initial stage both for acquiring new knowledge and integration process.
4. **Case study** – the teacher discusses concrete cases together with the students and they study the issue thoroughly. E.g., in the sphere of engineering safety it can be a discussion of a concrete accident or catastrophe, or in political science it can be a study of a concrete, e.g., Karabakh problem (Armenian-Azeri conflict).
5. **Brain storming** – this method implies forming and presenting as many radically different ideas and opinions on a given topic as possible. This method sets conditions for developing a creative approach towards a problem. This method is effective in a large group of students and consists of the following stages:
   - using a creative approach for defining a problem/issue;
   - for a certain period of time listing (mainly on the blackboard) students' ideas on the problem without any criticism;
   - determining the evaluation criteria for stating the correspondence of the idea to the aim of the research;
   - evaluating the chosen ideas according to the previously determined criteria;
   - selecting the ideas that most of all correspond to the given issue by applying the method of exclusion;
   - revealing the best idea for solving the given problem.

6. **Demonstration method** implies presenting information with the help of visual aids. It is quite effective in reaching the required result. It is frequently advisable to present the material simultaneously through audio and visual means. The material can be presented both by a teacher and a student. This method helps us to make different steps of perceiving the teaching material more obvious, specify what steps the students are supposed to take independently; at the same time this strategy visually shows the essence of an issue/problem. Demonstration can be very simple.
7. **Inductive method** determines such a form of conveying any kind of knowledge when in the process of learning the train of thought is oriented from facts towards generalization, i.e. while presenting the material the process goes from concrete to general.
8. **Deductive method** determines such a form of conveying any kind of knowledge which presents a logical process of discovering new knowledge on the basis of general knowledge, i.e. the process goes from general to concrete.
9. **Analytical method** helps us to divide the whole teaching material into constituent parts. In this way the detailed interpretation of separate issues within the given complex problem is simplified.
10. **Synthetic method** implies forming one issue from several separate ones. This method helps students to develop the ability of seeing the problem as a whole.
11. **Verbal or oral method** comprises a lecture, narration, conversation, etc. During the process the teacher conveys, explains the material verbally, and students perceive and learn it by comprehending and memorizing.
12. **Written method** implies the following forms of activity: copying, taking notes, composing theses, writing essays, etc.
13. **Laboratory method** implies the following forms of activity: conducting experiments, showing video materials, etc.
14. **Practical methods** unite all the teaching forms that stimulate developing practical skills in students. In this case a student independently performs different kinds of activity on the basis of the knowledge acquired e.g. field study, teaching practice, field work, etc.
15. **Explanatory method** is based on discussing a given issue. In the process of explaining the material the teacher brings concrete examples the detailed analysis of which is made in the framework of the given topic.

16. **Activity-oriented** teaching implies teachers' and students' active involvement in the teaching process, when practical interpretation of the theoretical material takes place.
17. **Designing and presenting a project.** While designing a project a student applies the knowledge and skills he has acquired for solving a problem. Teaching by means of designing projects increases students' motivation and responsibility. Working on a project involves the stages of planning, research, practical activity and presenting the results according to the chosen issue. The project is considered to be completed if its results are presented clearly, convincingly, and correctly. It can be carried out individually, in pairs or in groups; also, within the framework of one or several subjects (integration of subjects); on completion the project is presented to a large audience.
18. **E-learning** implies using the Internet and multi-media means in the process of teaching. It comprises all the components of the teaching process (aims, content, methods, means, etc.); the realization of these components takes place through specific means. There are three types of e-learning:
    - Full-time tuition; when the teaching process takes place during teachers' and students' contact hours, and conveying the teaching material occurs through an e-course;
    - Distant learning implies conducting the teaching process in the absence of a professor. The teaching course is conducted distantly; in the e-format.
    - Hybrid (full-time/distant) – teaching is mainly conducted distantly but a certain part of it is conducted during contact hours.

Conclusion

In the present study, it was illustrated that a good teaching method helps the students to question their preconceptions, and motivates them to learn, by putting them in a situation in which they come to see themselves as the authors of answers and the agents of responsibility for change. But whenever the teachers can teach by this method, they are faced with some barriers and requirements. Some of these requirements are prerequisite of the professors' behavior and some of these are prerequisite of the professors' outlook.

Research tools exist which are capable of measuring the main outcomes trainers identify. These tools are currently being used in a large-scale international comparative study that will be able to identify what training actually achieves. Trainers could use these tools to study which goals they achieve: whether or not their programmes achieve their intended goals, and whether or not they also achieve unintended goals. This could highlight whether their training processes are appropriate to the actual outcomes of their programme and may lead to a reconsideration, in some cases, of which goals for such programmes are realistic.

References

1. Bogdan, R., & Biklen, S. K. (2006). Qualitative research for education. An introduction to theories and methods (5th ed.). Boston: Allyn & Bacon.
2. Hubball, H. T., & Albon, S. (2007). Developing a faculty learning community: Enhancing the scholarship of teaching, learning and curriculum practice. Journal on Excellence in College Teaching, 18(2), 119-142.
3. Anderson A. The European project semester: A useful teaching method in engineering education project approaches to learning in engineering education. Journal of Engineering Education. 2012; 8:15–28.
4. Khodaparast Haghi A. New perspectives in engineering education: the promotion of traditional models to innovative solutions. Journal of Engineering Education. 2005;7 (28):

Chapter - 30

Human Resources Management in Higher Education

Dr. Mohd Husamuddin

Abstract

Human resource capacity has become a critical issue for contemporary universities as a result of increasing pressures from governments and global markets. As a consequence, particularly where the institution is the employer, changes are occurring in the expectations of staff and institutions about employment terms and conditions, as well as the broader aspects of working life, and this is affecting academic and professional identities. HR is a product of the human relations movement of the early 20th century, when researchers began documenting ways of creating business value through the strategic management of the workforce. The function was initially dominated by transactional work, such as payroll and benefits administration, but due to globalization, company consolidation, technological advancement, and further research, HR now focuses on strategic initiatives like mergers and acquisitions, talent management, succession planning, industrial and labor relations, and diversity and inclusion. This paper considers key issues and challenges in human resource management in higher education, and some of the implications of these changes.

Key Words: *Higher Education, Human Resource Management, Globalization.*

Introduction

Human resource management is the theory, techniques, methods, and tools for studying the adjustment of people and their relations in the organization, connection between work and its relations, matching the people and work in order to fully develop human resource management, tap people's potentials, motivating people, promoting the work efficiencies and meeting the organizational objectives. Human Resource Management used to be considered as other conventional administrative jobs. But over a period of time, it has evolved as a strategic function to improve working environment, plan out human resources needs and strike a balance between the organization and employers in order to increase organizational productivity and meet organizational goals. Not to exaggerate but in today's highly competitive world it has gradually become one of the most important functions of an organization.

Human Resource Management is the process of managing people in a company as well as managing the existing inter-personal relationships. These two processes are key in the success and growth of a business. Human resource management is the management process of an organization's workforce, or human resources. It is responsible for the attraction, selection, training, assessment, and rewarding of employees, while also overseeing organizational leadership and culture and ensuring compliance with employment and labor laws. In circumstances where employees desire and are legally authorized to hold a collective bargaining agreement, HR will also serve as the company's primary liaison with the employees' representatives (usually a trades union).

Today, society is increasingly knowledge-based, higher education and research now act as essential components of cultural socio-economic and environmentally sustainable development of individuals, communities and nations. The development of higher education must, therefore, feature among the highest national priorities. College and university education in India has produced scholars, engineers, technologists, doctors and management personal of quality comparable with the very best products of the best universities of the world. Teaching in higher education, mostly concentrates on giving information which is but one objective of education.

The Eleventh Five Year Plan (2007-08 to 2011-12) had aimed at achieving faster and more inclusive growth. Rapid GDP growth, targeted at 9.0 per cent per annum, was regarded necessary for two reasons: first, to generate the income and employment opportunities that were needed for improving living standards for the bulk of the population; and second, to generate the resources needed for financing social sector programmes, aimed at reducing poverty and enabling inclusiveness. HR has a pivotal role to play here. An analysis of the main HR problems in India could be done based on the certain challenges that mould the contours of the various sub-functions of HR. The 'attract, motivate and retain' mantra that the HR function seeks to deliver for the organization are based on these HR sub-functions.

- Management and Administration
- Employee Engagement and Talent Retention

- Employee Motivation
- Globalization of Business
- Effective Leadership
- Staffing
- Performance Management
- Managing Inter-Personal Relationships

Management and Administration

Educational Administration is the management with maximum efficiency of an institution or organization having the organized purpose of facilitating the teaching learning process. This definition of educational administration has three aspects:

- The first is management with maximum efficiency.
- The second is the institution or organization.
- The third is the facilitating the teaching learning process.

Thus, the educational administration is concerned not only with management of persons or groups of persons belonging to an organization with maximum efficiency, but also with the setting of the goals and policies of the organization.

The educational administration is also concerned with the development of programmes which prosper learning. It all means that educational administration is concerned on the one hand with the management with maximum efficiency, the persons involved in the educational organization that is the teachers, pupils, administrators etc. and on other with the formulation of goals, planning of programmes and implementation of policies.

Theories of management have proved to be of viable use and application in organizations settings and operations, such as academic organizations like a university. The word management generally implies the art and process of getting things done by others towards the achievement of preset goals and objectives (Keller, Parameswaran, & Jacob, 2011; Richard, 2011). Management involves the implementation of business objectives with a strategic aim of reaping in the gains of business, therefore on this note, the word 'management' as it is applicable in university and higher education management is 'business in nature'. That is when the term management is used and applied in a setting like university and institutions of higher learning; there must be expectation of 'profit and gains' as a result of the fact that management happens in business for the sole aim of profit advancement and survival (Wheelen & Hunger, 2011).

Employee Engagement and Talent Retention

Winning the hearts and minds of talent is of prime importance in the current context. Employees are no longer committed to their companies. Their dedication is towards their own professional growth and careers. Employee engagement means that HR has its eyes and ears close to the ground realities that an employee faces in the job. Issues like work-life balance, fun at work are considered part of the employee experience.

Human resource managers are on their toes to strike a balance between employer and employees keeping in mind the recent trends in the market. They may find themselves in dire consequences if they are not able to handle the human resource challenges efficiently.

- Multinational companies, state-owned enterprises, and private firms are all facing the problem of frequent changing leadership and high turnover rate.
- How to select employees, especially the senior managers? Is it a good idea for the state-owned firms to have all managers to retire at the age of 60?

Creativity and innovation by HR function can make a big difference in how an employee can actually be attracted, motivated and retained.

Employee Motivation

In a market which job-hopping has become the name of the game, keeping the workforce motivated is one of the key challenges of HR. Motivation no longer comes from just a lucrative pay package. Nowadays companies have to walk that extra mile to make the employee feel special to ensure that he doesn't walk out and into the arms of competition.

Talent segmentation and segregation with performance appraisal and rewards is essential to a good team of workers. In essence, as industries evolve, employers have to ensure that apart from the basics of 'roti, kapda and makaan', employees also expect job satisfaction, learning and development facilities.

Globalization of Business

Multinational Companies/Organizations have increasingly set up operations for manufacturing and services in India, bringing with them HRM practices from all around the world. The importation of new management practices has changed the nature of the labor market and the practice of HRM, and will potentially have an impact on Indian society.

These external forces are paralleled by unprecedented economic reform and the enactment of employment laws that are changing the nature of organizational forms and management practices within India. Outsourcing increases the interaction between HR managers in the West and India. Some insights into the common challenges our Indian colleagues face may improve support and collaboration between managers in both locations.

- Today's increasingly global, competitive marketplace has driven considerable changes in labor markets, and has transformed the practice of Human Resource Management.
- Expanded multinational operations within large companies, combined with increased technology and communication capability, have led to vast diffusion of global "best practices" in HRM.
- As a global company, the only way to succeed is to develop an effective global human resource management system with personnel capable of designing and implementing transnational business strategies.
- In most cases firms have historically gone from domestic, to international, to multinational, and finally to global operations. At each phase, the approach to human resource management changes significantly along with the changes in competitive strategy, company structure, the product or service being marketed, profit margin, and expenditure required for research and development.

It is really a huge challenge to understand the psychology of workforce, retain the best talents of the industry, motivate them to perform better and handle diversity while maintaining unity simultaneously, especially in countries like India, where it is still evolving.

Globalization has resulted in many positive developments but it has left many concerns for HR managers. In today's tough world and tight job market, coordinating a multicultural or diverse workforce is a real challenge for HR department.

Effective Leadership

Build an environment where employees enjoy the opportunity of presenting an opinion and discussing issues. Appreciate constructive criticism. It is important to be treated as a role model and to encourage members to work together for a common goal while focusing on the organizational goals largely. Make sure to understand what motivates your team members. It might vary from person to person and can be as diverse as the pay package, challenging assignments or career growth prospects. It is important to instill a sense of belonging in the team members. Always instruct and advise the team to work with each other closely rather than competing with each other. Leadership and management, at times, are considered similar. However, they have distinct differences. A manager strategizes and takes care of activities whereas management exercises control to handle the activities. A leader aims at building trust and oneness in the team. He is the one who stands for the team, supports them in crisis and protects them in adversity.

Staffing

Staffing is the core component of HRM. Staffing is about setting guidelines and procedures to guide recruiting and placement. The presence of these staffing procedures will aid in the effective advertising and reaching out to potential employees. On top of this, the person interviewing and selecting new staff should be able to identify candidates who are suitable for the various roles. The interview should be structured to ensure the success of the interview process as well as the candidate selection. Apart from hiring new employees, staffing also involves the management of existing employees. It touches on issues like disciplinary matters, monitoring of leave, absences and health and safety. Letting employees go is also covered under staffing. Therefore, an organization needs a robust system needs to make sure that all these elements are covered.

Performance Management

Another key component of HRM is performance management. The reason for this is that many employers use it to assess career progression and to determine pay increases. When a good performance management policy is in place, effective targets can be set and monitored regularly. These records are crucial when staffing levels need to be reduced or disciplinary proceedings are instituted.

Managing Inter-Personal Relationships

A secondary role of HRM is in the management of inter-personal relationships. This covers staff within departments as well as at an organizational level. The relationship between staff and management is an important factor in the success of an organization. It sets pace for how the organization will move forward in achieving their vision. As far as this secondary function is concerned, the objectives and outcomes, are designed to help employees and the management grow employees and ensure that the interactions within the organization are fulfilling for every member of staff from the bottom up. The ultimate focus of HRM is the people within an organization. Regular planning, monitoring and evaluation are important for the success of HRM. Successful implementation ensures that all employees know their role, career path and also feel part of an organization which is able to manage and reconcile their expectations as well as those of the organization and its objectives. In the current global work environment, all global companies are focused on retaining the talent and knowledge held by the workforce. All companies are focused on lowering the employee turnover and preserving knowledge. New hiring not only entails a high cost but also increases the risk of the newcomer not being able to replace the person who was working in that position before. HR departments also strive to offer benefits that will appeal to workers, thus reducing the risk of losing knowledge.

Successful Organization

A successful organization makes maximum use of the abilities and talents of each individual, not just a chosen few, or the few who chose to apply the effort necessary to do the job. While not everyone has the same impact on the success of the organization, everyone does contribute to that success. If anyone does not, either they are not doing their job or their job is not necessary to the success of the organization. Either case will have a negative impact on the organization because resources are being wasted. This element also means helping individuals develop their abilities and talents by creating an honest, open environment in which they can learn and grow. While such growth demands understanding and praise of people's successes, it also requires frank, honest appraisal of their mistakes and shortcomings. It is too easy to sympathize and emphasize and damn hard to honestly appraise. We must be careful not to substitute the trappings of human relations and emotions for an appreciation for human needs and those of the organization.

Conclusion

The system of the higher education certainly affects rest of the systems operating in the country. But while doing so, it also gets influenced by the situations and realities prevalent in other systems. With a view to ensure greater influences of higher education on the rest of systems, it is essential that a positive intervention is attempted. The recent government policy cut-in-allocation of the resources of higher education has further affected the efforts improvement of quality of higher education. The HR function of 21st century India has made a transition from being 'behind-the scenes' support appendage to becoming the critical differentiator in business. Rapid globalization has made companies realize people are the key to growth, the only strategic resource that any enterprise truly needs. This has led to companies routinely using their innovative HR practices as their USP (Unique Selling Proposition) to keep up with the times in the wake of a rapidly changing labor landscape. Companies now recognize that a 'Highly engaged employee' the key to success, across business sectors.

References

1. Amrik Singh, Academic Standards in Indian Universities: Ravages of Affiliation, Economic and Plitical Weekly, July 26-Audust 1,2003.
2. Kalam, abdul A.P.J. and Rajan, India 2020,New Delhi: Viking India,1998
3. Kuldeep Singh, Rao, Nair (1997), Selected Readings in HRD, New Delhi: Tata McGraw-Hill Publishing Company Limited.
4. J C Aggarwal (2000), Development and Planning of Modern Education, New Delhi: Vikas Publishing House.
5. Rao.T.V. (2010), Managers Who Make a Difference: Sharpening Your Management Skills. New Delhi: Random House India.
6. Lepousky.A (1965), Administration – The art and science of organization and management, Kolkata:Oxford& I.B.H. Publishing Company.
7. Rao.T.V. (1999), HRD Audit: Evaluating the Human Resource Function for Business Improvement. New Delhi: Response Books.
8. Mohanty. J (2005), Educational Administration and Supervision and School Management, New Delhi: Deep & Deep Publication Pvt. Ltd.
9. Prakash (2005), Educational Planning, New Delhi: Gyan Publishing house.
10. Premila Chandrasekaran (1997), Educational Planning and Management, New Delhi: Sterling Publishers Pvt Ltd.

Chapter - 31

Right to Education – A Fundamental Human Right of Children

Dr. Y. S. Kiran Kumar

"That mother and that father are enemies who don't give education to their children"[1]

"Education is the most powerful weapon which can change the world"[2]

Abstract

Education is the most potent mechanism for the advancement and all round development of the human being. It enlarges, enriches and improves the individual's image of the future. It is old saying that a human being without education is no less than an animal. The importance of education cannot be underestimated by any country in the world. There is another important saying that children of today are tomorrow citizen. The full and potential growth of children is indispensable for any nation. The child attains his or her full growth only by way of education.

Introduction

In our country there is no universal definition is available for age of child, even constitution does not define who is means by a child. Basically we can come to conclusion that a child means a male or female in age of 6 to 14 years. The same is mentioned in the Right of Children to Free and Compulsory Education Act 2009. In a civilized society the importance of child care and welfare cannot be under estimated because the welfare of child is welfare of the community.[3] The former Secretary General of the United Nations Mr. Kofi Annan observed that "there is no trust more sacred than one of the world holds with children".

International Scenario

Right of children is integral part of fundamental and human right. The beginning of the movement for the rights of the child can be traced back to mid 19th centaury by publication of an article in 1852 by Slaguoulk titled 'the rights of children'. Till recently majority of countries in the world have not given much importance to rights of children and their education. Due to change of time as many as 134 countries in the world have enacted legislations guaranting right to education acts for children.

For the first time regarding concern of the child is dealt by non governmental organization in way back 1923. Later the League of Nations passed a resolution in in 1924 in Geneva recognizing right of children over education. In 1948 the United Nations General Assembly approved expanded version of right of children over education and again another resolution is adopted in 1958 and ultimately in 1989 the countries have adopted the Rights of Child in recognsing the needs of children.

The Universal Declaration of Human Rights 1948 under Article 25(2) declares that "motherhood and childhood are entitled to special care and assistance. Article 26 (1) of U. D. H. R. goes on to say that "Everyone should have right to education". The same is repeated in International Covenant on Economic, Social and Cultural Rights which manded that the state parties should recognize everyone right to education. The United Nations Scientific and Cultural Organisation in 1962 affirmed that there should not be any discrimination with regard to children education. In 2000 the World Education Forum its convention held Senegal held that everybody has right to receive education. that In the regional level the European Convention guarantees the Right to Education.

National Scenario

According to Census Commission of India report India has 400 million child populations which is equal to that of entire population of North America. Among which 20 percent of children aged 6 to14 are still not seen enrolled for education.

In our country the awakening over the education is gained simultaneously with freedom movement. The great leaders such as Raja Ram Mohan Roy, Ishwar Chand Vidhya Sagar, Lala Lajpat Rai, Rabindranath Tagore, Madan Mohan Malviya, have recognized the importance education for bring social change and equilibrium in the society.

The importance of education is very much recognized by the Constituent Assembly while preparing the constitution but due to paucity of resources lead to placing the education in the part fourth of the constitution under articles 38, 39 (a),41 and 45 to avoid enforceability of them.

Constitutional and Judicial Perspective

In the post emergency period the apex court of the land, the Supreme Court of India embarked on liberal interpretation of the Article 21. The article 21 which deals with life and personal liberties have received a sort of strength on account of decision rendered by it in Maneka Gandhi v. Union of India[4] in this case, the court has expounded that for survival of the human being the life and personal liberty must to be guaranteed by the State under all circumstances and it is utmost positive duty of the state to protect it.

The Supreme Court has implied that the "Right to Education" as a fundamental right from the Article 21. The word "life" has been including 'education' as the education is major factor for promoting goodness and dignity in the life of any individual. In our country for the first time whether education is fundamental right or not aroused before two judge bench of the Supreme Court in Mohini Jain v. State of Karnataka[5].

The apex court of the land accepted that the Constitution of India does not expressly guarantee the right to education as such, as a fundamental right but reading cumulatively the Article 21 along with the Directive Principles of State Policy contained in articles 38, 39(a), 41 and 45 the court opined that "it becomes clear that the framers of the Constitution made it obligatory for the State to provide education for its citizens".[6]

The apex court further stated that without making the right to education under Article 41 a reality, the Fundamental Rights would remain beyond the reach of large majority of citizens. The apex court clearly remarked that

"We hold that every citizen has a 'right to education' under the Constitution. The State is under an obligation to establish educational institutions to enable the citizens to enjoy the said right. The State may discharge its obligation through State owned or State recognized educational institutions…Charging capitation fee in consideration of admission to educational institutions is a patent denial of a citizen's right to education under the Constitution".

The apex court by above judgment has taken very rigid and absolutic view and castigated burden upon the state to provide education at all levels. It is pertinent to mention that it is highly improbable to country like India where natural resources are abundant but their exploitation is very meager and state has to provide education free of cost at every level it nothing but sailing upon the impossible task.. The above judgment may sound to be good theoretically but it is very difficult to implement in present day globalization and liberalization and other post World Trade Organization existence.

It is pertinent mention that in the post globalization and liberalization period the apex court subsequently has taken reverse turn of above judgment in Unni Krishnan v. State of Andhra Pradesh[7]

The court has reiterated the proposition that having regard to the fundamental significance of education to the life of an individual and the nation, the right to education is implicit in and flows from the right to life guaranteed by Article 21, further the Court remarked that the parameters of this right is not absolute, have to be judged by taking into consideration of the Directive Principles of State Policy contained in Articles 41, 45, and 46. By embarking on new swift the apex Court has considerably lessened burdened of the State in providing educational facilities as follows:

1. Every Citizen has right to free education until he/she completes the age of 14 years.
2. Beyond that, the State has obligation to provide education is subject to the "limits of the economic capacity and development" of the State.[8]

The obligations created by Articles 41, 45 and 46 can be discharged by the State either by establishing institutions of its own, or by aiding, recognizing and or granting affiliations to private educational institutions. The court while taking note of the inadequate outlay on education on education and limited economic capacity of the State to finance education, it has ruled that private educational institutions, both aided and unaided are a necessity in India, but "commercialization of educational cannot and should not be permitted" under any circumstances.[9]

While denouncing the levy of "capitation fee" by certain professional colleges, the Court has however accepted that unaided private educational institutions can charge higher tuition fee: they "have to and are entitled to charge the higher fee, but not exceeding the ceiling fixed" by the state and state has every power to interfere in fixing the fees. In the same judgment the court opined that even the State has power to fix ceiling for charging of the fees by the private institutions.

By rendering the above judgment the court has indirectly accepted and recognized the fundamental right of every child for free and compulsory elementary education up to the age of fourteen years as provided in the Article 45. Meanwhile to ensure sufficient and effective realization of this aright as well as to reassert national will and commitment in this regard

Article 21-A was inserted by eighty-sixth Constitutional Amendment in 2002. Though the amendment was brought way back in 2002 until 2009 the succeeding governments have failed to enact any specific law for implementing given fundamental right of education. The United Progressive government as it promised in its manifesto has brought the constitutional amendment in and added article 21 A in which the right to education is recognized as the fundamental right and now this article 21 A provides that up to 14 years of age the State must provide education at free and if the citizens have denied of their this right they have right to enforce by approaching the apex court under articles 32 and various High courts under article 226 of the constitution. Though the Right to education became a fundamental right in 2002 but we suffered with dearth of specific law upto 2009 when the Government of India has passed much delayed and needed enactment in 2009 which is called as the Right of Children for Free and Compulsory Education Act in 2009 and which came into operation from 27th of August, 2009.

Right of Free and Compulsory Education Act 2009

This is another landmark enactment in post liberalization, privatization, and globalization period in our country. The act encompasses into thirty eight sections in seven chapters. The main features of the act are the state has to provide free and compulsory education to all children in the six to 14 age group,no child shall be held back, expelled, or required to pass a board examination untilcompletion of elementary education, a child above six years of age has not been admitted in any school or though admitted,could not complete his or her elementary education, then, he or she shall be admitted ina class appropriate to his or her age, provided that where a child is directly admitted in aclass appropriate to his or her age, then, he or she shall, in order to be at par withothers, have a right to receive special training, in such manner, and within such time limits,as may be prescribed, provided further that a child so admitted to elementary education shall be entitled to free education till completion of elementary education evenafter fourteen years of age. For the purposes of admission to elementary education theage of a child shall be determined on the basis of the birth certificate issued in accordance with the provisions of the Births and Deaths Registration Act, 1856 or on the basis of such other document, as may be prescribed.

The Act further enshrines that no child shall be denied admission in a school for lack of age proof, a child who completes elementary education shall be awarded a certificate. The Act mandates that the ratio of student-teacher has to be fixed and creating of 25 percent reservation for economically disadvantaged communities in admission to class one in all private schools. The Act mandates improvement in quality of education, school teachers will need adequate professional degree within five years or else will lose job, school infrastructure (where there is problem) to be improved in three years, else the authorities shall cancel recognition to such erring schools, the financial burden relating to improvement of infrastructure will be shared between state and central government. The act further provides that disputes regarding the educational matters have to be litigated in specially constituted educational tribunals.[10]

The Right of Children for Free and Compulsory Education Act 2009 is another kind of welfare legislation enacted by the parliament in post privatization, liberalization and globalization period and which enumerating far reaching provisions. This Act large extent is protecting the educational rights of the children but it is still not free from following lacunas.

1. The definition and meaning of educations is not defined in the Act.
2. The Act only speaks about 25% seats reserved in private schools for poor studens, but nol provision about government schools admission.
3. The Act mentions about children above the age of 6 years but does not cover children below the age of 6 years.
4. There is no provision about mental disorder or disable student education.
5. The Act only speaks about elementary or basic education but no provision about on secondary or higher education.
6. The Act does not speak about the development of infrastructural facilities in the schools.
7. The Act also silence about fair salaries to be made available for teacher working in the private management schools.
8. The central and state governments should accord sufficient budgetary provisions for meeting the requirements of the education.

If we overcome the above shortcomings of the Act the aims and objectives of the Right of Free and Compulsory Education Act is accomplished and which ultimately lead to accomplishment of the education human right of the children in our country.

References

1. Sharma, nidhi (2016-10-06). "1.75 crore rti applications filed since 2005: study". the economic times. retrieved 2018-04-07.

2. prs bill track the whistle blowers protection bill, 2011. www.prsindia.org. retrieved 2018-08-16.
3. http://www.rti.india.gov.in/cic decisions/decision 30112006 12.pdf
4. nayak, n. dinesh. "private institutions, ngos now come under rti act: information commissioner". thehindu.com.
5. pti. "khurshid sounds warning note on r.t.i ruling". the hindu. archived from the original on 10 june 2013. retrieved 4 june 2013.
6. pti. "political parties under rti: congress rejects cic order". the hindu newspaper. archived from the original on 27 october 2013. retrieved 4 june 2013.
7. subrahmaniam, vidya (12 august 2013). "first-ever amendment to historic rti act tabled in lok sabha". the hindu. retrieved 1 december 2014.
8. http://rti.gov.in/rticorner/guide 2013-issue.pdf.

Notes

1. Chanakya Chandraguptha – (c370-283BCE) Indian teacher, philosopher and royal advisor during Mauryan Empire.
2. Mandela Nelson – Anti Apartheid activist, former president of South Africa.
3. Law Relating to Women and Children by Dr. Mamata Rao 2005.Ist edition, 1988 P. 388.
4. AIR.1992 SC 1858 : (1992) 3 SCC 666.
5. Ibid, 1867.
6. AIR 1993 SC 2178.(1993) I SCC. 645.
7. Prof.Jain M.P.Indian Constitutional Law.Fifth Edition. Wadhwa and Company, Nagpur, 2007, P.1131.
8. Ibid.
9. The Gazattee of India, No.39, 27-08-2009.
10. Law Relating to Women and Children by Dr. Mamata Rao 2005.Ist edition, 1988 P. 388.
11. AIR.1992 SC 1858 : (1992) 3 SCC 666.
12. Ibid, 1867.
13. AIR 1993 SC 2178.(1993) I SCC. 645.
14. Prof. Jain M.P. Indian Constitutional Law.Fifth Edition. Wadhwa and Company, Nagpur, 2007, P. 1131.
15. Ibid.
16. The Gazattee of India, No.39, 27-08-2009.

Chapter - 32

Causes of Female Student Dropouts: An Analytical Study of Medak District

T. Neelima

Abstract

The saying goes that if the father is educated, only one person in the family is educated and if the mother is educated, the whole family is educated. Female literacy and women education play a pivotal role in any society, more so in the developing economies. An educated mother can play a constructive role in building a responsible and healthy family as well as contribute economically, politically and in many other ways to the society and nation at large. School education apart, the undergraduate (university) education where the students choose and study the subjects of their choice is an important stage in the career of any student. A graduate is eligible for holding many key government posts and for reaching higher echelons in private sector as well. So it is vital that women study and acquire at least a bachelor's degree. This will broaden their outlook and help them perform their roles in society in a better way. Unfortunately, it has been observed and recorded that many girl students, particularly in rural areas, after joining undergraduate courses drop out of college midway. A cause analysis of this particular phenomenon can yield useful results and help policy makers and stakeholders to take remedial steps to stem the tide.

Introduction

Before 1975, education at all levels was under the control of Directorate of Public Instruction (DPI). Because of the enormous growth of educational institutions, both at secondary and collegiate levels, the Directorate of Public Instruction was bifurcated into the Directorate of School Education and the Directorate of Higher Education in the year of 1975. After that, many junior colleges and degree colleges were established. As a result, the Directorate of Higher Education was further divided into the Directorate of Collegiate Education and the Directorate of Intermediate Education in the year 1989. Thus the Directorate of Collegiate Education came into existence on 1st November 1989. The Directorate of Collegiate Education has the main aim of developing college education in backward and rural areas. It also aims to strengthen the women's education at both UG and PG levels. In the year of 1969, the state government had introduced 10+2+3 system in education.

At present there are 127 (including autonomous) degree colleges in our Telangana State. The total strength of these colleges is 80,965. In that, boy's strength is 41,869 and girls 39096.

Objectives

1. To study the total enrolment number of girl students in the Government Degree Colleges of Medak District.
2. To assess the female student dropout data over the 3 Academic Years (2014-17).
3. To analyse the main causes of the female student dropout in GDCs.

Hypothesis

1. Female students join in large numbers in the UG courses in Medak District.
2. Many female students drop out of studies at UG level.
3. Personal reasons are the major causes for this scenario.

Methodology

1. Primary Data: - To collect the information from the Govt. Degree Colleges in Medak District (New).
2. Secondary Data: - College records, student attendance registers, etc.

Scope of The Study

This study is restricted to the new Medak District post district re-organisation in 2018.

Data Analysis

Thefollowing three tables reflect the student drop outs tendency of GDC's in Medak District (New).

GDC Medak Female Student Dropouts Data (2014 – 17)

Group	*2014 - 15*	*2015 - 16*	*2016 – 17*	*Dropouts*	*Percentage*
B.A. (HEP)	23	14	14	07	30%
B.A. (HPP)	15	11	11	04	26%
B.Com. (Gen)	42	35	32	10	23%
B.Com(Comp)	22	22	17	05	22%
B.Sc. (MPC)	23	15	13	10	43%
B.Sc. (BZC)	34	27	26	08	23%
B.Sc. (MSCS)	12	10	10	02	16%
B.Sc. (MPCS)	20	15	13	07	35%
B.Sc. (GZC)	26	24	21	05	19%
TOTAL	217	173	157	58	22%

GDC (W) Medak Female Student Dropouts Data (2014 – 17)

Group	*2014 - 15*	*2015 - 16*	*2016 – 17*	*Dropouts*	*Percentage*
B.A. (HEP)	58	50	41	17	29%
B.Com	31	20	15	16	51%
B.Sc. (MPC)	30	24	23	07	23%
B.Sc. (BZC)	50	43	22	28	56%
TOTAL	169	137	101	68	40%

GDC Narsapur Female Student Drop outs Data (2014 – 17)

Group	*2014 - 15*	*2015 - 16*	*2016 – 17*	*Dropouts*	*Percentage*
B.A.(HEP)	11	05	04	05	45%
B.Com	06	03	03	03	50%
B.Sc. (MPC)	-	-	-	-	-
B.Sc. (BZC)	07	07	06	01	14%
TOTAL	24	15	13	09	37%

College wise Female Student Drop Outs Percentage (2014 – 17)

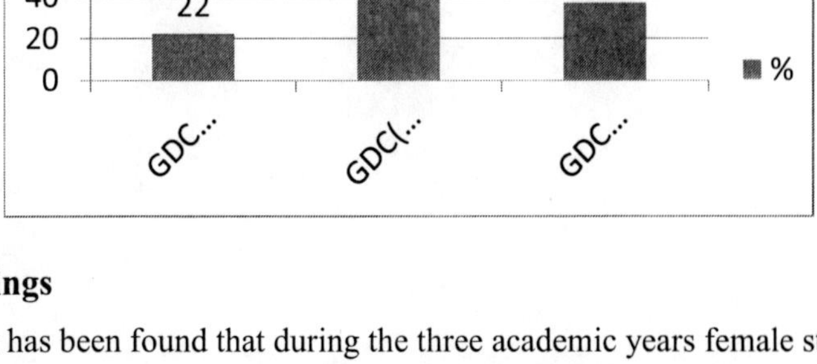

Findings

It has been found that during the three academic years female student drop out ratio touched (32%).The reasons cited by the students are mainly three - marriage, poverty and other family reasons. Parental pressure and other family pressures force the girls to get married before finishing their graduation and family obligations after marriage prevent them from completing their studies.Because of the Kalyana Lakshmi Scheme, parents wait till the girl reaches 18 years of age before they get her married.In the meantime the girls join Degree Courses.Many girls cite poverty as a reason for dropping out of studies.To earn extra money for the family, they do work in farms, etc. Therefore they avoid college and eventually they drop out of college altogether.

Conclusion

More skill oriented and job oriented courses should introduced at undergraduate level so that girl students are motivated to continue their studies in order to get good jobs.KG to PG free education should be given in our State.

Reference

1. Census 2011". The Registrar General & Census Commissioner, India. Retrieved 25 July 2014.
2. District Codes". Government of Telangana Transport Department. Retrieved 4 September 2014.
3. Jump up to:[a b c] "District Census Handbook - Medak" (PDF). Census of India. pp. 12–13. Retrieved 24 December 2015.
4. Indian. Of bindia. gov. in. Retrieved 2 January 2014.
5. Church of South India - Diocese of Medak. "Medak Cathedral". Retrieved 16 May 2014.
6. Monuments of Medak. www.telanganamuseums.com/. Department of Archaeology and Museums.

Chapter - 33

A study on Impact of Higher Education on Women's agency in Household and in the Society

Dr. P. Radhika, O. Pranathi

Abstract

"Education is a mental medicine that cures all the mental maladies of the society" asserts Plato. It is well accepted that education is only the weapon that can empower women to their best at all the phases of life. Higher education alone has the capacity to become a major liberating force against an epidemic of gender-based violence and systemic poverty which is one of core objectives of development goals. It enhances better understand of their rights, opportunities and gives them the wings to explore their careers in the way the wish. Investment in education alone shapes the ability of women to reach their full potential in the society.

Introduction

Present paper analyses the impact of female higher education on the agency of women which is one of the key factor of their wellbeing by explaining the importance of agency, and constraints in the World Bank framework. Secondary data from DHS (demographic health survey) data of India and other published sources are used.

As a hope of light decade into the new millennium, there are a number of reasons to feel optimistic about the women's education around the world. There is remarkable progress where we have succeeded in closing major gaps globally especially in developed and developing countries. Today, girls and boys around the world are able to equally participate in primary and secondary education. In tertiary education, a clear bias is emerging that favors women globally with enrollments increasing faster for women than for men, that is noticed due to increase in the policy interventions. When it comes to the matter of India, Higher Education plays a vital role in liberating women of their economic deprivations bestowing them the financial security and independence. Even though there is drastic increase in the literacy rate in India due to a number of policy interventions the female population who are 58,64,69,174 in number still lag behind in attaining education with low literacy rate of 65.46% according to the census of 2011. The DHS data also shows that there are a less number of women with higher education in India which is shown in table 1. This situation is much worse in the case of higher education. The female enrollment into higher education is 46% in 2016 shows that there is need to take interventions in this way.

Table: 1 Women with secondary or higher education

Country	*Survey*	*Total 15-49*
India	2015-16 DHS	60.1
India	2005-06 DHS	44.7
India	1998-99 DHS	29.6
India	1992-93 DHS	21.9

Source: DHS data.

Due to many reasons including early marriages, lack of awareness, parental pressure and economic backwardness girls are lagging behind in enrolling themselves in higher education which late impinges their income and wealth. Although income and wealth are said to be important factors for the women empowerment they are alone not sufficient for the wellbeing of women especially in the present developmental context of developing countries like India. The economic justice when complimented with social justice is most essential for the wellbeing of women (Sen 1980, 1984, 1985, 1987, 1992, 1999). Amartya Sen in his capability approach brings human beings to the centre of the debate of development and argues that wealth is not the end but is means to achieve the opportunity to live a good life. Even in today's world where gender gaps in human capital and physical assets are being narrowed down, differences in gender outcomes are emerging because girls and boys, who later become women and men, doesn't have equal capacity to exercise agency in all spheres, with women typically at a disadvantage.Agency as defined by world development report 2012 is an individual's (or group's) ability to make effective choices and to transform those choices into desired outcomes.Inthe process of agency men and women use their endowments and take advantage of economic opportunities to achieve desired outcomes. So, agency is said to be an important aspect to study the gender outcomes and to know why they differ amongst the two genders. The analytical framework, by world bank enables us to systematically analyze the roles of economic growth and markets, formal institutions (laws and services), and social norms in influencing women's capacity for agency (figure1).

They show how these determinants play a role in defining women's agency and how constraints in each of them can be mutually reinforcing. Economic growth, formal institutions which includes education, informal institutions, and markets interact to enable or constrain women's agency. Firstly, economic growth can improve the material conditions for exercising agency—through higher incomes, greater access to services, and expanded infrastructure. But the impact of higher aggregate incomes on women's agency partly hinges on women's ability to earn their *own* incomes; that ability increases their bargaining power within the household and their ability to accumulate autonomous assets. Economic growth alone will not eliminate gender differences in agency. Second, expanding women's rights can foster agency in some realms. But the expansion of rights for family formation and control over household resources has been limited. And the effectiveness of expanding rights in bringing about change depends on their applicability often linked to multiple legal systems—and their enforcement. Third, social norms shape women's agency.

Along with markets and institutions, they determine the endowments and opportunities that women have and whether they can exercise the choices to use them. Norms can constrain women's agency when they prevent laws, services, and incomes from benefiting women and men equally. Social norms are particularly binding when increases in women's agency would directly shift power balances in the household and in society. Reforms in markets and institutions, such as service delivery improvements, information provision, and creation of networks, can reduce the bind of social norms by affecting the costs and benefits of compliance. Fourth, women's collective agency can transform society. Women's collective agency both depends on and determines their individual agency. Women's ability to influence their environment goes beyond formal political channels, which can be limited by social norms and beliefs regarding gender roles and institutional structures. They can influence their environments through their participation in informal associations and through collective action, but their success depends in part on their individual ability to make effective choices which is diagrammatically shown in figure 1.

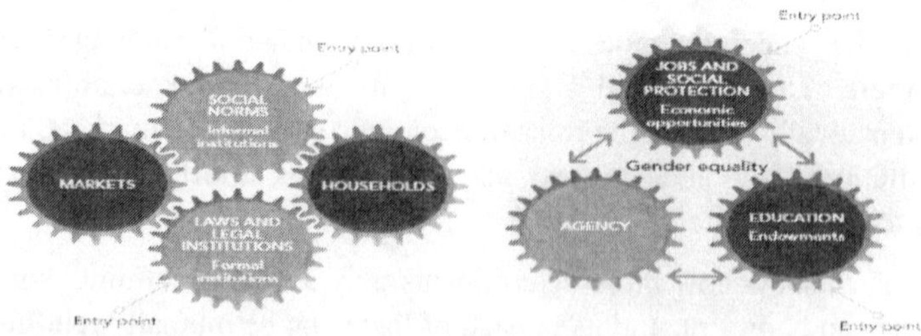

Source: world Bank.

Figure 1: Agency, endowments, economic opportunities, and drivers of change

The individual ability to make effective choices which is call 'agency' is what whole matters for the wellbeing of women at all the spears. Though it includes in it many aspects of women's agency, (a) women's own health care that include personal hygiene, reproductive health, nutritional intake which are important firstly, (b) secondly, making large purchases where as the they are the very stake holders of and are effected of the purchases, (c) visits to family, relatives, friends that define their social life and civic engagement are taken into consideration for the analysis. These are the three main areas where deprivations are widespread. These deprivations are highly related with educational attainment of women especially higher education. Women with higher education are said to have higher voices comparing to that of women with lesser education attainment which is explained in table 2.

Table: 2 Final say in all of the decisions [Women]

Country	*Survey*	*Education*			
		No education	*Primary*	*Secondary*	*Higher*
India	2015-16 DHS	60.2	62.3	63.2	71.5
India	2005-06 DHS	37.1	37.4	40.8	54.2

Source: DHS data.

The data shows that in 2005-06 only 37.1% of women without education, 37.4% of women with primary education. 40.8% of women with secondary education have autonomy in exercising their agency whereas 54.2% of women with higher education enjoy their voices. During 2015-16 there is raise in the agency of women's but still higher education has a major role in it as 71.5% of women with higher education exercise higher agency comparing to that of 63.2% with secondary, 62.3% with primary and 60.2% without education. Since, the data reveals that higher education in India has its remarkable impact on the agency of women leading to their better well-being, there is need to further policy interventions and community interventions in this field if we are really aiming at making our society a women-led developmental from dreaming of women development. Ensuring better infrastructure facilities for girls to attract them to institutions, inspiring them by regular interactions and exposure to successful female personalities in colleges, wide spreading knowledge regarding financial assistances from UGC, MHRD, CSRs, and NGOs can encourage female enrollment and curtail dropouts in higher education. Community participation also can also help in this cause since still social norms followed by family, clan, society and fear of girlhood persists in deciding the career and life of a girl today and women of tomorrow. Last but not the least, voice of girls for themselves which is very much important for their empowerment is to be enhanced at the lower level of education that can inculcate interest and passion towards higher education and career attainments. Let's hope higher female education in India sustain and succeed in enhancing higher voices to the unheard half of the sky.

References

1. All India Survey on Higher Education, MHRD, Govt. of India: www.aishe.gov.in
2. Author Accepted Manuscript by Hanmer, Lucia; Klugman, Jeni Exploring Women's Agency and Empowerment in Developing Countries © World Bank, published in the Feminist Economics22(1) 2015-10-27 CC BY-NC-ND 3.0 IGO
3. http://creativecommons.org/licenses/by-nc-nd/3.0/igo http://dx.doi.org/10.1080/13545701.2015.1091087
4. Alkire, Sabina. (2008). "Concepts and measures of agency." OPHI Working Paper Number 10,Queen Elizabeth House, University of Oxford.
5. Beaman L, Duflo E, Pande R, Topalova P.(2010). Political Reservation and Substantive Representation: Evidence from Indian Village Councils. In: Vol. 7. 2010th ed. Washington D.C. and New Delhi: Brookings Institution Press and The National Council of Applied Economic Research; 2010
6. Clots-Figueras, Irma. (2012). "Are Female Leaders Good for Education? Evidence from
India." American Economic Journal: Applied Economics 4(1), 212-44.
7. Census of India 2011.,Provisional Tables, Office of the Registrar General and Census Commission, India,New Delhi.
8. Desai, A.S. (1999) : Women in higher education and national development, University News, AIU, Vol 39, No 9
9. Dukkipati Uttara (2010): Higher education in India: sustaining long term growth, South Asia monitor, 141, 01
10. Educational Statistics at a glance (2014), MHRD, Government of India.

11. Kabeer, Naila. 1999. "Resources, Agency, Achievements: Reflections on the Measurement of women's Empowerment." *Development and Change* 30: 435–64.
12. Klugman, Jeni, Lucia Hanmer, Sarah Twigg, Tazeen Hasan, Jennifer McCleary-Sills, and Julieth Santamaria. 2014. Voice and Agency: Empowering Women and Girls for Shared Prosperity. Washington, DC: World Bank publications.
13. Mason, Karen (1998): "Wives' Economic Decision-Making Power in the Family: Five Asian Countries" in Karen Oppenheim Mason (ed.), the Changing Family in Comparative Perspective: Asia and the United States (Honolulu: East-West Center), pp 105-33.
14. Nath, S. (2014): Higher Education and Women participation in India, Journal of Business Management & Social Sciences Research, Vol 3, No 2, Pp 43-47.
15. Rao, R.K. (2001) : Women and Education, Kalpaz Publications, Delhi
16. Sen, Amartya K. (1999). Development as Freedom, Oxford, U.K.: Oxford University Press.
17. The DHS Program, STAT compiler. Funded by USAID. http://www. stat compiler. com. January 14 2019.
18. World Bank. *World Development Report2012: Gender Equality and Development.* Washington, DC: World Bank.
19. World Bank. *World Development Repor*2014a. "Gender at Work: A Companion to the World Development Report on Jobs." World Bank, Washington, DC. http:/ /w w w.worldbank .or g /content/dam/ Worldbank / document/Gender/ GenderAtWork web.pdf.

Chapter - 34

Nutrition Education for Adolescent Girls in the Slums of Twin Cities under IPP-VIII, Hyderabad

Dr. Kalpana Toran,
Dr. Kalapatapu Ravikiran Sharma,
Dr. Kavita Toran

Abstract

India Population Project (IPP) -VIII was launched with financial assistance from the World Bank to provide maternal & child health and family welfare services in select 100 slums of Hyderabad. This project adopted the task of addressing issues such as enforcing a positive change in the mindset of the wider community through an educational intervention. Mere availability of mass media or alternative communication channels always does not guarantee successful health education. The purpose of this study is to devise, carry out and measure the impact of educational intervention on the nutrition knowledge of adolescent girls in the selected 100 slums of twin cities under purview of IPP-VIII, Hyderabad.

Objectives

- To evaluate knowledge, attitude and practices (KAP) of adolescent girls on aspects relating to nutrition, early marriage, reproductive behaviour including sexuality and media using habits.
- To plan, devise and implement nutrition and health education programme for adolescent girls.
- To study the impact of nutrition education intervention programme.

Research methodology

The study was conducted in three stages. In the first stage, baseline data on 2500 adolescent girls (10-19 yrs) were collected using a specially designed comprehensive pretested interview schedule. In the second stage, an intensive nutrition education intervention was carried out covering all the adolescent girls living in slums for a period of six months mainly through IPC techniques. In the third stage, a repeat survey was conducted to find out the impact of nutrition education intervention in terms of improvement in knowledge level and consumption of nutrient rich foods.

Results

The study covered a sample of 2500 adolescent girls living in selected 100 slums. Though an effort was made to contact the same adolescent girls (follow up), only 2,326 could be covered during end line survey. The balance of 174 adolescent girls living in the same slums though covered as substitutes/replacement to make up the envisaged 2,500 sample were excluded for the purpose of analysis.

Suggestions

The study highlighted the need to project appropriate role models to these adolescent girls. Similarly, the informative Telugu booklet "Adolescent Health and Nutrition" needs to be popularised with every Telugu speaking adolescent girl keeping a copy of the same as a ready reckoner. The community-based IEC interventions must be conducted at regular intervals, instead of adopting an ad-hoc approach.

Conclusion

No doubt, adolescent girls are very receptive to IEC interventions. They tend to not just acquire higher knowledge but also translate this knowledge into appropriate action for their own good. So, IEC does generate a substantial long term impact in terms of better knowledge and suitable behaviour. But it is challenging to deploy adequate time, resources and attention towards a sizeable segment of society, namely the adolescent girls at the macro level. Therein lies the key to large scale behaviour change.

Background India Population Project (IPP) -VIII was launched with financial assistance from the World Bank to provide maternal & child health and family welfare service in 662 slums of Hyderabad.

The main goal of the project was to strengthen the family welfare program. The important objectives of the project were to reduce fertility among slum population, improve maternal & child health and decrease infant & maternal mortality rates, especially among slum population. The strategies to achieve the objectives were expansion of service delivery system, improving the quality of family welfare services, strengthening the management & administration, supporting innovative schemes and generating demand through IEC, women empowerment & community participation.

The main innovative approaches adopted under the project were forming Mahila Arogya Sanghams with built-in link volunteer's scheme, involvement of identified local NGOs, creating play schools, open schools, organising training activities and more importantly nutrition education programs for adolescent girls supported by community-based IEC activities.

Since majority of adolescent girls, especially representing lower segments of our society, are malnourished coupled with co-existence of social maladies like son preference, incidence of early marriage and high rates of maternal mortality; a strong focus on improvement in nutritional and health status of adolescent girls is warranted.

Moreover, several studies indicate that social indicators like belief systems regarding early marriages, poor dietary intakes and low social status of women in the community adversely impact the overall health and nutritional status of adolescent girls. Hence, the municipal corporation has taken up the task of addressing issues such as enforcing a positive change in the mindset of the wider community through an educational intervention. Mere availability of mass media or alternative communication channels always does not guarantee successful health education.

Purpose

The main purpose of the study was to devise, carry out and measure the impact of educational intervention on the nutrition knowledge of adolescent girls in the selected one hundred slums of twin cities under purview of IPP-VIII, Hyderabad.

Objectives

- To evaluate knowledge, attitude and practices (KAP) of adolescent girls on aspects relating to nutrition, early marriage, reproductive behaviour including sexuality and media using habits.
- To plan, devise and implement nutrition and health education programme for adolescent girls.
- To study the impact of nutrition education intervention programme.

Research methodology

The study was conducted in three stages. In the first stage, baseline data on 2500 adolescent girls (10-19 years) were collected using a specially designed comprehensive pretested interview schedule. In the second stage, an intensive nutrition education intervention was carried out covering all the adolescent girls living in slums for a period of six months, mainly through IPC techniques. In the third stage, a repeat survey was conducted to find out the impact of nutrition education intervention in terms of improvement in knowledge level and consumption of nutrient rich foods.

Results

The study covered a sample of 2500 adolescent girls living in selected 100 slums. Though an effort was made to contact the same adolescent girls (follow up), only 2,326 could be covered during end line survey. The balance of 174 adolescent girls living in the same slums though covered as substitutes/replacements to make up the envisaged 2,500 sample were excluded for the purpose of analysis.

Profile of adolescent girls

The mean age of the adolescent girls was 14.3 years and majority of the girls were unmarried. The educational levels of the adolescent girls revealed that 13.2 percent of them were illiterates, around 38% of them had primary education and 44% of them had high school (7 -10 years) education. Distribution of the respondents according to religion showed that the majority of them were Hindus (69.5%) and one third of them were Muslims. Among Hindus, greater proportions were either from backward castes (32.8%) or scheduled castes (28.3%). Regarding the type of family, 82.8% of respondents belonged to nuclear family.

Majority of respondents had 6-7 members in their family comprising on an average three males and four females. Regarding the educational background of the parents, almost half of the respondents had illiterate fathers and around two thirds of them had illiterate mothers.

Knowledge, Attitude and Practices (KAP)

Among the adolescent girls the knowledge regarding sexuality and related areas were found to be low. Majority of the girls did not know what safe sex means. The knowledge regarding STDs was found to be relatively better. The data revealed that 69.4 percent of the girls had awareness regarding STDs and 70.2 percent of the girls had awareness regarding abortion.

Information about knowledge of family planning is also an important component as far as adolescent girls are concerned. Almost half of the adolescent girls were aware about the female temporary methods. Regarding the knowledge of terminal methods of family planning, all of them knew about tubectomy and only 15.8% of them knew about vasectomy.

Out of the 40 married girls, 33 girls were pregnant. Out of the total pregnant girls, 48.5 percent have registered their pregnancy and all those who registered have used government services. All of them have received TT immunisation and IFA tablets. The preferred place of delivery among them was government hospital (48.5%) with private hospital being next in order of preference (42.4%).

IEC activities

Community-based IEC intervention activities were conducted for a period of six months in all the intervention areas mainly through IPC techniques. Besides regular media like television, radio, newspaper and magazine, the other IEC tools used in educational activities included cooking demonstrations, posters, informative booklet, innovative games and nutrition melas.

To inculcate the habit of taking more iron and calcium-based preparations and energy and protein rich recipes in their daily meals, cooking demonstrations were held in all the intervention areas. They were held in collaboration with Food and Nutrition Extension Board, Government of India. Adolescent girls were taught how to prepare simple iron and calcium rich recipes. They were also exposed to nutrient values of some commonly consumed food articles, choosing the energy and protein rich food articles, right cooking methods and some tips to preserve nutrients while cooking.

To infuse or build self-confidence and self-esteem among adolescent girls, some innovative games were developed. About 20 adolescent girls in each slum were exposed to participatory learning activities in the form of games. These innovative games are intended to build self confidence, knowledge and skills and to empower girls to begin to shape their own life.

The approach used in these games is called 'experimental learning'. It helps girls to participate in learning and learn from their own experiences, with facilitator-trainer as a guide. The games include 'my daily routine and my meal', 'I would like to introduce myself', 'role model or woman we admire', ' my grandmother, mother and myself'and 'good health practices during menstruation'. All the games are based on the experimental learning model. Situations and problems are presented, discussed and analysed. Problem- solving is emphasised. All the participants learnt things through a process of experience sharing activities, reflections and discussions. A facilitator's guide was prepared to aid the field investigators to conduct the games in the community for adolescent girls.

These games are intended to motivate young girls to change undesirable behaviours and adopt new behaviours, promote participation in the learning process. It is hoped that the experience gained by the participants would be applied in similar situations being encountered by them in future.

The informative booklet on' Adolescent Health and Nutrition' prepared in local language Telugu is being distributed to all willing and Telugu speaking adolescent girls. It is a ready reckoner to assess the nutritional status and nutrient requirements on their own. The booklet also contains information on growth and development during adolescence, recommended dietary allowances, balanced diet, menstruation and some commonly asked questions/queries by adolescent girls and their clarifications.

Four multi-coloured posters on education, nutrition, health & hygiene and age at marriage evoked positive response among subjects.

All the respondents were given information pertaining to their heights and weights, anaemia status, etc. Both moderately and severely anaemic girls were given IFA tablets through UHPs to correct anaemia.

In collaboration with three NGOs viz., Pratyamnaya, Sivaranjani Educational Society and CHAIN operating in the study area, seven 'nutrition melas' were conducted. More than 2,000 adolescent girls including other than sample population participated in these one-day melas. Besides cooking demonstrations, experts have taken sessions on following areas:

1. Adolescent growth & development,
2. Nutritional requirements & balanced diet,
3. Menstrual hygiene & health care and
4. Women empowerment.

Poster exhibition on nutrition was also held. The services of gynaecologist, paediatrician, public health specialist, nutrition and communication experts were utilised. Counselling sessions were held and many doubts with regard to nutrition, healthy cooking practices and menstruation were clarified by concerned specialists. Adolescent girls themselves presented some cultural items like songs, street play, etc. All the willing adolescent girls were given TT injections by the concerned UHP staff.

Aspects like adolescent growth and development, nutritional requirements, balanced diet, desirable food habits, right cooking methods, problems during menarche, age at marriage, care during pregnancy and lactation were dealt with in detail during IEC intervention. In addition, areas like building positive personality traits, countering the normal social depiction of adolescent girls in the society, inculcating health and hygiene habits were also included in IEC campaign. Though baseline data were available, based on the suggestions given by the participating NGOs and link volunteers, sensitive aspects like sexuality, family planning methods were excluded in the IEC campaign.

Knowledge, Attitude and Practices (KAP)

The knowledge about physical changes during adolescence has improved from 7.3 percent to 100 percent. In the same way, 56.4 percent of the girls after intervention stressed the need of early education on menstruation as against 43.8 percent in the baseline. About 70% of the subjects specifically mention that they received information on growth and development for the first time during IEC intervention.

Regarding the menstrual hygiene, almost three-fourths of the girls had knowledge of right method of using the sanitary pads. That means they were cleaning and drying pads properly or they were using commercially bought pads as absorbents. After the intervention, more than 85 percent of the girls reported right method of using the pads as against 75% in the pre-intervention period. Further, after the educational intervention it was also observed that they were changing their pads more often than they did it previously.

All the subjects were asked to recall the foods rich in nutrients like iron, calcium, protein and energy. The result clearly indicates that 77.6% could correctly identify the foods rich in iron, 55.2% could recall calcium rich foods and 62% could list the energy and protein rich recipes/food articles.

The consumption of various food items based on the previous day's diet was also analysed. It was found that more than 90 percent of the girls had consumed cereals and fats/oils on the previous day. More than 60 percent of the girls had consumed vegetables (73.6%) and pulses (63.5%). Only less than 30% of the girls had consumed milk, meat or fruits. The usage of all other food items like millets, oil seeds, rice flakes, condiments, jaggery, sprouted and fermented foods was found to be very low (less than 10%). Further, 37.9 percent of the girls were using iodised salt for cooking in their families. Even the consumption of various food items has changed after the intervention. The striking difference can be seen in the consumption of millets like ragi which is especially rich in iron and calcium. Only 3.5 percent of the girls had consumed millets in the baseline and the figure had gone up to 97.9 percent after IEC intervention. Further, an improvement was also observed in the consumption of iodised salt.

The majority of the families (52.9%) were cleaning rice in water thrice or more than that before cooking. Majority of them (83.4%) were also discarding ganji and excess water after cooking. They (93.2%) were also seen to sieve the flour before use. A small proportion of the families (7.7%) were even discarding excess water after cooking dal/vegetables. The awareness regarding the nutrient loss due to discarding of water was also not very high. Only 48.2% of the girls knew that there will be a loss of nutrients if they remove water. Almost all of them followed the practice of covering the vessels while cooking and 70.2% stated that they wash the vegetables before cutting. The post intervention results suggest an improvement in the practice of right cooking methods like discarding of ganji which has come down to 28.9%.

The legal minimum age at marriage is not widely known in the study population. Overall, only 60.6 percent of the girls reported correctly the minimum legal age at marriage for both boys and girls. The results of the post intervention survey indicated an increase in the awareness of legal age at marriage. After the intervention, the figure increased to 83.6 percent.

Data related to pregnancy, ante-natal care, delivery, immunisation and breast feeding were also collected from the sample population. Out of the total, 58.2 percent of the girls stated that they know what pregnancy is, and this figure rose to 60.7% after educational intervention.

Majority (68.9%) of the girls did not know when a woman should register the name for ante-natal checkups. During pre-educational intervention, only 13.3% reported that soon after the cessation of the menstrual cycle the woman should register for ante-natal checkups and this figure rose to 24.8% after intervention. Marginal increase in the knowledge was observed with regard to the need for pregnant women to take TT immunisation (36.8% - 45.8%), take adequate rest (85.4% -89.6%), avoid heavy work (11.6% -24.4%), need to protect themselves from anaemia (43.3% -51.0%) and take good food (38.9% -47.9%). Most of the girls could not identify the categories of women who fall under high risk. Only a small proportion of the girls during pre-intervention identified short stature (4.3%), young and old age pregnancy (5.1% and 3% respectively), high parity pregnancy (3.5%) etc as high risk cases. However, after intervention around 32% of adolescent girls could correctly identify all the high risk pregnant cases.

When it came to knowledge regarding the vaccine preventable diseases, the most well known disease was polio (72.2%). This figure rose to 90% after educational intervention.

Majority of the girls (80.6%) did not have a role model. A comparison of data on the pre- and post-intervention period also did not indicate any major change regarding their role models. The pattern regarding their role model almost remained the same (77.6%) except that a few more could spell out who their role model is.

Most of the girls graded themselves as cheerful (90.1%), cooperative (80.8%), truthful (75.9%), tidy (71.4%). However, only a very few rated themselves as courageous (27.9%) or possess self-confidence (34.4%). After the IEC intervention, though the trend remained the same, there was slight increase in each of these categories. The mean per cent score has also increased from 66.5 to 73.9.

On the whole, it was felt that the adolescent girls were in agreement with the accepted social norm, For example, most of the girls agreed that they are generally quiet (87.6%), emotional (80.5%), dependent (76.5%), subservient (76.7%), etc. However, only some girls stated that they are incapable (27.2%) or unimportant (39.4%). After the intervention, the mean percent score of girls holding negative concept regarding their social depiction came down slightly (65.3% to 58.7%).

Overall, the adolescent girls were found to follow good health and hygiene habits. In most of the categories, the percent distribution is above 80. A comparative analysis of pre- and post- intervention figures indicates that as per the expectation, the health and hygiene habits improved to an extent of 90.7% in follow up cases.

Nearly sixty per cent of the subjects mentioned that they had attended more than one program being organised under IEC intervention. Among those who were exposed to IEC intervention, nearly 82% of the subjects appreciated the information given under IEC intervention and 18.3% were undecided about the quality of information given to them.

Suggestions

The study highlighted the need to project appropriate role models to these adolescent girls. Similarly, the informative Telugu booklet "Adolescent Health and Nutrition" needs to be popularised with every Telugu speaking adolescent girl keeping a copy of the same as a ready reckoner. The community-based IEC interventions must be conducted at regular intervals, instead of adopting an ad-hoc approach.

Conclusion

No doubt, adolescent girls are very receptive to IEC interventions. They tend to not just acquire higher knowledge but also translate this knowledge into appropriate action for their own good. So, IEC does generate a substantial long term impact in terms of better knowledge and suitable behaviour. But it is challenging to deploy adequate time, resources and attention towards a sizeable segment of society, namely the adolescent girls at the macro level. Therein lies the key to large scale behaviour change.

References

1. National Nutrition Policy (1993), Department of women and child development. Ministry of Human resources development, New Delhi, Government of India.
2. White P (1976). Why all the fuss over nutrition education, Journal of Nutrition Education, 15 (3), pp. 105-109.
3. Israel RC, Dennis Foote and Janet Tognetti (1987). Operational guidelines for social marketing projects in public health and nutrition. Nutrition education series. Issue 14. Nutrition education programme, UNESCO.
4. Majorie Schurmann (1983). Community team work in nutrition education – Human Nutrition, Applied Nutrition. 37A. pp. 172-179.
5. Champakam S, Ramdasmurthy V and Balasubramanian SC (1972). Lessons in nutrition education. Journal of Nutrition Education 24. (5) Sept-Oct.

Chapter - 35

Relevance of Massive Open Online Courses in Higher Education

Dr. Vinod Kumar Singh

Abstract

Teaching is no longer a thing of the future but is a part of the present. It has created new horizons for individual learning, access to information resources, learning tools and services. There has been a significant qualitative change in the learning paradigm due to the introduction of technology and became a newer method of imparting education. The modern Indian education should aim to foster skills, talents and creative abilities among youth. Higher education plays an important role in overall development of the nation. Today India's higher education system is world's 3rd largest after USA and China. Though the government focuses on the improvement in providing quality education to its people, there are also number of challenges like globalization and fast development of science and technology in education etc. When these challenges are faced by the Indian education there is a natural question that whether our teachers and students are well equipped to face these demands of the modern education? Technology has closely knit the world. We cannot deny the fact that modern society is centers of information network. Worldwide webs have shrunk the world and are bringing about uniformity in our work, thoughts and aspirations. Earlier certain countries had iron curtains but today no country would like to isolate itself from the global knowledge and information network. Technologies have catalyzed the efforts of globalizing knowledge. Information technology is leading to common way of thinking and social trends. Today we aspire for the standards of the developed countries because we see the visuals every day. Education is an integral part of the social system and is meant for its progress. To meet the challenges of today's education we need to shift the chalk and talk methods of delivering the contents. Teachers need to update their knowledge and students need to be ready to receive the knowledge in the way it satisfies the need of the time. As a result the apex body of higher education introduces several programs for the improvement in the skills of teachers and students in the university level.

Massive Open Online Course is a new method of education for both teachers and students to enhance their skills and knowledge. This paper will discuss concept, historical background, structure, pedagogical process and relevance of MOOCs in today's classrooms.

Introduction

The modern Indian education should aim at grooming the skills, talents and creative powers of the youth. Today India's higher education system is world's 3rd largest after USA and China. Though the government focuses on the improvement in providing quality education to its people, there are also number of challenges like globalization and fast development of science and technology in education etc. When these challenges are faced by the Indian education there is a natural question that whether our teachers and students are well equipped to face these demands of the modern education? The advancement of science and technology has created a world-wide change in the methods of transferring and developing educational contents. All the educational authorities in the world try to fulfill the demands of the present educational system by shifting its methods and attitude to the needs of the time. To meet the challenges of today's education we need to shift the traditional methods of delivering the contents. Teachers need to update their knowledge and students need to be ready to receive the knowledge in the way it satisfies the need of the time. As a result the apex body of higher education introduces several programs for the improvement in the skills of teachers and students in the university level. Massive Open Online Course is a new method of education for both teachers and students to enhance their skills and knowledge.

Moocs as a teaching learning platform

Even though the technology of online learning is a new concept, it is almost 170 years old and has its origin in a correspondence course offered in Great Britain in which the teacher used to send the lessons and other learning materials to students. In the 21st century, the concept of MOOC is very new and gradually receiving popular in the higher education sectors. Massive Open Online Course is the new form of learning. As it is written, MOOC is composed of 4 words: massive-open-online-course and the structure and affordances of MOOC technology is understood from these words. 'Massive' here means large number of teachers and students can be engaged in this form of learning. There are no restrictions or limitations for the participation in this type of learning. The word 'open' here means that it is open to all irrespective of the participants' physical presence. It means these courses can be registered by anyone from anywhere provided that the users should be accessed to internet. MOOCs deliver online courses in synchronous mode schedule on a weekly calendar basis or on particular defined schedule. A user from anywhere in the world can take part in the lectures and do the prescribed exercises in his/her own time. Even it helps to attend and make up the missed lectures according to the users' convenience. The nature of the transaction of the course and its contents show the constructivist approach of pedagogy.

It is good to shed light on the history of MOOC. It was introduced during 2008 as a form of distance education having predefined structure of the course, learning objectives and specific learning contents. The term Massive Open Online course (MOOC) was coined by Dave Cormier and Alexander. This was initially a course which was basically developed in response to a course titled "Connectivism and Connective Knowledge" also known as CCK08 which was led by George Siemens of Athabasca university and Stephen Downes of the National Research council at the university of Manitoba.

Moocs-A Pathway for the Professional and Personal Enhancement

To meet the challenges of today's education, we need to shift the chalk and talk methods of delivering the contents. Teachers need to update their knowledge and students need to be ready to receive the knowledge in the way it satisfies the need of the time. As a result, the apex body of higher education introduces several programs for the improvement in the skills of teachers and students in the university level. Massive Open Online Course is a new method of education for both teachers and students to enhance their skills and knowledge.

In India, it has been observed that the teaching has become an activity of anybody due to the unsystematic preparation of university teachers. Among the students also it has been viewed that even the masters/research scholars are not able to transfer their knowledge clearly and contemplatively to others. It is evidence that the UG/PG courses offered from the university and colleges certify only the competence of students of their amount of cramming the knowledge and not the construction of knowledge and ability to teach. Therefore, we need professional and personal development for the teachers and students which enable them both for research and teaching. Each and every student must get opportunity to develop teaching competency and the teachers of higher education also be given professional development through different types of online courses or in-service programmes which have both real and virtual experiences. Open Educational Resources (OER) and MOOCs are prepared and designed to do so. MOOC works on the principle of A3 (Anyone, Anytime, Anywhere). It provides opportunity for its users to be more resourceful by being techno-savvy.

It is a true statement regarding Indian education system that higher education in India is going digital, triesto fulfil all sorts of demands of the learners in the knowledge scenario and MOOCs have proven a much-needed catalyst for the development of progressive programs that respond to the changing world.MOOC is a platform for everyone who is interested for the advancement of knowledge. There are lots of high quality technical, professional and personal development courses available for all sorts of people especially teachers, students, higher educational administrators, industry professionals, policy makers and all the life-long learners. In simple terms, MOOC is a platform of learning in which the learning materials are delivered online to virtually any person. These courses are specially meant for the aspiring learners according to their needs, knowledge and skill to enhance the professional and personal academic growth. Though there are wide varieties of online courses are available but MOOC still differ from them with respect to the objectives, structure and many other dimensions. It is totally free of cost and opens to all and provided by the leading universities across the world. The most important feature of this course is that, it does not require any basic academic requirements for participating in MOOC. The academic experience which a learner acquires through MOOC will enhance the regular academic experience of the learner. Most commonly MOOC will last to 5-8 weeks which require 2-6 hours study per week. The course materials are all provided online, course transactions and evaluations are made possible through online. But there are many well-structured and planned regular courses with a duration ranging from one year to two having few semesters. The learner has to enroll his/her name at the institutions hosting the MOOC courses through online. The learning contents of MOOC include video presentations of the experts in their field of study. And the course activities include watching video presentations, discussions, online blogging, writing and commenting on the videos watched, immediate feedbacks, peer reviews, summarizing the learning contents etc. The learners are free to watch and re-watch the learning content/ lectures/videos. The major advantage is that it allows the participants to learn at one's own pace and has the freedom to choose the study materials. The course interaction takes place in blogs, tweets and other social net-workings and online venues. The announcement of a particular course and its schedule, duration are usually made on academic websites, blogs.

Relevance of MOOCs in Higher Education

In India, it is a reality; most of the classroom environment is not student centric. Even though the curriculum of each course state that the content transaction strategies would be based on seminars, projects, small group interactions etc. Putting students at the centre of teaching learning activities demand many requirements. In this situation, a course which is fully student centric encourages self-learning satisfies the requirements of today's curriculum. Therefore, the UGC and higher education authorities should plan and implement MOOCs in universities in India. Today's knowledge societies, changing platforms of education due to the technological advancements in education, demand for online courses to enhance the quality learning. MOOCs allow students to select courses by choice and help to reduce geographical barrier. It has also the advantage of getting the opportunity to learn from famous universities and institutions. In the sphere of higher education, many universities make age limit for many courses. This confines the students from getting higher education and becomes a barrier for their aspiration for the lifelong learning. In this way people those who are interested in education become benefitted by MOOC and these courses allow the people to be updated.

MOOCs are getting more space in the higher educational scenario. The MHRD, UGC give priorities for MOOCs in the educational institutions. The demand for higher education is ever growing. To certain extent MOOCs can satisfy these demands by providing access through digitalizing the higher education. MOOCs have more scope in developing Asian countries like India and China through cultivating literacy among people and allows the students to have better world view.The relevance of MOOCs in higher education is based on its effects on our colleges or universities. Few are listed below:

- Increased institutional consciousness regarding the relevance of MOOCs in higher education-It is a positive sign that the apex bodies of Indian education system is planning and channelizing the funds for the accomplishment of digitalizing the education.The most predominant topic of conversation is that our educational agencies are seriously thinking and dreaming about the role of MOOCs—and digital education more broadly—in defining future models of higher education.
- An appreciation for the profession of teaching-MOOCs have effected and helped the teachers to focus on teaching and learning process, research and design new courses. This has initiated more

understanding and significance for the very profession of teaching among the teachers.

- Collaboration in the course design- A traditional classroom can be developed by the mere presence of the students and a teacher. But if we analyze a MOOC, it is the mutual co-operations of different people including various teachers as course developers/content writers/deliverers,software developers, learning researchers, librarians and videographers. Therefore, a successful designing of a MOOC definitely need a collaborative work and hence it leads to a co-operative learning scenario.
- Providing a space for experimentation-Many educationists especially who are engaged in digitalization of educational endeavors found that the organizational structures designed around MOOC creation provided safe spaces for experimentation and innovation in teaching and learning. The MOOC hype may change as the time and technology advance, but its momentum has paved the way for increased experimentation with thoughtful and bold ideas for higher education in a digital era.

The early impacts of MOOCs on higher education are a sign that this transition is difficult, but entirely possible. As the next waves of hype impact universities, likely in the form of adaptive learning and competency based education, the systems that are successful will be those that address the full spectrum of learning: liberal arts, vocational and life-long.The major challenge in the MOOCs are the language in which the course materials are delivered. Mostly the English speaking people get benefit of MOOC courses and when we apply these courses in India especially many of the non-English speaking students make distance from MOOCs. Many of the teachers and students are not aware about the value of MOOC certificates and its importance in the labour market. In the 21st century, where the learners are mostly the digital natives, MOOCs have always high significance.

Conclusion

We shall thank the new technologies and advancement in the ICT to make enormous changes in higher education. It is a good sign that the higher education is going digital. In recent years, Indian higher education is increasingly thinking about digitalizing the higher education. Introduction of MOOC in the field of higher educational institutions for the development of teachers and students is one of the hopeful steps in this regard. MOOCs can be offered in all the streams by the universities and Institutions because it has wide range of flexibility and dynamism for any type of learners.

Therefore, it is no doubt that MOOCs will become one of the futuristic learning trends in the areas of higher education.

References

1. Agarwal, Anant (2015). "MOOCs as Modern textbooks". *The Times of India*, 28 February p.16.
2. Altbach, P.G., Reisberg, L. and Rumbley, L.E. (2009). *Trends in Global Higher Education: Tracking an Academic Revolution*. Retrieved from:
3. http://unesdoc.unesco.org/images/0018/001831/1831168e.pdf.
4. Basu, K. (2012). *MOOCs and the Professoriate*. Retrieved from:
5. www.insidehighered.com/news/2012/05/23/faculty -groups-consider-howrespond-moocs
6. Dange, K. Jagannath and M. Somashekhara. (2016). "Massive Open Online Courses: A new form of learning, *University News*, Vol.54, No. 22, p. 26-31.
7. Joshith, V.P. (2016). "Open Educational Resources and Massive Open Online Courses as a model for professional development of Teachers", *University News*, Vol.54, No. 34,
8. p.22-26.
9. Mintz, Steven. (2014). "The Future of MOOCs". Retrieved from:
10. http://www.insidehighered.com/blogs/higher-ed-beta/future-moocs
11. McAuley, A., Stewart, B.,Siemens, G. and Cormier, D. (2010). The MOOC Model for Digital Practice. Retrieved from: www.open.ac.uk /about/main/the-ou-explained/history-the-ou.
12. Shankar, S. Prabhu. (2015). "Massive Open Online Courses: Perspectives on Futuristic Learning Trends", University News, Vol.53, No.44, p. 11-14.
13. Allison Dulin Salisbury (2014). Impacts of MOOCs on Higher Education. Retrieved from: https://blog.edx.org/impacts-moocs-higher-education.

Chapter - 36

The Changing Role of Teacher in Higher Education

Dr. K. Geetha

Abstract

The role of teacher in ancient Bharatavarsha was totally different. The teacher used to take care of each and every student who approaches him in quest of knowledge and provide him such guidance by following which the student could get accurate knowledge in depth at least of one subject. The teacher and the student together used to pray the God for betterment of the society in every aspect. The teacher used to train his students in such a way – shishyadicchet parajavam – he will enjoy his students winning over him. As per ancient tradition the teacher occupies a highly respectable position, almost equal, may even superior to that of God. The Guru desires – "Let this Adhyayana give protection to both of us. Let it give us equal enjoyment. Let us both cultivate this powerful knowledge. Let our study be (powerful) lustrous. Let us both free from malice and misunderstanding of each other" –

Introduction

At the time of convocation the teacher used to remind all the important points of human life to his disciples so that they should not deviate from the path of righteousness. *Purusharthas* were very important goals to achieve in human life. One has to learn so many things to reach these ultimate goals. The teacher used to say the following things in his convocational address to his disciples –

1. Speak truth.
2. Move in righteous path.
3. Do not deviate from the path of self learning.
4. Mother should be your first god.

5. Father should be your god
6. Teacher should be your god.
7. Guest should be your god.
8. Follow the path of persons with good conduct.
9. Donate for the needy.
10. Live like a best example in society.

These points carry the complete essence of ancient education system. The strongest desire of an *Acharya* according to *Tattiriyopanishad*, is to get students worthy of receiving instruction from him. The teacher and students together used to pray that all the good things happen to everyone. Let noble thoughts come from everywhere. Everyone should enjoy fruitful life of 100 years. No one should left over with pain and sorrow. The prayer always included the welfare of every living being. This is the ideology of *vasudaivakutumbakam*. The teachers used to give priority to their students than their own progeny. Drona blessed Arjuna with Astra Brahmasiras but not his son Aswathhama.

The development of inner nature or character of the student was deemed as one of the essential objects of education in ancient times. The rich and the poor have enjoyed equality in the Gurukula. *Sparthaabandhamanoharam* – these gurukualas are so beautiful which create competency in.

The disciple who receives knowledge from his Guru equals him and can produce students equal to him. The sincere efforts teachers and duties of students will surely establish peace and happiness in the world.

In present scenario of India the role of teacher is changing day by day with different types of responsibilities for the overall development of the students. The teacher has to update his subject knowledge according to the needs of the students. In 70s and 80s teacher used to sit and share the knowledge of the subject without moving from the chair with just narration and we still remember their gestures while teaching and the lessons taught by them with the lesson names. Their narration sometimes filled with picturesque descriptions where we carried away the students in to some different world. In 90s the influence of computers slowly started and 21st century one cannot show his talent without using computer knowledge. In recent years the development is teacher has to work with Google class rooms. May be in coming years virtual class rooms will fulfil the necessity of teacher who can teach virtually addressing different places students. The lack of permanent faculty is always a minus point to higher education. In present times the teacher has to use latest technology and update his subject knowledge. He has liberty to select authentic PPTs on particular topics from online for the benefit of the students. With digital class rooms he can directly access the YouTube and online lessons. He can write the notes on his subject topics and share Wikipedia which will reach to many needy students. Through subject blogs also many students are getting the benefits. Students are already getting the benefit of online courses through SVYAM, MOOCS and many other authorised centres.

Experts of different subjects are making online videos available for many subjects useful for the students to get through IIT, IAS, NET and CSIR exams and so on. Technology itself is acting as teacher if we have commitment to learn any subject. IIT Professors uploading their valuable lectures which is useful to the students to get acquainted with world class teaching professionals. Any good teacher can contribute lessons to address the needs of students. Now it is the trend and many scholars though not related to teaching profession are sharing their knowledge through internet. Now the student can get OXFORD University certificate after finishing online course. We should not forget even for online course also the master mind behind the programming is a Teacher.

Without a teacher we cannot shape the future generations as per the expectations of the society. After parents students mostly depend on their teachers. Government of India is taking so many steps to improve the quality of higher education. Meritorious teachers should be appointed otherwise a dull teacher would produce generations of dull students. For the welfare of any society a good teacher is always needed. Teacher must be energetic, active, enthusiastic and knowledgeable. The teacher should have the above the qualities to inspire the students. The teacher and student determine the future of the society.

The role of teacher is changing in many aspects but still it holds great importance. The teacher who influences his students will definitely motivate the student's to get success in education as well as personal life. From kinder garden level to higher education level students are always influenced and inspired by their teachers. No one can read their mind better than their teacher. Many a times he has to act as councillor when the situation demands so. The teacher should fill the minds of students with positive thinking. He should teach the student to celebrate the success as well as face the failure. We are not preparing students how to deal with failure and that is the primary cause of suicides of students. The student who got more than 90% in regular course is committing suicide for just not getting a seat in reputed course. Here the teacher can play the best role as a councillor. The stress from parents and society towards the students is leading for such mishaps. The teacher should teach how to maintain balance at any level of emotional stress. Parents mostly worry about the society which criticises the failure of their children. But the emotional support of teacher and parents is most essential need of the students. Everyone is interested in the success stories but these three people will build the courage of students. Suicides of students can be prevented by this emotional bondage of teachers and parents towards the students.

Unlike other professions teaching profession demands many sacrifices. To teach one effective class he has to spend so many hours in preparation. It is a serious profession demanding so many sacrifices and lot of time. Great commitment is needed in this profession. If a manufacturer makes a mistake only that product will go wrong. If an unsuitable person apt this profession it effects generations. The teacher should imbibe the morals and ethics which he wants to see in his students. Society always expects teacher with human values and ethics. Otherwise he will be the wrong example for the society. The students are expecting for a teacher who is sincere, knowledgeable, and a very friendly personality.

Conclusion

The present generation more focused towards their life compared to our elders. In modern society the goal of teaching is towards fulfilling the global needs. Here technology should be utilized appropriately such that only valid knowledge is imparted at the right time. To reach this goal now teachers are going through great stress. It is affecting their health. We have to deal this. Significant part of the education is seen as the process by which the teacher enlarges, enriches and improves the individual's image of the future. The teacher should play different roles as mentor, councilor, close friend, felicitator. "Faculty are supposed to make the sparks fly intellectually, and from time to time, we're supposed to make lightening strike." Ross Thomas.

Reference

1. Luntley, M. (1995), Reason, Truth and Self: Getting to Know the Truth about Postmodernism.
2. Marien, M. (2002), Futures Studies in the 21st Century: A Reality-based view: *Futures*, *34* (3-4), pp261-281.
3. Mei, C. W., & Siraj, S. (2017), Integrating Internship and Business Simulation into the Malaysian Business Studies Curriculum, (*MOJEM) Malaysian Online Journal of Educational Management*, *1* (1), pp1-16.
4. Young, M. F. (2002), *The Curriculum of the Future: from the new Sociology of*

Education to a critical theory of Learning, Routledge.

5. Young, M., Lambert, D., Roberts, C., & Roberts, M. (2014), *Knowledge and the Future School: Curriculum and Social Justice*. Bloomsbury Publishing.
6. Young, M., & Muller, J. (2015), Three Educational Scenarios for the future: Lessons from the Sociology of Knowledge in *Curriculum and the Specialization of Knowledge* pp76-91, Routledge.
7. Hughes, Arthur. (2008). Testing for Language Learners. UK: Cambridge University.
8. Kilickaya, Ferit. (2004). Authentic Materials and Cultural Content in EFL Classrooms. The Internet TESL Journal. Retrieved on December 2nd, 2013, from
9. http://iteslj.org/Techniques/Kilickaya-AutenticMaterial.html.
10. Maroko, Geoffrey M. (2010). The authentic materials approach in the teaching of functional writing in the classroom. Kenya: Kenyatta University Department of English and Linguistics.
11. Masood, Asif. (2013). Exploiting Authentic Materials for Developing Writing Skills at Secondary Level. Journal of Literature, Languages and Linguistics: An Open Access International Journal Vol.1 2013 pp15-25.

Chapter - 37

Amplificationon Curriculum Renewal for Value Based Education System

Kumaraswamy Manepalli MBA

Abstract

The paper has tried to explain the need for a new policy as its predecessors failed to realize fully the goals enshrine. "Though India has made significant progress in terms of enhancing access to and participation in all levels of education, the overall picture of education development in the country is mixed and there are many persisting concerns and challenges relating to access to and participation in education, quality of the education imparted, equity in education, system efficiency, governance and management, research and development, and financial commitment to education development," it says. The elements of a value-based education can be found not only in the subject matter, but in the learning styles which are employed, the scheduling of the classroom, extracurricular activities, and parental involvement. The VBE is therefore organized so as to secure the fullest possible development of body, mind and heart; and a fruitful channelization of the life-energy in pursuits that contribute to the growth of both internal and external personality. The Government of India would like to bring out a National Education Policy to meet the changing dynamics of the population's requirement with regards to quality education, innovation and research, aiming to make India a knowledge superpower by equipping its students with the necessary skills and knowledge and to eliminate the shortage of manpower in science, technology, academics and industry.

Key Words: *Value Based Education, Enshrine, Enhancing, Persisting, Pursuit*

I. Introduction

The National Policy on Education was framed in 1986 and modified in 1992. Since then several changes have taken place that calls for a revision of the Policy. The Government of India would like to bring out a National Education Policy to meet the changing dynamics of the population's requirement with regards to quality education, innovation and research, aiming to make India a knowledge superpower by equipping its students with the necessary skills and knowledge and to eliminate the shortage of manpower in science, technology, academics and industry.

The New Education Policy (NEP) "envisions a credible and high-performing education system capable of ensuring inclusive quality education and lifelong learning opportunities for all and producing students/graduates equipped with the knowledge, skills, attitudes and values that are required to lead a productive life, participate in the country's development process, respond to the requirements of the fast changing, ever-globalizing, knowledge-based economy and society," it adds.

The curricula also need to define the standards of educational performance and learning outcomes through which objectives of education are realized and the attainment of which can be assessed/monitored with a view to revision and upgrading of the curricula. In order to reform the examination system in our country, the **Mudaliar Commission** laid stress on the use of objective type tests and internal assessment. Kothari commission too repeated these reforms. This Commission boldly suggested that the certificate of the student should bear his complete performance but there should be no remark to the effect that he has passed or failed in the whole examination. This is very good suggestion and can be easily implemented.

As the first practical step in changing the present pattern of examinations, the All India Council for Secondary Education was set up by the Central Ministry of Education in October 1995. It gave top priority consideration to resolve the problem of examination system. The well-known International Commission on Education sponsored by **UNESCO** in 1992 gave their valuable comments and suggestions for reforming the system of examination.

The Programme of Action (POA) suggested several specific short-term and long-term measures for carrying out examination reform at the school level as well as at the university level. It also suggested that, "to formulate a national examination reform work the Department of Education would, inter-alia, constitute an inter institutional Committee with representations from **UGC, NCERT, AICTE** and state level organizations including Board of Secondary Education".

II. Need for A Value Based Education System [VBES]

HRD's New Education Policy emphasis on value-based education system

The suggestions in the document are based on the simple instrumental principle cause-and-effect: India needs to teach its students what is needed in the world; if a certain thing is taught, the students must be able to reproduce and apply it; where there is autonomy, there must be accountability; learning must lead to employability.

10 recommendations of Subramanian Committee on new education policy

Here are top 10 recommendations of the **Subramanian Committee** suggesting measures that the Govt must take to improve the education sector that caters to over 300 million students in the country The T.S.R. Subramanian committee, entrusted with preparing a new education policy for India submitted the report to the government in May suggesting measures that the country must take to improve the sector that caters to over 300 million students in the country. Here are top 10 recommendations of the report:

(1) An **Indian Education Service (IES)** should be established as an all India service with officers being on permanent settlement to the state governments but with the cadre controlling authority vesting with the **Human Resource Development (HRD)** ministry.

(2) The outlay on education should be raised to at least 6% of **GDP** without further loss of time.

(3) There should be minimum eligibility condition with 50% marks at graduate level for entry to existing B.Ed courses. **Teacher Entrance Tests (TET)** should be made compulsory for recruitment of all teachers. The Centre and states should jointly lay down norms and standards for TET.

(4) Compulsory licensing or certification for teachers in government and private schools should be made mandatory, with provision for renewal every 10 years based on independent external testing.

(5) Pre-school education for children in the age group of 4 to 5 years should be declared as a right and a programme for it implemented immediately.

(6) The no detention policy must be continued for young children until completion of class V when the child will be 11 years old. At the upper primary stage, the system of detention shall be restored subject to the provision of remedial coaching and at least two extra chances being offered to prove his capability to move to a higher class

(7) On-demand board exams should be introduced to offer flexibility and reduce year end stress of students and parents. A National Level Test open to every student who has completed class XII from any School Board should be designed.

(8) The **mid-day meal (MDM)** program should now be extended to cover students of secondary schools. This is necessary as levels of malnutrition and anemia continue to be high among adolescents.

(9) **UGC Act** must be allowed to lapse once a separate law is created for the management of higher education. The **University Grants Commission (UGC)** needs to be made leaner and thinner and given the role of disbursal of scholarships and fellowships.

(10) Top 200 foreign universities should be allowed to open campuses in India and give the same degree which is acceptable in the home country of the said university.

The National Policy on Education, 1986 emphasized on continuous and comprehensive evaluation and the introduction of semester system from the secondary stage. The National Policy on Education, 1986 recommended a new approach to examinations in the following words:

1. "Assessment of performance is an integral part of any process of learning and teaching. As part of sound educational strategy, examinations should be employed to bring about qualitative improvement in education.
2. The objective will be to recast the examination system so as to ensure a method of assessment that is a valid and reliable measure of student development and a powerful instrument for Improving teaching and learning; in functional terms, this would mean:
   - The elimination of excessive element of chance and subjectivity
   - The de-emphasis of memorization
   - Continuous and comprehensive evaluation that incorporates both scholastic and non-scholastic aspects of education, spread over the total span of instructional time.
   - Effective use of the evaluation process by teachers, students and parents.
   - Improvement in the conduct of examination;
   - The introduction of concomitant changes in instructional materials and methodology;
   - Instruction of the Semester system from the secondary stage in a phased manner, and the use of grades in place of marks.

Curriculum Renewal and Examination Reforms: NEP 2016 Policy Framework

Improving the assessment of student learning assumes greater importance in the context efforts to improve learning outcomes. Systems are in place for continuous formative and summative assessment, term-end and year-end examinations, and class X and class XII examinations. However, the overall assessment practices at the school level remainunsatis factory. In most cases the learning assessment is limited to testing the students' ability to reproduce content knowledge.

The whole assessment system needs to be revamped to ensure comprehensive assessment of the students, including learning outcomes relating to both scholastic and co-scholastic domains. There is also a need to institutionalize a system which tracks student progress in both the scholastic and co-scholastic domains across years.

The following policy ***initiatives*** will be taken:

1. Curricular reforms will be carried out to meet the emerging aspirations and align to national goals of social cohesion, religious amity and national integration. Curriculum should be outcome-based and aim for overall development of students through imparting life-skills in an increasingly technology driven environment. All students will be taught both fundamental duties and rights so that they can become responsible citizens both within the country and in the world.
2. National Council of Educational Research and Training (NCERT) will undergo a re-orientation to address issues of deteriorating quality of school education and periodic renewal of curricula and pedagogy to move from rote learning to facilitate understanding and encourage a spirit of enquiry.
3. For science, mathematics and English subjects, a common national curriculum will be designed. For other subjects, such as social sciences, a part of the curricula will be common across the country and the rest will be at the discretion of the states.
4. From Class V onwards, digital literacy will be introduced in the curriculum in a graded manner. However, ICT as a subject can start from class VI. ICT curricula at all levels will be revised to make these application oriented.
5. It is well recognized that concepts of science are best understood by students through demonstration and lab experiments. Hence for teaching of science subjects, practical components will be introduced gradually from class-VI onwards.

The new national education policy (NEP) was an election promise by the Modi government and repeated delays, including setting up of a new committee under former Indian Space Research Organisation (ISRO) chief

K Kasturirangan in June 2017, has raised a question mark whether it will be adopted before the term of the government ends in May, 2019.

The draft of the Kasturirangan Committee is ready and the Ministry of Human Resource Development plans to move forward towards an education policy soon. However, with the next elections drawing close, it is not clear whether the government has enough time to finalise thepolicy and implement it.The current education policy was framed in 1986 and revised in 1992, which is why there was a need to review it and bring in necessary changes.As per the report, the policy has been framed with a 20-year-vision."This has also been a reason for the delay as they keep updating the draft. Big restructuring in the regulatory framework is one of the focus. There will be increased stress on traditional knowledge, Indian languages and mathematics at school level,"

Conclusion

The current instructional practices and resource provisions are a hindrance to competence based curriculum which requires situations that can build the expected competencies in education system. Continuous assessment, standards in paper-setting, transparency in evaluation criteria, etc. are some steps that can be taken in this direction. In order to introduce flexibility and reduce year-end examination stress, the government will make an attempt to introduce on-demand board examination.

Reference

1. Ministry of Human Resource Development, Govt of India: Draft NEP 2016.
2. International Journal of Educational Management: Venkatesh Umashenkar (Institute for International Management and Technology, Haryana, India).
3. International Journal Of Inclusive Education- Mapping the field of inclusive education a review of the Indian literature:Nidhi Sngal.
4. Perspectives on Education and Development:V.prakash and K.Biswal, shripa publication, New Delhi.
5. Journal of Indian Education, Department of Teacher Education, NCERT, Sri Aurobindo Marg, New Delhi 110016.

Chapter - 38

Utilization of Digital Technology in Class Room

K.V. Satya Prakash

Abstract

Technology is getting updated very fast and the new generations of students too are much acquainted with it but the present day education systems are continuing old models of usual black or white boards with chalk pieces or markers thereby creating mismatches as well as gaps which are widening resulting in lack of understanding in students leading to increasing rates of failure or dropouts simultaneously rising frustrations among responsible Faculty despite effortsJust upgrading infrastructure would not itself create rapport of Professor with pupils but use of technical aids such as mobile or tablets and Virtual or Augmented Reality in the classrooms would surely connect the youngsters even with the old guards so that instant interest is generated for doing and learning, knowing and developing, etc., which are to be attained in endIn this scenario, the study highlights the urgent need to take advantage of advancements in the domain of technological developments and bring the same to augment resources in the course curriculum so that the teaching methodologies undergo drastic changes with a view to have real- time experienced trainings instead of lectures on subjects or topics in syllabuses for exams. The analysis also provides some case instances where some of the top educationists of most reputed institutions were interacting with the lower level colleges' Faculty as well as students using the internet, web cam, etc. technologies to the fullest extent apart from ensuring reaching benefits to all for optimizing 'Win-Win' situation which is to be achieved and required for the youth to advance further in their chosen careers or lives to become true updated literates to benefit the society at large so that the community develops along with the economy.

Introduction

Education is not just imparting what is there in the subjects or syllabuses without taking into consideration the interests and understanding levels of the students, especially the present day new generation youngsters who prefer to use the latest technology, more particularly mobiles. Transferring the same knowledge not through usual old methods but by using new technologies is a challenge to the teachers who are to ensure that their efforts bear fruits in the form of improving the skill quotients apart from increasing the success rates in exams and competitions.

Traditional to modern ways of learning

Old pedagogical methods seems outdated due to advancements in the technology, which interestingly is extensively used by the youngsters who form the majority of the students while Faculty generally may be indifferent to this trend and continue their usual ways of imparting resulting in widening gaps of learning among the youth who are unable to catch up in education.

Types of making students understand

There are three types of making students understand and these need to be used depending on the learners' capacity to grasp. The first one is the 'Coconut' method, which is usually to be administered on the learned group since the coconut is hard to break from outside and insides also difficult to take out to consume. This is the high level of teaching and for normal students the lessons go above their heads but to those who are mature enough to concentrate more to learn it gives results. Similarly, the next is the 'Banana' Method, in which slight effort is only required on the part of learners to absorb what is taught as the skin of banana is to be pealed to grasp the contents that can be taken without much difficulty. Lastly, there is this 'Grape' method, which is the simple way of making the pupils understand, i.e. the seedless grape can just be taken without much effort, thereby making it the easiest way to grasp the lesson quickly.

Learning by involving

There is a Chinese proverb that if one lectures, however best it is, the listeners do not remember it for long and if talk is combined with demonstration or showing then the audience 'may' absorb to some extent, but if pupils are involved with interest they would definitely learn. This aspect needs to be taken into consideration for serious learning to take place in the colleges for the benefit of the Faculty and students or else all efforts would be a futile exercise .

Synchronizing the methods with those of the learners

While in the past students used to make lot of effort in going to the libraries, get hold of the prescribed text books and write down notes for references, the present generation need to only take pictures in mobiles or Google to get access to the required contents or connect to worldwide groups through internet, WhatsApp or Face book to get variety of angles or analysis using technological tools but they alone cannot do it as they lack the knowledge of 'what' to get, which the teachers know due to experience in learning the hard way. Now- a- days there is no need to adopt old ways of learning through library, text books, writing notes, etc. or make much efforts as vast data are available to be accessed for taking in what is required at any time. Hence, it is essential for the Faculty to get updated with latest technology so that using it in the classrooms would enable generating interest among youngsters as they need simple ways of learning due to advancements and innovations, which are lesser costly, easier and user- friendly.

Use of Laptops in e- classrooms

Students were encouraged to buy and use laptops extensively as systems in the colleges are less in number and not sufficient for all. E- Classrooms concept has come into being thereby making the Faculty and students use e- learning through LCDs/ LEDs connecting them to laptops so that whatever is taught is also simultaneously captured. Classrooms as well as campuses are also 'wi- fi' enabled thereby providing internet connectivity to everyone, and due to digitalization, these are also called Digital Classrooms. Similarly for exams also, online tests are conducted so that students know their mistakes instantly and need not wait for long for results.

Experiments in the use of Mobile technology use or 'Tablets' and internet

IIT- Bombay are the pioneers in experimenting with the use of mobile technology or 'Tablets', which they collaborated with Data Wind Technologies to manufacture at low cost of Rs.1,000/- and after convincing the Ministry for Human Resources Development to give subsidy they not only got the supplies of these but also arranged to send them to all those colleges who were willing to be their Remote Centres of learning, free of cost. Then, they connected to the Remote Centres using broadband network and webcams so that the best Faculty at IIT interacted with the other colleges' Faculty and Students at those Centres by conducting various online Faculty or Students Development Programmes, using latest technologies easily with less or no cost to spread learning across all over the Country, where tests are conducted through 'Tablets' for instant results enabling participants to gain knowledge/ skills and certificates from IIT- Bombay.

Knowing understanding level of students and conducting tests by using 'Tablets'

It has been found that through the use of mobile technology, the 'tablets' are more effective in assessing the students learning abilities, particularly the understanding levels. Just like 'Audience Poll' in the TV Show 'Kaun Banega Crorepati', the teachers can instantly access to know the impact of their imparting lessons by asking pupils 'yes' or 'no' to whether they understood or not so that they can get data as to who understood and who did not, for proceeding further either to repeat in different way if all or many did not understand or to move on to the next if all or majority are following the topics, or to take extra classes for those weaker ones who are slow in catching with the rest of class. All objective- type tests can be held.

Experiments in Virtual Learning through 'A- VIEW'

Amrita University developed Amrita Virtual E- learning World or 'A-VIEW', which is advanced multi- model, multi- platform, collaborative e-learning solution allowing an instructor to teach or interact with large number of learners transcending geographies on real- time basis through live audio video streaming and synchronized content sharing with multiple users in many places.

IIT- Bombay too used this 'A- VIEW' to connect to different Remote Centres at various locations for conducting courses, and/ or tests and issuing IIT- Bombay certificates to the participants. For the 'Tablets' and for spreading IIT- Bombay expertise across the country, Dr. Deepak B. Pathak, Professor there, was conferred 'Padma Shree' during the year 2013 by the Government of India.

Virtual Reality (VR) and Augmented Reality (AR)

Despite some successful experiments by great institutes like the IIT-Bombay and Amrita University in the use of technology thereby creating interest among the young Faculty as well as students, there is still vast scope for using latest technologies in the classrooms such as the Virtual Reality (VR), and Augmented Reality (AR), which are briefed below to understand them Virtual Reality (VR) is an interactive Computer- generated experience taking place within a simulated environment. It incorporates mainly auditory and visual feedback. This immersive environment can be similar to the real world or it can be fantastical. Whereas, Augmented Reality (AR) systems may also be considered a form of VR that layers virtual information over a live camera feed into a headset or through smart phone or tablet device giving the user the ability to view three-dimensional image.

AR is an interactive experience of real-world environment where objects that reside in the real-world are 'augmented' by computer- generated perceptual information across multiple sensory modalities, like visual, auditory, etc.

Scope for bringing in VR and AR into classrooms

As it has been found that youngsters are going to 'play stations' for games using VR and AR, these technologies can also be brought into the classrooms. For example, as it is very costly and cumbersome occupying space to bring in the real machines in the college laboratories, they can be designed virtually or augmented to create a real- world environment in the labs or classes so that if students practice there they would gain similar practical exposure and experience just like they handled them really and can straight away work on them in field without any difficulty after graduating when they take up jobs in their chosen organizations. This has been proven to be right in the case of pilot training as initially they are trained in simulated environment on the ground where similar flying atmosphere and operations are created so that only after perfection they are allowed to fly or operate an aircraft in air due to high risk factors and costs.

Conclusions

It has been found that by and large youth are very much acquainted with the latest technologies as they are less costly, easy to operate and mostly user- friendly. It has been found that excepting for some experiments by IIT- Bambay and Amrita University to bring in the technology into classes to connect not only with their Faculty and Students but also to other colleges across the country using mobile technology or 'Tablets' and internet/ Webcams due to Amrita University developed Amrita Virtual E- learning World (A- VIEW), still there is lot of scope to use Virtual Reality (VR) and Augmented Reality (AR) in classrooms to make students employable in the companies after gaduating so that they would be able to adopt work-life without training apart from creating interest in them for involvement in the learning processes.

References

1. Author Prof. K.V. Satya Prakash's experiences at Alluri Institute of Management Sciences (AIMS), Warangal, a Remote Centre of IIT- Bombay and Amrita University's 'A- VIEW'.
2. Internet Resource through the On-line Website of IIT- Bombay- www.iitb.ac.in/ industry/ Outreach Programs/ Centre for Distance Engineering Education Program (CDEEP).

3. Internet Resource through On- line Website of Amrita University- www/ amrita.edu.
4. Interactions through internet with persons like 'Padma Shri' Dr. Deepak B. Pathak, IIT- B.
5. Personal Experiences with Faculty and Students of different streams in various colleges.

Chapter - 39

Impact of Open Source Technology in Higher Education

P. Swathi, V. Srujanamma

Abstract

Open Source Software is the major rival in the software market previously dominated by proprietary software products. Open source development has been around several years and is renowned for its extraordinary code quality. Open Source Software is the major rival in the software market previously dominated by proprietary software products. Some of the more popular open source projects include Linux, Apache and MySQL. Additionally, to its non-traditional distribution model that relies on software downloads from a website, the development of software code is collaborative and not handled by a single company but by a community of high-skilled, fascinated and encouraged developers. Open Source Software(OSS) is available in various forms including web servers, Enterprise Resource Planning systems (ERPs), Academic management systems and network management systems and the development and uptake of such software by both commercial and non-commercial companies and institutions is still on the rise. The availability of OSS applications for every common type of enterprise, minimal licensing issues and availability of source code as well as ease of access has made the technology even more attractive in learning and teaching of software based courses in institutions of learning. Through embracing this technology, institutions of learning have been able to minimize general operations cost that could have otherwise been incurred in procuring similar proprietary software. Students and teaching staff can nowadays interact and modify the readily available source code hence making learning and teaching more practical.

Keywords: *Information and Communication Technology(ICT), Apache Internet Information Server (IIS), MYSQL, Open Source Software (OSS), Open Source Technology.*

Introduction

Open Source Software is the major rival in the software market previously dominated by proprietary software products. Open Source Software(OSS) is available in various forms including web servers, Enterprise Resource Planning systems (ERPs), Academic management systems and network management systems and the development and uptake of such software by both commercial and non-commercial companies and institutions is still on the rise. The availability of OSS applications for every common type of enterprise, minimal licensing issues and availability of source code as well as ease of access has made the technology even more attractive in learning and teaching of software based courses in institutions of learning. Through embracing this technology, institutions of learning have been able to minimize general operations cost that could have otherwise been incurred in procuring similar proprietary software. Students and teaching staff can nowadays interact and modify the readily available source code hence making learning and teaching more practical.

Benefits

- Open Source solutions that are available off-the-shelf and high speed can considerably reduce the time for an offering to reach the market.
  Innovation.
- Companies that use Open Source get access to novel and innovative software, as well as enjoying participation in communities were this innovation occurs.
- Open source software is mostly high-quality software.

Challenges

- Ignoring license compliance can result in copyright infringement, stop shipment orders, and immediately impact revenue streams.
- Open Source software needs to be regularly monitored and updated to decrease the risk of security vulnerabilities.
- Proper compliance is fundamental and requires the organization to train personnel and set up governance. On the next level, the operational barrier is about how to become a more active participant in Open Source communities.

Open source programs for students and teachers

A. Focus Writer

How many browser tabs do you have open right now? Have you checked

Twitter in the last 10 minutes? Let's face it: technology was born to grab our attention. Beat down the distractions and get back to writing with Focus Writer, an application that helps students (and adults) dismiss the siren songs of social media and YouTube videos so they can craft a perfect five-paragraph essay. Launch Focus Writer and the application fills the screen with a blank white page and charming simulated-wood desktop backdrop. Focus Writer does one thing very well: it removes temptation.

B. Brackets

Cool kids code, and when introducing programming to young minds, HTML is an easy entry point for students of all skill levels. Brackets is a terrific text editor that excels at visual web design. Lightweight and feature rich, Brackets is deeply customizable thanks to its underlying HTML, CSS, and JavaScript framework. With live code previews, students will love the immediacy of writing HTML and instantly discovering how their changes render in a browser. For a fun and challenging learning project, have students pair Brackets and Reveal.js to craft a class presentation that will make PowerPoint look decidedly old school.

C. Red Note book

Youthful minds are not always organized minds. Students often struggle with managing notes and lesson materials. RedNotebook is a simple calendar-based journal that can help tame unruly piles of digital paper. The application is built around the idea of a daily diary. Individual journal entries may be tagged, searched, and identified via a visual world cloud. Students can use RedNotebook to organize notes by class or unit of study. A neat feature is the ability to export journal entries, as text or PDF, by date range or by tag. A student might use the export function to submit a collection of written work to a teacher for grading, or to forward notes to fellow students who missed class.

The open source way can distinguish you from other computer science students

- Demonstrate the way you work
- Increase your visibility
- Increase your value

Conclusion

Open source development has been around several years and is renowned for its extraordinary code quality. Some of the more popular open source projects include Linux, Apache and MySQL. Additionally, to its non-traditional distribution model that relies on software downloads from a website, the development of software code is collaborative and not handled by a single company but by a community of high-skilled, fascinated and encouraged developers. The community may be comprised of companies and individuals. The licensing models typically used promote the sharing and reuse of software source code with relaxed intellectual property restrictions. Open source development makes particular sense in the area of interoperability.

References

1. Aksulu, A., and M. Wade. 2010. A comprehensive review and synthesis of open source research. *Journal of the Association for Information Systems* 11: 576–656. [Web of Science ®],[Google Scholar].
2. Boehmke, Bradley C.; Hazen, Benjamin T. (21 February 2017). "The Future of Supply Chain Information Systems: The Open Source Ecosystem". Global Journal of Flexible Systems Management. 18 (2): 163–168. doi:10.1007/s40171-017-0152-x.
3. Hwang, Lorraine; Fish, Allison; Soito, Laura; Smith, MacKenzie; Kellogg, Louise H. (November 2017). "Software and the Scientist: Coding and Citation Practices in Geodynamics". *Earth and Space Science*. 4 (11): 670–680. Bibcode: 2017 E&SS....4..670H.
4. Moore, Madison (9 May 2016). "Journal of Open Source Software helps researchers write and publish papers on software - SD Times".

Chapter - 40

Attitude towards Computer Education among B.Ed. Students – A Study

Gollapudi Manikya Rao

Abstract

Computer play unique role in the modern world we can grater much information; it is useful in the field of education. It will make out work easy so introduced at all levels of education. It will make out work easy training course. If student trainees themselves don't possess and believes in computer education, they will not be in the right position to teach for their students in future. In India, Intel tech to the future was launched on 28th February 2000. It is a world – wide effort to help both in-service teachers and pre-service teachers integrate technology into classroom. The programmed enable pre- service teacher educators and teacher trainees to discover how to create technology enhanced unites in collaborative teams and develop tools that motivate students and help them become self - directed learners. They will understand how to use powerful productivity software, multimedia tools, and the internet to promote inquiry – based learning. Teacher educators are provided with training and resources for use in their pre-service courses. Teachers trainees working teams has they use technology to tap into vast reservoirs of information for the internet and digital sources and develop lesson plans that meet challenging standards' while promoting critical thinking and helping students grow and succeed with the speed of technology. Strengthening the pre- service teachers' content knowledge as well as presenting the content in a way which help them discovers how to turn the power of computer technology into teaching tools to captivate students, motivate them, and ultimately move them towards grates learning. The awareness of computer literacy among the students, teachers and parents is needed. Computer education has assumed immense significance in the education system of the country. Strengthening the pre – server's teachers' content of knowledge as well as presenting the content in a way which helps them to discover how to turn the powers of computer technology into teaching tools that captivate students, motivate them and ultimately move them towards greater learning. Hence, computer education should from an integral part of the teacher education programmed. Even though integration of computer education into the teacher education curriculum has started already is has not been implicated effectively in all the teachers education colleges. Hence, the present study attempt to assess attitude towards computer education among teacher trainees.

***Key words**: computer education, teacher educators, technology.*

Introduction

Computer is a device that computes, especially a programmable electronic machine that performs high-speed mathematical or logical operations or that assembles, stores, correlates, or otherwise processes information. Computers perform many of the routine activities in today's society. Computers have entered all walks of human life across the world. They are being used in various fields including education. Computers were introduced into this field to make the Teaching Learning Process (TLP) easier and more effective. Instructional material can be prepared and stored within the computer in the form of programmes, which are carefully structured to teach specific lessons.

The computer can ease the load of administrative duties, leaving the teacher more time to concentrate on teaching. For example, the computer can be used to assist in building timetable; to monitor and schedule teaching resources; to build up and maintain comprehensive student records in order to provide a complete student profile; and to accumulate information for assistance with career guidance (Hunt and Shelley, 1989).

Use of Internet and E-mail in Education

The Internet is an international network connecting a large number of smaller networks that link computers at academic, scientific, governmental and non-governmental and commercial institutions. The best known part of Internet is that WWW (World Wide Web) which stores information in multimedia form – sounds, photos, videos, as well as text etc.,

The Internet is a giant network of computers located all over the world that communicate with each other. At various stops on the highway, there are "sights" – similarly, at various places on the Internet, there are repositories of software and other information that you can download for free. This is call *file* transfer (Fisher, 1993).

The use of the Internet deserves special mention here. It is the newest and in the world of educational computing, it is being promoted by many as the most powerful tool for learning ever invented. What makes it so powerful is that is allows the child or young person to freely search for educational material or useful information, as well as doing communication with all sorts of people in different parts of the planet.

Importance of Computer Education in Teacher Education

The awareness of computer literacy among the students, teachers and parents is needed. Computer education has assumed immense significance in the education system of the country. Strengthening the pre-service teachers' content of knowledge as well as presenting the content in a way which helps them to discover how to turn the power of computer technology into teaching tools that captivate students, motivate them and ultimately move them towards greater learning.

The findings of this research will be helpful not only to teacher educators, but also educational administrators and planners, and parents as well. The findings may be useful in suggesting desirable changes in teacher education curriculum, to develop positive attitudes among the teacher trainees, and suggest remedies for the present problems.

The resources on the net are so large that even a well-established traditional library cannot match the Internet. The latest books or information is available on the Internet and this can be accessed from anywhere in the world. Trainees, teacher educators, researchers and anybody can use it for that matter. "Knowledge webs" give people distributed access to experts, archival resources, and authentic environments and shared investigations. Via information infrastructures, educators, and students can join distributed conferences that provide an instant network of contacts with useful skills (Sheela, 2005).

Electronic mail (e-mail) is the most commonly used service of the Internet. E-mail facilitates communication with people all over the world. It has made the geographical boundaries of nations shrink, as one can send mail to anyone connected to Internet wherever he/she is almost instantaneously. E-mail is mostly used for sending and receiving messages, scanned letters, text and image files, mails as attachments for the download, which reduces the postal delays and save time.

Need for the Study

Computers play unique role in the modern world. We can gather much information; it is useful in the field of education. It will make out work easy so introduced at all levels of education. Computers are introduced in teacher training course. If student trainees themselves don't possess and believe in computer education, they will not be in the right position to teach for their students in future.

They should know and understand what the computers are since success in developing computer awareness among pupils depends ultimately upon the teachers. The discussion implies that the level of computer education help by teachers should be positive. It they are having positive attitude they can lead their students in a progressive path. But if they are having negative attitude they create an unfavorable attitude in their students also. Which may student the technical progress of the nation towards prosperity.

There is a belief that arts students cannot teach the operation of computers in a right way, only science students who come from a back ground of mathematics can able to teach computers in a better way. This study will help the researcher to know how far Science and Arts students are aware of the computers, uses and application in the field of education.

The study will also help the researcher to know how far Men and Women are aware of computers. Are they holding favorable attitude towards computers in their curriculum? Does this curriculum help them to develop or improve their knowledge in computers.

Objectives of the Study

- To identify whether teacher trainers posses favorable attitude towards computer education.
- To identify whether the gender is influencing the teacher trainee's attitude towards computer education.
- To identify whether the educational discipline is influencing the teacher trainee's attitude towards computer education.
- To identify whether the locality is influencing the teacher trainee's attitude towards computer education.
- To identify whether the academic achievement is influencing the teacher trainee's attitude towards computer education.
- To identify the effect of use of computer technology in education.

Hypothesis

1. There is no significant difference between Male and Female attitude towards computer education among B.Ed. students.
2. There is no significant difference between Arts and Science attitude towards computer education among B.Ed. students.

3. There is no significant difference between Rural and Urban attitude towards computer education among B.Ed. students.
4. There is no significant difference between Post-Graduate and Graduates attitude towards computer education among B.Ed. students.

Limitation of the society

The investigation is only for B.Ed. Students.

- The scope of the study is limited to identify the teacher trainee's attitude towards computer education.
- The sample is limited to only 125 trainees including both male and female teacher trainees.
- This investigation is limited to the Visakhapatnam city, Visakhapatnam District only.

Design of the Study

This investigation was undertaken to find out whether teacher trainee holds favorable attitude towards computer education. This study was felt necessary as a revised B.Ed. curriculum has included computer education as an important component of teacher training. Before 2001 the emphasis was on class room teaching, curriculum and curriculum experiences into individuals with IT competency skills also. After a review of related literature on computer education, the investigator decided for this descriptive study comes under normative survey method using an attitude scale will serve the purpose.

The present investigation is conducted in three phases.

They are:

1. Preparation of suitable tool to know the attitude towards computer education among teacher trainees.
2. Collection of data.
3. Analysis and Report.

Selection of Items

The investigator according to the aims and objectives of the study prepares a large number of items.

For preparing the statements, the following areas were identified.

1. From point of view of teacher trainees.

2. From point of view of students.
3. Place of computer education.
4. General use of computers and in cost – economy.

The teacher trainees were expected to respond to the statements given in each area after writing the initial draft of the statements. The investigator got the statements evaluated by the panel of judges. The initial draft consisted of 55 statements and 50 statements are selected for the pilot study.

Table - 1

Area	*Item No.*	*No. of Items*	*Percentage %*
From point of view of B.Ed. Students	01 – 16	15	30
From point of view of students	16 – 24	9	18
Place of computers in education	25 – 38	14	28
General use of computer and in cost economy	39 – 50	12	24

Sample selected for the Study

A sample is a sample portion of a population selected for observation and analysis. It is a collected consisting of a part or subject of objective or individual population, which is selected for the express purpose of reorienting the population.

Table - 2 Description of the sample – variable wise

Variable	*Classification of variable*	*Sample*	*Total*
Gender	Male Female	55 70	125
Locality	Rural Urban	52 73	125
Academic Achievement	Post-Graduate Graduate	46 79	125
Education Discipline	Arts Science	56 69	125

A sample of 125 B. Ed. students covering Visakhapatnam city was chosen for the purpose. The technique of random sampling was used covering different variables.

The variables are

Analysis

Analysis of data means studying the tabulated material in order to determine inherent factor or meaning. It involves breaking down existing complex factors into simpler parts and putting the parts together in new arrangement for purpose of interpretation.

After the data has been collected, it must processed and analyzed to draw proper inference. Good, Barr, Seats writes, "Analysis is a process which enters into research is one form of another from the very beginning".

Statistical Analysis

1. Calculating frequency distribution of items under study.
2. Calculation methods of central tendency – Mean, Median, Mode, and establishing norms
3. Calculating percentiles and percentile ranks.

In the process of analysis of the data, the investigator usually makes use of many statistical devises necessary for purpose of their study. There are some other complicated devices of statistical analysis which researcher use particular experimental or complex or casual comparative studies of investigation.

Verification of first Hypothesis

The first hypothesis of the study states that "there is no significant difference between male and female towards attitude of computer education among B.Ed. Students".

Category	*N*	*M*	*S.D*	*D*	*SED*	*CR*
Male	55	68.08	9.22	4.88	1.54	3.18*
Female	70	72.96	7.55			

*Significant

The obtained 't' value i.e. **3.18** is greater than the table value 2.62 at 0.01 level. Hence the Null Hypothesis is rejected.

Verification of second hypothesis

The second hypothesis of the study states that "there is no significant difference between Arts and Science towards attitude of computer education among B. Ed. Students".

Category	*N*	*M*	*S.D*	*D*	*SED*	*CR*
Arts	56	71.32	9.48	0.91	1.62	0.56*
Science	69	70.41	7.97			

*Not Significant

The obtained't' value is **0.56** which is less than the table value 1.98 at 0.05 level. Hence the Null hypothesis is accepted.

Verification of Third Hypothesis

The third hypothesis of the study states that "there is no significant difference between Rural and Urban towards attitude of computer education among the B.Ed. Students".

Category	*N*	*M*	*S.D*	*D*	*SED*	*CR*
Rural	52	70.19	8.29	0.83	1.50	0.55*
Urban	73	71.02	8.18			

*Not Significant

The obtained't' value is 0.55 is less than the table value 1.98 at 0.05 level. Hence the Null Hypothesis is accepted.

Verification of Fourth Hypothesis

The fourth hypothesis of the study states that "there is no significant difference between Graduate and Post-Graduates towards attitude of computer education among B.Ed. Students".

Category	*N*	*M*	*S.D*	*D*	*SED*	*CR*
Post Graduate	46	71.98	8.28	1.83	1.56	0.53
Graduate	79	70.03	60			

*Not significant

The obtained't' value is **0.53** is less than the table value 1.98 at 0.05 level. Hence the Null Hypothesis is accepted.

The following table shows the mean values according to the Area

Area		*Mean Scores*
From point of view of B.Ed. Students	(Area-I)	24.01
From point of view of students	(Area-II)	13.21
Place of computers in Education	(Area-III)	19.04
General use of computers & in Cost Economy	(Area-IV)	14.44

Table shows the area wise mean scores for the whole sample. The sample has agreed mostly all questions in the Area – I "from point of view of B.Ed. Students".

The samples don't show the favorable attitude towards "point view of students" than Area – II. It is clear that some students do not have the favorable attitude towards computer education. All most all sample responded positively to the questions under Area – III i.e. place of computers in education". From these opinions, it is clear that all are accepted the role computers in education.

Conclusions

For proper existence in the modern world where technology is dominating and computers are taking over the control of day to day activity. A favourables attitudes towards computer education is the minimum expectation. This favourable attitude towards computer an education is also to be expected from prospective teachers i.e. B.Ed. Students. This study of attitude of B.Ed. Students towards computer education leads the investigator to draw the following conclusions is concluded most of the B.Ed. Students hold a favourable attitude towards computer education. This itself is a positive sign. The investigator is of the opinion that inclusion of computer education in teacher training program is effectively working on prospective teachers.

(1) It is also a good sign that these students irrespective of their education discipline are having favorable attitude towards computer education.

(2) There is influence of Gender on attitude towards computer education. Male and Female B.Ed. students hold opposing views towards Computer Education.

(3) It is also good sign that these students irrespective of their locality i.e. rural and urbanshown their favourable attitude towards computer education.

(4) There is influence of academic achievement towards attitude of computer education i.e. both post-graduate and graduate students shows their favourable attitude.

(5) The B.Ed. students have expressed favourable opinions regarding point of view of B.Ed. students and place of computer education. Unfavourable opinions hold regarding from point of view of students and in cost-economy point of view. Because the computer education is not available to a common man in our present educational institutions. Hence, it is a conclusion of investigator that the teacher trainees posses favourable attitude towards computer education and unfavorable towards in cost-economy point of view.

Findings

(1) There is difference in the attitude towards computer education in Male and Femaleteacher trainees. Female teacher trainees showed more favourable attitudes towards computer education than Male teacher trainees.

(2) It is also a good sign that teacher trainees irrespective of their locality shown favourable attitude towards computer education. There is no difference in attitudes of Rural and Urban people towards computer education.

(3) There is no difference in the attitude towards computer education in graduates and post—graduates. Post – Graduates as well as graduates shown favourable attitude towards computer education.

(4) It is also a good sign that these teacher trainees irrespective of their educational discipline i.e. Arts and Science are favourable towards computer education.

This study of attitude of teacher trainees towards computer education leads the investigator to drawn the following conclusion that most of the teacher trainees hold favourable attitude towards computer education. This itself is a positive sign. The investigator comes to the opinion that inclusion of computer education in teacher training program will be received favourable by the prospective teacher. For proper existence in the modern world, technology is gradually dominating and computers are taking over the control of day-to-day activity. A favourable attitude towards computer education is the minimum expectation. This favourable attitude is also to be expected from prospective teacher i.e. teacher trainees.

Discussion

This study shows that these students who have come to receive training as teachers are in favor of modernized technological class rooms. There seems to be willing to use the computer resources for class rooms teaching. Thus this is a sign of teachers in the process of modernization. When compare to the tradition teachers it is to be assumed that the present day teachers can easily catch up with the current change in education technology. The future class rooms are going to be dominated by computers and every individual learns the basis of operating computer.

Suggestions

On the basis of conclusions and findings the investigator had made some suggestions for improving the attitude towards computer education. They are:

1. The computer education among B.Ed. students should be more practical oriented.
2. The computer lab has to be maintained according to the norms given by NCTE.
3. More and more practical hours are to be allotted for developing positive attitude towards computer education.
4. Not only teaching operating systems and MS-Office. There is a necessity to know how lesson – plans are to be designed and prepared and how a lesson is presented in power point presentation effectively. Hence stress should be given in the utility of computer technology in their day-to-day lessons of the B. Ed. program.

Reference

1. Bala Guryswamy E - Programming in Basic. (1983).
2. J.W. Bes - : Research in Education.
3. J.C. Agarwas – Educational Research - An introduction.
4. A.C. Agarwal – Educational Philosophy.
5. Henry E. Garrett – Statistics in psychology and education
6. Jacquetta Megarray
7. David R.F. Walker – World year book of Education
8. James W. Armesey and Norman C Dahi - An inquiry into the use of instructional technology
9. Martin Greenberger - Computers and the world of future
10. Michal J Apter - The new Technology of Education
11. Roger E. Levier - The Emerging Technology
12. Singh UK and KN Udarshan – Media Education – Discovery Publishing House

Chapter - 41

Contemporary Classroom Management

Prof. T.V.R. Mohan, R.K. Chithiraa

Abstract

Class room management is a challenging task to the teachers' in the present century. Management means an act or skill of dealing with people or situations in a successful way. Managing is something different from controlling. So classroom management is all about how the teacher managing the students and the classroom situation in a successful way by using some strategies and methods. Classroom management is considered to be one of the most important skills of an effective and efficient teacher. All the teachers do not acquire this skill. Only very few, know how to manage the class and the students. Even though the teachers know the benefits of the classroom management, they can't practice it in their classes. In any B.Ed college, classroom management is prescribed as a subject and all the teacher trainees are well aware of its significance. Without passing that subject no teacher trainees will pass their final exams and become a teacher. Then, why the teachers fail to apply the subject classroom management in their classes? So there must be some drawbacks in the teaching of classroom management to the teacher trainees. The learners can learn many things in a well planned classroom. So any classroom should need this classroom management. But many teachers fail to be a good classroom manager. This paves the way for the raising of many problems in the class which cannot be controlled by the teachers. Many students loss their interest in learning and become uneducated due to the teachers without knowing the proper classroom management procedures. This paper focuses on the advantages of class room management, the condition of classroom without proper management, present century classroom, the reason for the failure of practicing classroom management by the teachers in their class and some solutions which Arguably says that by changing the teaching methodology of education programs the society will get a good teacher with all the skills of classroom management. Finally the paper suggests some tips to managing the 21st century classroom.

***Key Words**: Classroom Management, Condition of the Classroom, Suggestive Ideas to manage the Class, Benefits,*

Introduction

The Words Of Hardin give a clear idea about the classroom management.

> "The ultimate goal of classroom management should not be on simple obedience, but on having students behave appropriately because they know it's the right thing to do and because they can understand how their actions affect other people" (Hardin, 2008,p. 142).

The above quote clearly explains that classroom management can develop obedience and also it has the power to change the behavior of the learners. If its is a goal of the classroom management then the class without classroom management filled with indiscipline and disobedient students. So this quote proves the importance of classroom management. Every teacher should concern with different managements such as time, human resource, management etc..., but these all comes under this classroom management because classroom is a place where teacher and students spend most of their time. So to have a good time inside the class the teacher should manage the class in a better way.

Advantages of classroom management

"The greatest sign of success for a teacher…is to be able to say "The children are now working as if I did not exist." – Maria Montessori (qtd in Managing the classroom environment).

The above quotation suggests the advantages for the teachers who have the good classroom management. Not only the teachers but also the students also benefited by this management. Some of the benefits are listed below.

Iqac St.xavier College of Education

Proceedings of the International Seminar on Teaching to Teach and Learning to Learn in the Contemporary Classrooms

Time saving

The basic of classroom management it pre planned. If the teachers plan well in advance, then it will save time for both the teachers and the learners also learn many things within a period. In a well planned class the learners can learn many new things and it will not let the students to involve in any mischief activities.

Class room becomes a Resourceful area

The proverb "ideal mind is a devils workshop" will not happen in the case of the learners. Because the teachers are well planned then they can easily assign works to the learners one after another which makes the learners to busy with the task and gives no time to misbehave in the class. So the classroom becomes a resourceful area where there is no chance for the learners to do other works rather than learning.

Gain the heart of the learners

If a teacher is be a classroom manager they should know better about the minds of the individual learners. So the teacher can closely move with the students. This will impress many students. Then the students get hope on the particular teacher that they are the only soul in the world who knows very thing.

Role model

The teacher becomes a role model for the students only if they have a good classroom managing skill or else students will not respect them. A good teacher with good classroom management can influence many students to choose teacher profession in their future.

Class control

By planning a good classroom management the teacher can control the class indirectly.

Harmonies relationship

By using this classroom management the teacher can build a good conduct with the students which pave the way to the harmonies relationship between the learners and the teachers.

Class without proper management

All misbehave happens in the class without proper management. If the teacher leaves the students to do their works, definitely they will do useless things and not academic duties. Even the students who scored first mark will do the same if there is no control. The class without proper management will have the following problems.

1. The students will do the work of other subjects in the class.
2. They will do all the mischief activities like eating and sleeping in the class hours, fight with the fellow students, lack of attention in listening to the class, etc…

3. The students will do indiciplinary activities.
4. The students will evaluate the teacher's ability and they started to act according to the teachers.
5. The students won't respect the teachers. Sometimes they will argue with the teacher and they thought teacher as a inferior than them.

These are some of the problems faced by the class without management.

Present century classroom

Now the atmosphere of the classroom has totally changed. The students are well talented. They are more knowledgeable than the teachers by the help of internet and other web sources. By single click.

IQAC ST. Xavier College of Education

Proceedings of the International Seminar on Teaching to Teach and Learning to Learn in the Contemporary Classrooms

They get all the information. So they treated teachers as a secondary source. They primarily relay on the machines which easily gave them knowledge related ideas and messages.

So the teacher have to update themselves regularly if they fail to do it then they can't survive among those students as a teacher. The students can easily evaluate the capacity of the teacher. If the teacher fulfills the needs of the learners then they will definitely respect the teachers if not the opposite will be the result. Now day's teachers are forced to make use off all the periods. If they waste a single hour then students will not come under the control of the teacher.

Can the teachers use punishments to control the students? No it is not possible in the present century. Till the previous century all teachers used punishments like

1. Scolding
2. Beating
3. Make the students to stand outside of the class
4. Ask the students to stand on the bench
5. Giving imposition
6. Kneel down
7. Kneel down with hands up

8. Take the student to the principal and make others to know the mistake of the learner
9. Call the parents of the learner and complaint about their behavior.

Some decades ago these were some of the punishments commonly given by the teachers in all the schools. But in present days these punishments are banned by the government and it give full rights to the learners to complaint about the teacher if he or she does anything against the dignity of the learners. So the teacher's hands are tied up with Government rules. Now the teacher profession becomes a tough task and the teacher should be very careful when they deal with the learners because if the students started to hate the teacher then they will do anything against the teacher.

For example there are several criminal activities based on students attacking teacher, student snapped the teacher who gave punishment, etc…,

This all are because of using punishments to control the class. So if class room cannot be control by using punishments then how can the teacher control the class? The following suggestions would help the teachers to control or manage the class without punishments.

Suggestive ideas to manage the class

"A good teacher, like a entertainer first must hold their audience attention, then they can teach lessons."

IQAC ST. Xavier College of Education

Proceedings of the International Seminar on Teaching to Teach and Learning to Learn in the Contemporary Classrooms.

1. Understanding the learners
2. Conducting Seminars
3. Group discussion
4. Presentations
5. Quiz
6. Debate
7. Role play
8. Five minutes activities
9. Reinforcement
10. Using various models
11. Apply psychology
12. Teacher a good guide and a counselor

These are the some of the activities which make the class to be under the control of learning circumstance and help to avoid the chance of misbehave of the learners. Let see these points in detail.

1. Understanding the learners

The teacher should understand the needs and the feelings of the learners. Not all the students are problematic and all the problematic students are not easily identified by the teacher. So the teacher should observe the pros and cons of each student. Maintaining mutual understanding among the students is the first tasks to the teacher before get into the lessons. If the teacher fails to achieve this, then it will be very difficult for the learners to listen to the classes and the teacher to teach them. There is a subject called understanding the learners in education course. All the teachers had read the subject but they fails to apply it. The words of kuralt explain the duty of good teacher. He quotes that "A Good teacher know how to bring out the best in students" – Charles Kuralt.

2. Conducting seminars

Now seminars become a popular tactic in testing the understanding of the students at the college levels. This can be applying to the schools also. The teacher can assign a particular topic to an individual and ask them to teach the topic in the class. This is a very good example for learner centric approach.

Benefits

By conducting this activity the students can get a clear understanding about the topic assigned to them. They also get interest in participating in the classroom activities. After completing the seminars the students are motivated and have self confidence to do things like this.

3. Group Discussion

G. D. is a popular way of involving students in the classroom activities. The teacher can assign a topic regarding their subject or any social issue and ask the students to say a few words regarding the topic. In this G.D. the teacher can make the class into groups and give chance to each group to speak out their views on the topic.

Benefits

G. D. provides equal opportunities to all the students. Even the passive listeners in the class also have the chance to share their view. This makes the whole class to participate in the academic work. This is also a strategy in learner centric approach.

4. Presentations:

In presentations the teacher can leave the students to choose their own topics according to their area of interest. In this presentation the students can present their idea through oral, experiment or PPT.

Presentation etc…, but they should submit their topic in the form of written document before they present it.

Benefits

This is something like a research and if the teacher assigns a written work then the students will just copy from other student. But this presentation is based on their own idea if it is not then they will not present it well. So this activity will help the teacher to identify the interest of the learner as well as learners to get to know of their ability.

5. Quiz

Conducting quiz program is also a good technique to check the understanding of the learners. There is no necessary for the teacher to always ask the questions. It is better to leave the students to conduct the quiz program. Maybe two or three students in the class prepare question on a particular lesson and pose questions to the fellow students. For the next lesson the next three will conduct the quiz.

Benefits

By this activity both the students who organizing the quiz and who participate can get a clear idea about the lesson. This activity makes the active participation of all the students.

6. Debate

Debate is a kind of panel discussion. Here the teacher pose a topic among the students and ask them speak for and against the particular topic. The teacher may act as a judge.

Benefits

This strategy will help to develop the speaking skill of the learners.

7. Roleplay

After finishing the lesson the teacher may use the fore coming hours to conduct role play. The teacher may give certain role which is a character in the lesson they have completed and make the students to enact it in the classroom.

Benefits

This will help the learners to come out of their stage fear. Then they can understand the character well by empathized with it. It also helps to develop the language aspects of the learners such as stress, pause, and intonation.

8. Five Minute Activities

In particular sessions the students may feel very bore. For instance, after the lunch break, last period of the day and the day before a festival. So in these days it is very difficult to manage them and the teacher can't control them by using harsh words. Then they will hurt. So for these occasions the teacher can use some five minutes activities to make the students to enjoy the moments and also learn something.

Example for five minute activity

"Guess the local place

Procedure

(1) Divide the class into teams. Then set the children a challenge. They have to write three clues about a local building or place of interest. The trick is to write ambiguous clues so that the answer is not immediately obvious. Or could refer to more than one place.

(2) Team members take turns to read out a clue. If the rival team makes an incorrect guess they are out of the game. If they guess the place after one clue they score three points. After two clues they score two points and after three clues they score one point. If no other team can guess the place then the writer of the clues score three points.

For example : place clues Library

(1) It has many shelves

(2) Lots of people visit here

(3) It is usually very quite

This Activity is taken from the book McKay, Penny and GuseJenni, "five minute activities for young learners" (44).

9. Reinforcement

Encouragement is the key to enter into the heart of the learners. The teacher should encourage the students if they try to do things. The teacher should use positive verbal and non verbal reinforcement in the class. The words like very good, excellent, absolutely correct, and the positive nonverbal reinforcement like patting, clapping the hands, and move closer to the students.

Benefits

This will motivate the students to do things in better way to get the positive comments from the teachers. Normally the students like the teacher who encourage and appreciate them. So it will help the teachers to get a good and positive impression among the students.

10. Using Various Models

There are different models in teaching. They are

(1) Information processing models

(2) Social interaction models

(3) Personal development models

(4) Behavior modification models

Benefits

By applying these models in teaching, the teacher can easily understand the minds of the learners.

Thus these are some of the suggestive ideas to manage the classroom effectively. These ideas may be occur in any minds of the teachers but why the fails to practice it in their classrooms?

11. Apply Psychology

Psychology is also a subject in education courses which deals with several psychological topics. This subject deals with the study of the minds of the learners. If the teacher wants to be a democratic teacher then they should know the minds of the learners in their classes. They should know the minds of the learners in their classes. They should know the student's academic details as well as their personal details like their family background, the environment which the students come from, etc…,

Benefits

By Appling psychology in the classroom the students are feel free to communicate with the teachers. They directly say anything for example about their problems, to the teachers. They considered teachers as their friend and a good companion. The main advantage of this technique is the students don't comment back on the teacher. It's a universal truth that if the students like the teachers then they will respect them and considered them as in the words of Alexander the great, "I am indebted to my father for living, but to my teacher for living well" – Alexander the great. If they don't like the teachers then they won't respect them.

12. Teacher a good guide and a counselor

To be good guide and a counselor is more challenging tast but it leads to a complete teacher. Counseling can be given by the expert. But guidance can be given by any one. So any teacher can be a good guide. There are three types of guidance can be given by any teachers. They are

1. Personal guidance
2. Educational guidance
3. Vocational guidance

In personal guidance the teacher should analyze the different expectations, aspirations, pains and feelings of the learners. It is not related to academic side. It deals with the minds of the learners. In

IQAC ST. Xavier College of Education

Proceedings of the International Seminar on Teaching to Teach and Learning to Learn in the Contemporary Classrooms

The educational guidance the teacher the teacher should analyze and give solutions to the problems regarding the difficulties in studies, and other academic oriented problems or learning difficulties of the learners.

In the vocational guidance the teacher should give guidance or idea related to the profession.

Benefits

If the teacher applies this guidance and counseling skill in the classroom then they will easily identify the strength and the weakness of the learner. The role of the good teacher is to strengthen the strength and weaken the weakness of the learners. They consider the teacher is a resourceful person who knows everything in the world and they get the hope that their problems will be cure by the teachers. So this will help the students to listen to the classes without doing other activities because they like the teacher.

Reasons

In the teacher training and the education programs the student teachers had subjects like understanding the learners, instructional process & instruction skill development, psychology of teaching and learning, models of teaching, and education management. In all these subjects they have learnt how to perform as a good teacher in the class. After completing these courses the teacher trainees were allowed to go to the internship program. But even then they can't apply it while they become a teacher. This is because of the following reasons. They are :

(1) The teacher trainees learnt these things theoretically and not practically. So they don't know how to apply those things in practice.

(2) The internship program of the teacher trainees is very less (40 days). So within this short period of time the trainees cannot perform well and apply all these theories.

(3) The institutions are not ready to spend time on these kinds of activities. They just want the teachers to couch the students to score good marks. All they want is 100% result not more than that.

These are some of the major problems behind the failure of the applying the strategies of classroom management in the classroom.

Solutions

To solve the above mentioned problems the following suggestions will be helpful

(1) The professors those who teach the student teachers should follow the classroom management skill in the class. For example, if the

professor teaches models of teaching, only as a theory, then it will not work. To make it more effective the proof. can teach any lesson using that particular model. This is otherwise known as inductive way of teaching. This helps the learners to understand the concept of the model as well as the applicative part of it.

(2) The internship program for the teacher trainee should be increased to at least 60 days. 10 days they can go for observation and continuously 50 days of training as a teacher. This continuous training makes the teacher trainees to feel comfortable with the training program.

(3) The professors of the education department allow the student teachers to take class regarding their subjects using the management skills and models in education.

Thus these are some of the solutions to make the classroom management a successful one.

Conclusion

"A good teacher can inspire hope, ignite the imagination and instill a love of learning" (brad Henry). This quote proves that a good teacher can make the students to create love on learning. This paper says that the teacher is also a student once so it is in hands of the education teacher who teaches to

IQAC ST. Xavier College of Education

Proceedings of the International Seminar on Teaching to Teach and Learning to Learn in the Contemporary Classrooms

The student teachers produces a good teacher. Teaching is an art. Art is a practical one. Any teacher duty is to act in the class not to read the text. So they should know how to apply all the theories that they have read in their training periods. So it is more important to give practical knowledge to the teacher trainees rather than the theoretical knowledge.

As per the words of swami Vivekananda "education is the manifestation of divine perfection, already existing in man." (qtd in. "strategies of instruction", Major A. Balasruamanian. (18)). It is the duty of the teachers of the teacher trainees to teach them how to manage the classroom effectively. They evaluation of education program should needs some changes. The evaluation must be based on practical and not theoretical. So by using the above mentioned techniques and methodologies the society can get a effective teachers with a good classroom management skill.

Reference

1. Balasubramanian A. Major. "Strategies Of instruction". Print
2. Hardin, C.J. (2008). Effective classroom management (2nd ed). Upper Saddle River, NJ: Merrill Prentice Hall. Print.
3. McKay, Penny and JenniGuse. (2007). Five minute activities for young learners. Cambridge handbooks for language teachers, Cambridge UP India Pvt. Ltd., Cambridge house, New Delhi. Print.
4. www.brainyquote.com/quote/topic/pics/topic teacher.html. 10:30, 23 Jan 2015. Web.

Chapter - 42

The Foundation of Higher Education is Mother Tongue an Astute Study

Dr. C.S. Sukumar Reddy, Dr. G Gangaiah

Abstract

The early acquisition of education is delayed when the parent intends that it is entirely the responsibility of the teacher to initiate the child in acquiring education. In fact, the inspiration to get education comes more easily from the parents first. At present, the parents of any place are all most some how educated. They are able to make their children to learn primary level of education. The informal atmosphere at home can make children understand better to learning at school. Moreover, the amiable and understanding parents can motivate children better in learning with pleasure. Teachers have also an equally important role to play in inculcating love of learning education. Particularly, parents and teachers make their children to perceive the education is a life oriented skill. Teacher should try to utilize the early start given by the parents.

Introduction

Language shows us the prosperity of human being. Many people of us notice that many parents these days tend to speak to their children in English when in public. Whether they are fluent in that language or not, most end up speaking in butler English even. Its very strange that why they do like? Generally, many of them in a tendency that and embarrassing of communicating with their children in their mother tongue. There is nothing wrong with speaking another language. No doubt, everyone should be bilingual, or trilingual, or better yet… multilingual. Everyone feel proud themselves knowing more than two languages. But, it is an offence that the lack of importance we give our mother tongue. Whatever language it may be. When we honour our mother tongue then only we will be honorable. This must be perceived by everyone about their language. It's not like that we would want parents to discourage their children from learning English, or any other language. But it is a feel that it is important to make everyone to realise that knowing their mother tongue is a privilege.

Being taught in a known language is a key component of quality education for all learners - from the very early stages right through to adulthood. Early education in the mother tongue can prepare children for school and foster foundation skills, such as literacy and critical thinking, which are proven to significantly. Language is deeply connected to notions of culture and identity and the language children are taught in can often reflect broader societal inequalities.For example, in many countries the ethnic majority population, which often speaks the dominant language, enjoy better learning outcomes than minority groups that speak other languages. Inequality in education is actually increasing including for those marginalized by language. When pre existing barriers to education, such as poverty, or living in rural areas, combine with schooling in an unknown language, children are less likely to make it to school, and if they do, are less likely to say there. By experiments also that bilingual education which includes the mother tongue can lead to improve attainment levels more generally.

For the last fifteen years have seen the number of children and young people who are not in school fall by almost half. Every child should be able to access their right to education, and the world has made strides in the right direction, but it is imperative that, in addition to going to school, children are actually learning. If a child cannot speak or understand the language used in the classroom, the efficacy and quality of learning will obviously suffer. Provision of short in service trainings during school vacations often leaves bilingual teachers with limited language skills. Inadequate understanding of the bilingual teaching methodologies required by the adopted model. An added challenge is to find or train teachers proficient.

Advantages of Mother tongue learning

- Children tend to develop better thinking skills
- Many researches have shown that students who are taught in the same language spoken at home and the community for the first 8 years of their lives, develop better language abilities in other languages and even do better in other areas of study, leading some scientists to hypothesize that it might have to do with overall brain development.

- Children are more likely to enroll and succeed in school: If the language of instruction is the same as the child's mother tongue, there is a better chance for the child to 'fit in' and continue with education.
- Parents are more accessibility to participate in their children's learning:Parents will feel they can actually make a difference in their child's education if they are freely able to communicate this teachers and be able to help at home.
- Education in ones mother tongue can significantly improve the mental ability of students.
- Language skills would affect the thoughts, perceptions and actions of any one.
- Expand the reach of education. Many rural kids would have their parents and relatives with no knowledge of English. Forcing an English medium education can put them at a significant disadvantage.
- Improved learning outcomes during primary school. A few researchers have shown that having a mother tongue education enable the kids to easily grasp the course content as they are used to the vocabulary.
- **Advantages of mother tongue as the medium of education:** Education in mother tongue instantly, or even without noticing any difficulty, understood and bring about the thought process, which develops the mind through understanding of concepts behind what is being taught.
- It is easy to memorize information in the language we are naturalized by our surroundings, and it is believed it remains in our mind for a long time, and develops the greater pattern of understanding of information so gathered, and brings about the personal and individual's thinking about the subjects, rather than just believing and holding whatever is being taught and memorized, as perfect, which is what exactly happen in education in unknown, unfamiliar language. It is actually absurd to get education in unknown language.
- It is actually more beneficial to get informed about science and scientific theories in our own mother tongue, in which case people are more likely to be scientifically, and most importantly for society, logically develop the individual.

- Eventually education in mother tongue results in more scientific progress as well as betterment of society, unlike what is going on today, like corruption in educated class, immorality, anti social behavior i.e. carelessness towards society. Education in unknown and unfamiliar language creates enslaved mentality.
- It can help in preservation of our own mother tongue, and can develop the more vocabulary and terminology to denote many things that the language do not have any word for. Terminological advancement of a language can enhance the thinking ability of the people, and it is possible that these terminology will be used by general populace in the long run, which I think will increase the quality of thinking of the people, even if they are not very educated.
- Education in mother tongue looks more dignified, self-respecting, intelligent and justified to have instruction, which is quite opposite if we another language as medium of instruction. It is undignified, self-disrespecting, foolish, and unjustified, not only for us, but also for our mother tongue.
- According to researchers, education in the mother tongue helps improve the academicperformance of children. Studies have shown that children who had their mother tongue as the medium of instruction in the first three years of primary school scored higher in English tests in the fourth, fifth and sixth grade, than students who studied most of their subjects in English from grade one.
- Education in the mother tongue is said to make it easier for them to learn a second language.
- Also, children take pride in their identity and heritage, when they learn in their mother tongue.
- The advantage of studying in the mother tongue is that the student can focus on studying geography, history, mathematics and biology instead of struggling to decipher a foreign language.

Conclusion

If you want your children to think Indian and to grow in their identity, you must educate then in their mother tongue.Communicating in any language, one needs his own ideas to convey his point, and medium is to help the other understand. If one does not have a point to convey, an idea, there is no point in learning a official language or any other.

Chapter - 43

Preparation of Curriculum: A Futuristic Perspective

Dr. B. Prathima, Dr. M. Trimurthi Rao

Abstract

Curriculum is the content and experiences teachers provide to students for satisfying certain expected outcomes. The content to be taught, experiences to be provided, the method of providing contents, the expected outcomes of these content and evaluation method are essentially part of curriculum. In fact curriculum is an umbrella terminology which entails the whole process of education. Curriculum has to be designed as a tool for promoting critical consciousness among the students. It must help the students to identify the oppressive elements tacit in the system and there by liberate themselves from the oppressive forces. Unless education system succeeds in this mission, education will continue to be a tool for reproducing unequal society. If curriculum designers are able to provide learners with academic content that are enriched in quality and can be located from or across multiple sources, then learners will have increased chances of self-learning, reflective practice, critical thinking, rapid participation and collaboration in thoroughly comprehending complicated curricular areas. The data provided through a 'futuristic curriculum' is fundamental for all types of evaluation of successful learning- whether diagnostic, formative or summative- all of which are key components of a system that ensures self-paced, individual and differentiated learning.

This paper throw's light on the concept of curriculum and various definitions of curriculum, followed by an attempt to present the idea of futuristic curriculum, importance of the components and parameters of a futuristic curriculum, a vision of futuristic curriculum among the teachers working in higher education institutions. At the end three types of futuristic curriculum proposed by Young and Muller were discussed and an attempt was made to assess the trends and practices in curriculum construction.

Introduction

Curriculum is one of the main concerns of every educational system. Curriculum designers are concerned about what kind of curricula to be offered to learners. Teachers are concerned about the way curricula has to be transferred to the students. Parents are concerned about the potential of a curricula in shaping a safe future for their children. Students are concerned about the curricula they have to learn for their studies. Curriculum is generally understood as the content and experiences teachers provide to students for satisfying certain expected outcomes. Hence content to be taught, experiences to be provided, the method of providing contents the expected outcomes of these content and evaluation method are essentially part of curriculum. In fact curriculum is an umbrella terminology which entail the whole process of education. The word curriculum is derived from a Latin word 'currere' which means 'to run'. Later this Latin word has become a diminutive noun meaning 'race track'.

History of Curriculum

Longstreet and Shane (1993), opines that Curriculum is a historical accident. Curriculum was not developed to attain the pre-set goals of education. Rather it emerged due to the increasing complexities in the field of education. In course of time the word curriculum has attained a broad meaning. The literature shows that curriculum is defied in different ways. These definitions mainly include curriculum as a course of study, as an educational plan, as a document containing outline of programmes to be implemented, and finally curriculum as the sum total of experiences gained provided by an institution. The meaning of curriculum has changed drastically over a period of time. Recent developments in education, psychology, and sociology have been instrumental bringing changes that give new meanings and dimensions to curriculum.

Basil Bernstein, the renowned sociologist once wrote an essay on 'knowledge structures'. The work was precise and undoubtedly seminal but in a sense, incomplete. In it, Bernstein distinguished between horizontal and vertical structures of knowledge and within the horizontal he differentiated between 'weak' and 'strong' grammars. Later, some scholars, particularly Johan Muller and Michael Young, alongside Elizabeth Rata, Rob Moore, Leesa Wheelaham and Karl Maton, extensively worked upon Bernstein's concept in a much more organized endeavour to construct a body of knowledge within the purview of Sociology of Education drawing upon social realism. Barrett and Rata (2014) have wrote some recent papers elucidating this approach by addressing the challenges in curriculum preparation by looking back to the sociology of knowledge as produced by Marx, Durkheim, Mannheim and Bernstein through an analysis of the entanglement between power and knowledge – how the access to powerful knowledge can both explain and address the social reproduction of inequalities that schools tend to perpetuate. The school curricula and pedagogies are extensively related to fostering this unequal access to the powerful knowledge. Bernstein's work is crucial in the context of understanding the nature of educational inequality and central to progressive educational policies towards rendering educational equity through curriculum and pedagogy.

Curriculum has to be designed as a tool for promoting critical consciousness among the students. It helps the students to identify the oppressive elements tacit in the system and there by liberate themselves from the oppressive forces. Unless education system succeeds in this mission, education will continue to be a tool for reproducing unequal society. While talking about a curriculum for the future, politics of knowledge and curriculum should be a key point to direct our discussion.

Components of Futuristic Curriculum

The curricular components that require sustainable changes over a period of time for addressing the ever multiplying and continuous flux in societal expectations from education have been stated as follows:

- **Structure:** The structure or the framework of the curriculum needs to be revised in keeping with the vision of its liberatory role. Structural changes need to be brought about through proper researches for incorporating this as the base of curriculum. Policy makers and teachers need to be updated themselves about the latest developments in curriculum research to make the curriculum a tool for praxis.
- **Content:** The content of the curriculum should represent local identities, cultures and histories alongside globally important themes should be combined in a right balance. National curriculum frameworks should envisage guidelines for incorporating a well-balanced curricular content including adequate representations of all categories existing in society. The content should be regularly updated keeping abreast with latest developments and innovations in the respective subjects, disciplines and it should be seen that the official knowledge transacted through the textbooks should not lead to a hegemony that promotes and sustains existing inequalities.

- **Organization:** The next important step in developing a futuristic curriculum is in proper organization of selected concepts that are to be taught based on age-appropriate cognitive development, socio-cultural perspectives and so on. An advanced organization of core concepts based on levels of complexity, the immediate context in which the curriculum is implemented are some areas that need to be kept in mind, while constructing a future curriculum.
- **Pedagogy:** The methods and approaches to be undertaken in executing the curriculum is also a crucial aspect that needs to be addressed in coming eras. The curriculum should be such that it promotes the use of an interdisciplinary approach to deal with ideas and concepts. Curriculum must entail a culturally responsive and sustainable teaching learning in classrooms where multiculturalism and multilingualism are seen as advantageous resources instead of hindrances. The practices to be used by teachers should be based on model innovations, experimentations, blended learning using ample amounts of latest technologies in the educational context.
- **Time:** Content and appropriate time required for administering the particular curricular content must be prescribed in a futuristic curriculum. Based on factors like difficulty level, learners cognitive level, self-paced learning, and use of technology is the requirement for the next generation learners because time is a crucial factor in a highly competitive and fast paced future.
- **Assessment:** Assessment for learning need to be promoted instead of assessment of learning. Formative assessment and more specifically classroom assessment techniques need to be promoted as alternate means of assessment. These forms of formative, summative and diagnostic evaluation should be guided by dynamic rubrics suited for different categories of learners. Effective integration of technology will be an imperative need in the context of universalisation of higher education in future.
- **Materials/Resources:**Resources for a curriculum is expected to support the learner by extending their horizon of knowledge. In the contemporary society listing of the resources and imposing it to the students will not be practical. Inbuilt obsolescence of knowledge questions the perennial relevance of knowledge. Fast and the quick dissemination of knowledge with the support of internet provide opportunity for acquainting plurality of knowledge to students. Hence the futuristic curriculums should emphasise

upon the resources that are democratically selected by the teachers and students together.

Parameters of A Futuristic Curriculum

Curriculum has to be democratically developed to address the needs and desires of the people in a society. Curriculum for the future should be from the cultural context for the cultural context and by the people of that cultural context. Instead of proposing an assemblage of knowledge to the learners curriculum should provide a framework of experience for the learners that help them to identify the factors that keep them under subjugation and there by leading them to praxis that liberate them. In this process curriculum should provide a deep insight in to one's own abilities and opportunities to invest these abilities.

If curriculum designers are able to provide learners with academic content that are enriched in quality and can be located from or across multiple sources, then learners will have increased chances of self-learning, reflective practice, critical thinking, rapid participation and collaboration in thoroughly comprehending complicated curricular areas. The data provided through a futuristic curriculum is fundamental for all types of evaluation of successful learning- whether diagnostic, formative or summative – all of which are key components of a system that ensures self-paced, individual and differentiated learning. Therefore a futuristic curriculum must inevitably entail the following parameters:

- **Twenty-first Century Skills:**

  The primary learning outcomes expected out of the future curriculum, pedagogy and evaluation is to make learners well prepared for higher studies or the world of work after schooling. Such desirability is grounded upon a sound and standard-level of content knowledge alongside 21st century readiness in terms of other curricular components of deeper learning- creativity, innovation, self-directed learning and critical thinking skills coupled with ample opportunities for authentic learning in the contemporary digital era where a knowledge society has emerged due to technological boom.

- **Personalized Learning:**

  To provide personalized learning experiences for individual learners, futuristic educators must make use of technology and access diversified learning resources. Personalized learning includes self-pacing, customized content and a feedback mechanism for catering to the needs of individuals while empowering learners to control and take charge of their own learning.

- **Collaborative, Relevant and Applied Learning:**
  As professionals work in macro-societies learners need to work with the same efficacy in a digitized learning system. Collaboration with peers, teachers and community outside school is necessary for project-oriented learning that leads to creating knowledge products, fostering deeper learning and possesses value beyond the four walls of classroom.
- **Leveraging Technology:**
  Seamless technology integration into the learning processes is to be given for teachers in growing digital societies. Such futuristic educators possess skills of adopting a number of educational technologies and adapt to dynamic and plural learning structures to ensure that technology usage accentuates the process of learning.
- **Assessment Analytics as Feedback to Instruction:**
  Technology should be used as a tool for diagnostic, summative and formative assessment in schools. Schooling system must resort to digital processes and environments for using data to guide, improve and enrich the educational processes. Assessment analysis must be continuously undertaken by active use of digital evaluation processes that can guide teachers in selection of proper content, curriculum modification and strategies of instruction.

Types of Future Curriculum

Young et.al. (2014) employs the distinction made there between three possible kinds of curriculum futures: Futures 1, 2, and 3. **Future 1** advocates a radically knowledge-based curriculum in view of Young's contention that knowledge is power in an ever-changing world where epistemology is in a state of constant flux.

Future 2 includes differentiated curriculum informed by different kinds of relativist knowledge which try to validate the lived experiences and associated cultural knowledge including daily life and the professional frontier. Raewyn Connell (2012), the Australian sociologist documents in this regard that a curriculum that promotes social justice and equity, relies heavily upon local bodies of knowledge, experiences of the working classes and women, identities of the marginalized minorities and multiculturalism and multilingualism as resources. Therefore a futuristic curriculum that has social justice at its base must also entail inclusion of local cultures, local epistemology, class-based experiences, gender neutrality and multilingualism and multiculturalism as its pillars. In the Indian context, additionally other social realities like castes, religion and regional experiences should also be sufficiently reflected in a futuristic curriculum. In his earlier works too, Young confesses of perceiving curricula as social constructs merely open to revolutionary redefinition since there were no real knowledge constraints as such; only unequal distributions of power in society.

The central argument that nurtures **Future 3** is that curriculum must foster objectivity and bring learners closest to truth. In it, there is no claim for accessing unchanging or absolute truth however, for instance the truths that involve a direct reference to "the world's own register as Luntley (1995) calls it. Valid knowledge is a must for social realists, which is produced by scholars and researchers in academia. Such research communities have constructed a set of rules that bifurcate valid and invalid knowledge. Therefore this knowledge is not the absolute or ultimate one and is ***subjected to disintegration or modification*** in due course. However, it is the best repository of knowledge that future generations can access. This knowledge is considered more powerful form of knowledge than everyday knowledge on account of the superiority of cognitive functions and intellect that manufactures it. The most debatable arguments put forward by Young et.al. (2014) in this regard are: i) this objective knowledge extend to disciplines of Social Sciences and Art comprising primarily of subjects which have their bases in such disciplines, must be taught in school between 5-16 years of age compulsorily to all, for the sake of social justice and also because such a futuristic curriculum justifies meaningful schooling.

Trends and Practices

Michael Marien once remarked: "I aim to take a step toward the day when futures studies will become a basic part of the curriculum of every school, every college, and every university, and when everyone, everywhere, will take for granted that having some understanding of the principles of futures studies is an essential part of what it means to be an educated person." In agreement with the aforementioned statement, the writers Mei and Siraj (2017) suggest that the curriculum designers should consider the research findings from future trends studies as one of the vital tenets underlying the futuristic curriculum. The students should be exposed more to the futures and the possibilities they might face and also equip them with the problem solving skills and decision making skills.

- The future trends including a global entanglement of issues like food problems, the greenhouse effect, old area layer threat, land degradation, pollution and toxic waste, deforestation and desertification and many other problems need in depth studies to see their impacts upon education.

- Issues of social regression including multiplying family problems and increase in the number of homeless, deprived children post-war, and many other problems related to the technology advancement, are bound to occur in the future world.
- The role of future researches is vital in determining the future course of the education system. The curriculum experts should analyse a nation's basic philosophy, the needs of the future younger generation, and other possible solutions to dynamic challenges that evolve in a more complex post-modern society. These experts should also determine the curriculum and courses to be pursued in the schools with the main objective of providing a better preparation for the futuristic education of the youth. In this way, the youth is better prepared to face the future challenges that they continually encounter.
- The planners and designers have to deal with uncertainties partly due to the present socio-political and economical structure. To a certain extent, they have to face the challenges in dealing with curriculum decisions that they have never experienced before. In other words, they must somehow provide the knowledge and skills of recognizing the complexity and indefiniteness epitomizing current society or nation and how these complexities may further evolve in future. Hence, additional goals that have to go beyond the traditional purview of Mathematics and Natural Sciences; Future 3 curriculum, links in the future should be included into the planning and designing of curriculum activities that are guided by specific notions which are future-oriented in nature.
- Latest technologies have been applied in some curricula with practical activities such as flying an aeroplane – in concordance with the school's philosophy "free to learn whatever they want" and mobile learning – learn anywhere, anytime and anyplace has already been initiated in certain futuristic school systems.
- For the purpose of improving future pedagogy, for instance, the instructional environment must be flexible in order to widen the citizen-scientist-interfaced curriculum and provide various study experiences in the pedagogy of the sciences. The changes in the pedagogy of the social studies need to be accommodated by applying the hypothetical mode.

- The changes involving public and students that would in turn deal honestly with possible futures and foreseeable uncertainty must be premised in curriculum. This mode would create an atmosphere where instructors assist students to explore social problems, being open to questions of uncertainty, and involve students in decision-making activities.
- New conceptions in education (example: viruses as intelligent software-weapons, Nanotechnology and Biotechnology) have to be invented in response to new questions such as: What would cause a subject to be studied for both the present situation and for future needs? Which subject-areas would help the youth resolve both uncertain futures and current difficulties? What is the focal point of studies when there are nationwide and global networks of data shared by millions, daily? What can we do and what are we supposed to do to manage the psychological causes between technological means such as the Internet and the capability of humans to wisely use these means?

Conclusion

These are the emerging needs in the knowledge society and a futuristic curriculum can address these ever-growing needs of an education as forethought. The data provided through a 'futuristic curriculum' is fundamental for all types of evaluation of successful learning- whether diagnostic, formative or summative- all of which are key components of a system that ensures self-paced, individual and differentiated learning. In effect, a futuristic curriculum could transpire into a course of a better living in future.

Refernces

1. Barrett, B., & Rata, E. (Eds.) (2014), *Knowledge and the Future of the Curriculum: International Studies in Social Realism,* Springer.
2. Connell, R. (2012), Just education. *Journal of Education Policy*, *27*(5), pp 681-683.
3. Luntley, M. (1995), Reason, Truth and Self: Getting to Know the Truth about Postmodernism.
4. Marien, M. (2002), Futures Studies in the 21st Century: A Reality-based view: *Futures*, *34*(3-4), pp 261-281.
5. Mei, C. W., & Siraj, S. (2017), Integrating Internship and Business Simulation into the Malaysian Business Studies Curriculum, (*MOJEM) Malaysian Online Journal of Educational Management*, *1*(1), pp1-16.
6. Young, M. F. (2002), *The Curriculum of the Future: from the new Sociology of Education to a critical theory of Learning,* Routledge.

Chapter - 44

Influence of Imagination and Culture on Curriculum Development

Glaze George K

Abstract

Analysis of the value system among the school students shows a lack of synthesis between the actual aim of education and the expectations of the parents and the educators. The new socio cultural and economic changes resulted in a cultural lag which is reflected in the field of education as it is the place where the changing patterns are first experimented. A study of relationship between imagination and culture and its impact on curriculum would make us think about the need to remodel our present curriculum with the aim of bridging the cultural lag. Purpose of education according to the Indian tradition and the requirements of the modern globalized world form two almost opposite ideological strands. This adversely effected not only the value system but their knowledge levels as well.

Keywords: Education, Culture, Imagination, Curriculum, Indian Values

Introduction

The function of imagination is to fashion individual in to 'the seam of a collective narrative' [Popkewitz 2000 page168] and help the generate conceptions of personhood and identity. Imagination is obtained in a historical perspective. Imagination is an attempt to provide coherence between the ideas and action, to provide a basis for the content of social relationship and creation of categories with which to understand the world around.[Norreal A London-2002], it is not an attribute possed by few individuals. But a 'collective social fact'[Apaduri1996]. It is aggregate sense shared by a group of people. Thus it contributes to the development of nationalism.Colonialism as a state of mind possessed by the colonized, "not only s an extension of sovereignty and control by one nation and its government over another, but control of the minds of the conquered and the subordinated" [1977 P.17].

The feeling of cultural hegemony was created through imagination during colonial period.it was mainly done through colonial state through various ways, including specially designed curriculum. State can use its power for selection and management of school knowledge. Schools serve as agents of cultural and ideological hegemony, since they process not only knowledge but people as well [Carnoy & Samoff 1990]. They preserve and distribute what is perceived to be legitimate knowledge of specific groups. [Giroux 1983].

The aim of education according to Herbert Spencer is the 'training for completeness of life' and the molding of character of men and women for the battle of life. The unhappy incidents from the schools and colleges remind us about the need to rethink in this direction. Education has always been culture specific and culture is dynamic and inclusive. Hence there must be an ideal path where ideals of yesterday can meet the ideals of today to walk towards a brighter tomorrow. It is a humble attempt to find such a link which has to be supplemented by several other views from other minds.

Purpose of education according to Indian tradition

As per classical Indian tradition "*Sa vidya ya vimuktaye*", (that which liberates us is education). "He who is possessed of supreme knowledge by concentration of mind, must have his senses under control, like spirited steeds controlled by a charioteer" says the *Katha Upanishad.*

There is a direct relationship between the aim of education and the philosophy of the country. Methods of teaching, curriculum and our system of evaluation are shaped and molded according to the aim of education. If there is no clarity in the aims of education it will lead to wrong methods and result in physical, intellectual and moral weakness of the race.

According to Indian tradition education aimed at the following

- Formation of Character:Like Locke, ancient Indian thinkers held that mere intellectual attainments were of less consequence than the development of a proper moral feeling and character.Evil effects of divorcing power from virtue, intellectual and scientific progress from moral and spiritual values, were well realized by ancient Indians.
- Infusion of religiousness's teachers were religious and rituals were associated with education. Daily prayer and life of

brhamacharya made him realize the spiritual and natural world through his life.

- Fostering of self-confidence the ritual of pranayama infused divine cooperation with the student in achievement of his goal.
- Enforcement of self-restraint - self-restraint was needed in food, clothing and all sorts of pleasures. And it was not to be imposed one.
- Inclusion of civic and social duties—A graduate must teach the young generation even though there is no prospect for fee. He must be hospitable and charitable.
- Preservation of culture—Education is considered to be the chief means of cultural and social continuity. Specialization became a natural consequence of this ad it made education more deep rather than broad.

The strength of Vedic culture is proved by the facts

- Despite centuries of foreign rule over 75% of Indian population remains Hindu.
- Had it become obsolete, it would have given place to other religions and cultures.
- It influenced almost all other religions found in India.

Changed role of education

"I have travelled across the length and breadth of India and I have not seen one person who is beggar, who is a thief, such wealth I have seen in the country, such high moral values, people of such caliber, that I do not think we would ever conquer this country, unless we break the very backbone of this nation, which is her spiritual and cultural heritage, and therefore, I propose that we replace her old and ancient education system, her culture, for if the Indian think that all that is foreign and English is good and greater than their own, they will lose their self-esteem, their native culture and they will become what we want them, a truly dominated nation". Lord Macaulay's address to the British parliament, 2nd February, 1835.

Thus with a clear and well defined aim the curriculum and methods of education was redrawn during the colonial period.

With the globalization a new form of cultural imperialism started. In the context of India globalization has impacted upon the educational system in a complex and conflicting role. There is an increased emphasis on preparing global citizens who are ready to face the highly competitive world.

Globalization has put an extra pressure on the education system to create 'winners' who are ready to battle in the race for the survival of the fittest. It has led to the preparation of a curriculum that has to be internationally acceptable.

In the contemporary context, students are seen as customers as well as partners in the process of learning against their role as mere seekers of truth in the past.

Cultural influences on education

Cultural patterns always guided educational patterns both spiritually and materialistically. The very definition of culture by Taylor clearly tell us about this and he defines culture as "that complex whole which includes knowledge, belief, art, morals, law, custom and any other capabilities and habits, acquired by man as a member of society." Culture is transmitted from one generation to another and each generation modify the cultural heritage according to the needs of the society and transmit it to the next generation. This is a continuous process. Dynamism is one of the important characteristic of culture. Due to the rapid rise in transport and and communication, it is becoming more and more dynamic these days. But in comparison with the materialistic changes the changes in believes and value systems change very slowly. this has led to the cultural lag, the reflections of this effected the education more than any other fields as schools serve as the laboratories for testing the traditions values , believes, attitudes prevailing in a particular society.

Bridging of this cultural lag is one of the aims of education. Education as part of modernization has two aims viz., conservation and modification of culture. It is also an instrument of cultural change too apart from implementing knowledge and skill. A child adapts to his natural environment and social environment by knowing the customs, traditions and beliefs of his group. Development of his personality is reflected through his behavior and behavior is influenced by culture of his group. Culture influences education in several ways. The curriculum is prepared according to the culture of the society. Text books also promote democratic values. Various social activities are organized according to the cultural ideals.

In the present context where the needs of the global socio economic scenario does not comprehend with the ideals that we have inherited from our ancestors. The influence of our culture, negatively influence aims of our education in the present context.

Conclusion

A realization of this role transformation and the cultural influences will help us to understand the present problems. Indian philosophy always adopted middle paths. With the same kind of attitude we can try to find a proper solution for our ideological conflict. Awareness of cause will lead us to a better solution.

Reference

1. Mukhi, B.S., & Anand, R. (2015). Globalisation and its Impact on Indian Education System.*International Journal of Engineering Technology, Management and Applied Sciences, 3*(Special Issue), 216-220.
2. anand, m. (2015). globalisation and indian school education: impact and challenges. *European Scientific Journal, ESJ, 11*(10), 235-249.
3. Goddard, D., & Punch, K. F. (1996). Ideological conflict in education: Western Australia, 19831989. *Journal of Educational Administration*, *34*(4), 60-72.
4. Maheswari, V.K. (2012). The aims and ideals of education in ancient India.
5. sol.du.ac.in/mod/book/view.php?id=1449&chapterid=1335 (accessed on 04.02.2018).
6. https://latasinha.wordpress.com/2713-2/ (accessed on 04.02.2018).
7. Norreal A London (2002) Curriculum and pedagogy in development of Colonial imagination.

Chapter - 45

A Critical Reflection of Indian Higher Education in the Context of Infrastructure

Umme Salma

Abstract

Higher education will continue to play a vital role in increase in sustainable economic and social development. As a focal point of knowledge and its application, higher education makes a great contribution to the economic growth and development. It brings forth innovations and increasing higher skills. Higher education is crucial for every human being and more to person with differently-abled (PWD). According to All India Survey on Higher Education (AISHE) 2016-17, there are 70967 (PWD) students enrolled in higher education. The University Grants Commission (UGC) specified that persons with disabilities need special arrangements in the environment for their mobility and independent functioning. Many higher education institutions have architectural barriers and pose difficulty in functioning of differently-abled persons. However the government has put efforts in the form of schemes and instructions for the access to education of the differently-abled persons by providing disability friendly environment in higher education institutions but still the PWD students are facing challenges in their full participation in education. At all India level 4163 PWD teachers are working at higher education level. To maintain the quality in teaching and learning process in higher educational institutions, it is necessary to provide disable friendly infrastructure for student fraternity as well as teacher fraternity. Teaching and learning has to be taken place in a comfortable environment, both teacher and students should not face any physical hardship due to lack of proper infrastructure. The paper discusses the infrastructure facilities provided at the level of higher education in the purview of to meet the needs of both general and inclusive education student fraternity and teacher fraternity.

Keywords: *Infrastructure, Person with differently-abled, Education.*

Introduction

The higher education will continue to play a vital role in increase in sustainable economic and social development. As a focal point of knowledge and its application, higher education makes a great contribution to the economic growth and development. It brings forth innovations and increasing higher skills. It paves way in improving the quality of living by addressing social and global challenges. Higher education is crucial for every human being and more to person with differently-abled (PWD). According to All India Survey on Higher Education 2016-17, there are 70967 (PWD) students enrolled in higher education. Of them 40894 person with differently-abled are male students and 30073 are female students. The Persons with Disabilities Act, 1995 recommend that disabled persons should have access to education at all levels. Person with Disability (PWD) means a person suffering from a disability as defined in the "Persons with Disabilities (Equal Opportunities, Protection of Right and Full Participation) Act, 1995". As per Section 2 of this Act: "Person with disability" (PWD) means a person suffering from not less than forty percent of any of the following disabilities as certified by a medical authority; i. Blindness; ii. Low vision; iii. Leprosy-cured; iv. Hearing impairment; v. Locomotors disability; vi. Mental retardation; vii. Mental illness. (https://www.ugc.ac.in/oldpdf/xplanpdf/Differently Abled Persons. pdf).

University Grants Commission Guidelines Facilities For Differently -Abled Persons

The University Grants Commission (UGC) had started the scheme of assistance to universities/colleges to facilitate Teacher Preparation in Special Education (TEPSE) and Higher Education for Persons with Special Needs (Differently-abled-Persons) (HEPSN) during the Ninth Five-Year Plan, considered to give special education programs and infrastructure to differently-abled-persons. The infrastructure needs to be designed in a manner to enable them to easily access classrooms, laboratories, toilets, etc. Under this scheme UGC specified that persons with disabilities need special arrangements in the environment for their mobility and independent functioning. Many higher education institutions have architectural barriers and pose difficulty in functioning of differently-abled persons.

The universities and colleges under this scheme are expected to address this problem according to the Persons with Disabilities Act 1995, and ensure that all existing structures as well as future construction projects in their campuses are made disabled friendly. The institutes should create special facilities such as ramps, rails and special toilets, and make other necessary changes to suit the special needs of differently-abled persons. For this purpose, the UGC will make a one-time grant of up to Rs.5 lakh per university/college. (https://www.ugc.ac.in/oldpdf /xpla npdf/ DifferentlyAbledPersons. pdf).

In addition, the Ministry of Human Resource Development (MHRD) had issued various instructions from time to time to all the Centrally Funded Educational Institution to ensure barrier free environment in the buildings, which would include provision of ramps, rails, lifts, adaption of toilets for wheel chair users, braille signages and auditory signals, tactile flooring etc. It is also mandatory for All India Council for Technical Education (AICTE) approved institutions to have barrier free structure to encourage persons with disabilities for technical education (http://pib.nic.in/newsite/ PrintRelease.aspx?relid=175311).

However the government has put efforts in the form of schemes and instructions for the access to education of the differently-abled persons by providing disability friendly environment in higher education institutions but still the PWD students are facing challenges in their full participation in education. As it was noticed in the study conducted by Pivik et al, (2000) on barriers and facilitators to inclusive education, the results of this revealed that a major barrier identified by many of the students was physically getting in to school, environmental barriers included the following categories; doors, passage ways, elevators, washrooms, stairs and ramps, lockers, water fountain and recreational areas. The students were also asked to suggest possible facilitators to the barriers identified, in order to improve accessibility and promote full participation. It was suggested that facilitating inclusive school environment requires ensuring physical access, the opportunity for optimal learning and social experiences and providing a nurturing climate.

Table-1. Available Infrastructures in Higher Education Institutions

Percentage of Institutions having various Infrastructure			
Infrastructure	***University***	***College***	***Stand Alone Institutions***
Playground	88 %	91 %	91 %
Auditorium	80 %	58 %	65 %
Theatre	44 %	19 %	19 %
Library	94 %	97 %	98 %

(Contd...)

Laboratory	85 %	80 %	93 %
Conference Hall	93 %	75 %	80 %
Health Center	79 %	44 %	48 %
Gymnasium/ Fitness Center	76 %	36 %	30 %
Indoor Stadium	49 %	31 %	29 %
Common Room	84 %	89 %	89 %
Computer Center	90 %	85 %	91 %
Cafeteria	86 %	55 %	58 %
Guest House	82 %	39 %	45 %

Source: AISHE 2016-17

The available infrastructure facilities in Universities, Colleges and Stand Alone Institutions are presented by AISHE 2016-17. It was found that the Library, Conference Hall and Computer Center are available in 94%, 93% and 90% universities respectively. Followed by Playground, Cafeteria and Laboratory were available in 88%, 86% and 85% universities respectively. The percentage of universities found less 44% and 49% respectively on Theatre and Indoor Stadium. In Colleges, Library, Playground and Common Room are maintained by 97%, 91% and 89% colleges and 19%, 31% and 36% colleges maintained Theatre, Indoor Stadium and Gymnasium/ Fitness Center respectively. In Stand Alone Institutions (SAIs), 98%, 93% and 91% SAIs respectively have Library, Laboratory and Playground as well as Computer Center and Theatre, Indoor Stadium and Gymnasium/ Fitness Center were maintained by few Institutions 19%, 29% and 30% respectively.

The AISHE 2016-17 report has not provided the information about special facilities for persons with disabilities such as ramps, rails and special toilets which are very much essential and was also mentioned in the schemes formulated by the University Grants Commission.

Table -2. State-wise Enrollment of PWD in Higher Education

State Name	*Male*	*Female*	*Total*	*State Name*	*Male*	*Female*	*Total*	*State Name*	*Male*	*Female*	*Total*
Andaman & Nicobar Islands	14	6	20	Haryana	640	576	1216	Nagaland	13	12	25
Andhra Pradesh	1276	884	2160	Himachal Pradesh	438	140	578	Odisha	961	520	1481
ArunachaPradesh	32	7	39	Jammu and Kashmir	358	531	889	Puducherry	123	71	194
Assam	388	244	632	Jharkhand	368	200	568	Punjab	557	291	848
Bihar	1688	717	2405	Karnataka	2304	1404	3708	Rajasthan	1943	983	2926
Chandigarh	173	102	275	Kerala	1285	1233	2518	Sikkim	7	3	10
Chhatisgarh	484	240	724	Lakshadweep	0	0	0	Tamil Nadu	3077	2279	5356

(Contd...)

Dadra & Nagar Haveli	10	7	17	Madhya Pradesh	1757	1428	3185	Telangana	1980	1101	3081
Daman &Diu	0	1	1	Maharashtra	4298	2519	6817	Tripura	169	38	207
Delhi	2799	1365	4164	Manipur	79	41	120	Uttar Pradesh	8968	10874	19842
Goa	30	26	56	Meghalaya	35	16	51	Uttrakhand	511	248	759
Gujarat	1892	947	2839	Mizoram	8	7	15	West Bengal	2229	1012	3241
All India					40894	30073					70967

Source: AISHE 2016-17

According to AISHE 2016-17, at all India level 70967 persons with differently-abled student are enrolled, of them 40894 person with differently-abled students are male and 30073 are female in higher education level.

However, the research studies showed that person with differently-abled students are not satisfied with infrastructure facilities available for them. The study conducted by IJIP.In. (2016) on the student support services in higher education, it was found that most of the students were not so happy with the infrastructure and other facilities. Only 33.75 % students responded to provision of coolers in hostels. 46.87 % and 60.62 % of students were satisfied with cafeteria facilities and playground facilities respectively, while only 23.75 % students were satisfied with physical infrastructure. 29.37 % students agreed for support services for differently-abled students. The study concluded that students of the university are satisfied with library facilities, but wanted the regular addition of books in library. The physical infrastructure does not satisfy students, especially for differently-abled students.

Similarly, Tripathi and Kiran (2012) conducted a study on infrastructural facilities for differently-abled students. From the results it was found that differently-abled students are more neglected in Government institutions in terms of facilities. The infrastructure is not at all disabled friendly leading to a lot of inconvenience to them. It was also found that non-government institutions were providing more facilities in comparison to government institutions. The majority of non- government institutions have proper placed washrooms, accessories of washrooms at suitable height and provision of hand bars in their institutions. Majority of the non-government institutions have fixed seating arrangements in their academic institutions. None of these institutions have walking aids, internal phone and two-way radio transmitters. Majority of the Government institutional students have very low level of satisfaction regarding the availability of facilities.

Table -3. State-wise Number of Teachers among PWD in Higher Education

State Name	*Male*	*Female*	*Total*	*State Name*	*Male*	*Female*	*Total*	*State Name*	*Male*	*Female*	*Total*
Andaman & Nicobar Islands	0	0	0	Haryana	64	42	106	Nagaland	2	0	2
Andhra Pradesh	191	35	226	Himachal Pradesh	26	12	38	Odisha	72	29	101
Arunachal Pradesh	3	0	3	Jammu and Kashmir	24	8	32	Puducherry	24	4	28
Assam	46	9	55	Jharkhand	32	4	36	Punjab	83	51	134
Bihar	61	7	68	Karnataka	253	107	360	Rajasthan	137	41	178
Chandigarh	6	4	10	Kerala	93	38	131	Sikkim	4	0	4
Chhatisgarh	53	34	87	Lakshadweep	0	0	0	Tamil Nadu	270	237	507
Dadra & Nagar Haveli	2	0	2	Madhya Pradesh	191	56	247	Telangana	140	61	201
Daman & Diu	1	0	1	Maharashtra	335	143	478	Tripura	10	1	11
Delhi	128	63	191	Manipur	2	6	8	Uttar Pradesh	342	167	509
Goa	3	2	5	Meghalaya	2	0	2	Uttrakhand	38	16	54
Gujarat	142	40	182	Mizoram	4	0	4	West Bengal	133	29	162
All India					2917	1246					4163

Source: AISHE 2016-17

According to AISHE 2016-17 report, it is found that at all India level 4163 persons with disabilities teachers are working at higher education level, among which 2197 persons with disabilities are male and 1246 persons with disabilities are female. Along with the provision of infrastructure requirements for student fraternity; it is also required for teacher fraternity as well.

A Report by British Council 2014, Understanding India: The future of higher education and opportunities for international cooperation; the report indicated that the Indian higher education system is facing an unprecedented transformation in the coming decade. This transformation is being driven by economic and demographic change: by 2020, India will be the world's third largest economy. Currently, over 50% of India's population is under 25 years old; by 2020 India will outpace China as the country with the largest tertiary-age population. Despite significant progress over the last ten years, Indian higher education is faced with four broad challenges;

1. The supply-demand gap
2. The low quality of teaching and learning
3. Constraints on research capacity and innovation
4. Uneven growth and access to opportunity

To maintain the quality in teaching and learning process in higher educational institutions, it is necessary to provide disable friendly infrastructure for student fraternity as well as teacher fraternity. Teaching and learning has to be taken place in a comfortable environment, both teacher and students should not face any physical hardship due to lack of proper infrastructure.

Table- 4. Enrolment Details of PWD during last 5 years in Higher Education (India)

Year	*Male*	*Female*	*Total*
2016-17	40894	30073	70967
2015-16	39718	34717	74435
2014-15	34757	29541	64298
2013-14	31374	20580	51954
2012-13	45329	40904	86233

Source: AISHE 2016-17

According to AISHE 2016-17 report, the enrollment of person with differently-abled students have reduced notably, between 2012-13 the number of PWD students enrolled in higher education was 86233 and they reduced to 70967 in 2016-17.

Conclusion

The higher education paves way in improving the quality of living by addressing social and global challenges. Higher education is crucial for every human being and more to person with differently-abled (PWD). According to All India Survey on Higher Education (AISHE) 2016-17, there are 70967 (PWD) students enrolled in higher education. However the government has put efforts in the form of schemes and instructions for the access to education of the differently-abled persons by providing disability friendly environment in higher education institutions but still the PWD students are facing challenges in their full participation in education. Some studies found that the person with differently-abled students were not satisfied with infrastructure facilities available for them and differently-abled students are more neglected in Government institutions in terms of facilities. The AISHE 2016-17 reported that, at all India level 4163 persons with disabilities teachers are working at higher education level, along with the provision of infrastructure requirements for student fraternity; it is also required for teacher fraternity as well. To maintain the quality in teaching and learning process in higher educational institutions, it is necessary to provide disable friendly infrastructure for student fraternity as well as teacher fraternity. Teaching and learning has to be taken place in a comfortable environment, both teacher and students should not face any physical hardship due to lack of proper infrastructure.

References

1. AISHE 2016-17, Government Of India Ministry Of Human Resource Development Department Of Higher Education New Delhi.
2. British Council (2014). Understanding India - The future of higher education and opportunities for international cooperation. Retrieved from https://www.britishcouncil.org/sites/default /files/understanding india report.pdf
3. IJIP.In. (2016). Student support services in Higher Education: A Student Perspective, The International Journal of Indian Psychology, Volume 3, Issue 3, No. 9 P 130-131 Retrieved from https://www.ijip.in/index.php/?view = article&id=522.
4. Pivik K., Mccomas J. and Laflamme M., Barriers and Facilitators to Inclusive Education, *Council for Exceptional Children*, 69(1) 97-107.
5. Tripathi, P., & Kiran, UV. (2012). Infrastructural Facilities for Differently Abled Students - A Comparative Study of Government and Non-Government Institutions. *International Research Journal of Social Sciences,* Vol. 1(3), 21-25, November (2012).
6. https://www.ugc.ac.in/oldpdf/xplanpdf/ DifferentlyAbled Persons.pdf.
7. http://pib.nic.in/newsite/PrintRelease.aspx?relid=175311.

Chapter - 46

Student Centric Guidance and Counseling in Higher Education

Dr. Prashanthakumara T. M

Abstract

The present global scenario is being viewed in multiple perspectives in order to empower the various segments of our society. The accent is now gradually shifting from strengthening the more technological base of our transactions to promoting humanistic concerns .The present prime concern is to recast and reorient educational systems to make them vibrant and responsive to the needs and aspirations of global society. Education thus at all levels is being recognized as powerful tool for fulfillment of such realization. Education is very important for everyone to lead a successful life. The social and technical changes have a great effect on the student's progress. We are social beings and, so in some way or other we need help and guidance of others. Mother, father, grandparents, teacher and other elders, home, school and society guide youngsters for successful living. Due to explosion of knowledge industrialization and changes in socio economic set up the need of professional guidance and counseling is felt in the present day society.

Key Words: *Guidance, Counseling, Higher Education*

Introduction

One of the well known futurist , H.G.Wells stated, " Human History becomes more and more a race between education and catastrophe" our global society today is experiencing unprecedented changes and it has become evidently clear that changes in the future are going to be unpredictably fast. Increasing globalization and cultural pluralism has changed the focus of education form 'knowledge transmission to' human development.'

Meaning and Principles of Guidance

Literally guidance means "to direct" to point out 'and to show the path' it is the assistance or help rendered by a more experienced person to a less experienced person to solve certain major problems of individual (less experienced) i.e. educational, vocational, personal, etc., Guidance is concept as well as a process. As a concept guidance is concerned with the optimal development of the individual .As a process guidance helps the Individual in self understanding (Understanding one's strengths, limitations, and other resources) and in self direction (ability to solve problems, make choices and take decisions on one' own).

Guidance and Education

The aim of education is to achieve the fullest possible realization of possibilities inherent in the individual. The Education Commission (EC-1964-66) observes –Guidance should be regarded as an integral part of education and not as a special, psychological or social service which is peripheral to educational purposes. It is meant for all students not just for those who deviate from the norm in one direction or the other.

Guidance and Counseling

Guidance is term which is broader than counseling and it includes counseling as one of its services. Butter makes a logical separation of the counseling process i.e. (i) adjustment and (ii) distributive phase. In the adjustment phase, the emphasis is on social, personal and emotional problems of the individual, in the distributive phase the focus is upon educational, vocational and occupational problems the distributive phase can be most aptly described as guidance while the adjustment face can be considered as description of counseling.

Need and Importance of Guidance and Counseling

Guidance helps in understanding ones strength, limitations and other resources guidance helps an individual to develop an ability to solve the problems and take decisions (i.e. self understanding and self direction) Optimum development of individual, solving different problem of the individual, academic growth and development, vocational maturity, vocational choices, and vocational adjustments, social personal adjustment, better family life, good citizenship for conservation and proper utilization of human resources, for national development, etc.

School guidance and Counseling curriculum

This refers to a curriculum which is systematically organized according to grade level. It is designed to serve all students at the classroom or group level. The curriculum emphasizes decision making, self knowledge career exploration and career development. The curriculum is organized around three major areas:

- Learning to live
- Learning to Learn
- Learning to work

It will be the responsibility of the "Career Guidance and Counseling Cell" that proper record and details of the students passing out from school will be kept. Regular feedback from the students may also be taken, so that the good or bad experiences may be taken care of future planning.

Counseling cell for Adolescent

Adolescence is a period when an individual is overwhelmed by a number of simultaneous developments, therefore, to meet this situation proper guidance is needed in this period. Teacher and the school can encourage the development of effective maturity in adolescents by providing the counseling and guidance. In this connection, there shall be a counseling cell for adolescents in the school.

Further, a comprehensive and developmental guidance and counseling programme is not only preventive but also pro active in preventive orientation. It is an integral part of school programme, and complements other school activities. It is important for today's guidance and counseling programme to be developmental, so that it assists students who are growing up in complex word it should help them to develop into full human beings, capable of maximizing their potential in all personal, educational, social or career– related respects. A comprehensive guidance programme should be balanced, and encompass all the fundamental areas of guidance, viz; personal, educational, social and vocational, a vocational and health. Personal guidance is to help the individual in his – her physical, emotional, social rural and spiritual development.

Educational guidance at the tertiary stages must oriented students about purpose and scope of higher studies and helps them to stimulate their studies .Each college /university must have a guidance unit with due provision of guidance serve. Moral guidance helps in bringing these students in to proper track and help in their all round development. Health is regarded as wealth.

Total health i.e. preventive and curative is the goal of health guidance. The health guidance may be a co operative effort of the principal, doctors, counselor/psychologist, teachers, students and parents. From promoting preventive care the conditions of school hostel and canteen needs to be checked. Similarly Health education through formal classes and information is essential in school education stages. In the present day, the concern of health guidance also pertains to guidance in HIV /AIDs and also to avoid teenage pregnancies.

It should provide students with the assistance necessary for their maximum development. The programme should also decide what service to offer, such as information consultation referral, counseling placement, career follow up and evaluation services. The programme should use all staff member and determine their roles in it. It therefore demands consultation co ordination a programe should be define the role of guidance personnel, who should be fully informed about the programme. It should be create a team work approach in which every member of staff is considered responsible for contributing to the success of the programme.

For a guidance programme to the comprehensive, it should be also relevant for the client and not merely maintain a status quo. It must be purposeful and designed to meet the priority needs of the client thus needs should be met in an efficient and effective manner. Unless a programme is systematic, such benefits will not ensure. The programe leader and coordinator must ensured that the impact of the programe is felt and benefits the students the extent of the participation beneficiaries is highly dependent on the capabilities of the programme leader there are four phases in programe development ; Planning, designing implementation and evaluation.

Benefits of Guidance Counseling Programs

Students

- Increases self – knowledge and how to relate effectively to others.
- Broadens knowledge about the changing environment.
- Helps them reach their fullest academic potential.
- Provides opportunities for career exploration, planning and decision – making.
- Provides an opportunity for networking with services and this establishes an effective support system.
- Teacher responsible behavior.

Parents

- Provides parents with support for their child's educational and personal development.
- Increases opportunities for parental involvement in the education of the child.
- Equips parents with skills necessary to support their child.

Teachers

- Enables students to master effectively their subjects with an understanding of the important of each one.
- Provide an opportunity to work in collaboration with other teachers and parents

Administrators

- Enhances the image of the school in the community, reduces strikes, and improves the general appearance of the school.
- Allows for systematic evaluation.
- Provides a structure which can be monitored easily.

Conclusion

The Student' s life is getting complex day by day students in the twenty first century are facing many perplexing and difficult situations the Teacher must take the role of monitors to provide assistance to the students in every angle and guide them in the right path. The changing needs of the society must be indentified and addressed for the well being nations. Education is the primary agent of transformation towards sustainable development. Building the future citizens is the key task of education. Guidance and counseling programmes in the schools and colleges provide the necessary warm supportive, caring, learning environment for the students and ensure education for holistic development of the individuals.

References

1. Ramesh Chaturvidi (2005). Guidance and Counseling Skills. Journal of Indian Education Review. 27 (1).
2. Rashmi Agarwal (2009). Elementary Guidance and counseling. New Delhi: Tendon Publication.
3. Mangal S.K. (2006). Guidance and Counseling. New Delhi: Tendon Publication.

Chapter - 47

Integrating Technology in Classroom Studies

Geetha Sai Kumari

Abstract

Technology has transformed life as we know it, and the classroom looks much different than it did 50 or even 10 years ago. Traditional chalkboards have been replaced with digital whiteboards, and classrooms have a surplus of iPads. Is this advancement to the detriment of your students, or does it benefit their learning? According to the Pew Research Center, 92% of teachers said that the internet has a major impact on their ability to access content, resources, and materials. Although many technology-based teaching methods and resources effectively engage students and build their skills, many educators encounter difficulties when using technology in the classroom. Maybe a specific platform is too hard to introduce. Or maybe it won't run on your devices. Despite the challenges, we likely have to enjoy the benefits that education technology can deliver.

Key words: *Technology, iPads, Skills.*

Introduction

You may think technology is just a distraction, but it can help encourage active participation in your classroom. Using devices like a computer, tablet, or other type of technology in your classroom can help turn traditionally dull subjects into interactive and fun activities. Teachers have observed an increased frequency of students helping each other when they're using technology in the classroom. Many technology-based tasks involve other aspects, and this leads to situations where students need to seek help from their peers or the teacher. Additionally, when students are assigned to small groups, the students who are more technologically advanced can assist their inexperienced peers.

Use of Technology in Teaching and Learning

Technology users in fundamental structural changes that can be integral to achieving significant improvements in productivity. Used to support both teaching and learning, technology infuses classrooms with digital learning tools, such as computers and hand held devices; expands course offerings, experiences, and learning materials; supports learning 24 hours a day, 7 days a week; builds 21st century skills; increases student engagement and motivation; and accelerates learning. Technology also has the power to transform teaching by ushering in a new model of connected teaching. This model links teachers to their students and to professional content, resources, and systems to help them improve their own instruction and personalize learning.

Online learning opportunities and the use of open educational resources and other technologies can increase educational productivity by accelerating the rate of learning; reducing costs associated with instructional materials or program delivery; and better utilizing teacher time.

It is important to acknowledge that students are already interested and engaged in using technology, this creates many amazing opportunities for schools and teachers to benefit from integrating some forms of technology in the classroom and to make teaching and learning more effective. Here are some of the main benefits of using technology in the classroom.

1. Virtual or online learning

Some Institutions support online learning opportunities that range from supplementing classroom instruction on an occasional basis to enrolling students in full-time programs. These opportunities include dual enrollment, credit recovery, and summer school programs, and can make courses such as Advanced Placement and honors, or remediation classes available to students. Both core subjects and electives can be taken online, many supported by online learning materials. While some online schools or programs are homegrown, many others contract with private providers or other states to provide online learning opportunities.

2. Blended learning

Blended learning opportunities incorporate both face-to-face and online learning opportunities. The degree to which online learning takes place, and the way it is integrated into the curriculum, can vary across schools. The strategy of blending online learning with school-based instruction is often utilized to accommodate students' diverse learning styles and to enable them to work before or after school in ways that are not possible with full-time conventional classroom instruction. Online learning has the potential to improve educational productivity by accelerating the rate of learning, taking advantage of learning time outside of school hours, reducing the cost of instructional materials, and better utilizing teacher time. These strategies can be particularly useful in rural areas where blended or online learning can help teachers and students in remote areas overcome distance.

3. Students can learn useful life skills through technology

By using technology in the classroom, both teachers and students can develop skills essential for the 21st century. Students can gain the skills they will need to be successful in the future. Modern learning is about collaborating with others, solving complex problems, critical thinking, developing different forms of communication and leadership skills, and improving motivation and productivity. What is more, technology can help develop many practical skills, including creating presentations, learning to differentiate reliable from unreliable sources on the Internet, maintaining proper online etiquette, and writing emails. These are very important skills that can be developed in the classroom.

4. Benefits for teachers

With countless online resources, technology can help improve teaching. Teachers can use different apps or trusted online resources to enhance the traditional ways of teaching and to keep students more engaged. Virtual lesson plans, grading software and online assessments can help teachers save a lot time. This valuable time can be used for working with students who are struggling. What is more, having virtual learning environments in schools enhances collaboration and knowledge sharing between teachers.

5. Improves engagement

When technology is integrated into lessons, students are expected to be more interested in the subjects they are studying. Technology provides different opportunities to make learning more fun and enjoyable in terms of teaching same things in new ways. For instance, delivering teaching through gamification, taking students on virtual field trips and using other online learning resources. What is more, technology can encourage a more active participation in the learning process which can be hard to achieve through a traditional lecture environment.

6. Improves knowledge retention

Students who are engaged and interested in things they are studying, are expected to have better knowledge retention. As mentioned before, technology can help to encourage active participation in the classroom which also is a very important factor for increased knowledge retention. Different forms of technology can be used to experiment with and decide what works best for students in terms of retaining their knowledge.

7. Encourages individual learning

No one learns in the same way because of different learning styles and different abilities. Technology provides great opportunities for making learning more effective for everyone with different needs. For example, students can learn at their own speed, review difficult concepts or skip ahead if they need to. What is more, technology can provide more opportunities for struggling or disabled students. Access to the Internet gives students access to a broad range of resources to conduct research in different ways, which in turn can increase the engagement.

Conclusion

Technology can help teachers form a better relationship with their students and their colleagues. Technology will undoubtedly continue to evolve, and it's important to adjust your classroom style to align with its advancements. "Take the risk. Try something new. You never really know how effective a tool or approach will be until you try it. Using technology in your classroom also encourages critical thinking skills. Just dive in."

References

https://www.prodigygame.com

https://education.cu-portland.edu

https://www.inklyo.com/technology-in-the-classroom

Chapter - 48

21st Century Skills: Life Line for Student in the Modern Digital Era of Education:- Role of a Teacher

D. S. L. Aryani

Abstract

The digital transformation has overthrown conventional teaching; in today's scenario it is felt that majority of the digital innovations are going to have a significant impact on human life in general and Educational services in particular. It is becoming increasingly clear that knowledge alone is not enough for preparing students to thrive in the world; the important thing is that teachers should embrace the goal of providing students with the content and 21st century skills so that they can succeed in our complex and changing world. Teachers must standout out of the crowd in delivering their promises by sustaining & succeeding through their innovative capabilities, rapidity, flexibility, and making ceaseless adjustments in a continuously disruptive education system.

Keywords: *Conventional Teaching, Digital Transformation, Innovative Teaching, Sustainable Teaching, Disruptive Education Sector.*

Introduction

The 21st century dawned as the beginning of the Digital Age – a time of unprecedented growth in technology and its subsequent information explosion. Never before have the tools for information access and management made such an impact on the way we live, learn, work, shop and play. New technologies and tools multiply daily and the new technologies of today are outdated almost as soon as they reach the market. In this scenario as a teacher / educator we need to identify what can be done for students to help them face this ever changing world.

A thought often attributed to Albert Einstein holds that we cannot solve a problem using the same kind of thinking that created it. Today, we face challenges that literally are planetary in magnitude and complexity, and it is becoming increasingly clear that our thinking *is* the problem. If we want to change the kind of thinking we are doing, we need to change the educational systems we are using to create that thinking.

This paper addresses the question of how to prepare every child for the new global economy. The key elements of 21st century learning are presented and described. Self-assessment, professional development, collaboration with community, and high school reform are discussed as effective strategies.

Review of Literature:

Frank Levy and Richard Murnane (2003) Declining portions of the labour force are engaged in jobs that consist primarily of routine cognitive work and routine manual labour—the types of tasks that are easiest to program computers to do. Growing proportions of the nation's labour force are engaged in jobs that emphasize expert thinking or complex communication—tasks that computers cannot do.

Lemke, et al, (2003) Students who are being prepared for the 21st century will be involved in "continuous cycles of learning" that lead to deeper understanding of the subject area content and that develop the critical skills for meeting the challenges of the future.

Apple, (2008) provide opportunities for creating and verifying their own entries in collaborative sites and evaluating contributions of others. To precise they should be "creators as well as consumers of published information"

21st Century Skills

Numerous studies and reports have emerged over the past decade that seek to identify the life, career, and learning skills that define the skills needed for success in the 21st century world. While there are some differences in how the skills are categorized or interpreted, there are also many commonalities. Common skills across most of the studies include

The chart that follows demonstrates how the demands for skills have changed over the years (Autor, Levy and Murnane 2003).

Creativity and Innovation	Using knowledge and understanding to create new ways of thinking in order to find solutions to new problems and to create new products and services.
Critical Thinking and Problem Solving	Applying higher order thinking to new problems and issues, using appropriate reasoning as they effectively analyze the problem and make decisions about the most effective ways to solve the problem.
Communication	Communicating effectively in a wide variety of forms and contexts for a wide range of purposes and using multiple media and technologies.
Collaboration	Working with others respectfully and effectively to create, use and share knowledge, solutions and innovations.
Information Management	Accessing, analyzing, synthesizing, creating and sharing information from multiple sources.
Effective Use of Technology	Creating the capacity to identify and use technology efficiently, effectively and ethically as a tool to access, organize, evaluate and share information
Career and Life Skills	Developing skills for becoming self-directed, independent learners and workers who can adapt to change, manage projects, take responsibility for their work, lead others and produce results.
Cultural Awareness	Developing cultural competence in working with others by recognizing and respecting cultural differences and work with others from a wide range of cultural and social backgrounds.

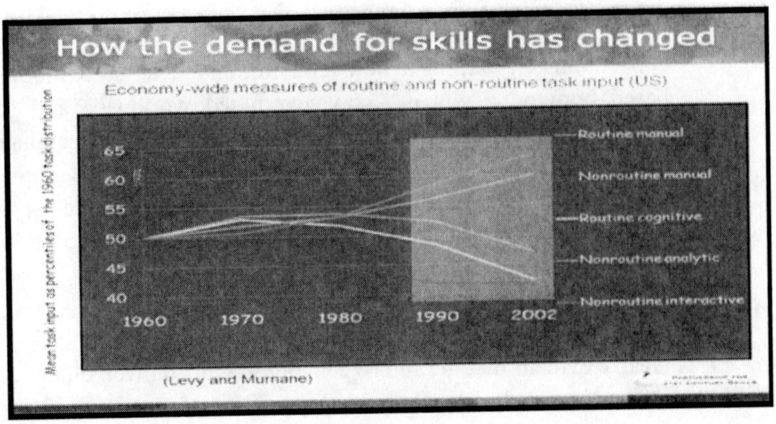

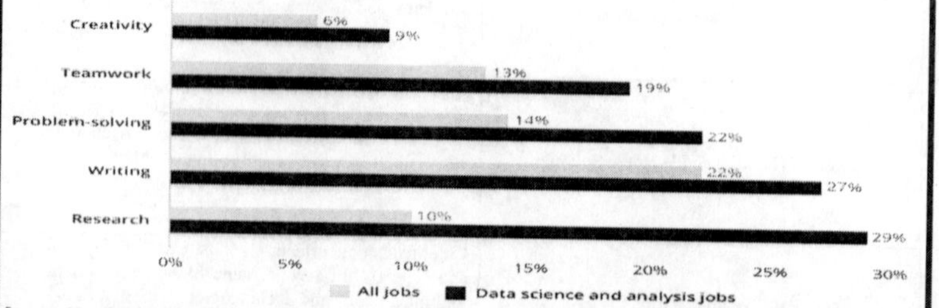

Figure 2. Data jobs require more soft skills
Percentage of posts requesting soft skills

Source: Matt Sigelman, "By the numbers: The job market for data science and analytics," Burning Glass Technologies, February 10, 2017.

Deloitte University Press | dupress.deloitte.com

What are the challenges for 21st Century Education?

We live in a world of crisis, in a knowledge society, and in an era in which time is fluid, nothing lasts, everything changes and is unstable and our present society has responsibility to build a generation for future , the challenges identified for 21st century education are.

- Society's educational systems must transform their objectives, curriculum, pedagogies, and assessments to help all students attain the sophisticated outcomes requisite for a prosperous, attractive lifestyle based on effective contributions in work and citizenship.
- 21st century education should prepare students for a world in which almost all types of routine cognitive tasks are done by computers and in which expert thinking and complex communications are the Core intellectual capabilities by which people attain prosperity and economic security individually, as a region, and as a nation.
- A crucial challenge for education in all countries is to align curriculum and learning to new economic and governance models based both on a global, knowledge-based workplace and on emerging world-level problems such as human-induced climate change. To accomplish this we must transform children's learning processes in and out of school and engage student interest in gaining 21st century skills and knowledge for work, citizenship, and a satisfying lifestyle.

How Teachers should Deal with this

It is clearly evident that the future generation must be well equipped with the skills which industry demands. The role of teacher is invincible and there is paradigm shift in the role of teacher.

The role of teachers in a 21st century classroom shifts from that of the "expert" to that of the "facilitator." The focus for instruction shifts from "knowing" to being able to use and apply information in relevant ways.

Teach our students in the way they learn, by using the 21st century skills they already possess. In order to do this, students must be considered at the planning, delivery, and assessment stages of instruction. The teacher should not be afraid to ask his/her students their opinions. Consider what they can contribute during the planning of a lesson. Give them a challenge and then guide them on their way to the solution.

21st century teaching involves a balance of the objectives of the teacher with the needs and input of the students. For that reason, learning objectives should be specific but flexible while allowing for customization.

To acquire 21st century skills, students must be encouraged to create new ideas, evaluate and analyze the material presented, and apply that knowledge to their previous academic experiences. This is achieved by changing the methods of instruction. If teachers consider their students' skills and facilitate learning, students will reach their greatest potential. This does, however, require a shift in thinking. Instead of delivering content, teachers should engage students in the content, which may also mean delivering instruction at a faster pace.

A one size fits all approach must be replaced with giving students options. Face to face interaction must be supplemented with online activities and also realise technology acts as a foundation and not what drives 21st century teaching and learning. Technology may actually hinder instruction until this paradigm shift occurs. Some of the steps which can be taken by teaching fraternity to make this paradigm shift are

- Connecting the content knowledge to real-world applications and problem situations that enable students to see how what they are learning connects with their lives and the world around them. The work that is asked of students must be authentic work that is relevant and that mirrors real life.
- Emphasizing deep understanding of the learning by focusing on projects and problems that require students to use the content knowledge in new ways and to extend their understanding through collaboration with others.
- Providing opportunities for students to become "creators as well as consumers of published information"

- Engaging students in solving complex problems that require higher order thinking and application of content and that result in new perspectives and solutions to problems.
- Providing opportunities for students to work collaborative as they gather information, solve problems, share ideas, and generate new ideas.
- Developing life and career skills by creating opportunities for students to become self-directed learners who take responsibility for their own learning and who learn how to work effectively with others.
- Helping students make connections between subjects, concepts and ideas and with others, including those outside of the classroom.
- Helping students understand and monitor the thinking process they are using by including meta cognitive activities that ask students to reflect on their use of thinking structures and effectiveness of thinking strategies they employed.
- Using Technology to help students access analyse organise and share what they are learning and allow students to independently locate appropriate tools for the task.

Conclusions

It's important to give students hands-on experiences in proving and applying what they know. The good news is there is no single "right" way to do this. You don't need fancy gadgets or huge budgets to make it happen. It does, however, take a different mindset where educators relinquish some control of the classroom to input from students and allow students to drive their own learning and try out what they know.

Many skills that had been considered valuable a decade ago, are considered obsolete today and there is no doubt that many valuable skills of today will be obsolete in a few years. Students should be prepared for jobs that didn't even exist before.

People who have 21st century skills in the future will be more likely to succeed while those who don't will either not find tremendous success or will find that their work and skills are at constant risk of being taken over by automation and artificial intelligence.

Children who have mastered the art of problem-solving by the age of 10, 12 or even 15 years will never be out skilled, and, thus, never be replaced by a smart machine when they're a part of the workforce.

References

1. 2007, June. “Apple - ACOT2 - Understanding of 21st Century Skills and Outcomes.” Understanding of 21st Century Skills and Outcomes. Apple, 2008. Web. 30 Mar. 2011. <http://ali.apple.com/acot2/skills/>.
2. Haines, Stuart T. “The Learning and Forgetting Curves.” Educational Theory and Practice. 25 Jan. 2006. Web. 30 Mar. 201.
3. http://edtheory.blogspot.com/2006/01/learning-and-forgetting-curves.html
4. Jukes, Ian, Ted D. E. McCain and Lee Crockett. Understandingthe Digital Generation: Teaching and Learning in the New Digital Landscape. Kelowna, BC: 21st Century Fluency Project, 2010. Print.
5. Key Findings: Are They Really Ready to Work? Rep. Conference Board, Oct. 2006. Web. 20 Mar. 2011.<http://www.p21.org/documents/key findings joint. pdf>.
6. Casner-Lotto, J., & Benner, M. (2006). Are they really ready for work? Employers' perspectives on the basic knowledge and applied skills of new entrants into the 21st century workforce. New York: The Conference Board, Inc., the Partnership for 21st Century Skills, Corporate Voices for Working Families, & the Society for Human Resource Management.
7. Pitler, Howard, Elizabeth R. Hubbell, Matt Kuhn, and Kim Malenoski. Using Technology with Classroom Instruction That Works. Alexandria, VA: ASCD, 2007.
8. Prensky, Marc, Clark Aldrich, and David Gibson. Games and simulations in online learning: research anddevelopment frameworks. Hershey, PA: Information Science Pub., 2007. Prensky, Marc. “Keynote Governors Institute for Innovation in Education.” December 19, 2007.(accessed December 22, 2007).
9. Lemke, Cheryl, Ed Coughlin, Vandana Thadani, and Crystal Martin. EnGauge (2003) 21st Century Skills: Literacy in the Digital Age. Rep. Los Angeles, CA: Metri Group, 2003. Print.
10. David H. Autor & Frank Levy & Richard J. Murnane, (2003). “The Skill Content of Recent Technological Change: An Empirical Exploration,” The Quarterly Journal of Economics, Oxford University Press, vol. 118(4), pages 1279-1333.
11. https://www2.deloitte.com/insights/us/en/deloitte-review/issue-21/changing-nature-of-careers-in-21st-century.html

Chapter - 49

Digitalization, Modernity and Inclusiveness; the Case of Special Needs Students in the Smart Class Rooms: A Study at the University of Hyderabad

Aysha Farhana

Abstract

The awe of digitilization of human life has an epoch impact over the fundamental institutions in the society. It has greatly influenced the formal education system existing today, largely designed around the various 'technological teaching aids' and through the smart classrooms per se. This has also created a situation wherein modernity is closely attached to these technologies. Schools and other educational institutions in large numbers are adopting the new technologies in teaching. The transition from traditional or conventional model of classroom teaching to smart class rooms are highly commendable, given that it helps students in better concept formation, concept elaboration, improvement in reading skills and in academic achievements. The new instructional materials comprising of 3D animated modules and videos are helpful in effective learning. The question that arises here is 'how and to what extent are these technologies benefitting the students with special needs in the same classrooms?'. The universal formal education system is envisaged around an 'abled body ideal' which is equally segregative and discriminatory. The wave of Inclusion movement in formal education, demanded for the regular education sector and teachers to take up the responsibilities of students with disabilities. This has taken a different leap as we suspect the effectiveness and inclusive capacity of the technologies deployed in the classrooms, in the name of teaching aids. The paper stresses upon the immediate need to address the technologies in classrooms around the question of inclusion and effectiveness of such technologies in teaching a heterogeneous group. The students who are admitted in regular schools instead of Special Needs Schools (SNS) and also students with any kind of learning disabilities shouldn't be segregated against the majoritarian imposition. This result in the inability of students to benefit from the learning activities designed for the abled body ideal in a mainstream setting. The needs of the user and the capability of the device shall be met. We shall speak this against the political and academic context of inclusive education and how power and knowledge are entangled in this case.

Introduction

"Education is the most powerful weapon which you can use to change the world".

-Nelson Mandela.

Education is an essential human virtue, a necessity of society, basis of good life and sign of freedom catering to human development. It does not confine itself to individual development but has larger social implications. The provisions Right to education and equality of educational opportunities are guaranteed by the constitution of India, it is disturbing that a major chunk of population of differently abled children and youth are denied their natural and civil rights and do not receive adequate schooling in an appropriate and conducive environment.

Do the technologies relegate the exclusiveness towards the special need students and provide inclusiveness to the special need students in the web of regular schools? Besides iPads and Chrome books and a plethora of free websites that enable students to collaborate, share and publish, the **technological explosion in the classrooms** has resulted in a wide (and increasing) variety of tools that extended the teacher's reach, making it easier to distinguish and dispose at the varied needs of students even in a busy classroom.Tech-infused alternatives and granular education activities such as note-taking, math and reading allow students with specialized needs to use their **abilities** (strengths) to work around their **disabilities** (challenges).

Technology in the classroom has become the great equalizer, providing students of all skill levels, the tools needed to fully participate in learning activities. Has this situation created inclusive spaces? This is something that we shall address at the earliest.

Special Need School and the Need of Technology

A special school is a school catering for students who have special educational needs due to learning difficulties, physical disabilities or behavioral problems. Special schools are specifically designed, staffed and resourced to provide appropriate special education for children with additional needs. Students attending special schools generally do not attend any classes in mainstream schools at the same time. Student to teacher ratios are kept low, often 6:1 or lower depending upon the needs of the children. It also have other facilities such as soft play areas, sensory rooms or swimming pools, necessary for student's development. The recent trend indicates a growth in students who are enrolling in inclusive schools. However, there will always be some children, whose learning needs cannot be appropriately met in a regular classroom setting and will require specialized education and resources to provide the level of support they require. The educational standards claim that students with disabilities should be provided equal opportunities to realize their potential. Due to the progress in the IT industry, digital technologies are easily accessible and widespread, which provide students with new opportunities. *Technology makes it possible for a classroom to be enhanced with individual learning events, allowing instructors to provide greater flexibility and differentiation in instruction. Teachers can use technology to offer a variety of learning opportunities and approaches that engage, instruct, and support special education students with a myriad of tactics designed to appeal to individual learners.* ***Digitalization of Classroom*** across the world means that 'traditional' teaching is evolving and technologies are taking over classrooms. Consistent engagement with students is a challenging task for even the most experienced educators and now there is plethora of technologies that assist learning. But, to what extent can technology assist teachers in enhancing learning environments and keeping the students engaged? The digital revolution in the education sphere means students have access to the best resources at the click of a button in any remote location. In this current digital climate, technology takes the front seat and the education sector is by no means behind. The notion of an 'abled body ideal' is the biggest challenge that the educational spaces face. What are the implications of such an exclusionary model of education? Who are the agents of it? Aren't we imposing a certain degree of normativity upon the differently abled? We, as a socio-political civil society has to address all of them with at most sensibility.

Methodology of the Study

Central universities witness the amalgamation of heterogeneous students in the pursuit of education and are to supposedly provide an inclusive environment especially for the differently abled students. Being of this kind, the University of Hyderabad, a premier institute in education is our area of study where more than hundreds of differently abled students are pursuing various courses under UG, PG, MPhil and PhD. The study shall cover 15 students from different departments of University of Hyderabad. The researchers will be following the interview method with an open ended questionnaire.

Objectives of the Study

The objectives of the study are:

- To understand the impact of smart class rooms in learning with respect to special needs students.
- To understand the role of various agencies in making the spaces inclusive or vice-versa.
- To analyze the need for discourse around the spaces generated around differently abled students in education.

Data Analysis

Whether attended special needs school and the reactions of parents while sending to regular schools.

12 out of 15 has attended Special needs school in their elementary or high school learning. The reactions of parents were mixed, most of them received encouragements but there were factors like fear, lack of awareness etc. The interventions of certain NGO's are also commendable in persuading the parents to send children to schools; both regular and special schools.

Challenges faced on a daily basis in classroom learning.

Students had various types of difficulties in classroom with respect to learning most of which was falling under the factor, i.e. unavailability and inaccessibility of study materials that are provided in the classrooms. Majority of them found difficulties in smart classrooms as power point presentations weren't helpful. They also had issues with spellings on the board, certain equations with respect to students from science and economics background.

Devices and technologies that are used currently for academic purposes.

Majority of samples were relying on smart phones and laptops or computer systems for learning. They could easily install differently able friendly android apps like ID-Pro and Invision eye and the inbuilt talkback system in phones are also used. The free software N.V.D.A (Non Visual Desktop Access) and JAWS (Job Access With Speech) a commercial software is used widely amongst the students. There are other devices like the audio recorders, Braille-me, Narrators etc. 99% students rely upon E-books for learning .

Are university facilities adequate and efficient?

Most of the sample under study felt it was quite satisfactory and can improve in many terms. Rest of them was facing issues with like lack of materials, outdated scanners and technology in assistive labs etc.

Technology as an indicator of modern education

There was an 100% agreement with respect to this notion of technological advancement and developmental notions of education. They were of the opinion that technology enables to understand the world better and also helps to be independent and self reliant given their physical state.

Is there a need for attending both Special schools and regular schools?

Majority of the sample under study felt the need for both the schooling. The elementary education was necessary and also the trainings in special schools to learn Braille, basic math, sign language, assistive technologies etc. They highlighted the need for knowledge to compete with the larger system.

Effectiveness of smart class rooms.

Only 4 pupil felt smart classroom teaching as an effective method with respect to their learning capabilities, that too not fully satisfactory. Majority had issues with PowerPoint presentations/ seminars, the videos like movies, short films, documentaries with low quality sound system and no music at all was not helpful. The subtitles displayed with movies or videos of foreign or unknown languages could not be followed. Overall there was a feeling of missing out and exclusion.

Do these spaces cater to your needs or are they another form of imposition?

There was a mixed response to this query as most of them believed that technology can improve. If provided with advanced, quality assistive technologies and adequate care and efforts from the teacher to explain the content in such spaces, ensures the equal participation of students who are differently abled.

What are the governmental aids and support that you are receiving now?

The students hailing from the state of Telangana and Andhra Pradesh received aids from home governments respectively. They were provided free laptops with installed software (N.V.D.A) at the graduation level and there were exceptions in writing exams under various provisions. The university also has a committee, E.C.D.A.P (Empowered Committee For Differently Abled Persons) constituted as per government guidelines.

How can things improve from a Special Needs perspective?

There was a wide arena of suggestions that we received regarding this. Majority of samples was of the opinion that government and institutions should provide advanced technology to students with different needs. Periodical workshops and trainings for teachers and caretakers were also necessary. Proper awareness and inclusive spaces were also to be created.

The role of teachers in making learning more inclusive and less discriminatory.

Everybody agreed to the fact that the instrumental agent in class room learning, specifically in smart class rooms were the teachers. They opined that teachers should make learning a two-way process which shall ensure the equal participation of all.

Do these spaces cater to more exclusionary practices? How to overcome them?

75% of the respondents did not feel it as a spatial issue, rather it was the system and it's functioning that made things much worse. Pupil felt the need for equal participation and timely intervention of the system to rectify and facilitate. The suggestions were abundant regarding the mode of examinations, availability of study materials and technical knowledge.

Findings

- Majority of students has availed both special education and regular schooling. Parental choice was instrumental in many cases as parents were reluctant to send children to inclusive schools due to fear, uncertainties etc. The role of certain NGO's, rotary clubs and projects like Enable India is highly commendable in enrolling differently abled students into schools. It was helpful for them to receive early trainings in assistive technologies, sign language, Braille, computer training etc and also knowledge to compete with other students. The elementary trainings in special schools enable them to effectively use technologies and also make presentations using software.
- The challenges that the students face on a daily basis were many. They mainly faced difficulties due to unavailability of books, especially in regional languages for students hailing from humanities background. Students had extreme difficulties in understanding PPT's, that were used as a mode of lecturing, which if not read out or explained deeply and the graphical contents were not benefitting. Certain spellings, visual images with low clarity audio or no audio at all were also challenging. They felt missed out in those spaces as it was impossible to seek personal assistance whenever something was played or projected. The lack of E-materials, E-books also heavily affected students as scanning was a tedious and time consuming task.

- The students from science and economic background faced high difficulties in comprehending equations, graphs, images etc.
- The sheer neglect and sympathy led to depression at early ages which imparted them low self esteem and low confidence in participating in the classroom activities and learning.
- Outdated technology and devices were a great issue faced by all.
- Everybody relied upon smart phones and laptops or computer system for learning. Assistive technologies like recorders, Braille me, talkback and software like JAWS, N.V.D.A were commonly used as screen readers.
- The university facilities were quite satisfactory but there is lot more to be done. The spaces have to be more differently able friendly. Timely upgradation of technology and devices in special labs, provision for Braille catalogs and more books in library are the need of the hour. All students should be given permission to write exams using laptops, as practiced in two departments currently. The University E.C.D.A.P conducts workshops and programs which helps students to have an institutional support.
- The state governments of both Andhra Pradesh and Telangana are providing aids like free laptops for students at graduate level which enables them to access internet and other technologies required for graduate and master's level education.
- The improvement question was really crucial as everybody had certain basic requirements with regard to learning. The need for awareness both at faculty level and student level is important to create inclusive spaces.
- The primary agent in education, teachers, had major role in educating an individual. They were to be equipped with basic training with respect to the needs of differently abled students in inclusive schools. Teachers have to acknowledge the specific needs of students and should encourage and notify students to participate equally in class rooms and competitions or seminars.
- Learning shall be a two way process, should take extra efforts like special classes, reading out and explaining imageries, provide adequate e-materials etc.
- From a special needs perspective, there is more way to go. The free and compulsory universal education was a milestone in ensuring justice to the underprivileged, minorities and the marginalized. Aren't we lacking inclusive spaces when it comes

to the differently abled question? We propose certain suggestions that would curtail to cultivate more inclusionary practices.

- Parents and children should be persuaded and encouraged to attend both special schools and inclusive schools which would help to reduce the cracks in inclusionary practices.
- The NGO's working towards the enrollment of visually challenged or other differently abled should be supported by respective authorities.
- There shall be periodical trainings and workshops for teachers in inclusive schools to understand the specific needs of students.
- The power point presentations and other technological modes of teaching shall ensure availability of soft (E-materials) and hard copies (Braille handouts) of the same to students with visual challenges.
- Government shall provide more technical and assistive technologies with in-built software or install them for students who can't afford commercial software and screen readers.
- Students shall be provided with headphones during audio-video projections in smart class rooms to ensure equal participation.
- The devices like scanners, systems, recorders in special labs shall be up-to-date , so that students don't have to spend long hours for scanning books etc.
- There shall be provisions for extra classes for students in need which enables to cover certain portions with ease.
- Libraries should ensure availability of E-copies and materials for students. There shall be Braille catalogs of books and codes shall be written in shacks in Braille for students to search books without an external help.
- There shall be a discourse about the new spaces in making, due to the advent of technology into educational spaces.

Conclusion

The study which has focused upon the struggles and challenges faced by the visually challenged students at the University of Hyderabad in learning, with respect to modern smart class rooms has yielded may insightful thoughts on the need for discourse around differently abled bodies in the age of digitalization. The functionalist perspective of education was in close proximity with the notions of 'development' and progress of an individual and of society at large. The developmental discourse was high and large in its sense, that we somehow felt as hurried upon with inadequate precautions. This has been the case of differently abled students at such spaces who were equally meant to be the stakeholders of this new and advanced system of learning, as against the conventional ones. The situation had grave consequences upon them in various forms, the sheer neglect from the side of various agencies catered to low self-esteem and confidence amongst the students at the earliest stages of learning. The lack of proper materials, outdated technology and inaccessibility to certain spaces has worsened things either. The community is hopeful for improvement and change at the earliest as they believe things have the potential to change into its fullest. There shall be a constructivist design of action regarding education and realizing the potential of pupil in an egalitarian manner.

Reference

1. Alexandra Dikusar, "The use of Technology in Special education" August 9- 2018.
2. Boe, E E, Bobbit, S.A & Cook , L H. (1997). Wither didst thou go? Retention, Reassignment Migration and attrition of Special and General Education Teachers from a National Perspective. The Journal of Special Education, 30(4), 371-389.
3. Kristin Stanberry, Marshall H. Raskind. 'Assistive Technology for Kids with Learning Disabilities: An Overview' in "The Use of Technology in Special Education" published on *September* 15, 2017.
4. "What Are the Advantages of Technology in Special Education?" by research group, University of Texas, in "The Use of Technology in Special Education" *September* 15, 2017.
5. De Monchy, M., Pijl, S. J. & Zandberg, T. (2004). Discrepancies in judging social inclusion and bullying of pupils with behaviour problems. European Journal of Special Needs Education, 19(3), 317 - 330.
6. Wolpe, A. M. (1985). Schools, discipline and social control. In L. Barton & S. Walker (Eds.), Education and social change (pp. 152-72). London: Croom Helm.

Chapter - 50

A Comparative Study on Achievement Motivation and GRIT among Government and Private School Children

Dr. Eswari Vadlamudi

Abstract

Children are inherently inquisitive and full of wonder. When this curiosity is tapped into in education, students become critical thinkers, embrace the spirit of enquiry and excel in academics. The present study focuses on a comparison between traditional schools; where rote learning and uninspiring classrooms leave us far from quality education vs. alternative education schools, which branch off into different ideals for pedagogy, student-teacher relationship, environment and all-round development of a child. The major objective of the study is to observe the levels of curiosity and exploration & mood introspection in students of diverse education systems. The second objective is to know if there is any relationship between mood introspection and exploration and curiosity. These objectives are also studied in relation to the selected independent variables like time spent in school, in coaching classes etc. Simple random sampling method and descriptive research design has been used. The researcher has used reliable and valid scales to measure dependent variables. The data interpretation is yet to be done. For the same, the researcher is using SPSS Version 21 to calculate measures of central tendency, correlation and t-test.

***Key Words**: Mood introspection, curiosity, exploration, curriculum, academic excellence, critical thinking.*

Introduction

Achievement motivation is defined as a behavior that is directed to differentiate the high and low ability of a person and what is the ability of a person to focus on his or her preferred goal. The motivation of a person can be either positive or negative depending on the past experiences and choices, performances and knowledge. The achievement motivation of a person can be determined by the situation in the way of the perceived goals. Different predictions of tasks, choices and performance are derived and tested for each case (John G. Nicholls 1984).

Achievement motivation plays a key role in determining the interests of a person and there are three common properties to determine the success or failures, that is locus, stability and controllability. The perceived stability of causes influences changes in expectancy of success; all 3 dimensions of causality affect a variety of common emotional experiences, including anger, gratitude, guilt, hopelessness, pity, pride, and shame. Expectancy and affect, in turn, are presumed to guide motivated behavior. The theory therefore relates the structure of thinking to the dynamics of feeling and action. Analysis of a created motivational episode involving achievement strivings is offered, and numerous empirical observations are examined from this theoretical position. The strength of the empirical evidence and the capability of this theory to address prevalent human emotions are stressed, and examples of research on parole decisions, smoking cessation, and helping behavior are presented to illustrate the generalizability of the theory beyond the achievement-related theoretical focus (Weiner, 1985)

A study examined a process model of relations among children's perceptions of their parents, their motivation, and their performance in school. Children's perceptions of their parents on dimensions of autonomy support and involvement were measured with the new children's perceptions of parents scale. Three motivation variables under control understanding, perceived competence, and perceived autonomy were hypothesized to mediate between children's perceptions of their parents and their school performance. Analyses indicated that perceived maternal autonomy support and involvement were positively associated with perceived competence, control understanding, and perceptions of autonomy. Perceived paternal autonomy support and involvement were related to perceived competence and autonomy (Wendy S. Grolnick, 1991).

The final goal in this study is the nature of reading motivation was to examine whether there were different groups of students who had different motivational profiles and whether these profiles were differentially related to reading activity and reading achievement. However, in the study of done by Linda Baker and Allan Wigfield (1997), we learn that there would be groups of individuals with high motivation on a number of the variables and groups of individuals with low motivation or lack of motivation on several of the dimensions. Of particular theoretical interest was whether there would be groups defined by higher motivation on some of the dimensions and lower motivation on others. One such group could be high in intrinsic motivation for reading but low in extrinsic motivation, for example. Evidence for such profiles and of their differential relations with reading activity and achievement would clearly demonstrate the importance of recognizing motivation as a multidimensional construct.

Achievement motivation creates a high energy in a person to pursue a certain activity and make it the main goal with a spirit of competence. And these goals can be categorized into two claases: (1) learning goals – this enables a person to understand or to be a master of something new and (2) performance goals :in this case a person needs to know the opinion of people either negative or positive. (Dweck & Elliott, 1983; NichoUs, 1984; Nicholls & Dweck, 1979).

One additional non-cognitive variable that has received widespread attention and that has been widely touted as an important predictor of success and performance is a personality trait referred to as grit. Grit is defined as "perseverance and passion for long-term goals". Despite the widespread enthusiasm for grit as a potentially novel predictor and determinant of performance there are sound empirical and theoretical reasons why a critical reappraisal of the nature of the grit construct, its contribution to our understanding of performance, and its general position within the nomological network may be warranted. Proponents of grit as a predictor of performance have argued that between-person differences in grit can help to explain why two individuals with the same level of ability in a particular domain are often observed to perform at substantially different levels. (Duckworth, Peterson, Matthews, & Kelly, 2007; Duckworth & Quinn, 2009).

It is commonly observed that people who are consistent towards their goals and wants to achieve them are commonly happy and satisfied with their lives because they are academically successful, creating a clear path for their future. The country we live in makes it so difficult to accept people in our society, therefore the children are pressurised to get an A grade , which in turn makes the child conscious about their future and makes their life complicated. The child gets degraded and compared to other children or cousins which make him /her lose confidence in their own selves. Therefore this research will throw a light on the topic of grit among individuals in professions such as doctors, teachers, engineers, lawyers and bankers (Bisma Mazhar Khan and Ali Mahmood Khan, 2017).

Grit and achievement motivation can be studied hand in hand as grit helps an individual to see the end goal even though it may take many years of patience and hard work. Grit has been a source to help an individual to achieve success in various ways in an individual's lifespan. Grit can be developed and improved, it is often seen as an aspect of one's personality. Grit is also used to determine a student's personal and professional life. The personality of a person is also based on the previous experiences faced by the individual either good or bad determines the personality. A person may or may not have changes in his /her personality because of these experiences (Duckworth, 2006, Allen & Lewis, 2006,)

Grit is comprised of motivation, self-control, a positive mindset, and goal-directedness and researchers have realized that each of these qualities can be influential in student success.Duckworth (2016) shares that as a child she heard the term genius frequently, but it was most often in the context of her dad telling her what she was not. A few years ago, Duckworth became a recipient of the prestigious MacArthur Fellowship, for which one cannot apply and which is often referred to as the genius grant. Duckworth coined the term grit after the young girl (played by Kim Darby) in the famous John Wayne movie by the same name True Grit (Hathaway, 1969, remake 2010), but grit itself has been around since the dawn of humankind.

In other studies, Pappano (2013), found that "how students approach learning may be as critical as what they learn", thereby demonstrating that intellectual performance may be "more malleable than we thought". According to Kidd, Palmeri, and Aslim (2013), researchers who created the marshmallow experiments found that children who were assigned to reliable experimenters (e.g., adults whom they could trust to keep their commitments) were likely to wait up to four times longer than their counterparts who were assigned to unreliable experimenters (who did not keep their word).

Therefore, Grit can be cultivated by stakeholders including parents, teachers, mentors, and employers when the four psychological assets found in really gritty people (purpose, practice, interest and hope) are present (Duckworth, 2016).

Grit as a predictor of achievement

Grit enables us to understand the hunger in an individual to achieve something. There are few factors which can determine that grit is a predictor of achievement and they are tenacity, persistence, resilience, stamina, and perseverance. Each of these by itself could certainly be considered as a predictor of achievement, but the combination of qualities can "create[s] a whole that is greater than the sum of its parts." (Goodwin & Miller, 2013)

If grit is found to play an important role in designing a student's academic performance, the study will provide new insights to higher education institutions on different methods of enhancing student academic performance, which in turn will help increase student persistence and retention. Higher education practitioners can use grit to predict which students are more likely to struggle in college, thus identifying at-risk students and provide support to increase their academic performance, which is directly related to student persistence and retention.

Objectives

(1) To study the profile of the respondents.

(2) To study the levels of Achievement Motivation and GRIT.

(3) To know the levels of relationship between Achievement Motivation and GRIT.

(4) To know if there exists any difference in Achievement Motivation and GRIT based on gender.

(5) To know if there exists any difference in Achievement Motivation and GRIT based on deprivational types.

(6) To understand the co-relation with age and Achievement Motivation.

(7) To understand the co-relation with age and GRIT.

Hypotheses

H1: Levels of Achievement Motivation and GRIT are co-related with each other.

H2: Levels of Achievement Motivation and GRIT are co-related with age.

H3: There exists a difference in Achievement Motivation and GRIT based on deprivation type.

H4: There exists a difference in Achievement Motivation and GRIT based on gender.

Population and sample

The present study aims at those individuals who are currently studying in government and private schools ranging from the age groups 9 to 15 years from the cities of Hyderabad and Secunderabad. To get the sample, the researcher used random sampling method. The sample size has been determined by the institution as the research is conducted at an Under Graduate level.

Research Design

For the present study, the researcher used descriptive research design as it can reveal potential relationships thus setting the stage for more elaborate investigation later.

Data Collection

Data was collected from government and private schools following survey method. Surveys are usually questionnaires that are given away to them to fill personally.

Results

In the present study 50% students are from government schools and 50% students are from private schools, for the present study, the age group of the respondents are mostly between 9 – 15 years. Among them the male students were 48% and the female students were 52%. It can be seen that 80% of the students were from a nuclear family background while 20% were from joined families.

The mean scores of Achievement Motivation is 136.65 and standard deviation of achievement motivation is 16.98 while the mean scores of GRIT is 1.94 while standard deviation is 0.78. the researcher used co-relation to analyse the relationship between Achievement Motivation and GRIT, and the results show that there is a positive co-relation between two variables (r =0.294, significance =0.02)

Age was also co-related with Achievement Motivation and GRIT. The results indicate that there is positive co-relation between age and GRIT (r =0.175, significance = 0.040) but there exists no relationship between age and achievement motivation.

The t-test was used by the researcher to know the difference in achievement motivation and grit based on gender. However, the results show that there is no difference in both the variables with regard to gender. The mean scores of Achievement Motivation indicate that females have higher achievement motivation (mean = 138.65) than males (mean = 134.47). The mean scores of GRIT indicate that females have higher grit (mean = 26.71) than males (mean = 25.93).

The t-test was used by the researcher to know the difference in Achievement Motivation and grit based on deprivational type. However, the results show that there is no difference in Achievement Motivation with regard todeprivational type. The mean scores of Achievement Motivation for complete deprivation type is higher (mean = 140.00) whereas for partial type (mean = 137.37).

The t-test shows that there is significant difference in the levels of GRIT based on type of deprivation (T = -2.419, DF =58, Significance = 0.01). The mean scores clearly show that respondents who are experiencing partial deprivation have higher levels of GRIT (mean =27.35) than those who have complete deprivation (mean = 25.00).

Research Design

Research design is the logical and systematic planning in directing the research. The present study is performed using a quantitative methodology with a non-experimental comparative design, and propose to analyze my data using measures of central tendency, dispersion, correlation and t-test. Non-experimental comparative design is also known as correlational research design. Within correlational research, researchers are primarily interested in determining non-causal relationships amongst variables. More specifically, the correlational research design is a type of non-experimental study in which relationships are assessed without manipulating independent variables or randomly assigning participants to different conditions.

Chapter - 51

Utilizing technology (Digital Classes) in the class room of Government schools in Telangana state

Shaik. Asif Ali

Abstract

Digital class has a significant role to play in teaching learning process. Digital class has formally been adopted as a learning tool in education system at primary school and higher education level. The digital classes take teaching learning process more meaningful and enjoyable.Digital classes extend learning opportunities worldwide. The opportunity to customize learning sequences for each student will make education more productive special needs will be more quickly diagnosed, learning gaps will be addressed, and progress will be accelerated.

Introducation

Digital learning is powering benefits that are changing the opportunity set for teachers. There are also additional benefits that are proving to be game changers for educators.

Collaborative Learning

Digital learning powers collaboration. Social learning platforms like Edmond make it easy for teachers to create and manage groups.

Personalized learning

The opportunity to help every student learn at the best pace and path for them is the most important benefit of digital learning. Learning can be enhanced based on the learners own passions, strengths, needs, and abilities.

High Engagement Learning

The shift to digital can boost student motivation. Anyone who has witnessed the engagement of game- based learning can appreciate the potential to create learning experiences that boost persistence.

Competency Based Learning

Students show what they know and progress based on demonstrated mastery. Competency based learning changes everything about school, the transition from age chorots to individual progress models will take longer, this is a generational shift.

Assessment for Learning: Digital learning provides continuous feedback from content –embedded assessment, games, simulations, and adaptive learning. When students can track their own progress it can improve motivation and agency.

Implementation of Digital classes in Telangana State

The Govt of Telangana launched its digital classroom programme in 3352 high schools in the state. The state Government provided technical support and all equipment's and terminals to run the digital classes effectively in the Telangana state.

SIET (State Institute of Educational Technology)

State Institute of Educational Technology at Hyderabad focuses on research and production of audio and video programs. The main objective of this institution is to support the department of school Education in the implementation of Educational policies and programs. Its programmes are

1. Educational Video Programmes.
2. Educational Radio Programmes.
3. Interactive Multimedia Learning Objects.

Educational Video programmes

The Educational Video programmes primarily assist in the universalization of Elementary Education.(UEE).They cover a very wide area which include instruction in 3 Rs programmes of immense value acts mainly as stimulants to create interest and awareness in children,. Stories songs Dance Ballerts, Experimental Demonstration etc. are used as formats in programme making not only develop the skills and talents in participating children.

Themes like national integration, health and nutrition, sanitation, preservation of environment, energy conservation and population education are treated with over all aim of widening the horizons.

Activities of Siet

Conduct of workshops and training programmes for persons involved in the use of media material.

Production of video programmes for SSA (School Education Dept.) Mana TV channel and other departments.

Conclusion

Digital learning allows the teacher to instruct students in a subject in such a manner that learning takes place through seeing and hearing, lecture and demonstration methods. The digital classes are useful to school teachers and students equally. Digital classes provide the clarity in learning for the students. It enables the students to understand the lesson effectively .So the Digital classes r boon to the govt school students for the overall development The State Government initiated digital classes to the government school students to empower the teaching learning process in government schools. The preparation of digital lessons as per the state syllabus in the SIET under the guidance of eminent academicians by the teachers.

The Digital classes telecasted thorough the Mana TV according to the State syllabus. The Day wise time table is drawn to provide digital classes for school students as per the academic planner. The Govt school students are gaining the benefits of Digital classes along with preparation plan and motivational sessions for SSC exams every year. The students are enjoying the digital classes and it's a boon for the Government school students. The Digital classes are very useful for the overall development of the students.

Chapter - 52

Higher Education in India: Emerging Challenges Teaching Learning Strategies With Respect To Student Centric Approaches

Kalpana Yerragokula

Abstract

The present study deals with the teaching learning strategies with respect to Student centric approaches especially throughout the India we have followed The traditional methods which means content oriented that is nothing but Whatever the teacher's teaching in the classrooms the learners have to follow But later in 1956 according to Benjamin. S. Blooms in "Blooms Taxonomy of Educational Objectives" Behaviouristic approach the importance shifted to Learning outcome which means based on course objectives, institutional Objectives and chronological age and psychological maturity of the learner Some expected learning outcomes are expected by the teachers and later now in according to Lev. Vygotsky the CONSTRUCTIVIST APPROACH the Importance shifted to the LEARNING PROCESS of the learner according to Jean Piaget the learning process is takes place in four steps i.e., Schema, Accommodation, Assimilation and Equilibration and Thorndike said about the learning principles (i) law of readiness, (ii) law of Exercise and (iii) law of result will lead the learner to learn the concept so many psychologists have given lot of learning strategies and principles strategies and techniques are in the part of approach so with in the classroom transaction according to the need and desirable of the learner the technique and strategy may be changes so present deals with above things in detail.

Keywords: - Teaching-Learning Strategies, Student Centric Approaches, Learning Process.

Introduction

Foundation of modern education was laid down by the thinkers like Aurobindo Ghosh, Rabindra Nath Tagore, Mahatma Gandhi, Moulana Abul

Kalam Azad, and Sarvepalli Radha Krishnan. Almost all the pedagogies related with content knowledge deal with learning and knowledge. Thus to make any alternate pedagogy successful and meaningful in a given context, there is a need to understand the epistemic and epistemological dimensions of learning. We know that without understanding learning (i.e. process as well as a product) properly we cannot understand the pedagogy that we want to implement in the class room for teaching and learning of any concept especially science. Pedagogy includes both the teaching as well as a learning process of learners. Teaching-Learning is a collaborative process in which sometimes teacher may work as a student and student may work as a teacher and they share knowledge with each other. Earlier, nature of knowledge in general and nature of knowing in particularly was considered as a fixed entity. However, in the contemporary understanding of nature of understanding of nature of knowledge and nature of knowing is dynamic entity. In static entity the knowledge to be transferred to learner's mind, makes her passive receiver of knowledge. The knowledge is personal and individual; the learners construct their knowledge through interactions with physical world, collaboratively in socio-cultural settings and linguistics. Today the pedagogy gives the importance of the voice of learners and their questions, their abilities of making argumentation and justification, synthesizing and analyzing knowledge and their involvement in the process of inquiring the concept in a collaborative set up rather than their ability of rote memorization.

Definitions of Education

According to Plato: - Education develops in the body and soul of the pupil all the beauty and all the perfection he is capable of According to Aristotle: - Education is the creation of sound mind in a sound body. It develops man's faculty specially his mind so that he may be able to enjoy the contemplation of supreme truth, goodness and beauty. According to Rousseau: - Education is the child's development from within. According to Froebel: -Education is enfoldment of what is already enfolded in the germ. It is the process through which the child makes the internal-external.

Definitions of Learning

According to Kingsley and R. Garry (1957) Learning is a process by which behavior is originated or changes through practice or training. According to Kimble (1961) Learning is relatively permanent change in behavioral potentiality that occurs as a result of reinforced practice. According to Henry P. Smith (1962) Learning is the acquisition of new behavior or the strengthening or weakening of old behavior as the result of experience. According to Gardner Murphy (1968) the term learning covers every modification in behavior to meet environmental requirements. According to Crow and Crow (1973) Learning is defined as "The acquisition of habits, knowledge and attitudes. It involves new way of doing things, and it operates in an individual attempts to overcome obstacles or adjust to new situations. It represents progressive changes in behavior. It enables him to satisfy interests to attain goals.

Significance of the Study

Each learner is unique if we observe no two individuals are same even in identical twins they look like same but they can differentiate in eye balls and finger prints and height, weight, color and intellectual, emotional and socio-cultural differences, when come to the learning styles each learner have different learning styles so some have read number of books, some have worked on many projects at the previous stages of learning, while some have traveled to many places. Different learners interact with different people and they observe and interpret their environment differently. All these factors contribute to the differences in their experiences. Based on above traits the teachers and policy makers need to use various strategies to transact the curriculum which is highly student centric. It has to considers the chronological age and psychological maturity of the learners and as well as it gives importance to the needs and desires of the learner ultimately it concentrates to develop the learner in every area, i.e. Physical, Intellectual, Emotional, Moral, Spiritual, Aesthetic and also fulfills the society need which expects good citizen to serve the nation. Within the class room the teacher gives importance to the diverse of the class according to john Dewey school is the miniature of the society. Any class have three kinds of students above average, average and below average so here any selected approach or strategy need to consider all the above features and do the justification to each and every learner within the classroom then we can consider that approach or strategy is student centric. Some of the student centric approaches are constructivist approach, collaborative approach, concept mapping, experiential learning, Peer learning, Team teaching, problem solving approach, 5E-learning model, Group Learning, Inquiry approach.

Nature of Curriculum in student centric Approach or Strategy

The role of teacher is to provide learning environment and stimulating experiences to learners. From the learner-centered viewpoint, teachers must trust in the innate abilities of learners; in their capacity to direct their own exploration and learning. Learner-centered curriculum views learning from a constructivist perspective. Learning takes place when learners engage with stimulating environment, get involved in inquiry and make meaning for themselves out of interactions with environment. Learner-centered educators are interested in knowing, 'what is happening within' the learner between stimulus and response. The learner-centered educators are interested in parameters such as the state of learner's cognitive structures, her meaning-making abilities, and her creative spirit. For 'constructivist curriculum' developers, it is the learning environment and experiences, that are of crucial importance and can be generated by taking into consideration the context of learner as well as teaching-learning environment. The curriculum must engage learners with stimulating experiences by arranging suitable learning environment.

'Constructivist curriculum' is based on the following assumptions:

- Knowledge is actively constructed, invented, created, or discovered by learners. It is not passively received and stored by learners.
- Knowledge cannot be separated from the process of meaning-making or knowing or learner's experiences. It is based on learner's conceptual structures and prior experiences.
- Learners are constantly constructing and reconstructing their cognitive structures, both as a result of newly acquired knowledge and as a result of their reflection on previously acquired knowledge.
- Social interaction with peers and adults in a cultural context are extremely important in individual's construction of knowledge.
- Concept formation progresses from concrete to abstract slowly.
- Learners have different learning styles, and teaching–learning should accommodate these.
- The teacher in constructivist curriculum is provider of the learning environment and a facilitator of learning.
- The analysis of syllabi prepared by NCERT in 1988, 2000 and 2005 reveals that there is a shift in approach to syllabus development. There is a shift from information loaded content to 'activity-based' integrated science syllabus to 'learner-centered' syllabus.

Student Centric Strategies Exploring Learners

1. Encouraging Learners to Raise and ask Questions:-
   - Asking questions is one of the most valuable skills. Learning process should lead to a situation where the learner gets involved in COGNITIVE- CONFLICT.

- Welcome and value each question. No question should be stamped as simple or silly question
- Each learner of the class has to raise at least one question during learning process.
- Asking a good question requires thinking and knowledge. Not only their answers but also quality of their questions will be assessed in the class. This would motivate them to concentrate on learning and thinking.

2. Creating the Habit of Listening to the Learners
   - Asking and listening are closely tied together in teaching-learning process
   - Teacher listen students by providing open-ended questions
   - Listening to the students is one of the most powerful tools of teachers
   - Teacher should understand the ....
   - The students thinking process
   - Find the learning gap between their thinking and existing concepts
   - To know the organization of thought process of the students
3. Creating Opportunity to Listening to the Learners
   - Each learner is unique with varied levels of interest and abilities. Learners come from diverse social and educational background so each learner may respond differently to the same learning situation.
   - Take time to observe and assess the ideas of all learners including those who seldom participate in teaching- learning process this will help to know the complex way of thinking and also help the teacher to choose an appropriate approach to teaching-learning process.
4. Encouraging The Learner To Collect Materials From The Local Resources Activities to collect materials:-
   - Develop resources (collect the written material reference books, journals and articles etc...)Library, physical equipment for laboratory for conducting the experiments to related disciplines
   - Opening a special clubs to related disciplines
   - Organizing the field trips/ industrial tours and educational trips

- Conducting various projects
- Making static and working models

Above mentioned activities can generate interest in the learners, motivate them for learning and give them chance to move out of the boundaries explore their knowledge on their own.

5. Motivating the learners to bring their previous knowledge into the classroom
   - Learners' experiences and observations of real life situations and their previous knowledge should be used in teaching-learning process.
   - Teacher should nurture a learning environment where learners' can get motivated to share their previous experience and knowledge without fear and take initiative to participate such kind of classroom leads to quality learning.
   - Before starting the lesson teacher should ensure that the learners are ready to learn this is according to Ivan Pavlov's law of readiness principle
   - Encourage the learner's to share their experiences, clear their doubts and their existing ideas with the class and seek out the knowledge from sources other than the text books,i.e. their personal experiences, from the peers , home and surroundings, outside of the classrooms.
6. Naive concepts

   When learner undergo an new experience ,they try to make its connections with the existing ideas to construct a meaning for particular concept, if it does not fit with the existing ideas, then these ideas are altered to make connection with other experiences for better construction of a contextual concept. The process of information to explore to their naïve concept with the help of three strategies, i.e. (i) Catch (ii) Challenge (iii) Change

   (i) Catch: Encourage the learners to talk, enter into conversation, discussion, and argumentation

   (ii) Challenge:
   - Ask learners to generate, collect and give evidences of their learning
   - Give them opportunity to perform experiments, activities and projects, concept maps with their ideas

   (iii) Change:
   - Provide learning situations to support new ideas

- Relate the learning situation to daily life experience
- Help them to reflect on their new understanding

Conclusion

Teaching-Learning Strategy which is too used in any class room transaction it is direction to the teacher to deliver the content, many strategies are there according to the nature of the concept. Suppose if it is "The life history and contribution of scientist –C.V. Raman" a teacher can give oral lecture, pictorial representation, motion picture and taking the students to exhibition etc… so one strategy is not for one particular topic strictly any strategy can use any where according to the demand on the situation so in present study we discussed about the student centric approach or strategy nature and type of curriculum for that and as well as most predominant approach is constructivist approach we discussed and students involvement while construct the new knowledge about particular topic mentioned, here teacher have complete freedom to select any teaching strategy and the strategy is in flexible in nature so this help the learner to construct on his own by previous experience because it become student centric.

Issues Faced By The Learners' During Construction of Knowledge

- Lack of previous knowledge about the existing concept.
- No sufficient time to the learner to constructs the knowledge.
- No individual differences have been considered.
- Imbalanced student-teacher ratio.
- Force by the management to complete the syllabus.
- No additional training to the faculty for difficult concept
- No teachers' involvement in the curriculum selection.

Suggestions

1. The teacher has to take care of the existing ideas of the learners and the difference in nature of their ideas with the scientific explanations.
2. The teacher develop the habit of listening to learners , giving value to their ideas and motivating them to bring their own idea about their observations and interpretations of phenomena in their own context.
3. A constructivist teacher must be trained as a critical analysis of syllabi, textbooks and reflective practitioner of her own teaching-learning practices.

4. The teachers need to identify the individual differences to share their views in the teaching learning process.
5. The teachers need to identify the individual interests, abilities and aptitudes of the every learner and encourage them accordingly.
6. The teachers should provide sufficient time to build the relationship with the concept i.e. (cognitive structuring) experience, explore and reflect with it.
7. The teachers need to understand the diverse needs of the class students and use new Innovative methods.
8. In the process of construction the previous knowledge of the learner will help to frame a mental representation about present concept and it will lead to the future.

References

1. Appleton, K. (1997). Analysis and Description of Student's Learning During Science Class Using a Constructivist Based Model, Journal of Research in Science Teaching, 34 (3), pp. 303-318.
2. Anderson, L.W., & Krathwohl, D. R., et al. (eds.) (2001). A Taxonomy for Learning, Teaching, and Assessing: A Revision of Bloom's Taxonomy of Educational Objectives, Boston: Allyn & Bacon.
3. Ausubel, D.P. (1963). The Psychology of Meaningful Verbal Learning. NY: Grune & Stratton.
4. Ausubel, D.P. (1968). Educational Psychology: A Cognitive View. NY: Holt, Rinehart & Winston.
5. Beiser, Arthur (1991). Modern Technical Physics, 6th Edition. USA: Addison - Wessly.
6. Bloom, B.S. & Krathwohl, D. R. (1956). Taxonomy of Educational Objectives: The Classification of Educational Goals, Handbook I: Cognitive Domain.NY: Longmans, Green.
7. Catherine, W.U. & Julie Gess Newsome, (2008). Active Learning Strategies, The Science Teacher, 75 (9), pp. 47-52.
8. Chiappetta, E.L., Koballa, T.R. & Collette A.T. (1998). Science Instructions in the Middle and Secondary Schools. New Jersey: Prentice-Hall, Inc.
9. Driver, R., Asoko, H., et al. (1994).Constructing Scientific Knowledge in the Classroom, Educational Researcher, 23(7), pp. 5-12.
10. Glasgow, N.A. & Hicks, C.D. (2003). What Successful Teachers Do: 91 Reseach-Based Classroom Strategies for New and Veteran Teachers. Thousand Oaks, California: Crowin Press, Inc.
11. Hewitt, P.G.(1992). Conceptual Physics, 2nd Edition. USA: Addison- Wessly.
12. Krathwohl, D.R., Bloom, B.S. and Masia, B.B. (1973). Taxonomy of Educational Objectives: The Classification of Educational Goals Handbook II: Affective Domain. NY: David McKay Company, Inc.

13. NCERT (2007). Chemisty Part – I Textbook for Class XI. New Delhi: National Council of Education Research and Training.
14. Page 10 of 10
15. NCERT (2007). Chemistry Part – II Textbook for Class XI. New Delhi: National Council of Education Research and Training.
16. Web resources
17. bertil.roos@pedag.umu.sehttp://www.onlineassessment.nu/onlineas_webb/products/NERA_paper_040217.pdf
18. Douglas College (British Columbia). The ASSURE Model for Selecting Instructional Media, http://www.douglas.bc.ca/dls/pdf/assuremodel.pdf.
19. http:www.education.nic.in/cd50years/q/6j/BJ/6JBO401.htm>
20. http://etc.usf.edu/broward/mod2/module2.html
21. http://knol.google.com/k/low-cost-teaching-aids-for-rural-schools-in-india
22. http://nobelprize.org/nobel_prizes/physics/laureates/1930/raman-bio.html
23. http://olc.spsd.sk.ca/DE/PD/instr/strats/coop/lesson.pdf.

Chapter - 53

Developing Creative Writing Skill among Degree College Students through The Authentic Materials

Gidde Rajinikanth

Abstract

Writing skill is one of the major skills among all the language skills which have a prominent role in this present day of the world. Writing is an effective way to communication to the others, and it carries the information with clarity and clearly. Creative writing means "Creative writing is any writing that goes outside the bounds of normal professional, journalistic, academic, or technical forms of literature, typically identified by an emphasis on narrative craft, character development, and the use of literary tropes". Objectives are Developing creative writing skills of degree level students through the use of authentic materials. To create awareness of the importance of writing skills in English. To make the learning joyful with the introduction of authentic materials in the classroom. To make the learners compose considerably well in the target language. To make the learners learn to write effectively in any context through the use of authentic materials. Hypothesis are Students from Degree level may have difficulties in creative writing skills. Students' background may be the reason in lacking behind in creative writing skills. Authentic material may help the learners to improve their creative writing skills at the degree level. The introduction of authentic material the learners may improve their writing skills'. The research tools will be standardised before the actual research process being conducted.

***Key words**: creative writing, Degree college students, Authentic Material.*

Introduction

Writing skill is one of the major skills among all the language skills which have a prominent role in this present day of the world. Writing is an effective way to communication to the others, and it carries the information with clarity and clearly. In the part of writing skills, creative writing is essential to everyone. It should be developed among the students in early age of schooling. Creative writing is to edit the existed information, to imagine, to explain the any situation, with the sources of available materials which may be anything.

So, what is creative writing? Chambers Dictionary denes creative as 'Having the power to create, that creates, showing, pertaining to, imagination, originality' and writing as 'The act of one who writes, that which is written, literary production or composition'. Therefore, the **term 'creative writing' may be dened as:**

"Having the power to create an imaginative, original literary production or composition

And can be applied to Avery broad spectrum of writing genres". "Creative writing is any writing that goes outside the bounds of normal professional, journalistic, academic, or technical forms of literature, typically identified by an emphasis on narrative craft, character development, and the use of literary tropes".

In every college, no one is trying to help the students to develop their creative writing skill; it is lack them behind in effective writing skills. The students must learn the compositions on their own. From this creative writing development they may learn academic writing skills in an effective way. The students show interest in writing their personal likes and dislikes. So, it is point that children learn the creative writing skills when a peaceful, interested and free from instructions are provided. So many students are not aware of creative writing, and its important in their further studies and so on.

Significance of the study

With the development of science and technology into all the fields, the essence of learning English is being rocketed up as well. As an individual, English has become everyone's part of life and one cannot detach English from his life. With the bearing in mind the essence of learning English is encouraged by all the people from different walks of life. Earlier, English medium education was confined only to the urban areas is now slowly being spread to the rural areas of the state. This spread of English itself shows the important that it has gained in the recent times.

English, in the rural areas id being neglected even though it's important is being stressed upon by many scholars. Students from the rural areas find learning of English a herculean task. This made the learner to distance themselves from the learning of English. Therefore, keeping in mind the need of learning English it is to be taught in more interesting way. Therefore, in order to ignite the interest of learning English in the minds of the learners' it can be done so by the use of authentic materials. With the use of authentic materials in the classroom, the learners may be motivated and show a sense of interest in learning English and would enjoy learning English.

Though there are many methods and techniques have been introduced in the field of teaching and learning of the English language education, but a little progress has been achieved in the productive skills than the passive skills. It is too less especially in writing skills. Unfortunately it is considered that one who fluency in speaking and reading, he has knowledge of English, but apart from listening skill ,writing skill is totally neglected in secondary level. So there is a need to develop the creative writing among the students at secondary level with innovative methods and material, instructions of teaching. A wide range of opinion about teaching creative writing skills is that formal way of teaching the writing skills is not much effective. This will be more effective with the use of authentic materials.

The present study on developing creative writing skills through the use of authentic materials. These authentic materials can be used for developing language skills. In all the four language skills, speaking skills is considered to be an important one for it is used for medium of communication. The authentic materials that are being introduced in the class would help the degree level learners to enhance their speaking skills which are essential for learners in more than one way.

Conceptual background of the study

In a Chinese proverb that quoted as "A picture is the worth of thousand words". It means that a picture can give the whole meaning of a situation what we want to say or interpret or to write something. It is taken into the consideration if we use the pictures in a language classroom it will be very effective to the learners to learn the skills. We cannot say most of the things that we were asked to present. But by watching and observing a picture, a number of ideas, thoughts, perceptions, views experiences float into the mind, it easy to say something by watching and observing.

As well as the pictures and the other materials such as realia (materials from the real life situations), advertisements, newspapers, audio-visual aids and everything that cannot mean the purpose of academics. So that the present study was taken to intend to develop the creative writing skills of degree college level students through the highly effective activities for teaching writing skills. The activities were designed by different types of materials which were collected from the outside of the classroom. The activities were introduced with a lot of interest and great effort.

Review of related studies

There are many references to authentic material in the ELT literature. Books and journals contain thorough explanations of why it should or should not be included in lessons, and how it is to be used or best exploited. But those authors who support the use of authentic material have in common one idea: "exposure". In other words, the benefit students get from being exposed to the language in authentic materials.

The definition of authentic materials used in this paper is taken from Peacock (1997): materials that have been produced to fulfil some social purpose in the language community.

Widdowson's (1990) differentiation of the terms "authentic" and "genuine material" has been a seminal one in the field so I should like to mention it here: *Authentic* would be material designed for native speakers of English used in the classroom in a way similar to the one it was designed for. For example, a radio news report brought into the class so students discuss the report on pollution in the city where learners live.

Most of the time, though, this material is used in a *genuine* way, in other words, not in the way it was intended, but in a somewhat artificial way. For example, news article where the paragraphs are cut up and jumbled so students have to put them back together in the correct order.

Another view is the difference between artificial and authentic materials (see Shortall, 2001).

The definitions of authentic materials are slightly different in literature. What is common in these definitions is 'exposure to real language and its use in its own community'.

Rogers (1988) defines it as 'appropriate' and 'quality' in terms of goals, objectives, learner needs and interest and 'natural' in terms of real life and meaningful communication (p. 467).

Harmer (1991), cited in Matsuta (n.d., para. 1) defines authentic texts as materials which are designed for native speakers; they are real text; designed not for language students, but for the speakers of the language.

Jordan (1997, p. 113) refers to authentic texts as texts that are not written for language teaching purposes. Authentic materials is significant since it increases students' motivation for learning, makes the learner be exposed to the 'real' language as discussed by Guariento & Morley (2001, p. 347).

Objectives of the study

The present study has focused on mainly on:

(a) Developing creative writing skills of degree level students through the use of authentic materials.

(b) To create awareness of the importance of writing skills in English.

(c) To make the learning joyful with the introduction of authentic materials in the classroom

(d) To make the learners compose considerably well in the target language.

(e) To make the learners learn to write effectively in any context through the use of authentic materials

Research methodology

Statement of the problem

The researcher has to look into the problem in degree college students and needs to take the study to develop the creative writing skills among the students.

Approach to the study

The present study should be qualitative in nature. So it will adapt the qualitative approach to the research. A qualitative "approach" is a general way of thinking about conducting qualitative research. It describes, either explicitly or implicitly, the purpose of the qualitative research, the role of the researcher(s), the stages of research, and the method of data analysis.

Universe: Degree college level

Population: heterogeneous group of 8th class students

Sample: 120 students and Government colleges

Sampling technique: Random sampling technique will be used in the research process.

Research questions

1. What are difficulties in learning creative writing among the students at degree college level?
2. What are the possible reasons for the learners to lack behind in creative writing?
3. Can authentic material be helpful in improving the students' creative writing skills at secondary level?
4. How far authentic materials helpful in improving the students' creative writing skills at secondary level?

Variables

A variable is anything that can vary, i.e. changed or be changed, such as memory, attention, time taken to perform a task etc.

Variable are given a special names that only apply to experimental investigations. One is called the dependent variable and the other the independent variable. In an experiment, the researcher is looking for the possible effect on the dependent variable that might be caused by changing the independent variable.

Independent variables: Variable the experimenter manipulates (i.e. changes) – assumed to have a direct effect on the dependent variable.

1. Students
2. Interventions
3. Teaching methods
4. Students background

Dependent variables: Variable the experimenter measures, after making changes to the Independent Variable that are assumed to affect the Dependent Variable.

1. Behaviour
2. Competence in creative writing
3. Learning conditions
4. Out comes

Hypotheses

1. Students from degree college level may have difficulties in creative writing skills.
2. Students' background may be the reason in lacking behind in creative writing skills.

3. Authentic material may help the learners to improve their creative writing skills at the Degree college level.
4. The introduction of authentic material the learners may improve their writing skills

Research tools

- Interview with the teachers
- Informal interaction with the students
- Pre-test
- Intervention
- Post-test.

Standardisation of tools

The research tools will be standardised before the actual research process being preceded.

Techniques of data analysis

Appropriate techniques will be followed for analysing and interpret the data.

Such as, T-test, ANOVAs.

References

1. Birnie, B. F. (2015). A Teacher's Guide To Organizational Strategies For Thinking And Writing. Maryland: The Rowman & Littlefield Publishing Group, Inc.
2. Currier D. (2008). Essay on the importance of writing – need feedback please. Asian ESL Journal. Retrieved from Gloria, Essay Writing Feedback/ EssayForum.com on 8/17/2010 Journal 80 pp. 183-199.
3. Gall, M. D., Borg, W. R., Gall, J. P. (2003). Educational Research: an Introduction 7th Edition. New York: Longman.
4. Gay, L. R., et al. (2006). Educational Research Competencies for Analysis and Applications: Eight Edition. Columbus Ohio. Pearson Merril Prentice Hall.
5. Gebhard, J.G. (1996). Teaching English as a Foreign Language: A Teacher Self-Development and Methodology Guide. Ann Arbor: The University of Michigan Press. Ghaith, Ghazi. (2002). Writing. Retrieved December 2nd, 2013, from
6. http://www.thefreedictionary.com/writing.
7. Hosseini, Monirosadat; Taghizadeh, Mohamad Ehsan; Abedin, Mohamad Jafre Zainol; Naseri, Elham. (2013). In the
8. Importance of EFL Learners' writing Skill: Is there any Relation between Writing Skill and Content Score of English Essay Test?. International Letters of Social and Humanistic Sciences. 6 (2013) pp. 1-12.

9. Hughes, Arthur. (2008). Testing for Language Learners. UK: Cambridge University.
10. Kilickaya, Ferit. (2004). Authentic Materials and Cultural Content in EFL Classrooms. The Internet TESL Journal. Retrieved on December 2nd, 2013, from.
11. http://iteslj.org/Techniques/Kilickaya-AutenticMaterial.html.
12. Maroko, Geoffrey M. (2010). The authentic materials approach in the teaching of functional writing in the classroom. Kenya: Kenyatta University Department of English and Linguistics.

Chapter - 54

Health Education on Anaemia to Rural Adolescent Girls in Erstwhile Medak District

Dr. Kalapatapu Ravikiran Sharma,
Dr. Kalpana Toran, Dr. Kavita Toran

Introduction

Iron Deficiency Anaemia (IDA) is the most common nutritional disorder, which affects people from all segments. Adolescent girls are highly vulnerable to nutrition disorders, especially IDA. To prevent and control the problem of anaemia among adolescent girls, multicentric health education was conducted under the auspices of UNICEF to provide IFA supplementation. The health education has clearly demonstrated the efficacy of once –a-week IFA tablet containing 100 mg of elemental iron and 0.5 mg of folic acid in raising the haemoglobin level similar to that seen with the same dose level of iron given daily and thus reduce anaemia prevalence. Side effects were far fewer with weekly supplementation compared to daily iron administration.

In this context, ahealth education study was conducted for two years in the erstwhile Medak district with a sample size of 3071 rural adolescent girls.

Purpose of study

The purpose of this study is to undertake health education on anaemia to adolescent girls in the backward mandals of erstwhile Medak district.

Research methodology

A wide variety of methods were used during both the phases of this health education intervention. During the first stage, anthropometry, clinical trials, biochemical tests and interview schedules were used to assess the nutritional anaemia status and knowledge, attitude and practices (KAP) of respondents. Consultation-cum-planning meetings, orientation training programs, collection of baseline data, development and distribution of IEC materials, formal evaluation, individual counselling and monitoring were done. This health education project was executed in four stages during both the phases.

Results

The behavioural change was substantial in the sense that there was an increase in normal hb level for children to an extent of 68%. Dwelling on awareness change, it was found that the most remarkable improvements were registered with respect to consumption of IFA tablets at 93% and consumption of iron rich foods at 92.6%. Highly appreciable shifts were also registered in awareness change regarding adolescent anaemia control program at 81.5%. The corresponding figure regarding consumption of de-worming drug stood at 80.2%, while it stood at 75.2% for problem of anaemia and for Hb level at 66.4%.

Background

Iron Deficiency Anaemia (IDA) is the most common nutritional disorder, which affects people from all segments. Adolescent girls are highly vulnerable to nutrition disorders, especially IDA. To prevent and control the problem of anaemia among adolescent girls, multicentric studies were conducted under the auspices of UNICEF to provide IFA supplementation. The studies have clearly demonstrated the efficacy of once–a-week IFA tablet containing 100 mg of elemental iron and 0.5 mg of folic acid in raising the haemoglobin level similar to that seen with the same dose level of iron given daily and thus reduce anaemia prevalence. Side effects were far fewer with weekly supplementation compared to daily iron administration.

In this context, this study was launched for two years in the backward Medak district at 16 schools with a sample size of 3071 rural adolescent girls who were all in an age range of 10-15 years with the mean age being 12.5 years.

Purpose of study

The purpose of this study is to prevent and control anaemia in adolescent girls in the backward mandals of erstwhile Medak district.

Objectives of study

- To assess the feasibility and acceptability of supervised weekly supplementation of iron and folic acid to adolescent girls to prevent and control anaemia through joint involvement of the departments of education and health.
- To improve the knowledge, attitude and understanding of adolescent girls regarding ill effects of anaemia and convince them of the usefulness of weekly supplementation of iron and folic acid through appropriate IEC interventions.
- To assess the impact of the programme in reducing the prevalence of anaemia using haemoglobin as an indicator and scale-up the programme in the entire district in a phased manner.

Research methodology

A wide variety of methods were used during both the phases of the intervention. During the first stage, anthropometry, clinical trials, biochemical tests and interview schedules were used to assess the nutritional anaemia status and KAP of respondents. Consultation-cum-planning meetings, orientation training programs, collection of baseline data, development and distribution of IEC materials, formal evaluation, individual counselling and monitoring were completed. The project was executed in four stages during the both the phases.

Results

The behavioural change was substantial in the sense that there was an increase in normal hb level for children to an extent of 68%. Dwelling on awareness change, it was found that the most remarkable improvements were registered with respect to consumption of IFA tablets at 93% and consumption of iron rich foods at 92.6%. Highly appreciable shifts were also registered in awareness change regarding adolescent anaemia control program at 81.5%. The corresponding figure regarding consumption of de-worming drug stood at 80.2%, while it stood at 75.2% for problem of anaemia and for Hb level at 66.4%.

The overall IEC utilisation rate of this intervention turned out to be only 24.66%. Little media were used quite well at a rate of 55.15% with personnel coming in a distant second at 24.60%. The electronic media and print media were meagrely used at a rate of 10.10% and 7.50% respectively, though these mass media could have been more effective in dissemination of messages which were oriented towards preventive healthcare.

Electronic media

Television was grossly neglected in terms of IEC utilisation as it showed a marginal score of 11.3%. Radio was even more neglected with an IEC utilisation score of just 8.9%.

Little media

The most encouraging score was reported by the research-based set of folders/pamphlets/leaflets/brochures/flip books/booklets which together recorded 61.1% in terms of IEC utilisation. Posters/exhibits also contributed to some extent with a score of 49.2%.

Print media

Newspapers were marginally used for IEC dissemination with a score of just 7.5% while magazines were completely ignored.

IEC activities

Demonstrations alone stood out among all IEC activities with regard to utilisation score at 44.7%. The combo of innovative games/singing/painting/story telling/quiz were utilised at a rate of 9.3% while self-awareness surprisingly registered its slight presence at 5.4%.

Personnel

The resource rich set of AWW/dhai/education committee members/ WHV /RMP/private doctors/VAO were utilised for IEC activities with a score of 38.3% while an IEC utilisation rate of 10.9% was reported by the volunteering community of NGO/NSS volunteers/youth club.

Critical comments

It is really incomprehensible that a healthcare intervention highly focused on preventive healthcare as well as supportive healthcare has been able to utilise health education only to some extent even though it is common knowledge that IEC is the cornerstone of the aforementioned healthcare dimensions.

Teachers are key resource persons in any health education intervention of this nature and should hence be provided some monetary incentive to carry out such an important task. The girls can play a proactive role in IEC dissemination on their own provided they are thoroughly educated on all aspects of anaemia. New methods such as role play, docudrama and local folk forms can be adopted to spread the IEC messages which are rooted in local dialect, local culture and local norms. The use of such unconventional training methods in dull educational settings can add novelty as well as spice to the learning experience.

Suggestions

- Counselling and reassurance should be repeatedly adopted to ensure good compliance with regard to IFA tablet consumption by Adolescent Girls, especially during the first month after the commencement of supplementation.
- Anaemiacan be prevented and controlled only if basic facilities such as clean drinking water, containers to store water and tumblers to drink water are provided.
- Health department should ensure regular supply of IFA tablets at any cost.
- Systematic planning of IEC activities must be done to promote IFA tablet consumption and encourage intake of Iron Rich Foods.
- IEC activities should be integrated into the normal educational activities.
- Teachers and health staff should be imparted orientation and refresher training for successful implementation of the IEC intervention.

Conclusion

Since there is a significant rise in hemoglobin levels, the once-a-week IFA supplementation to adolescent school girls is a prerequisite for prevention and control of anaemia. Such an approach can click only through sustained IEC activities by teachers and health staff. The focus of this health education intervention needs to be on those interpersonal forms of health communication like cooking demonstrations and student to student learning as evidenced in this study. It is very important that the routine academic activities in educational institutes should not be disturbed by this health education initiative.

Chapter - 55

Nutrition Education for Adolescent Girls in the Slums of Twin Cities under IPP-VIII, Hyderabad

Dr. Kalpana Toran,
Dr. Kalapatapu Ravikiran Sharma
Dr. Kavita Toran

Abstract

India Population Project (IPP) -VIII was launched with financial assistance from the World Bank to provide maternal & child health and family welfare services in select 100 slums of Hyderabad. This project adopted the task of addressing issues such as enforcing a positive change in the mindset of the wider community through an educational intervention. Mere availability of mass media or alternative communication channels always does not guarantee successful health education. The purpose of this study is to devise, carry out and measure the impact of educational intervention on the nutrition knowledge of adolescent girls in the selected 100 slums of twin cities under purview of IPP-VIII, Hyderabad.

Objectives

- To evaluate knowledge, attitude and practices (KAP) of adolescent girls on aspects relating to nutrition, early marriage, reproductive behaviour including sexuality and media using habits.
- To plan, devise and implement nutrition and health education programme for adolescent girls.
- To study the impact of nutrition education intervention programme.

Research methodology

The study was conducted in three stages. In the first stage, baseline data on 2500 adolescent girls (10-19 yrs) were collected using a specially designed comprehensive pretested interview schedule. In the second stage, an intensive nutrition education intervention was carried out covering all the adolescent girls living in slums for a period of six months mainly through IPC techniques. In the third stage, a repeat survey was conducted to find out the impact of nutrition education intervention in terms of improvement in knowledge level and consumption of nutrient rich foods.

Results

The study covered a sample of 2500 adolescent girls living in selected 100 slums. Though an effort was made to contact the same adolescent girls (follow up), only 2,326 could be covered during end line survey. The balance of 174 adolescent girls living in the same slums though covered as substitutes/replacement to make up the envisaged 2,500 sample were excluded for the purpose of analysis.The study highlighted the need to project appropriate role models to these adolescent girls. Similarly, the informative Telugu booklet "Adolescent Health and Nutrition" needs to be popularised with every Telugu speaking adolescent girl keeping a copy of the same as a ready reckoner. The community-based IEC interventions must be conducted at regular intervals, instead of adopting an ad-hoc approach.

Conclusion

No doubt, adolescent girls are very receptive to IEC interventions. They tend to not just acquire higher knowledge but also translate this knowledge into appropriate action for their own good. So, IEC does generate a substantial long term impact in terms of better knowledge and suitable behaviour. But it is challenging to deploy adequate time, resources and attention towards a sizeable segment of society, namely the adolescent girls at the macro level. Therein lies the key to large scale behaviour change.

Background India Population Project (IPP) -VIII was launched with financial assistance from the World Bank to provide maternal & child health and family welfare service in 662 slums of Hyderabad.

The main goal of the project was to strengthen the family welfare program. The important objectives of the project were to reduce fertility among slum population, improve maternal &child health and decrease infant & maternal mortality rates, especially among slum population. The strategies to achieve the objectives were expansion of service delivery system, improving the quality of family welfare services, strengthening the management & administration, supporting innovative schemes and generating demand through IEC, women empowerment & community participation.

The main innovative approaches adopted under the project were forming Mahila Arogya Sanghams with built-in link volunteer's scheme, involvement of identified local NGOs, creating play schools, open schools, organising training activities and more importantly nutrition education programs for adolescent girls supported by community-based IEC activities.

Since majority of adolescent girls, especially representing lower segments of our society, are malnourished coupled with co-existence of social maladies like son preference, incidence of early marriage and high rates of maternal mortality; a strong focus on improvement in nutritional and health status of adolescent girls is warranted.

Moreover, several studies indicate that social indicators like belief systems regarding early marriages, poor dietary intakes and low social status of women in the community adversely impact the overall health and nutritional status of adolescent girls. Hence, the municipal corporation has taken up the task of addressing issues such as enforcing a positive change in the mindset of the wider community through an educational intervention. Mere availability of mass media or alternative communication channels always does not guarantee successful health education.

Purpose The main purpose of the study was to devise, carry out and measure the impact of educational intervention on the nutrition knowledge of adolescent girls in the selected one hundred slums of twin cities under purview of IPP-VIII, Hyderabad.

Objectives

- To evaluate knowledge, attitude and practices (KAP) of adolescent girls on aspects relating to nutrition, early marriage, reproductive behaviour including sexuality and media using habits.
- To plan, devise and implement nutrition and health education programme for adolescent girls.
- To study the impact of nutrition education intervention programme.

Research methodology

The study was conducted in three stages. In the first stage, baseline data on 2500 adolescent girls (10-19 years) were collected using a specially designed comprehensive pretested interview schedule. In the second stage, an intensive nutrition education intervention was carried out covering all the adolescent girls living in slums for a period of six months, mainly through IPC techniques. In the third stage, a repeat survey was conducted to find out the impact of nutrition education intervention in terms of improvement in knowledge level and consumption of nutrient rich foods.

Results

The study covered a sample of 2500 adolescent girls living in selected 100 slums. Though an effort was made to contact the same adolescent girls (follow up), only 2,326 could be covered during end line survey. The balance of 174 adolescent girls living in the same slums though covered as substitutes/replacements to make up the envisaged 2,500 sample were excluded for the purpose of analysis.

Profile of adolescent girls

The mean age of the adolescent girls was 14.3 years and majority of the girls were unmarried. The educational levels of the adolescent girls revealed that 13.2 percent of them were illiterates, around 38% of them had primary education and 44% of them had high school (7 -10 years) education. Distribution of the respondents according to religion showed that the majority of them were Hindus (69.5%) and one third of them were Muslims. Among Hindus, greater proportions were either from backward castes (32.8%) or scheduled castes (28.3%). Regarding the type of family, 82.8% of respondents belonged to nuclear family.

Majority of respondents had 6-7 members in their family comprising on an average three males and four females. Regarding the educational background of the parents, almost half of the respondents had illiterate fathers and around two thirds of them had illiterate mothers.

Knowledge, Attitude and Practices (KAP)

Among the adolescent girls the knowledge regarding sexuality and related areas were found to be low. Majority of the girls did not know what safe sex means. The knowledge regarding STDs was found to be relatively better. The data revealed that 69.4 percent of the girls had awareness regarding STDs and 70.2 percent of the girls had awareness regarding abortion.

Information about knowledge of family planning is also an important component as far as adolescent girls are concerned. Almost half of the adolescent girls were aware about the female temporary methods. Regarding the knowledge of terminal methods of family planning, all of them knew about tubectomy and only 15.8% of them knew about vasectomy.

Out of the 40 married girls, 33 girls were pregnant. Out of the total pregnant girls, 48.5 percent have registered their pregnancy and all those who registered have used government services. All of them have received

TT immunisation and IFA tablets. The preferred place of delivery among them was government hospital (48.5%) with private hospital being next in order of preference (42.4%).

IEC activities

Community-based IEC intervention activities were conducted for a period of six months in all the intervention areas mainly through IPC techniques. Besides regular media like television, radio, newspaper and magazine, the other IEC tools used in educational activities included cooking demonstrations, posters, informative booklet, innovative games and nutrition melas.

To inculcate the habit of taking more iron and calcium-based preparations and energy and protein rich recipes in their daily meals, cooking demonstrations were held in all the intervention areas. They were held in collaboration with Food and Nutrition Extension Board, Government of India. Adolescent girls were taught how to prepare simple iron and calcium rich recipes. They were also exposed to nutrient values of some commonly consumed food articles, choosing the energy and protein rich food articles, right cooking methods and some tips to preserve nutrients while cooking.

To infuse or build self-confidence and self-esteem among adolescent girls, some innovative games were developed. About 20 adolescent girls in each slum were exposed to participatory learning activities in the form of games. These innovative games are intended to build self confidence, knowledge and skills and to empower girls to begin to shape their own life.

The approach used in these games is called 'experimental learning'. It helps girls to participate in learning and learn from their own experiences, with facilitator-trainer as a guide. The games include 'my daily routine and my meal', 'I would like to introduce myself', 'role model or woman we admire', ' my grandmother, mother and myself'and 'good health practices during menstruation'. All the games are based on the experimental learning model. Situations and problems are presented, discussed and analysed. Problem- solving is emphasised. All the participants learnt things through a process of experience sharing activities, reflections and discussions. A facilitator's guide was prepared to aid the field investigators to conduct the games in the community for adolescent girls.

These games are intended to motivate young girls to change undesirable behaviours and adopt new behaviours, promote participation in the learning process. It is hoped that the experience gained by the participants would be applied in similar situations being encountered by them in future.

The informative booklet on' Adolescent Health and Nutrition' prepared in local language Telugu is being distributed to all willing and Telugu speaking adolescent girls. It is a ready reckoner to assess the nutritional status and nutrient requirements on their own. The booklet also contains information on growth and development during adolescence, recommended dietary allowances, balanced diet, menstruation and some commonly asked questions/queries by adolescent girls and their clarifications.

Four multi-coloured posters on education, nutrition, health & hygiene and age at marriage evoked positive response among subjects.

All the respondents were given information pertaining to their heights and weights, anaemia status, etc. Both moderately and severely anaemic girls were given IFA tablets through UHPs to correct anaemia.

In collaboration with three NGOs viz., Pratyamnaya, Sivaranjani Educational Society and CHAIN operating in the study area, seven 'nutrition melas' were conducted. More than 2,000 adolescent girls including other than sample population participated in these one-day melas. Besides cooking demonstrations, experts have taken sessions on following areas:

1. Adolescent growth & development,
2. Nutritional requirements & balanced diet,
3. Menstrual hygiene & health care and
4. Women empowerment.

Poster exhibition on nutrition was also held. The services of gynaecologist, paediatrician, public health specialist, nutrition and communication experts were utilised. Counselling sessions were held and many doubts with regard to nutrition, healthy cooking practices and menstruation were clarified by concerned specialists. Adolescent girls themselves presented some cultural items like songs, street play, etc. All the willing adolescent girls were given TT injections by the concerned UHP staff.

Aspects like adolescent growth and development, nutritional requirements, balanced diet, desirable food habits, right cooking methods, problems during menarche, age at marriage, care during pregnancy and lactation were dealt with in detail during IEC intervention. In addition, areas like building positive personality traits, countering the normal social depiction of adolescent girls in the society, inculcating health and hygiene habits were also included in IEC campaign. Though baseline data were available, based on the suggestions given by the participating NGOs and link volunteers, sensitive aspects like sexuality, family planning methods were excluded in the IEC campaign.

Knowledge, Attitude and Practices (KAP)

The knowledge about physical changes during adolescence has improved from 7.3 percent to 100 percent. In the same way, 56.4 percent of the girls after intervention stressed the need of early education on menstruation as against 43.8 percent in the baseline. About 70% of the subjects specifically mention that they received information on growth and development for the first time during IEC intervention.

Regarding the menstrual hygiene, almost three-fourths of the girls had knowledge of right method of using the sanitary pads. That means they were cleaning and drying pads properly or they were using commercially bought pads as absorbents. After the intervention, more than 85 percent of the girls reported right method of using the pads as against 75% in the pre-intervention period. Further, after the educational intervention it was also observed that they were changing their pads more often than they did it previously.

All the subjects were asked to recall the foods rich in nutrients like iron, calcium, protein and energy. The result clearly indicates that 77.6% could correctly identify the foods rich in iron, 55.2% could recall calcium rich foods and 62% could list the energy and protein rich recipes/food articles.

The consumption of various food items based on the previous day's diet was also analysed. It was found that more than 90 percent of the girls had consumed cereals and fats/oils on the previous day. More than 60 percent of the girls had consumed vegetables (73.6%) and pulses (63.5%). Only less than 30% of the girls had consumed milk, meat or fruits. The usage of all other food items like millets, oil seeds, rice flakes, condiments, jaggery, sprouted and fermented foods was found to be very low (less than 10%). Further, 37.9 percent of the girls were using iodised salt for cooking in their families. Even the consumption of various food items has changed after the intervention. The striking difference can be seen in the consumption of millets like ragi which is especially rich in iron and calcium. Only 3.5 percent of the girls had consumed millets in the baseline and the figure had gone up to 97.9 percent after IEC intervention. Further, an improvement was also observed in the consumption of iodised salt.

The majority of the families (52.9%) were cleaning rice in water thrice or more than that before cooking. Majority of them (83.4%) were also discarding ganji and excess water after cooking. They (93.2%) were also seen to sieve the flour before use. A small proportion of the families (7.7%) were even discarding excess water after cooking dal/vegetables. The awareness regarding the nutrient loss due to discarding of water was also not very high. Only 48.2% of the girls knew that there will be a loss of nutrients if they remove water. Almost all of them followed the practice of covering the vessels while cooking and 70.2% stated that they wash the vegetables before cutting. The post intervention results suggest an improvement in the practice of right cooking methods like discarding of ganji which has come down to 28.9%.

The legal minimum age at marriage is not widely known in the study population. Overall, only 60.6 percent of the girls reported correctly the minimum legal age at marriage for both boys and girls. The results of the post intervention survey indicated an increase in the awareness of legal age at marriage. After the intervention, the figure increased to 83.6 percent.

Data related to pregnancy, ante-natal care, delivery, immunisation and breast feeding were also collected from the sample population. Out of the total, 58.2 percent of the girls stated that they know what pregnancy is, and this figure rose to 60.7% after educational intervention.

Majority (68.9%) of the girls did not know when a woman should register the name for ante-natal checkups. During pre-educational intervention, only 13.3% reported that soon after the cessation of the menstrual cycle the woman should register for ante-natal checkups and this figure rose to 24.8% after intervention. Marginal increase in the knowledge was observed with regard to the need for pregnant women to take TT immunisation (36.8% - 45.8%), take adequate rest (85.4% -89.6%), avoid heavy work (11.6% -24.4%), need to protect themselves from anaemia (43.3% -51.0%) and take good food (38.9% -47.9%). Most of the girls could not identify the categories of women who fall under high risk. Only a small proportion of the girls during pre-intervention identified short stature (4.3%), young and old age pregnancy (5.1% and 3% respectively), high parity pregnancy (3.5%) etc as high risk cases. However, after intervention around 32% of adolescent girls could correctly identify all the high risk pregnant cases.

When it came to knowledge regarding the vaccine preventable diseases, the most well known disease was polio (72.2%). This figure rose to 90% after educational intervention.

Majority of the girls (80.6%) did not have a role model. A comparison of data on the pre- and post-intervention period also did not indicate any major change regarding their role models. The pattern regarding their role model almost remained the same (77.6%) except that a few more could spell out who their role model is.

Most of the girls graded themselves as cheerful (90.1%), cooperative (80.8%), truthful (75.9%), tidy (71.4%). However, only a very few rated themselves as courageous (27.9%) or possess self-confidence (34.4%). After the IEC intervention, though the trend remained the same, there was slight increase in each of these categories. The mean per cent score has also increased from 66.5 to 73.9.

On the whole, it was felt that the adolescent girls were in agreement with the accepted social norm, For example, most of the girls agreed that they are generally quiet (87.6%), emotional (80.5%), dependent (76.5%), subservient (76.7%), etc. However, only some girls stated that they are incapable (27.2%) or unimportant (39.4%). After the intervention, the mean percent score of girls holding negative concept regarding their social depiction came down slightly (65.3% to 58.7%).

Overall, the adolescent girls were found to follow good health and hygiene habits. In most of the categories, the percent distribution is above 80. A comparative analysis of pre- and post- intervention figures indicates that as per the expectation, the health and hygiene habits improved to an extent of 90.7% in follow up cases.

Nearly sixty per cent of the subjects mentioned that they had attended more than one program being organised under IEC intervention. Among those who were exposed to IEC intervention, nearly 82% of the subjects appreciated the information given under IEC intervention and 18.3% were undecided about the quality of information given to them.

Suggestions

The study highlighted the need to project appropriate role models to these adolescent girls. Similarly, the informative Telugu booklet "Adolescent Health and Nutrition" needs to be popularised with every Telugu speaking adolescent girl keeping a copy of the same as a ready reckoner. The community-based IEC interventions must be conducted at regular intervals, instead of adopting an ad-hoc approach.

Conclusion

No doubt, adolescent girls are very receptive to IEC interventions. They tend to not just acquire higher knowledge but also translate this knowledge into appropriate action for their own good. So, IEC does generate a substantial long term impact in terms of better knowledge and suitable behaviour. But it is challenging to deploy adequate time, resources and attention towards a sizeable segment of society, namely the adolescent girls at the macro level. Therein lies the key to large scale behaviour change.

References

1. National Nutrition Policy (1993), Department of women and child development. Ministry of Human resources development, New Delhi, Government of India.
2. White P (1976). Why all the fuss over nutrition education, Journal of Nutrition Education, 15 (3), pp. 105-109.
3. Israel RC, Dennis Foote and Janet Tognetti (1987). Operational guidelines for social marketing projects in public health and nutrition. Nutrition education series. Issue 14. Nutrition education programme, UNESCO.
4. Majorie Schurmann (1983). Community team work in nutrition education – Human Nutrition, Applied Nutrition. 37A. pp. 172-179.
5. Champakam S, Ramdasmurthy V and Balasubramanian SC (1972). Lessons in nutrition education. Journal of Nutrition Education 24. (5) Sept-Oct.

Chapter - 56

Right to Education – A Fundamental Human Right of Children

Dr. Y. S. Kiran Kumar

Abstract

Education is the most potent mechanism for the advancement and all round development of the human being. It enlarges, enriches and improves the individual's image of the future. It is old saying that a human being without education is no less than an animal. The importance of education cannot be underestimated by any country in the world. There is another important saying that children of today are tomorrow citizen. The full and potential growth of children is indispensable for any nation. The child attains his or her full growth only by way of education.

In our country there is no universal definition is available for age of child, even constitution does not define who is means by a child. Basically we can come to conclusion that a child means a male or female in age of 6 to 14 years. The same is mentioned in the Right of Children to Free and Compulsory Education Act 2009. In a civilized society the importance of child care and welfare cannot be under estimated because the welfare of child is welfare of the community.[1] The former Secretary General of the United Nations Mr. Kofi Annan observed that "there is no trust more sacred than one of the world holds with children".

International Scenario

Right of children is integral part of fundamental and human right. The beginning of the movement for the rights of the child can be traced back to mid 19th centaury by publication of an article in 1852 by Slaguoulk titled 'the rights of children'. Till recently majority of countries in the world have not given much importance to rights of children and their education. Due to change of time as many as 134 countries in the world have enacted legislations guaranting right to education acts for children.

For the first time regarding concern of the child is dealt by non governmental organization in way back 1923. Later the League of Nations passed a resolution in in 1924 in Geneva recognizing right of children over education. In 1948 the United Nations General Assembly approved expanded version of right of children over education and again another resolution is adopted in 1958 and ultimately in 1989 the countries have adopted the Rights of Child in recognsing the needs of children.

The Universal Declaration of Human Rights 1948 under Article 25(2) declares that "motherhood and childhood are entitled to special care and assistance. Article 26 (1) of U.D.H.R. goes on to say that "Everyone should have right to education". The same is repeated in International Covenant on Economic, Social and Cultural Rights which manded that the state parties should recognize everyone right to education. The United Nations Scientific and Cultural Organisation in 1962 affirmed that there should not be any discrimination with regard to children education. In 2000 the World Education Forum its convention held Senegal held that everybody has right to receive education. that In the regional level the European Convention guarantees the Right to Education.

National Scenario

According to Census Commission of India report India has 400 million child populations which is equal to that of entire population of North America. Among which 20 per cent of children aged 6 to14 are still not seen enrolled for education.

In our country the awakening over the education is gained simultaneously with freedom movement. The great leaders such as Raja Ram Mohan Roy, Ishwar Chand Vidhya Sagar, Lal Lajpat Rai, Rabindranath Tagore, Madan Mohan Malviya, have recognized the importance education for bring social change and equilibrium in the society.

The importance of education is very much recognized by the Constituent Assembly while preparing the constitution but due to paucity of resources lead to placing the education in the part fourth of the constitution under articles 38, 39 (a), 41 and 45 to avoid enforceability of them.

Constitutional and Judicial Perspective

In the post emergency period the apex court of the land, the Supreme Court of India embarked on liberal interpretation of the Article 21. The article 21 which deals with life and personal liberties have received a sort of strength on account of decision rendered by it in Maneka Gandhi v.

Union of India[2] in this case, the court has expounded that for survival of the human being the life and personal liberty must to be guaranteed by the State under all circumstances and it is utmost positive duty of the state to protect it.

The Supreme Court has implied that the "Right to Education" as a fundamental right from the Article 21. The word "life" has been including 'education' as the education is major factor for promoting goodness and dignity in the life of any individual. In our country for the first time whether education is fundamental right or not aroused before two judge bench of the Supreme Court in Mohini Jain v. State of Karnataka[3].

The apex court of the land accepted that the Constitution of India does not expressly guarantee the right to education as such, as a fundamental right but reading cumulatively the Article 21 along with the Directive Principles of State Policy contained in articles 38, 39(a), 41 and 45 the court opined that "it becomes clear that the framers of the Constitution made it obligatory for the State to provide education for its citizens".[4]

The apex court further stated that without making the right to education under Article 41 a reality, the Fundamental Rights would remain beyond the reach of large majority of citizens.The apex court clearly remarked that

"We hold that every citizen has a 'right to education' under the Constitution. The State is under an obligation to establish educational institutions to enable the citizens to enjoy the said right. The State may discharge its obligation through State owned or State recognized educational institutions...Charging capitation fee in consideration of admission to educational institutions is a patent denial of a citizen's right to education under the Constitution".

The apex court by above judgment has taken very rigid and absolutic view and castigated burden upon the state to provide education at all levels. It is pertinent to mention that it is highly improbable to country like India where natural resources are abundant but their exploitation is very meager and state has to provide education free of cost at every level it nothing but sailing upon the impossible task.. The above judgment may sound to be good theoretically but it is very difficult to implement in present day globalization and liberalization and other post World Trade Organization existence.

It is pertinent mention that in the post globalization and liberalization period the apex court subsequently has taken reverse turn of above judgment in Unni Krishnan v. State of Andhra Pradesh[5]

The court has reiterated the proposition that having regard to the fundamental significance of education to the life of an individual and the nation, the right to education is implicit in and flows from the right to life guaranteed by Article 21, further the Court remarked that the parameters of this right is not absolute, have to be judged by taking into consideration of the Directive Principles of State Policy contained in Articles 41, 45, and 46. By embarking on new swift the apex Court has considerably lessened burdened of the State in providing educational facilities as follows:

1. Every Citizen has right to free education until he/she completes the age of 14 years.
2. Beyond that, the State has obligation to provide education is subject to the "limits of the economic capacity and development" of the State.[6]

The obligations created by Articles 41,45 and 46 can be discharged by the State either by establishing institutions of its own, or by aiding, recognizing and or granting affiliations to private educational institutions. The court while taking note of the inadequate outlay on education on education and limited economic capacity of the State to finance education, it has ruled that private educational institutions, both aided and unaided are a necessity in India, but "commercialization of educational cannot and should not be permitted" under any circumstances..[7]

While denouncing the levy of "capitation fee" by certain professional colleges, the Court has however accepted that unaided private educational institutions can charge higher tuition fee: they "have to and are entitled to charge the higher fee, but not exceeding the ceiling fixed" by the state and state has every power to interfere in fixing the fees. In the same judgment the court opined that even the State has power to fix ceiling for charging of the fees by the private institutions.

By rendering the above judgment the court has indirectly accepted and recognized the fundamental right of every child for free and compulsory elementary education up to the age of fourteen years as provided in the Article 45. Meanwhile to ensure sufficient and effective realization of this aright as well as to reassert national will and commitment in this regard Article 21-A was inserted by eighty-sixth Constitutional Amendment in 2002. Though the amendment was brought way back in 2002 until 2009 the succeeding governments have failed to enact any specific law for implementing given fundamental right of education. The United Progressive government as it promised in its manifesto has brought the constitutional amendment in and added article 21 A in which the right to education is recognized as the fundamental right and now this article 21 A provides that up to 14 years of age the State must provide education at free and if the citizens have denied of their this right they have right to enforce by approaching the apex court under articles 32 and various High courts under article 226 of the constitution. Though the Right to education became a fundamental right in 2002 but we suffered with dearth of specific law upto 2009 when the Government of India has passed much delayed and needed enactment in 2009 which is called as the Right of Children for Free and Compulsory Education Act in 2009 and which came into operation from 27th of August, 2009.

Right of Free and Compulsory Education Act 2009

This is another landmark enactment in post liberalization, privatization, and globalization period in our country. The act encompasses into thirty eight sections in seven chapters. The main features of the act are the state has to provide free and compulsory education to all children in the six to 14 age group,no child shall be held back, expelled, or required to pass a board examination untilcompletion of elementary education, a child above six years of age has not been admitted in any school or though admitted,could not complete his or her elementary education, then, he or she shall be admitted ina class appropriate to his or her age, provided that where a child is directly admitted in aclass appropriate to his or her age, then, he or she shall, in order to be at par withothers, have a right to receive special training, in such manner, and within such time limits,as may be prescribed, provided further that a child so admitted to elementaryeducation shall be entitled to free education till completion of elementary education evenafter fourteen years of age. For the purposes of admission to elementary education theage of a child shall be determined on the basis of the birth certificate issued in accordance with the provisions of the Births and Deaths Registration Act, 1856 or on the basis of such other document, as may be prescribed.

The Act further enshrines that no child shall be denied admission in a school for lack of age proof, a child who completes elementary education shall be awarded a certificate. The Act mandates that the ratio of student-teacher has to be fixed and creating of 25 percent reservation for economically disadvantaged communities in admission to class one in all private schools. The Act mandates improvement in quality of education, school teachers will need adequate professional degree within five years or else will lose job, school infrastructure (where there is problem) to be improved in three years, else the authorities shall cancel recognition to such erring schools, the financial burden relating to improvement of infrastructure will be shared between state and central government. The act further provides that disputes regarding the educational matters have to be litigated in specially constituted educational tribunals.[8]

The Right of Children for Free and Compulsory Education Act 2009 is another kind of welfare legislation enacted by the parliament in post privatization, liberalization and globalization period and which enumerating far reaching provisions. This Act large extent is protecting the educational rights of the children but it is still not free from following lacunas.

1. The definition and meaning of educations is not defined in the Act.
2. The Act only speaks about 25% seats reserved in private schools for poor studens, but nol provision about government schools admission.
3. The Act mentions about children above the age of 6 years but does not cover children below the age of 6 years.
4. There is no provision about mental disorder or disable student education.
5. The Act only speaks about elementary or basic education but no provision about on secondary or higher education.
6. The Act does not speak about the development of infrastructural facilities in the schools.
7. The Act also silence about fair salaries to be made available for teacher working in the private management schools.
8. The central and state governments should accord sufficient budgetary provisions for meeting the requirements of the education.

If we overcome the above shortcomings of the Act the aims and objectives of the Right of Free and Compulsory Education Act is accomplished and which ultimately lead to accomplishment of the education human right of the children in our country.

Notes

1. Chanakya Chandraguptha – (c370-283BCE) Indian teacher, philosopher and royal advisor during Mauryan Empire.
2. Mandela Nelson – Anti Apartheid activist, former president of South Africa.
3. Law Relating to Women and Children by Dr. Mamata Rao 2005.Ist edition, 1988 P.388.
4. AIR.1992 SC 1858 : (1992) 3 SCC 666.
5. Ibid, 1867.

6. AIR 1993 SC 2178.(1993) I SCC. 645.
7. Prof. Jain M. P. Indian Constitutional Law. Fifth Edition. Wadhwa and Company, Nagpur, 2007, P. 1131.
8. Ibid.
9. The Gazattee of India, No.39, 27-08-2009.
10. Law Relating to Women and Children by Dr. Mamata Rao 2005. Ist edition, 1988 P. 388.
11. AIR.1992 SC 1858 : (1992) 3 SCC 666.
12. Ibid, 1867.
13. AIR 1993 SC 2178.(1993) I SCC. 645.
14. Prof.Jain M.P.Indian Constitutional Law.Fifth Edition. Wadhwa and Company, Nagpur, 2007, P. 1131.
15. Ibid.
16. The Gazattee of India, No.39, 27-08-2009.

Chapter - 57

Causes of Female Student Dropouts: An Analytical Study of Medak District

T. Neelima

Abstract

The saying goes that if the father is educated, only one person in the family is educated and if the mother is educated, the whole family is educated. Female literacy and women education play a pivotal role in any society, more so in the developing economies. An educated mother can play a constructive role in building a responsible and healthy family as well as contribute economically, politically and in many other ways to the society and nation at large. School education apart, the undergraduate (university) education where the students choose and study the subjects of their choice is an important stage in the career of any student. A graduate is eligible for holding many key government posts and for reaching higher echelons in private sector as well. So it is vital that women study and acquire at least a bachelor's degree. This will broaden their outlook and help them perform their roles in society in a better way. Unfortunately, it has been observed and recorded that many girl students, particularly in rural areas, after joining undergraduate courses drop out of college midway. A cause analysis of this particular phenomenon can yield useful results and help policy makers and stakeholders to take remedial steps to stem the tide.

Introduction

Before 1975, education at all levels was under the control of Directorate of Public Instruction (DPI). Because of the enormous growth of educational institutions, both at secondary and collegiate levels, the Directorate of Public Instruction was bifurcated into the Directorate of School Education and the Directorate of Higher Education in the year of 1975. After that, many junior colleges and degree colleges were established. As a result, the Directorate of Higher Education was further divided into the Directorate of Collegiate Education and the Directorate of Intermediate Education in the year 1989.Thus the Directorate of Collegiate Education came into existence on 1st November 1989. The Directorate of Collegiate Education has the main aim of developing college education in backward and rural areas. It also aims to strengthen the women's education at both UG and PG levels. In the year of 1969, the state government had introduced 10+2+3 system in education.

At present there are 127 (including autonomous) degree colleges in our Telangana State. The total strength of these colleges is 80,965. In that, boy's strength is 41,869 and girls 39096.

Objectives

1. To study the total enrolment number of girl students in the Government Degree Colleges of Medak District.
2. To assess the female student dropout data over the 3 Academic Years (2014-17).
3. To analyse the main causes of the female student dropout in GDCs.

Hypothesis

1. Female students join in large numbers in the UG courses in Medak District.
2. Many female students drop out of studies at UG level.
3. Personal reasons are the major causes for this scenario.

Methodology

1. Primary Data: - To collect the information from the Govt. Degree Colleges in Medak District (New).
2. Secondary Data: - College records, student attendance registers, etc.

Scope of The Study

This study is restricted to the new Medak District post district re-organisation in 2018.

Data Analysis

The following three tables reflect the student drop outs tendency of GDC's in Medak District (New).

GDC Medak Female Student Dropouts Data (2014 – 17)

Group	*2014 - 15*	*2015 - 16*	*2016 – 17*	*Dropouts*	*Percentage*
B.A. (HEP)	23	14	14	07	30%
B.A. (HPP)	15	11	11	04	26%
B.Com. (Gen)	42	35	32	10	23%
B.Com(Comp)	22	22	17	05	22%
B.Sc. (MPC)	23	15	13	10	43%
B.Sc. (BZC)	34	27	26	08	23%
B.Sc. (MSCS)	12	10	10	02	16%
B.Sc. (MPCS)	20	15	13	07	35%
B.Sc. (GZC)	26	24	21	05	19%
TOTAL	217	173	157	58	22%

GDC (W) Medak Female Student Dropouts Data (2014 – 17)

Group	*2014 - 15*	*2015 - 16*	*2016 – 17*	*Dropouts*	*Percentage*
B.A. (HEP)	58	50	41	17	29%
B.Com	31	20	15	16	51%
B.Sc. (MPC)	30	24	23	07	23%
B.Sc. (BZC)	50	43	22	28	56%
TOTAL	169	137	101	68	40%

GDC Narsapur Female Student Drop Outs Data (2014 – 17)

Group	*2014 - 15*	*2015 - 16*	*2016 – 17*	*Dropouts*	*Percentage*
B.A.(HEP)	11	05	04	05	45%
B.Com	06	03	03	03	50%
B.Sc. (MPC)	-	-	-	-	-
B.Sc. (BZC)	07	07	06	01	14%
TOTAL	24	15	13	09	37%

College wise Female Student Drop Outs Percentage (2014 – 17)

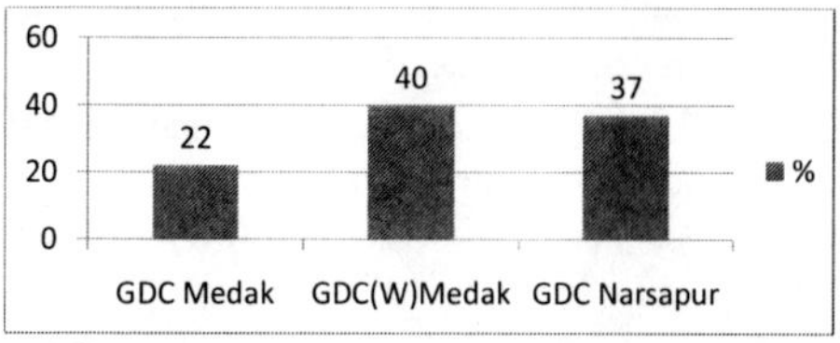

Findings

It has been found that during the three academic years female student drop out ratio touched (32%).The reasons cited by the students are mainly three - marriage, poverty and other family reasons.

Parental pressure and other family pressures force the girls to get married before finishing their graduation and family obligations after marriage prevent them from completing their studies.

Because of the Kalyana Lakshmi Scheme, parents wait till the girl reaches 18 years of age before they get her married.In the meantime the girls join Degree Courses.

Many girls cite poverty as a reason for dropping out of studies.To earn extra money for the family, they do work in farms, etc. Therefore they avoid college and eventually they drop out of college altogether.

Suggestions

More skill oriented and job oriented courses should introduced at undergraduate level so that girl students are motivated to continue their studies in order to get good jobs.

KG to PG free education should be given in our State.

Reference

1. Indiana Department of Education. (2008). Dropout and mobility report. Available: http://www.doe.in.gov/stn/pdf/2007-DM. pdf.
2. Ingels, S. J., Dowd, K.L., Taylor, J.R., Bartot, V.H., Frankel, M.R., Pulliam, P.A., and Quinn, P. (1995). User's manual, NELS:88 second follow-up: Transcript component data file. NCES 95377. Washington, DC: U.S. Department of Education, National Center for Education Statistics.
3. Jerald, C.D. (2006, June). Identifying potential dropouts: Key lessons for building an early warning data system. White paper prepared by Craig D. Jerald for Staying the Course: High Standards and Improved Graduation Rates, a joint project of Achieve, Inc., and Jobs for the Future. Washington, DC: Achieve, Inc.
4. Joftus, S. (2002). Every child a graduate: A framework for an excellent education for all middle and high school students. Washington, DC: Alliance for Excellent Education.
5. Jordan, W.J., Lara, J., and McPartland, J.M. (1999). Rethinking the cause of high school dropout. Prevention Researcher, 6, 1-4.
6. Kaufman, P. (2004). The national dropout data collection system: History and the search for consistency. In G. Orfield (Ed.), Dropouts in America: Confronting the graduation rate crisis. Pp. 107-130. Cambridge, MA: Harvard Educational Publishing Group.
7. Kaufman, P., McMillen, M., and Bradby, D. (1992). Dropout rates in the United States: 1991. NCES 92129. Washington, DC: U.S. Department of Education, National Center for Education Statistics.
8. Klem, A.M., and Connell, J.P. (2004). Relationships matter: Linking teacher support to student engagement and achievement. Journal of School Health, 74(7), 262-273.

Chapter - 58

A study on Impact of Higher Education on women's agency in household and in the society

Dr. P. Radhika, O. Pranathi

Abstract

"Education is a mental medicine that cures all the mental maladies of the society" asserts Plato. It is well accepted that education is only the weapon that can empower women to their best at all the phases of life. Higher education alone has the capacity to become a major liberating force against an epidemic of gender-based violence and systemic poverty which is one of core objectives of development goals. It enhances better understand of their rights, opportunities and gives them the wings to explore their careers in the way the wish. Investment in education alone shapes the ability of women to reach their full potential in the society. Present paper analyses the impact of female higher education on the agency of women which is one of the key factor of their wellbeing by explaining the importance of agency, and constraints in the World Bank framework. Secondary data from DHS (demographic health survey) data of India and other published sources are used.

Introduction

As a hope of light decade into the new millennium, there are a number of reasons to feel optimistic about the women's education around the world. There is remarkable progress where we have succeeded in closing major gaps globally especially in developed and developing countries. Today, girls and boys around the world are able to equally participate in primary and secondary education. In tertiary education, a clear bias is emerging that favors women globally with enrollments increasing faster for women than for men, that is noticed due to increase in the policy interventions. When it comes to the matter of India, Higher Education plays a vital role in liberating women of their economic deprivations bestowing them the financial security and independence. Even though there is drastic increase in the literacy rate in India due to a number of policy interventions the female population who are 58,64,69,174 in number still lag behind in attaining education with low literacy rate of 65.46% according to the census of 2011. The DHS data also shows that there are a less number of women with higher education in India which is shown in table 1. This situation is much worse in the case of higher education. The female enrollment into higher education is 46% in 2016 shows that there is need to take interventions in this way.

Table: 1 Women with secondary or higher education

Country	*Survey*	*Total 15-49*
India	2015-16 DHS	60.1
India	2005-06 DHS	44.7
India	1998-99 DHS	29.6
India	1992-93 DHS	21.9

Source: DHS data.

Due to many reasons including early marriages, lack of awareness, parental pressure and economic backwardness girls are lagging behind in enrolling themselves in higher education which late impinges their income and wealth. Although income and wealth are said to be important factors for the women empowerment they are alone not sufficient for the wellbeing of women especially in the present developmental context of developing countries like India. The economic justice when complimented with social justice is most essential for the wellbeing of women (Sen 1980, 1984, 1985, 1987, 1992, 1999). Amartya Sen in his capability approach brings human beings to the centre of the debate of development and argues that wealth is not the end but is means to achieve the opportunity to live a good life. Even in today's world where gender gaps in human capital and physical assets are being narrowed down, differences in gender outcomes are emerging because girls and boys, who later become women and men, doesn't have equal capacity to exercise agency in all spheres, with women typically at a disadvantage.Agency as defined by world development report 2012 is an individual's (or group's) ability to make effective choices and to transform those choices into desired outcomes.Inthe process of agency men and women use their endowments and take advantage of economic opportunities to achieve desired outcomes. So, agency is said to be an important aspect to study the gender outcomes and to know why they differ amongst the two genders. The analytical framework, by world bank enables us to systematically analyze the roles of economic growth and markets, formal institutions (laws and services), and social norms in influencing women's capacity for agency (figure1).

They show how these determinants play a role in defining women's agency and how constraints in each of them can be mutually reinforcing. Economic growth, formal institutions which includes education, informal institutions, and markets interact to enable or constrain women's agency. Firstly, economic growth can improve the material conditions for exercising agency—through higher incomes, greater access to services, and expanded infrastructure. But the impact of higher aggregate incomes on women's agency partly hinges on women's ability to earn their *own* incomes; that ability increases their bargaining power within the household and their ability to accumulate autonomous assets. Economic growth alone will not eliminate gender differences in agency. Second, expanding women's rights can foster agency in some realms. But the expansion of rights for family formation and control over household resources has been limited. And the effectiveness of expanding rights in bringing about change depends on their applicability often linked to multiple legal systems—and their enforcement. Third, social norms shape women's agency.

Along with markets and institutions, they determine the endowments and opportunities that women have and whether they can exercise the choices to use them. Norms can constrain women's agency when they prevent laws, services, and incomes from benefiting women and men equally. Social norms are particularly binding when increases in women's agency would directly shift power balances in the household and in society. Reforms in markets and institutions, such as service delivery improvements, information provision, and creation of networks, can reduce the bind of social norms by affecting the costs and benefits of compliance. Fourth, women's collective agency can transform society. Women's collective agency both depends on and determines their individual agency. Women's ability to influence their environment goes beyond formal political channels, which can be limited by social norms and beliefs regarding gender roles and institutional structures. They can influence their environments through their participation in informal associations and through collective action, but their success depends in part on their individual ability to make effective choices which is diagrammatically shown in figure 1.

The individual ability to make effective choices which is call 'agency' is what whole matters for the wellbeing of women at all the spears. Though it includes in it many aspects of women's agency, (a) women's own health care that include personal hygiene, reproductive health, nutritional intake

Source: world Bank.

Figure 1: Agency, endowments, economic opportunities, and drivers of change

which are important firstly, (b) secondly, making large purchases where as the they are the very stake holders of and are effected of the purchases, (c) visits to family, relatives, friends that define their social life and civic engagement are taken into consideration for the analysis. These are the three main areas where deprivations are widespread. These deprivations are highly related with educational attainment of women especially higher education. Women with higher education are said to have higher voices comparing to that of women with lesser education attainment which is explained in table 2.

Table: 2 Final say in all of the decisions [Women]

Country	***Survey***	***Education***			
		No education	***Primary***	***Secondary***	***Higher***
India	2015-16 DHS	60.2	62.3	63.2	71.5
India	2005-06 DHS	37.1	37.4	40.8	54.2

Source: DHS data.

The data shows that in 2005-06 only 37.1% of women without education, 37.4% of women with primary education. 40.8% of women with secondary education have autonomy in exercising their agency whereas 54.2% of women with higher education enjoy their voices. During 2015-16 there is raise in the agency of women's but still higher education has a major role in it as 71.5% of women with higher education exercise higher agency comparing to that of 63.2% with secondary, 62.3% with primary and 60.2% without education. Since, the data reveals that higher education in India has its remarkable impact on the agency of women leading to their better well-being, there is need to further policy interventions and community interventions in this field if we are really aiming at making our society a women-led developmental from dreaming of women development. Ensuring better infrastructure facilities for girls to attract them to institutions, inspiring them by regular interactions and exposure to successful female personalities in colleges, wide spreading knowledge regarding financial assistances from UGC, MHRD, CSRs, and NGOs can encourage female enrollment and curtail dropouts in higher education. Community participation also can also help in this cause since still social norms followed by family, clan, society and fear of girlhood persists in deciding the career and life of a girl today and women of tomorrow. Last but not the least, voice of girls for themselves which is very much important for their empowerment is to be enhanced at the lower level of education that can inculcate interest and passion towards higher education and career attainments. Let's hope higher female education in India sustain and succeed in enhancing higher voices to the unheard half of the sky.

References

1. All India Survey on Higher Education, MHRD, Govt. of India: www.aishe.gov.in
2. Author Accepted Manuscript by Hanmer, Lucia; Klugman, Jeni Exploring Women's Agency and Empowerment in Developing Countries © World Bank, published in the Feminist Economics22(1) 2015-10-27 CC BY-NC-ND 3.0 IGO http://creativecommons.org/licenses/by-nc-nd/3.0/igo http://dx.doi.org/10.1080/13545701.2015.1091087
3. Alkire, Sabina. (2008). "Concepts and measures of agency." OPHI Working Paper Number 10,Queen Elizabeth House, University of Oxford.
4. Beaman L, Duflo E, Pande R, Topalova P.(2010). Political Reservation and Substantive Representation: Evidence from Indian Village Councils. In: Vol. 7. 2010th ed. Washington D.C. and New Delhi: Brookings Institution Press and The National Council of Applied Economic Research; 2010.
5. Clots-Figueras, Irma. (2012). "Are Female Leaders Good for Education? Evidence from.
6. India." American Economic Journal: Applied Economics 4(1), 212-44.
7. Census of India 2011. Provisional Tables, Office of the Registrar General and Census Commission, India,New Delhi.
8. Desai, A.S. (1999) : Women in higher education and national development, University News, AIU, Vol 39, No 9.
9. Dukkipati Uttara (2010): Higher education in India: sustaining long term growth, South Asia monitor, 141, 01.
10. Educational Statistics at a glance (2014), MHRD, Government of India.
11. Kabeer, Naila. 1999. "Resources, Agency, Achievements: Reflections on the easurement of women's Empowerment." *Development and Change* 30: 435–64.
12. Klugman, Jeni, Lucia Hanmer, Sarah Twigg, Tazeen Hasan, Jennifer McCleary-Sills, and
13. Julieth Santamaria. 2014. Voice and Agency: Empowering Women and Girls for Shared Prosperity. Washington, DC: World Bank publications.

14. Mason, Karen (1998): "Wives' Economic Decision-Making Power in the Family: Five Asian Countries" in Karen Oppenheim Mason (ed.), the Changing Family in Comparative Perspective: Asia and the United States (Honolulu: East-West Center), pp 105-33.
15. Nath, S. (2014): Higher Education and Women participation in India, Journal of Business Management & Social Sciences Research, Vol 3, No 2, Pp 43-47.
16. Rao, R.K. (2001) : Women and Education, Kalpaz Publications, Delhi.
17. Sen, Amartya K. (1999). Development as Freedom, Oxford, U.K.: Oxford University Press.
18. The DHS Program, STATcompiler. Funded by USAID. http://www. statcompiler. com. January 14 2019.
19. World Bank.*World Development Report2012: Gender Equality and Development*. Washington, DC: World Bank.

Chapter - 59

Reforming Higher Education in India

P. Sujatha

Abstract

India's higher education system is the third largest in the world, next to the USA and china. Education system in India has expanded at a first place by adding nearly, 40,026 colleges, 864 recognized universities, but enrollment ratio of students was only about 26 percentage in 2016-17. The problem that confront higher education in India today are low rates of enrollment ,a huge gap between education and employability, decreasing teaching quality, lack of finance, Privatization, lack of project based learning, political pressure on institutional administration. Hence it is an hour to review as well as introduce some radical reforms in higher education system. A focus on enforcing higher standards of transparency, strengthening of the vocational and doctoral education pipeline, and professionalization of the sector through stronger institutional responsibility would help in reprioritizing efforts and working around the complexities. Our goal to be a world power, the resolving and restructuring of higher education is must, then only we will be able to harness the human potential and resources of nation to the fullest and channelize it for the growth of the nation. Thus a complete revamp is needed to meet the present demand and address the future challenges that India is about to face. This paper contains challenges of higher education system in India, objectives, method of study, findings and reforms that are needed to the higher education system in India.

***Keywords**: Education, Challenges, Employability, world market, Reforms.*

Introduction

The system of higher education now existing in India was originally implanted by the British rulers in the mid-19th century to serve the colonial economic, political and administrative interests, and in particular, to consolidate and maintain their dominance in the country. It was inherited by the state managers after independence (in 1947) as a colonial legacy, and has been expanded phenomenally during the last five decades.

The massive system of higher education in India consists of 214 (198 state and 16 central) universities, 38 institutions 'deemed-to-be universities,' 11 institutes of national importance, 9,703 colleges, and 887 polytechnics. The system now employs 321,000 teachers and caters to 6,755,000 students. Critical appraisals undertaken by the governmental committees and independent academicians have highlighted the crisis confronting the system: 'over-production of "educated" persons; increasing educated unemployment; weakening of student motivation; increasing unrest and indiscipline on the campuses; frequent collapse of administration; deterioration of standards; and above all, the demoralizing effect of the irrelevance and purposelessness of most of what is being done.' While the politicians and policy makers have often spoken about the need for radical reconstruction of the system, what has been achieved in reality is only moderate reformism. After a long period of protected expansion with state patronage until the mid-1980s, a complex turn of events has thrown higher education into a vortex of change. The foremost among such events was the adoption by the Government of India in 1990 of structural adjustment reforms.

Influenced by the World Bank-International Monetary Fund combine, structural adjustment has meant the gradual withdrawal of state patronage for higher education and a coterminous privatization of that sphere. However, with the government dithering about the long-term policy to be adopted in this regard, higher education in India is now passing through a period of stunted growth and uncertain future. The conventional university system in India, confronting as it is a systemic crisis, has proved itself to be incapable of introducing any significant educational innovation or effectively implementing any educational reform. Given the mounting pressure for increasing accessibility and overdemocratization, the trend in the universities is toward reducing everything to the lowest common denominator or leveling down quality rather than raising it.

The Indian university system is extraordinarily rigid and pronouncedly resistant to change: The impetus to change does not come from within the system. When experiments or innovations are introduced from outside, they are resisted; if enforced, they are ritualized.

The fate of such innovations as the merit promotion scheme, faculty-improvement program, vocationalization of courses, semesterization of courses, curriculum-development centers, annual self-appraisal report, college-development council, academic-staff college and refresher and orientation courses are too well known. It is indeed ironic that higher education, which is expected to function as an agency of change, should itself be resistant to it. The void created by the paralysis and drift of the conventional university system is being filled by private entrepreneurial initiatives. Thus, significant educational innovations and experiments are currently taking place in institutions outside the university orbit and in the private sector. In view of the rapid expansion of and increasing variety in knowledge and skills, there is enormous scope for educational innovations and initiatives. The private institutions have been more responsive to the demands of the economy and industry and the changing employment scenario. They have also shown their ability to match relevance with flexibility both in costs and regulation. This does not, however, mean that all private institutions are necessarily good.

Some of them are brazenly commercial establishments out to swindle gullible people looking for better-quality education at affordable prices. As in any commercial operation in a market economy, such establishments get exposed. Privatization of higher education is apparently a fledgling but welcome trend: Higher education requires it to maintain creativity, adaptability and quality. The economic trail of liberalization and globalization demands it. Considering the chronic paucity of resources, gradually unburdening itself of the additional responsibility for higher education may be advisable for the government. Instead, it could better utilize the scarce resources for realizing the goal of universalization of elementary education and for improving the quality of school education. Privatization of higher education, however, is not without social costs. In a polity such as India's, where structured inequalities have been entrenched, privatization is sure to reinforce existing inequalities and to foster inegalitarian tendencies.

This requires the social supervision of the private sector and effective measures for offsetting imbalances resulting from unequal economic capacities of the population. Thus, we again confront a dilemma: Theoretically, how do we advance equality without sacrificing quality? Practically, how do we control the private sector without curbing its creativity and initiative? That is the challenge in higher education at the beginning of the new millennium.

Reforms to expand the system

India's higher education sector has moved from a period of slow growth and low gross enrolment ratios (GERs) to an era of unprecedented expansion. Over the past 15 years, student enrolment has quadrupled to reach 34 million with a GER of 24 percent in 2015-2016. The size of India's education system has now surpassed the United States, becoming the world's second largest after China.

Massification of the education system has heavily relied on non-state funding. Market friendly reforms introduced by the state include cost recovery measures in public institutions and the promotion of the private sector to own and operate universities. While privatization started slow, private universities are proliferating, and now account for more than 60 per cent of the enrolment share both in terms of institutions and enrolment. Massification in India is also accompanied by persisting social inequalities and widening regional inequalities in enrolment in higher education.

Reforms to improve quality

India established external quality assurance agencies and internal quality assurance mechanisms to enhance higher education quality. Although accreditation is mandatory to obtain public funding, a majority of private higher education institutions still remain non-accredited. Ranking has been another effort to enhance quality. Indian institutions do not fare well in the world ranking of universities. In response, India initiated a national ranking process with the National Institutional Ranking Framework (NIRF) in 2015. The first results published in April 2016 and 2017 clearly indicated that the top ranking institutions are mostly public funded central universities. It is currently believed that creating world class universities will boost India's position in the global rankings. This prompted India to plan to support the creation of 20 world class universities in the immediate future. It appears that India, like many other developing countries, is on a fast track towards the reorientation of existing institutions into world class universities.

Reforms to enhance relevance

Despite the sector's growth, many employers in India have lost confidence in the quality of the qualifications awarded by the country's universities. It is questioned whether these universities offer the skills and competencies to its graduates as expected in the labour market. In order to regain the credibility and enhance the relevance of university qualifications, India is now in the process of developing a National Higher Education Qualification Framework (NHEQF), which is focusing on learning outcomes, employability skills and competencies. This follows the 2013 development of a national skills qualification framework (NSQF).

Conclusion

The massification of higher education is accompanied by a widening of regional disparities, persisting social inequalities and commercialization of the sector. The challenge now is to address the issues of equity and diversity to provide affordable, quality higher education in a period of market-led reforms. It is expected that the national policy on education currently in development will hopefully address some of these concerns.

References

1. A crisis of confidence in higher education?". universityworldnews.com. 2011-07-24. Retrieved 2011-08-23.
2. A study in apathy. 11 September 2013. Archived from the original on 16 September 2013.
3. Ahmad Sheikh, Younis (2017). "Higher Education in India: Challenges and Opportunities" (PDF). Journal of Education and Practice. 8.
4. Asia's Best Science and Technology Schools". Cgi.cnn.com. 22 June 2000. Archived from the original on 31 May 2012. Retrieved 1 September 2010.
5. Encyclopædia Britannica
6. Fake and Cheat Universities in India, Think Ahead.
7. Government of India. Ministry of Human Resource Development.(2016) All India Survey on Higher Education: Higher Education Statistics at a Glance
8. Matt Lynley (9 July 2012). "The World's Best Engineering Schools". Business Insider.
9. MBA global Top 100 rankings – FT". ft.com. Retrieved 2009-03-04.
10. Medical Meccas: An Oasis for India's Poorest | Newsweek Health for Life | Newsweek.com". Newsweek.com. 2006-10-30. Retrieved 2008-11-03.
11. MHRD, Annual Report on Higher Education in India- 2015-2016.
12. Ranjan Ravi, Naveen (2015). "Structure and Organisation of Higher Education in India : A Macro-Perspective" (PDF). Indian Journal of Educational Studies : An Interdisciplinary Journal. 2.
13. Roy Chowdhury, Sunandan (2017). Politics, Policy and Higher Education in India SpringerLink. doi:10.1007/978-981-10-5056-5. ISBN 978-981-10-5055-8.
14. Roy, Chowdhury, Sunandan. Politics, policy and higher education in India. Singapore. ISBN 9789811050565. OCLC 1002303793.
15. Times Higher Education". Times Higher Education. 2006-10-06. Retrieved 2010-09-01.

Chapter - 60

Gender Issues in Indian Higher Education: An Analytical Study

Nithya Kalmekolan

Abstract

Higher education is very important for the overall development of a nation. Education creates human capital which is the core for economic progress of every society. One of the major challenges is to provide access to higher education. The representation of SC, ST, OBC, women and minority communities in colleges and universities remains lower than their population size. This is attributed to the inequalities in the Indian society due to caste, hierarchy, gender, etc. The demands of these sections regarding access to higher education cannot be ignored. Access to higher education is a major step towards gender mainstreaming in few countries where women are still looked down as second grade citizens since ages. Further, cultural perceptions of the roles which women are expected to fill are reflected in the extent to which women participate in formal education and the type of education to which they have access. This has an impact on the professions since it is gender based rather on their personal capabilities. Access to education is a crucial indicator of women's status in the society and gender equality facilitates the progress of society. This paper is an attempt to discuss about the higher education system and gender related issues in the system as one of the major challenges. It argues that control and domination on women and resources would only result in partial and unilinear development of the society. Women offer immense potential to contribute to the skill base of the country but they sadly represent an under-utilized resource. This paper also highlights the importance of education for women empowerment. There is a need to bring about cultural transformation along with gender sensitization in order to achieve gender equality. Once we realize the significance of women contribution in various fields of development then there cannot be any look back about women and their role in the higher education of the country.

Keywords: *Higher education, Gendered Education, Indian Context*

Introduction

For over centuries, the education system in India was based on the Gurukula system where in the teaching and learning processes were under the guidance of the Guru, the teacher. This sort of education was restricted to a few elite families, whereby the vast mass of society was barred from educational access. Some historians speculate that these centers had a remarkable resemblance to the European medieval universities that came up much later. Incidentally, a major change in the design of higher education was brought by the European rulers like the British. Obviously, the foreign influence on Indian higher education has been on the rise over the years.

To be specific, the British established the formal system of higher education which focused on languages, literature, philosophy and history. These knowledge centers focused on generating English-speaking people for the British administrative services, army and trade. In the post-independence period, the higher education system in India grew rapidly, albeit modeled after British system. By 1980, there were 132 universities and 4738 colleges, enrolling around five per cent of the eligible age group in higher education. However, the number of such institutions in India became four times more than the number of institutions both in the United States and the entire Europe by now. These institutions are there established in both the sectors, public and private, of development in India.

Higher Education

As usual, the higher education plays an important role in the overall development of any country. It is through the quality of education that a nation develops its human capital. Education provides an opportunity to reflect on the cultural, moral, social, economic and spiritual issues. And, higher education is certainly a key to build a knowledge-based society. Given its vast population size, India has emerged as the third largest higher education system in the world. The consistent growth rate of India in last two decades is attributed to the higher education system which has been able to generate skilled manpower for the rapid industrialization and knowledge based economy.

Besides, India has become the main hub of Information Technology (IT) & IT enabled services industry. Although the education system has been able to support service industry to some extent, the Research & Development (R & D) at various industries and universities have not kept pace with developed countries which has created a huge divide within the society. The progress in education which has been made in last two decades during the era of globalization has not reached all sections of the society. Particularly, the gender-based discrimination has continued unabated in the field of education in almost all countries that practice patriarchy. Due to patriarchy, Indian women still lag behind their counterparts in the society. Thus, educational progress in the country is yet not achieved on expected lines.

At the other level, the present educational predicament in poverty, environment, energy, security concerns within India is mainly due to lack of indigenous cost effective technology to address these issues. This directly correlates to quality of higher education in India especially quantity and quality of R & D in higher education systems. Universities and colleges have become training centers for the service based industry of the country with short term economic development of the society rather than focusing on long term development of a society which is stable, reliable and prosperous. The challenges faced by higher education system in India are limited access and participation in higher education, lack of autonomy, lack of financing, no proper research infrastructure, burden of affiliation, etc.

There is a burning issue of unemployment in India and this is attributed to the weak quality of higher education system in the country. The challenges in higher education are no longer nation-centric. They have already attained global dimensions, particularly after trade in services has been brought under the purview of the WTO regime. With the explosive growth of knowledge in the past decades and with the development of handy tools of information and communication technologies as well as of other scientific innovations, competition has become a hallmark of growth throughout the World. Hence, knowledge is not only going to be the driver of Indian economy, but also, it is going to permeate into all the strata of Indian society for a better quality of life and living conditions. Therefore, India has to rise to the occasion urgently and reorient its higher education system to be competitive, vibrant, meaningful and purposeful. Besides, there is absolutely no substitute to the quality of higher education, although the country has been faced for a long time with the serious problem of meeting the quantity needs of our society. It is, therefore, essential that a careful balancing of the two as a priority to meet the twin requirements of the society in the foreseeable future.

It is true that enhancing social access to higher education is still important in the country. But, the major challenge before the Indian higher education system is to bring equity in quality of education across the length and breadth of the country. This is more close to the hearts of students in rural, semi urban and urban areas, because they also wish to participate in the new economic revolution. Several social, economic and political reasons seem to act as constraints to access and equity in higher education in India. Poverty leads to high drop-out rates even at primary, middle and secondary school levels. Lower status of women, lack of implementation of existing programmes, lack of easy access, inadequate utilization of resources, absence of political will and inadequacies in coordinated actions across all equity fronts within institutions seem to be the other reason. Financial constrains also often form a significant factor in advancing equity.

In an environment of global competitiveness it is important that Indian products of the higher education institutions are considered as competent as graduates of any other country. This is not only about their scholastic attainments, but also in terms of the value system and richness of their personality. The quality and standard of the Indian higher education institutions needs to be enhanced in order to compete at the global level. This could be achieved through creativity, innovation and regular monitoring. This calls for suitable assessment and accreditation mechanisms to be available in the country in order to ensure the quality and standard of the academic programmes at higher educational institutions. This assessment has to be continuous and the process has to be transparent to gain the acceptance of the society at large.

Gender Issues in Higher Education

Evidently, there is a huge gap between the two genders when it comes to literacy and education rate. As per the 2011 Census, the female literacy rate is only 65.46%, as opposed to 82.7% in China, and 79.7% in the world. The percentage of girls who complete secondary education determines the proportion of girls accessing higher education. Although women offer immense potential to contribute to the skill base of the country, they sadly represent an under-utilized resource. Some of the gender issues include the following:

- Access, Retention and Completion: Early marriage, pressure to work, family honor, household responsibilities and related issues inhibit girls from access and completing school.
- Lack of infrastructure and facilities: Due to non- availability of schools and colleges at a walking distance especially in backward areas, parents are unwilling to send their daughters to such institutions. The availability of women faculty, secure spaces for

women students to wait between classes and provision of separate toilets and sanitation facilities, make a huge difference to women.

- Cultural Perception: In most of the societies, there is a belief that education isn't important for the role a woman has to play in the family. Cultural and religious norms governing gender relations exert a strong influence on their access to higher education.
- Gender-based Violence: Increase in public and domestic violence, as well as sexual harassment and abuse within educational institutions negatively impacts girls performance within schools and their ability to access higher education.
- Lack of Supervision and personal guidance: There is not enough machinery to look after different programmes in the field of women education. These programmes require attention and proper guidance for getting them into the right direction.
- Financial constraints: Most of the women who come from financially weak families choose to educate their sons over daughters due to limited financial resources. Prevalence of dowry system in India has resulted in investing in son's education over daughter's.
- Less availability of female teachers: Female teacher availability determines enrolment levels. Most of the parents in traditional societies are more willing to send their daughters to school if there are more women teachers than the others.

In other words, the location (urban or rural) of institutions also affects girls more than boys, in areas where roads and public transportation systems have not penetrated. Availability of institutions or universities within reach is an important determinant. Travelling long distances in public transport is an important security issue and this is particularly significant in societies where girls are not permitted to travel alone or have to be escorted.

Government policies work only as long as the people are made for being supportive. Only when one is ready to participate fully and honestly in the programs that the government launches can one expect better results and expect our demands to be heard. The patriarchal thinking of the society needs to give way to a more feminist based way of life. One needs to use all the able population in order to progress in the right direction. Or else despite having all the right resources, one will end up where it began 70 years ago.

Further, the government can be impressed upon to spend more on education. Nothing short of free and quality education for all and the provision of accessible schools for girls in every area of the country, will ensure that all girls gain equal access to education. Besides, the Government schools are increasingly becoming centers of poor quality education for the marginalized sections of society, especially girls, which in turn is connected to the high dropout rates of girls. Hence the infrastructure and quality of teaching in government schools can be brought up to the mark.

Also, educational projects should target girls as the main beneficiary. A multi pronged approach and a conscious decision should be made to enroll and retain the maximum possible number of girls in schools. Access, equity, accountability and quality should form the four guiding principles, while planning for higher education development in India in the twenty-first century.

Gendered Education

As it is well-known, gender is a social construct that impacts attitudes, roles, responsibilities and behavior patterns of boys and girls, men and women in all societies. Gender relations vary from society to society. It is a women's and people's issues shaped by power relations in patriarchal societies like India. Gender issue also deals with human concerns encompassing diversities and differences in any society. It has been the most endemic form of discrimination operating across cultures in developed and developing societies. Incidentally, education has the inbuilt potential of initiating social change in the context of gender relations.

Meanwhile, conscious and pluralistic interventions have been put forward by the Government of India to address gender equality in education at the centre and state level. A landmark initiative was undertaken in 1986, with the enactment of the National Policy on Education (NPE) and its revised Programme of Action (PoA) 1992. This philosophy has also been reflected in the National Policy on Empowerment of Women 2001. The policy focuses on promoting gender sensitive curriculum for addressing gender discrimination at all levels of education. The National Policy emphasizes on "Encourage, Educate and Employ", all irrespective of their socio-economic background. Gender concerns in education have also been reflected in curriculum frameworks developed by apex national organization like National Council of Educational Research and Training (NCERT).

Besides, the curriculum frameworks of 1975, 1988, 2000 and 2005 have made specific efforts to focus attention on gender disparities in education. The journey has been from mere concern to substantial inclusion. While a lot of efforts have been made on integrating gender concerns in education, globalization, liberalization and expansion in information technology have once again made it mandatory for revisiting gender concerns in education in a proactive manner as an important developmental agenda. There is now an emerging need to reflect and focus in a proactive manner on transforming traditional attitudes, beliefs and behavioral patterns that impact gender relations at family, community, school and work place levels. Gender debates and discourses can be operationalised within the overarching concern for democratizing education.

In this context, constitutional commitments, policy initiatives, schemes and programmes have been conceptualized by Centre and State Governments at different points of time to address gender barriers in education. One of the promising initiatives is the Rashtriya Madhyamik Shiksha Abhiyan (RMSA) that attempts to universalize education at the secondary level. This stage of education serves as a bridge between elementary and higher education. The RMSA is envisaged to achieve an enrolment rate of 75% from 52.26% in 2005-06 at secondary stage of implementation of the scheme by providing a secondary school within a reasonable distance of any habitation. The other objectives include improving quality of education through making all secondary schools conform to prescribed norms, removing gender, socio-economic and disability barriers, providing universal access to secondary level education by 2017, i.e., by the end of 12th Five Year Plan and achieving universal retention by 2020. Yet, most of these objectives still remain expectations, if one goes by the experiences of the RMSA.

Another latest initiative of the Indian government is Rashtriya Uchchatar Shiksha Abhiyan (RUSA) whose main aim is to improve access, equity and quality in higher education through planned development of higher education at the state level. The other objectives of RUSA include creating new academic institutions, expanding and upgrading the existing ones, developing institutions that are self-reliant in terms of quality education, professionally managed, and characterized by greater inclination towards research and provide students with education that is relevant to them as well as the nation as a whole. Also to improve equity in higher education by providing adequate opportunities of higher education to SC/STs and socially and educationally backward classes and promotes inclusion of women, minorities, and differently-abled persons.

Conclusion

To conclude it, education improves a woman's awareness of her own worth, and the worth of daughters. The number of children which women consider desirable decreases with increase in education, for instance. They are less likely to be influenced by family pressure and are aware of opportunities and fulfillment beyond motherhood. A high level of socio-economic development is associated with women's access to higher education. Educated women are in better control of their own lives and are better able to take care of their children. They have wider opportunities and higher earning power. As more and more girls are educated, they can be the catalysts of social development.

Further, gender mainstreaming is one of the accepted strategies for promoting gender equality. It is a process of creating knowledge and awareness of and responsibility for gender equality among all the professionals engaged in tertiary education. It is a means to achieve the goal of gender equality in higher education institutions through sensitization and educating key stakeholders that the costs of women's marginalization and gender inequalities are borne by all in the education sector as a whole (from pre-primary to tertiary and life-long learning). Mainstreaming also ensures attention to the goal of gender equality is central to activities such as education policy, curriculum, research, advocacy, facilities and planning, resource allocation, implementation and monitoring of tertiary education programmes.Since half of the society constitutes the human resources, women and their issues deserve immediate attention. While the state and government can intervene at the educational policy formulation and execution levels, the civil society and family level interventions are also important if the gender issues are to be addressed. In a way, comprehensive attempts have to be made so that the women have their partnership in the field of higher education and thereby grab their employment opportunities in proportion to their population share.

References

1. Recommendations of UGC Golden Jubilee Seminars (2003). Higher Education in India: Issues, Concerns and New Directions, UGC, New Delhi.
2. Ramachandran, Vimala (2010). Gender Issues in Higher Education - Advocacy Brief. UNESCO Bangkok: UNESCO Asia and Pacific Regional Bureau for Education.
3. Srivastava, Gouri. (n.d.). Gender Concerns in Education. Retrieved from http://www.ncert.nic.in/departments/nie/dse/activities/advisory board/PDF/Gender concerns. pdf.
4. National Curriculum Framework, NCERT, New Delhi.
5. Rashtriya Madhyamik Shiksha Abhiyan (RMSA): Overview. Retrieved January 14, 2019, from http://mhrd.gov.in/rmsa.
6. Rashtriya Uchchatar Shiksha Abhiyan (RUSA): Objectives. Retrieved January 14, 2019, from http://mhrd.gov.in/rusa.

Chapter - 61

The Changing Role of Teacher in Higher Education

Dr. K. Geetha

Abstract

How to help students learn academic content? is to be answered by concentrating on the various techniques of instruction – lecture, organise a laboratory class & run a small group discussion. 'Gone Are Those Days' when being a teacher was enough to command respect. In higher education, approaches to teaching are becoming more student – centered, which demands different teaching competences. Person as a teacher, expert on content knowledge, facilitator or learning processor, organizer and scholar/ lifelong learner.

Introduction

Anyone in higher education who claims to know how the role as teachers is going to change is obviously deluding himself. The future is not his to know. Nevertheless in a spirit of genuine curiosity and purposeful inquiry, it may be useful to examine the issue of the teacher's changing role by considering three major questions: *The role of teacher in ancient Bharatavarsha was totally different. The teacher used to take care of each and every student who approaches him in quest of knowledge and provide him such guidance by following which the student could get accurate knowledge in depth at least in one subject. The teacher and the student together used to pray the God for betterment of the society in every aspect. The teacher used to train his students in such a way he will enjoy his students winning over him. As per ancient tradition the teacher occupies a highly respectable position, almost equal, may even superior to that of God. The Guru desires – "Let this Adhyayana - study give protection to both of us. Let it give us equal enjoyment. Let us both cultivate this powerful knowledge.*

Let our study be (powerful) lustrous. Let us both free from malice and misunderstanding of each other"

At the time of convocation the teacher used to remind all the important points of human life to his disciples so that they should not deviate from the path of righteousness. *Purushaarthas* were very important goals to achieve in human life. One has to learn so many things in the path of life to reach these ultimate goals. The teacher used to say the following things in his convocational address to his disciples.

1. Speak truth.
2. Move in righteous path.
3. Do not deviate from the path of self learning.
4. Mother should be your god.
5. Father should be your god.
6. Teacher should be your god.
7. Guest should be your god.
8. Follow the path of persons with good conduct.
9. Donate for the needy.
10. Live like a best example in society.

These points carry the complete essence of ancient education system. The strongest desire of an *Achaarya* according to *Tattiriyopanishad*, is to get students worthy of receiving instruction from him. The teacher and students together used to pray that all the good things happen to everyone. Let noble thoughts come from everywhere. Everyone should enjoy fruitful life of 100 years. No one should left over with pain and sorrow. The prayer always included the welfare of every living being. This is the ideology of *vasudaivakutumbakam*. The teachers used to give priority to their students than their own progeny. Drona blessed Arjuna with Astra Brahmasiras but not his son Aswathhama.

The development of inner nature or character of the student was deemed as one of the essential objects of education in ancient times. The rich and the poor have enjoyed equality in the Gurukula. *Sparthaabandhamanoharam* – these gurukualas are so beautiful which create competency in students. Even now the competency is there but those students who cannot compete are leaving their lives. The increasing rate of suicides not only in professional courses, even in higher education is not at all acceptable to the society.

The disciple who receives knowledge from his Guru equals him and can produce students with same calibre. The sincere efforts of teachers and acceptance of students will surely lead to best society and establish peace and happiness in the world.

In present scenario of India the role of teacher is changing day by day with different types of responsibilities for the overall development of the students. The teacher has to update his subject knowledge according to the needs of the students. In 70s and 80s teacher used to sit and share the knowledge of the subject with just narration and we still remember their gestures while teaching. We can recollect the lessons taught by them with along with the titles. Their narration sometimes filled with picturesque descriptions where we carried away in to some different world. In 90s the influence of computers slowly started and 21st century one cannot show his talent without using computer knowledge. In recent years the development is teacher has to work with Google class rooms. In his absence also his class will run by the recorded lessons of the teacher. May be in coming years virtual class rooms will fulfil the necessity of teacher who can teach virtually addressing different places students. The lack of permanent faculty is always a minus point to higher education. In present times the teacher has to use latest technology and update his subject knowledge. He has liberty to select authentic PPTs on particular topics from online for the benefit of the students. With digital class rooms he can directly access to the You Tube and online lessons. He can write the notes on his subject topics and share to Wikipedia which will reach to many needy students. Through subject blogs also many students are getting the benefits. Students are already getting used to online courses through SVYAM, MOOCS and many other authorised centres.

Experts of different subjects are making online videos available for many subjects useful for the students to get through IIT, IAS, NET and CSIR exams and so on. Technology itself is acting as teacher if we have commitment to learn any subject. IIT Professors uploading their valuable lectures which are useful to the students to get acquainted with world class teaching professionals. Any good teacher can contribute lessons to address the needs of students. Now it is the trend and many scholars though not related to teaching profession are sharing their knowledge through internet. Now the student can get OXFORD University certificate after finishing online course. We should not forget even for online course also the master mind behind the programming is a Teacher.

Without a teacher we cannot shape the future generations as per the expectations and needs of the society. After parents students mostly depend on their teachers. Government of India is taking so many steps to improve the quality of higher education. Meritorious teachers should be appointed otherwise a dull teacher would produce generations of dull students. For the welfare of any society a good teacher is always needed. Teacher must be energetic, active, enthusiastic and knowledgeable. The teacher should have the above the qualities to inspire the students. The teacher and student determine the future of the society.

The role of teacher is changing in many aspects but still it holds great importance. The teacher who influences his students will definitely motivate the student's to get success in education as well as personal life. From kinder garden level to higher education level students are always influenced and inspired by their teachers. No one can read their mind better than their teacher. Many a times he has to act as councillor when the situation demands so. The teacher should fill the minds of students with positive thinking. He should teach the student to celebrate the success as well as face the failure. We are not preparing students how to deal with failure and that is the primary cause of suicides of students. The student who got more than 90% in regular course is committing suicide for just not getting a seat in reputed course. Here the teacher can play the best role as a councillor. The stress from parents and society towards the students is leading for such mishaps. The teacher should teach how to maintain balance at any level of emotional stress. Parents mostly worry about the society which criticises the failure of their children. But the emotional support of teacher and parents is most essential need of the students. Everyone is interested in the success stories but these three people will build the courage of failure students. Suicides of students can be prevented by this emotional bondage of teachers and parents.

Unlike other professions teaching profession demands many sacrifices. To teach one effective class he has to spend so many hours in preparation. It is a serious profession demanding so many sacrifices and lot of time. Great commitment is needed in this profession. If a manufacturer makes a mistake only that product will go wrong. If an unsuitable person apt this profession it effects generations. The teacher should imbibe the morals and ethics which he wants to see in his students. Society always expects teacher with human values and ethics. Otherwise he will be the wrong example for the society. The students are expecting for a teacher who is sincere, knowledgeable, and a very friendly personality.

Conclusion

Altogether the teacher role is expanding and changing to meet the demands of a new era. He might even strive to meet new standards of quality, to become a superior teacher or even an excellent teacher.The present generation more focussed towards their life compared to our elders. In modern society the goal of teaching is towards fulfilling the global needs. Here technology should be utilized appropriately such that only valid knowledge is imparted at the right time. To reach this goal now teachers are going through great stress. It is affecting their health. We have to deal this. Significant part of the education is seen as the process by which the teacher enlarges, enriches and improves the individual's image of the future. The teacher should play different roles as mentor, councillor, close friend, felicitator. "Faculty are supposed to make the sparks fly intellectually, and from time to time, we're supposed to make lighting strike." – Ross Thomas.

Conclusion

1. Atkinson, J W. 1964. An introduction to motivation.
2. Mc Dougall, W. 1921. Social psychology.
3. www.wikipedia.com/pedagogy
4. www.wikipedia.com/andragogy
5. www.learning.com
6. Mangal, S., Uma mangal. 2009. Essential of Education Technology. PHI
7. Mr. Vishal G. Jadhav, foundation of education

Index

A

Academic abilities, 63,66
Absence of teachers, 100
Academic Authority, 258
Academic concepts, 112
Academic dialogue, 50
Academic experts, 261
Academic Leader, 47, 48
Academic Leadership, 46
Academic management systems, 370
Academic quality, 126
Academic-staff college, 520
Academic Technology Group, 90
Academic tutor, 25
Academic websites, 346
Achievement Motivation, 459, 460, 461
Action learning, 23
Active Learning Method, 48
Activities of Siet, 465
Activity-oriented, 305
Administration of Research Tool, 38
Administrative work pressure, 65
Adobe Captivate, 89
Adobe Photo Shop, 87
Adolescent girls, 334, 335, 336, 341, 486, 487, 492
Adolescent growth & development, 338, 496
Adolescent Health and Nutrition, 334, 338, 341, 492
Advanced Placement, 434
Advancement of Technology, 53
Advantages of classroom management, 386
Advantages of Mothertongue learning, 400
Advantages of project method, 214
Advisory Board, 130
Against child marriage, 73
Albert Einstein, 438
Alexander the great, 394
Alfred Adler, 113
Algorithmic approaches, 240
Ali Mahmood Khan, 457
Allan Wigfield, 456
Allen Blue, 165
All India Council for Technical Education, 96, 421
All India Survey, 425
All India Survey on Higher Education, 419
All objective-type tests, 366
Amartya Sen, 328, 514
American Institutions, 125
American Society for Education, 287
Amrita University, 366, 367
Amrita Virtual E-learning World, 366, 367
Analytical frame work, 514
Analytical method, 304
Ananda Marga Gurukula, 95
Anderson and Krathwohl Taxonomy, 45
Andhra Pradesh, 452
Annual self-appraisal report, 520

Annual Survey of Education Report, 97
Ante-natal care, 340, 498
Ante-natal checkups, 340, 498
Apache Internet Information Server, 369
Aparna Mukherjee, 299
Approximation theory, 240
Aricultural sciences, 125
Arjun Sengupta committee, 212
Armenian- Azeri conflict, 303
Artistic perfection, 225
Artistic perfection is not necessary, 225
Art of planning, 107
Ashoka University, 136
Ashton & Newman, 28
Asian countries, 347
Assessment for Learning, 464
Association of Indian Universities, 133
Astra Brahmasiras, 352
Aswathhama, 352, 534
Attendance management, 59
Attitude of the parents, 175
Audacity, 87
Audience Poll, 366
Audio and Video- Creating and Editing, 86
Audio editing software, 87
Audio mixing and editing, 88
Audio pod cast, 156
Audio- Visual quality, 169
Augmented Reality, 58, 366, 367
Aurobindo Ghosh, 467
Australia, 94, 121, 123, 134, 136
Australian sociologist documents, 408
Authentic assessment, 183
Authentic material, 480, 481
Authoring tools, 88
Automata theory, 240
Automatic route, 132
Autonomous schools, 95
Availability of qualified teachers, 262
Azim Premji University, 137

B

B. Ed.level, 34
B. Ed. Students, 381
Babson College, 137
Bachelor degree, 238
Bachelor of Education programme, 37
Backward castes, 494
B A German(Hon.), 219
Balanced diet, 496
Bangladesh, 123
Bank Clerk, 157
Banking Approach, 113
Bar Council of India, 96
Bargaining power, 329, 515
Baseline data, 339
Basic human skills, 263
Beginning Teacher Standards, 187
Behaviorist Approach, 108
Behavior modification models, 393
Bell Hooks, 191
Benefits for teachers, 199, 435
Benefits of Guidance, 430
Benefits of Technology, 58, 200
Berkeley, 136
Bernstein, 405
Besides Walter Beimdick, 221
Better class management, 67
Bhutan, 123
Big Data, 57
Biochemical tests, 487
Births and Deaths Registration Act, 305, 319
Bisma Mazhar Khan, 457
Black for Cautions, 45
Black money, 100
Blank signed cheques, 97
Blended Learning, 48
Blue for Process, 45

BML Munjal University, 137
Board of Secondary Education, 358
Bob Lingard, 77
Borrowed term, 107
Braille handouts, 453
Brainstorm Ideas, 45
Brain storming, 303
Brazil, 126
Brazilian educator and philosopher, 190
Breast feeding, 340, 498
Brighter tomorrow, 414
Bright students, 63
British administrative services, 526
British Council, 424
British rulers, 519
Bruce Crauder, 242
Business Administration, 98
Business Plan, 160

C

C. V. Raman, 473
Cafeteria, 422
Calicut University, 192
Cambridge, 95, 118
Canada, 93, 121
Capitation fee, 317,259
Carleton College, 136
Carl Jung, 113
Case study, 303
Census Commission, 502
Census Commission of India, 316
Central Board of Secondary Education, 95, 127
Central Council of Homeopathy, 96
Central Council of Indian Medicine, 96
Central Ministry of Education, 358
Century Skills, 438
Chambers Dictionary, 478
Changed role of education, 415
Character theory, 240
China, 50, 93, 119, 125, 126, 343, 344
Chrome books, 446
Classical Indian tradition, 414
Class management, 66
Classroom activities, 452
Classroom activities or techniques, 107, 406
Classroom conversations, 206
Classroom discourse, 193
Classroom discussion, 109
Classroom environment, 241, 347
Classroom Learning, 289,291
Classroom Management, 385, 395
Classroom Response Systems, 230
Classroom supervision, 38, 39
Classroom Teaching, 35
Class without proper management, 387
Clean Drinking Water, 489
Clinical trials, 487
Coaching classes, 98
Co-curricular activities, 278, 279, 280
Collaboration skills, 208
Collaboration Tools, 231, 232
Collaboration with community, 438
Collaborative Learning, 24, 463
Collaborative Learning Approach, 109
Collaborative work, 303
Collection of baseline data, 487
Collection of data, 377
College-development council, 520
College laboratories, 367
College records, 510
Commerce Department, 158
Commerce Lab, 159
Commerce Ministry, 121
Commerce Quiz, 160
Commercial cross-border education, 138
Commercialization of educational, 318
Commercial software, 449
Common Course, 192

Common European Frame work of Reference, 219
Communication abilities & skills, 208
Communication Skills, 192, 238
Compact discs, 246
Competency Based Learning, 464
Components of Futuristic Curriculum, 405
Computer Assisted Instruction, 48
Computer Center, 422
Computer education, 376, 379, 380, 382
Computer knowledge, 251
Computer lab, 383
Computer skills, 197
Computer technology, 375, 376
Concept formation progresses, 470
Concept Mapping Approach, 112
Concept maps, 112
Concepts of drama didactics, 220
Concurrent List, 54
Confederation of Indian Industry, 127
Conference Hall, 422
Congenial context, 186
Connectivism and Connective Knowledge, 345
Constituent Assembly, 316
Constitutional Amendment, 319
Constitutional and Judicial Perspective, 502
Constitution of India, 317, 75, 262
Constructivist curriculum, 470
Constructivist Learning Approach, 110
Contemporary Classrooms, 388, 389, 391
Content knowledge, 239
Content Management System, 86
Context facilitate learning, 184
Contextual teaching, 184
Contextual teaching and learning, 182, 183
Conveyance management, 59
Cool kids code, 371
Cooperative Learning Approach, 109
Cooperative learning method, 76
Co- Ordinate Live Video, 201
Council of Indian School Certificate Examination, 95
Counseling cell for Adolescent, 429
Counseling curriculum, 429
Counseling Programs, 430
Creation of learning resources, 84
Creative drama pedagogy for classroom, 207
Creativity, 208
Creativity-related skills, 76
Critical comments, 488
Critical pedagogy, 176, 177, 178, 190
Critical Reasoning, 192
Critical teaching, 191
Critical thinking, 176, 191
Critical thinking skills, 76, 208
Cross-border education, 138
Cultural and political upliftment, 82
Cultural patterns, 416
Cultural Perception, 529
Curriculum-development centers, 520
Curriculum issues, 97
Curriculum materials, 74
Curriculum Renewal, 360

D

Daily basis in classroom learning, 448
Dark rooms, 97
Data Analysis, 299, 448
Data Collection, 460
Data collection and Analysis, 279
Data related to pregnancy, 340, 498
Data Wind Technologies, 365
Deakin University, 134
Decision making capabilities, 208
Deductive method, 304
Definitions of Learning, 468

Degree Courses, 511
Delhi University, 219, 224
Delivery, 498
Delpit, 177
Democratic culture, 194
Demographic health survey, 327, 513
Demonstration method, 304
Dentist Council of India, 96
Department of Commerce, 134, 157
Dependent variables, 482
Designing and presenting a project, 305
Desirable food habits, 338
Development of democratic schools, 191
Differently Abled Persons, 450, 531, 420
Difficult situations, 431
Digital Age, 437
Digital board, 66
Digital cameras, 198
Digital classrooms, 353, 365
Digital concept mapping tools, 83, 92
Digital content, 91
Digital Education Revolution, 83
Digitalization of Classroom, 447
Digital painting, 87
Digitized learning system, 408
Diploma and post-diploma, 96
Directive Principles of State Policy, 318, 503, 504
Directorate of Collegiate Education, 323, 324, 510, 512
Directorate of Higher Education, 323, 511
Directorate of Intermediate Education, 323, 512
Directorate of Public Instruction, 323, 509
Directorate of School Education, 323, 511
Direct Teaching Approach, 113
Disciplinal Approach, 113
Disciplines of Social sciences, 75
Disinterested Students, 62
Disobedient students, 64
Distance Education Council, 96
District Institute of Education, 245
Dr. Deepak B. Pathak, 366
Dr. Radhakrishnan, 54
Drama-based pedagogy, 206
Dramaclass by Steinweg, 225
Drama pre-school by Waldmann, 223
Drama-specific rhythm, 222
Drama teaching, 220
Drama text student, 221
Draw Pad, 87
Drona blessed Arjuna, 352, 534
Duckworth, 457, 458
Duke center for instructional Technology, 234
Duke University, 137
Duke University school of Nursing, 234
During Construction of Knowledge, 473
Durkheim, 405
Duties of appropriate authorities, 260

E

Early marriage, 328, 491, 528
E-books, 451
Economic backwardness, 328
Economic Condition, 175
Economic development, 94
Educational assessment, 183
Educational attainment of women, 330
Educational field, 201
Educational guidance, 394
Educational institutions, 64
Educational levels, 494
Educational organization, 309
Educational patterns, 416
Educational plan, 278
Educational Radio Programmes, 464
Educational resources, 434
Educational status, 173

Educational technologies teachers, 197
Educational Technology, 196
Educational tool, 232
Educational Video Programmes, 464
Education Commission, 428
Education genre, 90
Education in mother tongue, 402
Education in stitutions, 100
Education-led technology, 97
Education Satellite, 77
Education Sector, 94
Education Technology, 59
Edward de Bono, 45
Effective Leadership, 309, 311
Effectiveness of smart classrooms, 449
Eight years Elementary Education Cycle, 258
Eighty-sixth Constitutional Amendment, 504
E-learning, 305
E-learning, Massive Open Online Courses, 48
Electronic Content, 85
Electronic goods, 250
Electronic media, 487
Electronic media, 488
Electronic or mechanical, 197
Elementary trainings, 451
Elimination theory, 240
Elizabeth Rata, 405
E-materials, 451
Emotional expression, 297
Employee Engagement, 310
Employee Motivation, 309, 310
Empowered Committee, 450
Enable India, 451
Enables students to learn, 199
Enables students to learn at their own pace, 199
Encourage collaboration, 199
Encourages individual learning, 199, 436
Energetic youth, 101
Enforcing a positive, 335
Engaged Pedagogy, 191
English-language skills, 242
English medium school, 193
English speaking people, 348, 526
English text books, 192
Enhance Student Engagement, 231
Enterprise Resource Planning systems, 369, 370
Entrepreneurship training, 96
Epistemological risk, 27
Equal Opportunities, 420
Eric Lysoon, 165
Essay Writing & Elocution, 160
Establishment of Student Bank, 156
Establishment of Student Store, 156
European Convention, 316
European medieval universities, 526
Experiential learning, 469
Explanatory method, 304
Explosion of Knowledge, 49
Explosion of Population, 49
Extracurricular activities, 357

F

Facebook, 170
Face-to- Face Course, 234
Face-to-face instruction, 287, 288
Faculty Development Programs, 65
Family honor, 528
Family planning methods, 339
Fazal Rizvi, 77
Feedback to Instruction, 408
Fee management, 59
Female higher education, 327
Female sample, 280
Female teacher trainees, 377, 382
Finance Commission, 260, 261
Financial assistances, 331, 517
Financial burden, 505

Financial commitment, 357
Financial constraints, 529
Findings of the study, 39
First Education Commission, 54
First year degree students, 239
Five Minute Activities, 392
Five Year Plan, 308, 531
Flash Statistics, 46
Flexible And Negotiated Assessment, 24
Flexible Curriculum, 23
Flipped Classroom, 48
Flipping the Classroom, 233
Floppy diskettes, 246
Food and Nutrition Extension Board, 337, 495
Foreign curriculum, 129
Foreign direct investment, 132
Foreign Educational Institutions, 129, 130, 132
Foreign education institution, 127
Foreign Education Providers, 129, 134, 132
Foreign influence, 526
Foreign investment, 137
Foreign language skills, 238
Foreign scholars, 134
Foreign students, 126
Foreign universities, 125, 126, 129, 132, 135
Foreign Universities branches, 134
Foreign universities degree, 127
Foreign university, 126, 130
Four year bachelor degree programme, 126
Framework of Blended Approach, 286
Frank Levy and Richard Murnane, 438
Franklin and Marshall College, 242
Franz- Josef Payrhuber, 221
Freedom in learning, 25
Free open source software, 87
Full Participation, 420
Fundamental Rights, 317, 503
Futuristic Curriculum, 407, 409

G

Gain the heart of the learners, 387
Gardner Murphy, 469
Garrison and Vaughan, 284, 285
Gathering and sharing information, 111
Gather Student Feedback, 201
Gender-based Violence, 529
Gender gaps, 328
Gender Issues in Higher Education, 528
General Agreement on Trade in Services, 118, 121
General use of computers, 378
Geneva, 502
Genre theory approach, 220
Geographical barrier, 347
Geographic Information System, 261
George Mason, 231
George Siemens, 168
German-as-a-foreign-language, 219
German educationalist, 221
Germany, 93
Giroux, 177
Global human resource management, 311
Globalization and Modernization process, 48
Globalization of Business, 309, 310
Good guide and a counselor, 394
Good Lesson- Qualities, 35
Google classrooms, 48, 535
Government& Aided Managements, 259
Governmental aids and support, 450
Government Degree College, 241, 277, 324, 510
Grammatical and semantic structures, 225
Gram Panchayats, 258
Graphic editing, 87
Grass root level, 234

Great Britain, 55, 344
Green for Creativity, 45
Gross enrolment ratios, 521
Gross National Product, 54
Group Learning, 469
Growth of Higher Education Sector, 147
Guidance and Counseling, 428
Guidance and Education, 428
Gujarat, 261
Gurukula, 352
Gurukula system, 164, 526

H

H. G. Wells, 427
Haemoglobin level, 486
Harmonies relationship, 387
Harvard Business School, 134
Haryana, 260
Hase and Kenyon, 25
Health care, 496
Health education, 430
Helping students, 442
Henry P. Smith, 468
Herbert Spencer, 414
Herta- Elisabeth Renk, 221
Heutagogical Learning Environment, 27
Heutagogy looks, 20
High degree of self-efficacy, 25
High Engagement Learning, 464
Higher Education, 425, 49, 50, 72
Higher educational institutions, 301
Higher education institutions, 138, 532
Higher Education System, 302
Higher female education, 331
Higher order thinking skills, 45, 111
History of Curriculum, 404
History or Economics, 62
Hoic- Bozic, 288
Hooks, 177
Hostel management, 59
Howard- Jones, 208
How Teachers should Deal with this, 440
Human History, 427
Human Resource Development, 359, 362, 46
Human Resource Management, 307, 308, 311
Human resource potential, 151
Human values and ethics, 354
Hyderabad, 333, 460, 491, 493

I

IIT- Bambay, 367, 365
IIT Professors, 353
Imagination, 208
Imbalanced student-teacher ratio, 474
Immunisation, 340, 498
Imperial College, 137
Implementation of Digital classes, 464
Implicit enactment, 222
Importance of Computer Education, 375
Importance of Higher Education, 211
Importance to technology, 98
Important developmental agenda, 531
Import videos, 87
Improper Teaching Materials, 175
Improves engagement, 199, 435
Improves Knowledge retention, 199, 436
Independent variables, 482
Indiana University, 231
Indiana University Bloomington, 135
Indian Council for Agriculture Research, 96
Indian Council of Cultural Relations, 121
Indian educational institutions, 127
Indian education sector, 129, 48
Indian Education Service, 359
Indian Education System, 94
Indian graduates, 154
Indian Institute of Technology, 125, 127
Indian Institutes of Management, 127
Indian Nursing Council, 96

Indian research centre, 134
Indian Space Research Organisation, 361
Indian Students Studying Abroad, 121
Indian university system, 520
Indian Yearbook of Education, 55
India Population Project, 333, 334, 491, 492
Indira Gandhi National Open University, 96, 127
Indirect, Guided Approach, 113
Individualized Instruction, 48
Indo- US collaborations, 125
Inductive method, 304
Industrialized countries, 125
Informational handouts, 156
Information and Communication Technologies, 22, 48, 77, 284
Information Communication Technology, 245
Information processing models, 393
Information technology, 77, 283, 526
Information Visualization Tools, 232
Informative booklet, 337
Innovation and creativity, 99
Inquiry approach, 469
Inquiry Based Learning, 112
Institute of Advanced study, 37
Institutional administration, 284
Instructional hours, 259
Instructional technology, 197
Integrated Approach, 113
Integrating technology, 202
Interactive Approach, 113
Interactive Multimedia Learning Objects, 464
Interdependent Learning groups, 183
Interest in international security, 118
International Commission on Education, 358
International dimension, 118
International Monetary Fund, 520
International rankings, 126
International schools, 95
International Seminar, 389
International Seminar on Teaching, 386, 388, 393, 396
International students, 124, 126
Internet-based, 167
Internet technologies, 283
Internship program, 395
Intervening task, 185
Introduction of technology, 343
Iron Deficiency Anaemia, 485, 486
Ishwar Chand Vidhya Sagar, 316, 502
Islamic Madrasah School Boards, 95

J

Jameela Begum, 75
James E. Rogers Collegeof Law, 135
Japan people, 298
Java Script framework, 371
Jean- Luc Vaillant, 165
Jharkhand, 98
Jindal Global University, 135
Job Access With Speech, 449
Joe Kincheloe, 191
Johan Muller, 405
John Dewey, 183
Joint Degree Programmes, 135

K

K. N. Panikkar, 77
Kalyana Lakshmi Scheme, 511
Kanpur, 125
Kaplan and Haenlein, 164
Karabakh problem, 303
Karl Maton, 405
Karnataka, 257
Kasturirangan Committee, 362
Kaun Banega Crorepati, 366
Kavita A. Sharma, 77
Keeps students focused, 199

Kelly, 457
Kendriya vidyalaya, 101
Kerala, 54, 192, 259
King's College, 136
Kingsley and R. Garry, 468
Kofi Annan, 315, 501
Kurt Weill, 224

L

Laboratory, 422
Laboratory method, 304
Lack of awareness, 328
Lack of Facilities, 97
Lack of infrastructure, 66
Lack of proper monitoring, 175
Lack of quality education, 96
Ladson- Billings, 177
Lambada and Yerukala, 174
Language community, 480
Language learning, 240, 241
Language learning ability, 239
Language pedagogy, 194
Laptops or computer, 452
Large purchases, 516
Larger classroom sizes, 108
Launch Focus Writer, 371
Leadership and management, 312
Leadership qualities questionnaire, 278
League of Nations, 316, 502
Learned English bilingually, 192
Learner capacity, 26
Learner Centered Approach, 108
Learning and teaching process, 285
Learning by involving, 364
Learning community, 287
Learning Flexibility, 289
Learning goals, 457
Learning Management System, 57, 86, 89
Learning Mathematics, 242, 243
Learning model, 469
Learning plays, 224
Lecture method, 108
Leesa Wheelaham, 405
Less availability of female teachers, 529
Lesson Preparation, 35
Leveraging Technology, 408
Liberal Arts and Humanities, 135
Limitations of the study, 167
Linda Baker, 456
Linked In, 170
Literary Canon, 192
Literary interpretation of drama text, 225
Literature Review, 54
Little media, 488
Lok Sabha, 129
London, 137
Lucid Chart, 90

M

M. Bhaskaran Nair, 77
Mac Arthur Fellowship, 458
Madan Mohan Malviya, 316, 502
Madhya Pradesh, 260
Mahabubnagar, 247
Mahabubnagar district, 247, 248
Maharashtra, 98
Mahatma Gandhi, 467
Mahila Arogya Sanghams, 335, 493
Main objective of the study, 37
Maintenance of economic competitiveness, 118
Majority of students, 451
Make education affordable, 100
Makes student more excited, 199
Male and Female B. Ed. students, 381
Malnutrition affects, 101
Management of the Indian education, 149
Management quota system, 102
Managing Inter- Personal Relationships, 309, 312

Mandatory Schedule, 256
Manipur, 259
Mannheim, 405
Marginalized sections, 191
Maria Montessori, 386
Marketing corporate, 90
Massive Open Online Course, 344, 345
Maternal & child health, 334
Maternal mortality, 335
Maternal mortality rates, 334
Mathematical terms, 241
Mathematics, 237
Mathematics and Natural Sciences, 410
Mathematics Education, 238
Mathematics problem, 242
Mathematics skills, 184
Mc Donnell Academy, 136
Mc Laren, 177
Mc Loughlin and Lee, 164
Meaning and Principles of Guidance, 428
Means of Financing Educational Development, 54
Meat or fruits, 497
Medak District, 324, 485, 486, 510
Medical Council of India, 96
Medium of education, 401
Meghalaya, 259
Menstrual hygiene & health care, 338
Menstrual hygiene, 496
Mental enactment, 222
Mental maladies, 513
Mental medicine, 327, 513
Meritorious teachers, 353, 536
Methodological Approaches, 48
Methodology of the Study, 447
Michael Apple, 191
Michael Marien, 409
Michael Young, 405
Michigan State University, 137
Microsoft Office, 86, 92
Microsoft Power Point, 88
Mid-day meal, 256, 360
Migration, 119
Millennium Declaration of United Nations, 262
Minimal licensing issues, 370
Misuse of mobile phones, 63
Misuse of newly found freedom, 63
Mobile phones, 198
Mobile technology, 365
Modern communication satellites, 246
Modern education, 449
Modern French philosopher, 29
Modern world, 375
Monitory mechanism, 250
Moulana Abul Kalam Azad, 467
M S- Office, 383
Mudaliar Commission, 358
Muhammad Azeem Ashraf, 71
Mulgeta Zemuy Zegergish, 71
Multicentric studies, 486
Multilingual skills, 238
Multimedial presentations, 114
Multinational Companies, 310
Multi-platform, 366

N

Nagaland, 259
Nalanda, 147
Nalgonda, 158
National Association of Software, 127
National coalition, 212
National Commission, 258
National Council for Teacher Education, 33, 96
National Council of Educational Research and Traing, 95, 125, 361, 530
National Curriculum Framework, 46
National Education Policy, 357
National education policy, 361

National Focus Group on Teaching of Science, 44
National Higher Education Qualification Framework, 522
National Institute of Open Schooling, 95
National Institutional Ranking Framework, 522
Nationalize education sector, 100
National Level Test, 359
National Mission on Education, 48, 77, 357, 360, 530
National Policy on Empowerment of Women, 530
National Research council, 345
National Sample Survey, 212
National Skill Development Mission, 96
National skills qualification frame work, 522
Navodaya vidyalaya, 101, 96
Need and Importance, 428
Need and significance of the study, 183
Need of Technology, 446
Negative concept, 341
Negative Side of Using Technology, 201
Neo- Marxist school of thought, 189
Nepal, 123
New Education Policy, 358
New Zealand, 121, 134
Ninth Five- Year Plan, 420
Nizamabad district, 277, 279
No Board Examinations, 259
No corporal punishment, 259
Non-academic challenges, 62
Non-commercial companies, 370
Non-experimental comparative design, 461
Non-government institutions, 423
Non-participant groups, 280
Non-ranked Indian institutions, 126
Non-repatriation of profits, 130
Non-university sector, 138
Non Visual Desktop Access, 449
Normal Educational Activities, 489
North America, 316, 502
Nutritional requirements & balanced diet, 338
Nutritional requirements, 496
Nutrition disorders, 486
Nutrition education, 334, 336

O

Obstruction theory, 240
Offering Joint Degrees, 126
Oklahoma State University, 242
Old-age homes, 97
On-demand board examination, 362
On-demand board exams, 359
Online Course, 234
Online exam, 59
Online lessons, 535
Online Projects, 231
Online videos available, 353
Open digital education, 58
Open Educational Resources, 345, 58
Open Source Application, 90
Open source development, 369, 371, 372
Open Source Software, 369, 370, 86
Open source Software concept, 90
Open Source solutions, 370
Open Source Technology, 369
Open source vector drawing, 87
Operational Definitions, 167
Organisation for Economic Co-operation and Development, 119
Organising Student Activity, 71
Organizing Commerce Fests, 156, 160
Orientation training programs, 487
Our Sages, 211
Oxford, 118

P

Paperless classroom, 292
Parental choice, 451

Parental involvement, 357
Parental pressure, 325, 328
Patha Bhavan, 95
Paul Hindemith, 224
Paulo Friere, 190
Pearson coefficient, 277
Pearson Moment Correlation, 290
Pedagogic skills, 62
Peer Group Learning, 48
Peer learning, 469
Performance goals, 457
Performance Management, 309, 312
Performed enactment, 222
Personal development models, 393
Personal guidance, 394
Personalized Learning, 407, 463
Persons with Disabilities Act, 420
Person with differently-abled, 419, 420
Peterson, 457
Pharmacy Council of India, 96
Photo blog, 90
Photo Shop, 87
Physical environment, 175
Pilot study, 378
Pilot training, 367
Place of computer education, 378
Playground, 422
Political and administrative interests, 519
Political science, 189
Poor Women's education, 97
Population and sample, 459
Post Colonial India, 192
Post-colonialism, 243
Poster Making, 160
Post- Graduate, 377
Post-graduate and graduate students, 381
Post-intervention period, 498
Power Point, 230
Power Point Presentations, 156
Practical methods, 304
Practical risk, 27
Practical training, 36
Pre-and post-intervention period, 341
Pregnant women, 340
Preparation of suitable tool, 377
Pre-school education, 59, 359
Presentation Software, 229
Present century classroom, 388
Pre-service education, 34
President Barack Obama, 126
Principle of Alignment, 72
Principle of Community, 72
Principle of Connection, 72
Principle of Interest, 72
Principles of State Policy, 317
Print media, 488
Private sector, 101
Private tuitions, 259
Privatization of higher education, 521
Problem- Based Learning, 182, 185, 303
Problem-solving abilities, 208
Problem Solving Approach, 111, 469
Production-oriented approach, 221
Product Moment Correlation, 289
Professional and personal academic growth, 346
Professional development, 438
Profile of adolescent girls, 336,494
Programme of Action, 358, 530
Promoted active learning, 27
Promotion of scholarship, 47
Proprietary software, 86, 89
Protection of Child Rights, 258
Protection of Right, 420
Providing opportunities, 442
Psychoanalytical Approach, 113
Psychological causes, 411
Psychology of teaching, 395
Public domain software, 86
Public education systems, 74

Public health specialist, 338
Public sector, 101
Published information, 441
Purdue University, 242
Purpose of education, 414
Purpose of Internationalization, 118
Purpose of study, 485
Purpose of the study, 166

Q

Qualities of a good lecture, 107
Quality education, 99
Quality improvement, 177
Quality in Education, 24, 174, 527
Quality schools, 40
Quality training, 40
Quiz program, 391

R

Rabindranath Tagore, 211, 316, 467, 502
Raja Ram Mohan Roy, 316,502
Random sample method, 247
Ranga Reddy Dist, 288
Rape and sexual harassment, 99
Rashtriya Madhyamik Shiksha Abhiyan, 531
Rashtriya Uchchatar Shiksha Abhiyan, 531
Rat race for ranking, 66
Red for Feelings, 45
Red Note book, 371
Reflective Learning, 23
Reforms to enhance relevance, 522
Regional languages, 174
Reid Hoffman, 165
Remote Centres, 365, 366
Reporting and Recording, 213
Report of the Education Commission, 56
Reproductive behaviour, 491
Research and Enterprise, 125
Research Design, 299
Research Instruments, 299
Research Methodology, 37, 302
Research methodology, 481, 493
Research Questions, 37, 482
Reservation system, 102
Review of Literature, 438
Review of related studies, 480
Rice flakes, 497
Right of children, 315
Right of Children for Free and Compulsory Education, 501, 505, 506
Right of Free and Compulsory Education Act, 320, 505, 506
Right to Education, 316, 317
Right to Education Act, 146
Right to Education Protection Authority, 258
Right to Free and Compulsory Education, 262
Robbins Committee, 55
Rob Moore, 405
Robust image editor, 87
Rogers College of Law, 135
Role of Teacher in Education, 84
Rollins College, 135
Roma Paul, 299
Ross Thomas, 354
Routine manual labour, 438
Rural and Urban attitude, 377
Rural and urban students, 55
Rural kids, 401

S

S. K. Mangal, 77
S. Radhakrishnan, 211
SAARC region, 124
Sarva Shiksha Abhiyan, 257
Sarvepalli Radha Krishnan, 212, 468
Sayantan Mandal, 71
Scheduled castes, 494
School-based instruction, 434
School Board, 359

School Education, 44
School guidance, 429
School Management Committees, 261
Science and Arts students, 376
Science and Technology, 234
Science and Technology Education, 147
Science-based world, 44
Science Curriculum, 44
Scientific temper, 212
Screening procedure, 259
Secondary Education, 46
Secondary Education Commission, 44
Secondary School Level, 247
Secretary General, 315
Secunderabad, 460
Selection of the problem, 213
Self-determined learning, 28
Self-regulated learners, 182, 185
Semesterization of courses, 520
Service Education, 34
Shiv Nadar University, 137
Shortage of manpower, 357
Sibnath Deb, 299
Significance of the Study, 469
Sikkim, 260
Simon Bailey, 168
Sitting in on lessons, 36
Six Thinking Hats, 45
Skill development, 74
Small Web Formats, 89
Snowden and Halsall, 20
Social and Cultural Rights, 316
Social interaction models, 393
Social media, 164, 166
Social Sciences, 289
Software application, 198
Software Package, 82, 92
Solving ability in Mathematics, 240
South Africa, 93
South Asian region, 123
South East Asia, 121
South Korea, 46
Speaking and writing activities, 193
Special Need School, 446
Special Needs perspective, 450
Special Needs Schools, 445
Specific objectives of the study, 37
Spirit of openness, 26
Sri Aurobindo, 211
Sri Aurobindo International Centre of Education, 95
St. Louis, 136
S T. Xavier College of Education, 388, 389
Stages in Teaching Practice, 34
Stand Alone Institutions, 422
Standardisation of tools, 483
Standard of education, 66
Standards in paper-setting, 362
Stanley Hall, 298
State Commission, 258
State government Boards, 95
State Institute of Educational Technology, 464
Statement of the Problem, 36, 278, 166
State Open School, 96
State Open Universities, 96
State University, 134
Statistical Analysis, 379
Statistical Package, 289
Statistical Tool, 248
Statutory authorities, 131
Stephen Downes, 345
Stopwatch, 185
Strength of Vedic culture, 415
Strongly Agree, 289
Strongly Disagree, 289
Strong Regulatory Mechanism, 127
Structural arrangements, 243
Student and Faculty Mobility, 49

Student attendance registers, 510
Student bank, 157
Student Bank concept, 157
Student-based information, 59
Student-centered approach, 185
Student Centered Instruction, 46
Student dropout, 324
Student learning, 106, 114
Student portfolios, 106
Students Development Programmes, 365
Student- Teacher Ratio, 64
Study Management, 289
Subramanian Committee, 359
Successful organization, 313
Suicides, 97
Suicides of students, 354
Supervision over noise making, 40
Supplementary materials, 193
Supreme Court, 260, 317
Supreme Court of India, 317, 502
Swami Vivekananda, 211
Swimming pools, 447
Synchronizing the methods, 364
Synergistic conversations, 206
Synthetic method, 304

T

Tabulated material, 378
Talent Retention, 310
Tape recorders, 246
Tata Trust, 136
Taxila, 147
Teacher centered approach, 107
Teacher centred learning, 164
Teacher Education, 33, 44, 375
Teacher Educational Institutes, 247
Teacher Education Institution, 34, 246
Teacher Entrance Tests, 359
Teacher Preparation in Special Education, 420
Teacher Pupil Ratio, 260
Teacher Related Problems, 175
Teachers training programme, 36
Teacher trainees, 93, 377
Teacher-training college, 36
Teacher training programs, 184
Teacher tube videos, 156
Teaching and Learning, 247
Teaching and learning in multiple context, 182
Teaching and learning methods, 302
Teaching as a Transmission, 70
Teaching learning materials, 256
Teaching Learning process, 190, 207, 374
Teaching learning situation, 114
Teaching lessons independently, 36
Teaching lessons under supervision, 36
Teaching practice, 34
Teaching Practice– Evaluation, 35
Teaching strategies, 206
Teaching with Games, 233
Teaching with Tablet Computers, 233
Team Building Activity, 160
Team teaching, 469
Technical education, 133
Techniques of data analysis, 483
Technological, explosion in the classrooms, 446
Technological Approach, 114
Technological era, 114
Technology advancement, 212
Technology-based tasks, 433
Technology in education, 196, 201
Technology integration, 197
Technology in the classroom, 114, 433
Telangana, 174, 288, 452
Telangana Social Welfare Department, 156
Telangana Social Welfare Residential Degree Colleg, 156
Telangana State, 174, 324, 464

Telugu booklet, 334, 492
Telugu speaking adolescent girl, 341, 492
Textbooks, 365
The Gross Enrolment Ratio, 148
Theory of Constructivism, 70
Timetable management, 59
Tirupati, 37
Tool development and Data collection, 38
Top-ranked foreign institutions, 126
Trade agreements, 137
Traditional Approach, 107, 287
Traditional books, 91
Traditional classroom, 57, 287, 348
Traditional classroom learning, 286
Traditional education, 201
Traditional mode of education, 190
Traditional printed material, 91
Traditional professional development, 202
Traditional sector, 56
Traditional teaching, 19
Traditional textbooks, 82
Traditional to modern ways of learning, 364
Transactional theory, 239
Transmission, 226
Transparency and accountability, 146
Transparency in evaluation, 362
Trends and Practices, 409
Trends in Internationalization, 119
Tribal community, 175
Tribal education, 174
Tribal schools, 174
Tribal societies, 298, 174
T V Show, 366
Twenty-first Century Skills, 407
Twin cities, 335
Types of making students nderstand, 364

U

Uma Mangal, 77
Undergraduate level, 49
Undergraduate programmes, 133
Understanding India, 424
Unfavorable attitude, 376
Union Territories, 257, 261
Unique Selling Proposition, 314
United Arab Emirates, 121
United Kingdom, 123
United Nations, 315, 501
United Nations General Assembly, 316
United Progressive government, 319, 504
United States, 50, 119, 121, 123, 125, 126, 206
United States, 522
Universal Declaration of Human Rights, 316, 502
Universal education, 452
Universalisation of Elementary Education, 257, 464
Universities and Colleges, 147
University education, 301
University expenditure, 54
University facilities, 449
University Grants Commission, 50, 54, 95, 127, 129, 132, 360, 420, 422
University level, 343
University level Institutions, 146
University of Arizona, 135
University of California, 135, 136
University of Chicago, 134
University of Colorado, 230
University of Delaware report, 231
University of Hyderabad, 447, 448, 453
University of Manitoba, 345
University of Michigan, 136
University of Queensland, 136
University of Texas at Dallas, 135
University of Wisconsin, 242
University teachers, 345

Updation of knowledge, 65
Use of Internet, 374
Use of Laptops in e-classrooms, 365
Using Technology, 442
Utility of Student Store, 159
Uttar Pradesh, 261

V

Vaidyanathan and Nair, 175
Value Based Education System, 358
Various learning resources, 74
Various learning theories, 202
Various Models, 393
Verbal or oral method, 304
Verbal skills, 219
Verification of first Hypothesis, 379
Verification of Fourth Hypothesis, 380
Verification of second hypothesis, 379
Verification of Third Hypothesis, 380
Vernacular languages, 194
Very ill-disciplined, 64
Video-based learning, 57, 58
Video cameras, 198
Video editor, 87, 88
Video games are good for learning, 233
Video Pad, 87, 88
Video programmes, 465
Vikramshila, 147
Virginia Polytechnic Institute, 134
Virtual classroom, 292, 48
Virtual Reality, 58, 366, 367
Visakhapatnam city, 377, 378
Visual images, 451
Visualize new academic concepts, 114
Visual Understanding Environment, 90
Vocational adjustments, 428
Vocational choices, 428
Vocational education, 96, 394
Vocationalization of courses, 520
Vocational maturity, 428
Vocational studies, 184

W

Washington University, 136
Well-paid and risk-free jobs, 99
Well trained teachers, 82
West Bengal, 261
Whats App or Facebook, 365
White for Facts, 45
Wijayanthi & Listiani, 284
Winfield and Crimmins, 208
Withdrawal forms, 157
Women's own health, 330, 515
Women empowerment, 338, 492, 496
Women with primary education, 516
Wooden screen, 185
Wood stock School, 95
Working Days, 259
Working with parents, 36
World Bank, 98, 246, 327, 329, 333, 334, 492, 513, 514, 520
World class universities, 101
World development report, 514
World Education Forum, 316
World Tech Team, 198
World Trade Organization, 118, 318, 503
Writing and Presentation, 192
Writing Skills, 238
Written method, 304
Wrong societal outlook, 98

X

Xavier College of Education, 391, 393, 394, 396

Y

Yapiciand Akbayin, 288
Yashpal Committee, 133, 134
Yashpal Committee Report, 49
Yellow for Benefits, 45
Yes Sayer Brecht, 225
Young and old age pregnancy, 340, 498
Young people, 114
You Tube, 88